Tort Law

Robert R. Cummins, Esq.
Southern College

PRENTICE HALL PARALEGAL SERIES

Prentice Hall
Upper Saddle River, New Jersey 07458

Library of Congress Cataloging-in-Publication Data

Cummins, Robert R.
Tort law / Robert R. Cummins.
p. cm.
Includes index.
ISBN 0-13-660994-5
1. Torts—United States. I. Title. II. Series.
KF1250.Z9C86 1999
346.7303—dc21 98-16766
CIP

Acquisitions Editor: Elizabeth Sugg
Director of Production and Manufacturing: Bruce Johnson
Managing Editor: Mary Carnis
Editorial/Production Supervision and Interior Design: Inkwell Publishing Services
Cover Director: Jayne Conte
Manufacturing Buyer: Edward O'Dougherty

Simon & Schuster / A Viacom Company
Upper Saddle River, New Jersey 07458

Printed in the United States of America

10 9 8 7 6 5 4 3 2 1

ISBN 0-13-660994-5

PRENTICE-HALL INTERNATIONAL (UK) LIMITED, *London*
PRENTICE-HALL OF AUSTRALIA PTY. LIMITED, *Sydney*
PRENTICE-HALL CANADA INC., *Toronto*
PRENTICE-HALL HISPANOAMERICANA, S.A., *Mexico*
PRENTICE-HALL OF INDIA PRIVATE LIMITED, *New Delhi*
PRENTICE-HALL OF JAPAN, INC., *Tokyo*
PRENTICE-HALL OF SOUTHEAST ASIA PTE. LTD., *Singapore*
EDITORA PRENTICE-HALL DO BRASIL, LTDA., *Rio de Janeiro*

CONTENTS

Preface v

1
Foundations of Tort Law 1

Tort Defined 2
History 4
Sources 6
Purpose 10
Categories 12

2
The Tort of Negligence 17

Negligence Explained 18
Elements of Negligence 19
Duty of Reasonable Care 20
Breach of the Duty of Reasonable Care 29
Proximate Cause 29
Damages 41

3
Proof of Negligence 47

Legal Proof 48
Unavoidable Accident 50
Act of God 50
Degrees of Negligence 51
Burden of Proof 57
Res Ipsa Loquitur 59
Joint Tortfeasors' Liability 62
Survival Actions and Wrongful Death 63

4
Defenses to Negligence 67

Contributory Negligence 68
Last Clear Chance 76
Comparative Negligence 78
Assumption of Risk 80

5
Intentional Torts 91

Intent 92
Harm to Person 93
Harm to Property 108

6
Defenses to Intentional Torts 117

Consent 119
Defense of Self, Persons, and Property 121
Legal Process 124
Mistake 125
Necessity 126
Privilege 127
Reasonable Discipline 128
Recapture of Land and Chattels 132
Statute of Limitations 133
Warrantless Arrest 133

7
Immunity from Tort Liability 137

Public Policy 138
Intra-Family Immunity 139
Charitable Immunity 144
Governmental Immunity 145
Immunity of Infants and Minors 154
Immunity of Mental Incompetents 155
Privileged Communication 158

8
Premises Liability 161

General Duty of a Landholder 162
Entry upon Land 168
Lessor and Lessee 179
Vendor and Vendee 183

9
Doctrine of Nuisance 189

Doctrine of Nuisance 190
Private Nuisance 193
Substantial and Unreasonable Interference 200
Absolute Nuisance 203
Public Nuisance 204
Remedies 205
Negligence and Strict Liability 209

10
Vicarious Liability 211

Doctrine of Vicarious Liability 212
Master-Servant Relationship 216
Independent Contractor 223
Joint Enterprise 228
Automobile Ownership 232
Dram Shop Liability 232

11
Product Liability 237

History 238
Parties 242
Warranty 245
Negligence 245
Strict Liability 249
Unreasonably Dangerous 255
Defenses 259
Consumer Product Safety 260

12
Strict Liability 263

Liability without Fault 264
Animals 265
Fire 270
Abnormally Dangerous Things 273
Scope of Liability 276

Table of Cases Cited 279
Table of Restatement Citations 281
Glossary 283
Index 287

PREFACE

The arena of human conflict covered by the field of torts pervades virtually every other area of the practice of law. It is the rare paralegal or legal assistant who is *never* exposed to a factual or legal situation involving the field of tort law either directly or indirectly. As a paralegal educator for many years, I have long recognized the need for a textbook in the field of tort law that presents its basic principles in a comprehensible style and format. This text strives to present those fundamental principles in a clear and concise manner, allowing the paralegal and legal assistant student to enter the profession with a firm foundation in the precepts of the field. I have structured the text to include the major subjects of tort law and presented them in an order that leads the student to build on the principles already learned. I have selected case law, references to the *Restatement (Second) of Torts*, and comments from *Prosser and Keeton on the Law of Torts* to support and illustrate the material. Each chapter includes a discussion of the fundamental principles of law on the chapter topic, as well as case law, supporting commentaries, review questions, and an opportunity to apply the principles presented in the chapter.

ORGANIZATION

I have organized this text into 12 chapters to offer the paralegal and legal assistant student a logical approach to the various areas of tort law. Chapter 1 presents the student with an overview of the field of torts. Chapters 2, 3, and 4 provide in-depth analyses of negligence law, problems of proving negligence, and the defenses available. Chapters 5 and 6 present the issues and problems involved in intentional torts, an area of tort law that is quite distinct from the concept of negligence.

The remaining six chapters are concerned with special situations that arise from injury to a person or property in a particular manner other than through negligence or intentional tort. Tort immunity, premises liability, nuisance, vicarious liability, product liability, and absolute liability, are all areas of tort law that arise from the fundamental tort principles considered in the first six chapters. It is important for the student to become familiar with those basic principles before considering the special situations.

Each chapter begins with an epigram related to the subject matter under consideration. The quotes are designed to elevate the student's thought process and stimulate a discussion of the topic. The list of Chapter Topics provides an overview of the areas to be considered within the broad subject matter of the chapter. The Chapter Objectives described are my concept of what the student will be able to accomplish after careful consideration of the chapter content. In every chapter, each of the legal terms defined in the body of the text is displayed in the margin. The purpose here is twofold: first, to offer a convenient reference for the meaning of each term; and second, to emphasize the importance of terminology for the paralegal. Students who master the terminology of the law can more easily assimilate the concepts of the law.

The Cases in Point featured in each chapter offer the student an opportunity to see how the principles of tort law under consideration have been applied by the courts. The cases have been selected for their fact settings and the presentation of legal reasoning. In addition to the case law examples, I have included commentary and support from the two major sources of tort principle, the *Restatement* and *Prosser*. The *Restatement* is the quintessential statement of the "black letter" of tort law. Prosser and Keeton are acknowledged legal scholars in the field of torts and offer a concise commentary on its principles.

Following a summary of the chapter are questions for review of the materials that are designed to put each topic in perspective, and a section entitled Focus Your Skills that provides the student with an opportunity to apply the principles of the chapter topic. The scenarios presented suggest the occasionally bizarre factual settings to which the principles of tort law must be applied.

For the paralegal and legal assistant student, this textbook will provide a fundamental knowledge of the basic principles of tort law, along with invaluable hands-on experience in applying the concepts. The student who is trained to think analytically and can apply principles to facts will achieve success in the field of tort law.

Acknowledgments

Every textbook is a mosaic of the efforts of many individuals, only one of whom is the author. Without the contributions of many other people, the completion of this project would not have been possible. Quality comes from expert advice. Many thanks to Melinda G. Hess, JD of the College of St. Mary; Susan M. Taylor, JD of Indiana University and Ivy Tech State College; among many other colleagues. The support and encouragement of my loving wife, Margaret Ann, deserves my heartfelt gratitude. Her patient understanding and calm assurance helped me throughout this project. I wish to extend my gratitude to Ms. Rosalind Beck for her indefatigable efforts in editing this manuscript into a readable and concise work. Her suggestions kept me focused on grammatical accuracy and the needs of the student. I wish to thank my research assistant, Ms. Linda Langlois, for her quality legal research. These individuals keep me mindful of the fact that the professor can learn from the student.

I am especially grateful to Prentice Hall for providing the opportunity for me to put my love of the field of tort law into print. My editor, Ms. Elizabeth Sugg, provided the support and vision that made this effort a reality. I thank her and the entire Prentice Hall family for their support and expertise.

FOUNDATIONS OF TORT LAW

The law can ask no better justification than the deepest instincts of man.

Justice Oliver Wendell Holmes

A study of the law of torts begins with a definition of the term *tort*, along with an appreciation of the history of tort law and an understanding of its place in American jurisprudence. To fully understand the tort concept, the paralegal student must understand the categories of tort law and have a fundamental knowledge of its sources.

Chapter Topics

1. Tort Defined
2. History
3. Evolution
4. Purpose
5. Categories

Objectives

After completing this chapter, you will be able to:

1. Define the basic concept of tort law.
2. Discuss the history of torts.
3. Understand the sources of tort law.
4. Summarize the purposes behind the law of torts.
5. List the various categories of tort law.

Tort Defined

Legal scholars have attempted for centuries to define the term *tort*. Most efforts at defining the term describe what a tort is *not*. A tort has been defined as something that is "not a contract" and as something that is "not a crime." A crime is considered an offense against the public, while a tort is considered an offense against an individual. An understanding of what a tort *is not* is of some value in appreciating its nature, but paralegal students are best served by understanding what a tort *is*.

The term originates from the Latin term *torquere,* meaning to twist. The twisting is the bending of the rules of proper human behavior resulting in harm to another person. The term tort refers to a violation of a civil rule of conduct causing injury to another. Thus, a **tort** is a civil wrong resulting in injury to the person or property of another. It is any civil wrong that infringes on an individual's private rights. An individual's private rights are the enjoyment of one's property and the maintenance of one's physical well-being. The infringement may be through an intentional act or omission, or as the result of unintentional behavior. The intentional or unintentional behavior that results in harm to another is called **tortious conduct**, or conduct that is harmful to another's individual rights.

Tort law provides a remedy for civil wrongs in the American system of jurisprudence. The remedy is in the form of a **cause of action**, which is the legal right of the injured party to bring a lawsuit against the wrongdoer. The wrongdoer, the person whose behavior resulted in injury to another, is referred to as

tort

tortious conduct

cause of action

tortfeasor

the **tortfeasor**. The "feasor" part of the term comes from the Latin *facere* meaning to make or do. Thus, the term refers to one who does a tort.

Figure 1-1: Case in Point: *Stimson*

Stimson v. Michigan Bell Telephone Company
77 Mich. App. 361, 258 N.W.2d 227, 231 (1977)

Former employee brought action against former employer to recover for acute nervous breakdown, subsequent hospitalization and inability to secure employment, and subsequent embarrassment, humiliation, and loss of esteem resulting from alleged denial of promotions and discharge based on sex. Husband sought to recover for loss of consortium. The Circuit Court, Wayne County, Harry J. Dingeman, Jr., J., denied former employer's motion for summary judgment and motion to strike plaintiff's complaint and former employer appealed. The Court of Appeals held that: (1) to the extent that complaint sought to recover for nervous breakdown and subsequent embarrassment and humiliation and loss of esteem, the action was barred by the Worker's Disability Compensation Act, but (2) to the extent that former employee sought to recover for discharge and failure to obtain promotions, the action was not barred by the Act.

Reversed and remanded.

PER CURIAM.

Defendant appeals from an order of the Wayne County Circuit Court denying its motion for partial summary judgment and/or to strike portions of plaintiffs' complaint.

On July 9, 1974, plaintiffs filed suit pursuant to the Michigan Fair Employment Practices Act, M.C.L.A. s 423.301 et seq.; *M.S.A. s* 17.458(l) et seq. (hereinafter, the "FEPA"), and the United States and Michigan Constitutions, charging defendant with discriminating against her, on the basis of sex, as to grade and wage promotions and her eventual discharge. Plaintiff alleged that because of such discrimination, she suffered an acute nervous breakdown, required hospitalization, was unable to secure employment, and experienced embarrassment, humiliation and a loss of esteem among her peers because of her inability to support herself. Mr. Stimson alleged that he suffered a loss of consortium due to his wife's injuries. Plaintiffs sought back pay, future pay and compensatory and punitive damages....

...A tort is broadly defined as "a private or civil wrong or injury." *Black's Law Dictionary*, p. 1660. It consists of the existence of a legal duty owed the plaintiff by the defendant, breach of the duty, a proximate causal relationship between the breach and plaintiff's injury, and damages.... A civil damage action based on the alleged violation of a plaintiff's civil rights is in the nature of a tort action.

liability

The goal of tort law is to assign financial responsibility, referred to as **liability**, to the tortfeasor for tortious conduct that has resulted in injury to an individual's property or person.

HISTORY

English common law

Tort law originated in the **English common law**. The English common law is the ancient, unwritten law of England as practiced following the Norman Conquest in 1066; it formed the basis for the law that prevailed in the American colonies before the Revolutionary War. Common law developed through the decisions of the courts of England over many centuries. It is the foundation of many of the principles and rules that are followed in American jurisprudence today. Torts were considered wrongs against an individual, and the victim was permitted to retaliate against the wrongdoer. Tort law preceded criminal law in permitting vengeance by individuals for personal wrongs. Personal revenge was later replaced by a system of monetary compensation, becoming the first recovery of damages for tort.

trespass

writ

trespass on the case

The law of torts is rooted specifically in the thirteenth century concept of **trespass**. At that time trespass was considered any serious breach of the King's peace by act of force or violence that resulted in injury to person or property. To obtain redress for such a breach, the victim petitioned the King's court through a formal process by submitting a **writ**. Writs are still used in many of our modern systems of civil procedure as a form of petition to a court. Two writs were available to the victim of a breach of the King's peace. The writ of trespass existed for a breach of the King's peace by a direct and forceful act causing injury to the victim's person or property. The writ of trespass evolved into the contemporary body of law involving intentional torts (discussed in Chapter 5). The writ of **trespass on the case** existed for a breach of the King's peace in the form of a wrongful act indirectly causing an injury. Trespass on the case was the forerunner of our modern concept of negligence, where redress is sought on the basis of fault (discussed in Chapter 2). The redress provided by the King's court was in the form of monetary damages compensating the victim for the loss or injury and punishing the wrongdoer.

Figure 1-2: Case in Point: *Mueller*

Mueller v. Brunn
105 Wis.2d 171, 313 N.W.2d 790, 794 (1982)

HEFFERNAN, Justice.

...The plaintiffs, Albert R. Mueller and Delores J. Mueller, his wife, hereinafter plaintiffs, have petitioned for review of a decision of the court of appeals which reversed an order of the trial court and directed that the plaintiffs' action against the Town of Vernon be dismissed. We reverse the court of appeals.

The plaintiffs, who are property owners in Waukesha county, commenced an action alleging that Donald B. Brunn and Marion F. Brunn, his wife, the vendors of the property purchased by plaintiffs, made material misrepresentations because they stated that they had no knowledge of any defects in respect to the adequacy and quality of the well, while, in fact, plaintiffs allege, the sellers had notice of salt contamination prior to the execution of the real estate contract...

...Trespass on the case is the ancestor of the present day action for negligence where problems of legal and factual cause arise.

As agrarian medieval England evolved into the urban industrial society of the eighteenth century, its culture's growing complexity demanded an expanded system of recovery. Recovery for injury to an individual's person and property turned from the ancient writs toward a system of recovery based upon the dual concepts of intentional torts and negligence. These concepts allowed compensation for many more wrongs than had been contemplated by the ancient writs. As we will see in subsequent chapters, the nature of recovery for tort continues to change and expand along with our modern society.

Figure 1-3: Case in Point: *Waller*

Waller v. First Savings & Trust Co.
103 Fla. 1025, 138 So. 780 (1931)

DAVIS, J.

The facts upon which this suit is based, as disclosed by the allegations of the declaration, are most unusual, and, so far as we know, unprecedented in this state.

The declaration alleges that on April 24, 1930, the plaintiff and his wife were residing in a dwelling in Hillsborough county, owned by the plaintiff, and that on said date one John Hodasz, for whose estate the defendant had been appointed administrator, intentionally injured and damaged said dwelling house by placing a bomb, or other high explosive, underneath or near to said residence, and had willfully and intentionally caused the same to be exploded, with the intention of injuring and damaging the plaintiff, and that such explosion did damage the plaintiff's dwelling house to the amount of $3,000.

The declaration further alleges that, in addition to injuring said dwelling house, the said Hodasz caused plaintiff to suffer other pecuniary damage and loss, in that the explosion inflicted very serious injuries upon the plaintiff's wife, necessitating the amputation of her left leg between the ankle and the knee, seriously injuring her right leg and causing the loss of sight in one eye, and injuring her right arm and hand so that she cannot use them, and so maiming her that she will be practically an invalid the balance of her life, rendering it impossible for her to perform the duties of a wife, and thereby depriving plaintiff of her companionship and services, and making it necessary that he have some one with her at all times to wait upon her. That plaintiff was forced to expend $800 for hospital bills for the treatment of his wife, and that he will be required to expend other large sums for her care and treatment in the future. The declaration further alleges that after the commission of said wrongful act, the said John Hodasz died, and that the First Savings and Trust Company of Tampa, a corporation, was duly appointed administrator of his estate and duly qualified, and is now acting as such administrator. The action was brought against said corporation as administrator of the estate of John Hodasz, and claimed damages in the sum of $50,000....

...The theory of the English common law is that a tort action is to be regarded as punitive in character, while under the intendment of the Declaration of Rights contained in the Florida Constitution, there is recognized and preserved in organic language a legal remedy for tortious wrongs, with a provision that the courts shall always be open to afford that remedy to the person wronged, the effect of which is to change the nature of tort actions as recognized in our legal system, from that of an action almost wholly punitive, to one largely remedial, in character.

Sources

The paralegal student must understand how the common law roots of tort law continue to influence contemporary court decisions. In fact, the common law is the single most significant source of today's tort law. These principles of common law tort are modified in many instances by courts and legislatures to meet the demands of a complex technological society, but you will see those fundamental roots underlying even our modern system of tort recovery.

Evolution

natural law

An understanding of the evolution of the law of torts begins with an appreciation of the role of **natural law**. A natural law is a fundamental legal principle that is essential to an ordered social existence. Natural law forms the rules that dictate socially unacceptable human behavior. The English common law was founded on principles dictated by natural law. As the social order evolved from agrarian to urban and from regional to national, legal principles were adapted accordingly. For centuries the courts have recognized the need for the law to keep pace with the values of society, constantly redefining acceptable social conduct.

treatise

hornbook

A valuable research tool for the paralegal student is the legal **treatise**. A treatise provides an exposition on an area of the law in greater depth than that offered by encyclopedias or periodicals. It serves to organize the vast body of case law into chapters and sections arranged for ease of study. *Prosser and Keeton on the Law of Torts* is considered a **hornbook**, which is a treatise used by law students to study well-settled principles found in landmark cases.

In his learned treatise on the law of torts, Professor Keeton acknowledges that the principle underlying the evolution of tort law is the concept of socially responsible conduct (see Figure 1-4).

Today, the United States Congress and the legislatures of the individual states have enacted many statutes that either embody the common law or mod-

Figure 1-4: *Prosser and Keeton on Torts*, Social Responsibility

> So far as there is one central idea, it would seem that it is that liability must be based upon conduct which is socially unreasonable. The common thread woven into all torts is the idea of unreasonable interference with the interest of others.
>
> W. Page Keeton et al., *Prosser and Keeton on the Law of Torts* at 6 (5th ed. 1984)

ify it to meet contemporary needs. Since the landmark decision of Chief Justice John Marshall in the case of *Marbury v. Madison*, 5 U.S. (1 Cranch) 137 (1803), the courts have exercised the power of **judicial review**. Judicial review is the power of a court to review legislative enactments to determine their validity. It enables courts to interpret the meaning of statutes dealing with the law of torts in light of common law principles superimposed upon the realities of our modern society. The effect of the vigilance of the United States Congress, state legislatures, and the courts on the law of torts is to provide a seasoning of the underlying tort principles in existence for the past 600 years.

judicial review

Resources

primary authority

secondary authority

Authorities. Constitutions, statutes, and case law provide the resources within which modern tort law can be found. For legal research into the law of torts, these resources are considered **primary authority**, meaning that they are statements *of* the law. Primary authority is distinguished from **secondary authority**. Secondary authority consists of statements *about* the law. Secondary authorities present an explanation, analysis, or criticism of the law and often provide insight regarding trends. Therefore, the paralegal student can find the body of the law of torts located in primary authorities and obtain an explanation and critique of the law from secondary sources.

constitution

Constitutions. A **constitution** is the highest law of the land. It establishes the form for the organization of government and provides for the rights and privileges of the citizens it protects. The United States Constitution is the written instrument that forms our Union and establishes the fundamental law of the United States. Each state has its own constitution to provide for the organization of the state government and protect the individual rights and freedoms of the state's citizens. The individual rights guaranteed by the U.S. Constitution or any of the state constitutions are the very rights that tort law seeks to protect. A right that originates in a constitution and protection in the law of torts is called a **constitutional tort**. For example, § 1983 of Title 43 of the United States Code provides a civil tort action remedy for any person who has been deprived of his or her individual rights.

constitutional tort

Figure 1-5: 42 U.S.C. § 1983

§ 1983. Civil action for deprivation of rights

Every person who, under color of any statute, ordinance, regulation, custom, or usage, of any State or Territory or the District of Columbia, subjects, or causes to be subjected, any citizen of the United States or other person within the jurisdiction thereof to the deprivation of any rights, privileges, or immunities secured by the Constitution and laws, shall be liable to the party injured in an action at law, suit in equity, or other proper proceeding for redress.

The federal statute provides a cause of action for any citizen of this country for any deprivation of rights guaranteed by the U.S. Constitution.

statute

Statutes. A **statute** is a formal written act of a legislative body that creates a law. Enactments of the U.S. Congress form the body of federal statutes found in the United States Code. The legislative acts of the individual states can be found in each state's code. Acts of Congress and the state legislatures must comply with the principles established by their respective constitutions. Federal law and individual state statutes express principles of tort law. An example of this can be seen in the modification of the tort principle of sovereign immunity (discussed in detail in Chapter 7). While the U.S. government cannot be sued without its permission according to the principle of governmental immunity, the Federal Tort Claims Act enacted in 1946 established certain conditions under which the federal government may be sued for tort.

case law

common law

Case Law. **Case law** is made up of court decisions issued by appellate courts reviewing the decisions of lower courts. Also referred to as the **common law** to distinguish it from statutory law, it is made up of the court decisions that form the principles and rules of proper behavior relating to the government and its citizens. As applied to the law of torts, it is the principles or rules that apply to actions for redress of civil wrongs resulting in injury to an individual's person or property. Case law is found in the court reports of the various federal and state jurisdictions. **Court reports** are published volumes of case law, and can be found in multivolume sets containing the written opinions of the appellate courts within a jurisdiction. For example, the Federal Reporter (Fed.) and the Federal Reporter, Second Edition (Fed. 2d) contain all of the written opinions of the United States Circuit Courts of Appeal. An example of a court reporter at the state level can be found in the Michigan Reports, which contain all of the case law decided by the Michigan Supreme Court.

court reports

finding tools

Finding Tools. Legal research in tort law involves the use of both primary and secondary authority. Access to those authorities can be facilitated by the use of **finding tools**. Finding tools are legal research aids to locate primary and secondary sources of the law. The resources containing primary and secondary authority along with their finding tools are summarized in the list provided in Figure 1-6.

Figure 1-6: Tort Law Research

PRIMARY AUTHORITY

<u>FEDERAL CASE LAW</u>

United States Reports
Supreme Court Reporter
United States Supreme Court Reports
Lawyer Edition
Federal Reporter 2d
Federal Supplement

<u>STATE CASE LAW</u>

North Western Reporter
North Eastern Reporter
Southern Reporter
South Western Reporter
Pacific Reporter
Local State Reporters

<u>FEDERAL STATUTORY LAW</u>

United States Code
United States Code Annotated
United States Code Service
Code of Federal Regulations
Loose-Leaf Services

<u>STATE STATUTORY LAW</u>

Local State Statutes
Loose-Leaf Services

SECONDARY AUTHORITY

<u>ENCYCLOPEDIAS</u>

American Jurisprudence 2d (Am. Jur. 2d)
Corpus Juris Secundum

<u>LAW REPORTS</u>

American Law Reports (ALR, ALR2d, ALR3d, ALR4th, ALR5th, ALR FED)

<u>TREATISES</u>

American Jurisprudence Proof of Facts
American Jurisprudence Trials
Attorney's Textbook of Medicine
Aviation Tort Law
Courtroom Medicine
Prosser and Keaton on the Law of Torts

<u>RESTATEMENTS</u>

Restatement of Torts 2d

FINDING TOOLS

DIGESTS

American Digest System
Regional Digests
State Digests

CITATORS

Shepard's—Statutes
Shepard's—Cases

While this list is not intended to be comprehensive, it is sufficient to acquaint the paralegal student with the basic resources for researching the law of torts. Loose-leaf services and the law reviews published by various law schools throughout the country can also be used to research specific areas of tort law.

PURPOSE

In the latter half of the twentieth century a rapid expansion occurred in the law of torts. That expansion has led to criticism of tort law in light of its intended purpose, and that criticism has led to the replacement of some time-honored tort principles by whole systems of recovery based upon injury compensation without regard to fault. An analysis of the aims of tort law is necessary to understand its foundations, to appreciate its evolution, and to recognize its shortcomings. The purpose of tort law has historically been classified in terms of punishment, deterrence, and compensation.

Punishment

As was mentioned in the section on History, tort law preceded criminal law. Breaches of the King's peace in the form of wrongs to the individual were treated with principles of tort law involving personal vengeance against the tortfeasor rather than with criminal prosecution. Ancient tort remedies were based upon monetary punishment of the wrongdoer.

exemplary damages

Modern theories of tort law generally do not include a penalty to teach the tortfeasor a lesson or to make an example of the offender, with the sole exception of punitive or **exemplary damages**. Exemplary damages are the last remnant of ancient tort law designed to punish the tortfeasor. Exemplary damages consist of a monetary award above that required to compensate a plaintiff for his or her loss. They are used in prescribed instances when the wrong to the plaintiff occurred under circumstances of willful, malicious, or fraudulent behavior on the part of the tortfeasor. The goal is to punish the wrongdoer and to make an example of the consequence for egregious conduct. Federal law and the laws of individual states set forth the particular circumstances under which exemplary damages may be awarded (see Chapter 2). Punishment of the tortfeasor through exemplary damages has been criticized because of the windfall recovery to the plaintiff in such cases. For that reason, the circumstances of the application of exemplary damages are severely limited.

Punishment remains the basis of modern tort recovery in the sense that liability involves a determination of responsibility for wrong behavior. In the modern tort action, there is an element of accountability in making the tortfeasor monetarily responsible for his or her actions. Such accountability retains a punitive element in the sense that monetary responsibility penalizes the wrongdoer for the offending behavior.

Deterrence

Another purpose of modern tort law involves an attempt to reduce the number of acts of tortious conduct by imposing financial responsibility on the tortfeasor. Theoretically, the number of tortious acts will decrease if such activity carries a heavy economic burden. Individual tortfeasors will be deterred from acting in a tortious manner out of fear of economic sanction. While the goal of attempting to reduce the incidence of tortious conduct through deterrence may be valid, it is somewhat diluted in application today because of the protection provided by insurance.

The deterrence of harmful conduct is an important goal of tort law. The imposition of monetary sanctions creates a standard of conduct for individuals which states that a person must behave so as to avoid injury to the property or person of another. Civil liability in the form of monetary damages will be imposed for a violation of that standard of conduct. The application of this principle will be examined in the discussion of each particular tort. It appears doubtful that a person will be deterred from the violation of a standard of conduct when he or she does not intend the act. In such cases, tort law can do little to deter tortious conduct.

Compensation

The most critical purpose of modern tort law is compensation for the victim of tortious conduct. The theory of compensating a tort victim for loss involves the award of money as payment or reparation for injury to person or property. A recovery of money to compensate a victim of tortious conduct is called **compensatory damages**. (This topic is discussed in greater detail in Chapter 2.)

compensatory damages

In its most basic form, compensation involves shifting the cost of an injury from the victim to the tortfeasor. The fault of the tortfeasor provides the legal excuse for the shift of responsibility, making the tortfeasor pay for injuries that are his or her fault. While no serious argument can be mounted to sustain the position that a tortfeasor should be able to avoid compensating individuals injured as a result of his or her tortious behavior, insurance cushions the financial responsibility somewhat. Compensation costs for a tort injury are shifted from the victim to the tortfeasor, and in turn to the insurance carrier. In the case of liability of the tortfeasor for tortious conduct resulting from a commercial activity, the cost of compensation for injury is passed on to the consumer by increasing the prices for goods or services. It is the consumer who ultimately pays for the insurance that provides tort injury compensation. The net effect is that the individual consumer eventually pays the cost for every injury caused by tortious conduct in a commercial setting.

CATEGORIES

plaintiff

defendant

Perhaps the most fundamental axiom in the law is that there shall be no wrong without a remedy—and so it is with the law of torts. Tort law establishes a remedy for wrongs provided that the basic elements of the cause of action exist. The parties to a tort action consist of the **plaintiff**, the party to a lawsuit that commences the action, and the **defendant**, the party in a lawsuit against whom an action has been brought. The plaintiff in a tort action is the party that has sustained an injury to person or property. The defendant to a tort action is the tortfeasor, the party responsible for tortious conduct.

A cause of action for tort must contain these basic elements:

- legal right residing with the plaintiff,
- corresponding duty in the defendant,
- violation of that duty, and
- damage to the plaintiff as a result of the violation of that duty

omission

Thus, in any action for tort, the basic question will involve the proper discharge of a duty by the defendant. The discharge of that duty may involve an act or it may involve the failure to act when there exists a legal duty to do so, called an **omission**. The failure of proper discharge of a duty is the central question.

The body of tort law is divided into the following basic categories:

- negligence
- intentional torts
- strict liability

intent

The distinction between negligence, intentional torts, and strict liability rests with the issue of **intent**. Intent involves a state of mind at the time one carries out an action to bring about an intended result. The categories of tort law are distinguished by how each requires a level of intent or fault upon the part of the tortfeasor.

The tort of negligence is discussed in detail in Chapters 2 and 3. It is rooted in the ancient writ of trespass and involves a lack of intent to cause injury to the plaintiff's person or property.

intentional tort

An **intentional tort** arises when the defendant intends to violate a duty owed to the plaintiff, resulting in injury to the plaintiff's person or property. Intentional torts are discussed in detail in Chapter 5. Traditionally, these are intentional torts:

- assault and battery
- false imprisonment
- false arrest
- infliction of emotional distress
- fraud and misrepresentation
- conversion
- trespass to land and chattels
- invasion of privacy
- defamation
- malicious prosecution
- abuse of process

These torts stem from the original writ of trespass and continue to provide a cause of action in modern tort law.

Remedies for torts involving liability for actions regardless of intent are categorized as strict liability or absolute liability torts, and are the subject of Chapter 12. These torts are not considered to be intentional, nor are they based upon a theory of negligence. They are subject to compensation and imposition of liability for injury to person and property regardless of fault or intent.

There are several types of tort action that do not easily fit into the categories of negligence, intentional torts, or strict liability. Those special torts consist of actions for:

- premises liability
- nuisance
- vicarious liability
- product liability

These types of tort action involve the violation of a duty to the plaintiff resulting in some form of injury, yet they may contain elements common to both negligence and intentional torts. They are considered in Chapters 8 through 11.

SUMMARY

The law of torts is the ancient of ancients when measured against other forms of legal action. Springing from the English common law following the Norman

Conquest of England in 1066, the law of torts has survived as a remedy for injury to person and property. It has been a part of the common law of the United States since the colonial era and has evolved along with changes in society. The law of torts has kept pace with America's transformation from a young, agrarian economy to a modern, technologically sophisticated global power. Today, tort law serves as the basic form of redress for injuries sustained by an individual to either person or property.

Many former tort actions have given way to systems of recovery that have moved away from the fundamental principles of tort law. This text considers the principles of tort law as they exist today. Those systems of tort reform that deviate substantially from basic tort principles are the proper subject of other works and so shall they remain.

Review Questions

1. Define a *tort.*
2. What are the private rights of an individual that the law of torts seeks to protect?
3. Define *tortious conduct.*
4. What is a tortfeasor?
5. Discuss the origins of the law of torts.
6. What is the distinction between the writ of trespass and the writ of trespass on the case?
7. What role has judicial review played in the development of tort law?
8. List the primary sources of tort law.
9. List the three principal aims of the law of torts.
10. What are the three broad categories of tort law?

Focus Your Skills

Olympian State University, situated on the sandstone bluffs overlooking the picturesque Sasquatch River, has long been regarded as the state's premier breeding ground for doctoral candidates. Year after year, OSU Cybernauts (the school's mascot was chosen from the popular computer game, *Quarks & Cybernauts®*, featuring virtual space travel) are chosen to enter postgraduate programs at the country's most prestigious research universities.

Wally Moone, President of the campus Cybernaut Computer Club, hoped to be chosen for an elite computer research program. Wally was affectionately known around campus as a cyber-geek, a fact that should have removed him from active consideration as an acceptable date. Yet surprisingly, Wally found himself the object of the attention and affections of OSU's stellar pom-pom girl and Homecoming Queen-elect. Her name was Hellene Mars, and she was the secret fantasy of every male on campus. To a man, the OSU campus was baffled as to how she could be attracted to such a cyber-nerd as Wally Moone. Speculation ran rampant concerning the source of her admiration for Wally. The conventional wisdom had it buried deep in some Freudian recess of her psyche, to be reached only through years of intensive psychotherapy.

A not-so-secret admirer of Ms. Mars was one Blanford "Butch" Thor, captain of the rugby team and acknowledged to be leather-tough. Never one for subtlety, Butch let it be known that he considered Hellene to be his private preserve and would pound the sand out of anyone who dared interfere with his pursuit of her.

Leaving the computer lab late one balmy May evening after a particularly arduous session reformatting floppies, Hellene and Wally were confronted by a very intoxicated Butch (whether it was beer or love or both, no one was quite sure). The sight of Hellene and Wally together had an effect on Butch similar to waving a red flag before a bull. The cyber-struck Wally quickly became the target of a poorly executed swing aimed at the Moone face. When it came to athletic agility, Wally was smart enough to duck. The sluggishly launched roundhouse punch went sailing right over Wally's head and struck Hellene squarely on the point of her Martian chin. The blow caused her to be separated from everything but her name. It took out four front teeth, broke her jaw, and left her with a permanent look of walleyed astonishment that defied surgical correction. Any thoughts that she may have had of a movie career were left on the campus of OSU.

In memorandum form, advise whether a possible tort claim exists. Your analysis should be based upon your knowledge of the fundamental principles that underlie tort law. A determination should be made as to the common law roots of any tort that may have occurred on the OSU campus that fateful May evening.

2 The Tort of Negligence

There is occasions and causes why and wherefore in all things.

William Shakespeare, *Henry V*

The doctrine of negligence is the most frequent basis for lawsuits involving injuries to person and property in the United States today. Legal scholars consider it to be the most complex concept in the law. Negligence is based upon a determination of what is considered acceptable conduct. *Unacceptable conduct* may support an action for negligence; *acceptable conduct* will not. Defining acceptable conduct is difficult, yet it remains the task of the trier of fact in any action for negligence. The unreasonableness of the tortfeasor's conduct establishes legal responsibility for unacceptable acts or omissions. This chapter provides an analysis of an action for negligence. The fundamental question for the paralegal student is: Did the defendant-tortfeasor act reasonably under the circumstances?

Chapter Topics

1. Negligence Explained
2. Elements of Negligence
3. Duty of Reasonable Care
4. Breach of Duty of Reasonable Care
5. Proximate Cause
6. Damages

Objectives

After completing this chapter, you will be able to:

1. Define the tort of negligence.
2. Understand the duty of reasonable care, the reasonable person standard, and the sources of the duty.
3. Discuss the concept of a breach of the duty of reasonable care.
4. Understand the concepts related to the requirement of proximate cause.
5. Profile the issue of damages in a tort action.

Negligence Explained

Negligence is a term that has been a source of confusion to both the public and the courts. It can be used to describe behavior that is a careless lack of acceptable conduct; or it can be used to refer to the tort that sustains an action for negligence. The tort of negligence consists of four elements, only one of which refers to unacceptably careless conduct on the part of the tortfeasor.

negligence

In its more limited sense, **negligence** is the failure to use the care a reasonable person would under the same circumstances. The term refers to lack of acceptable conduct forming the requirement of a duty of reasonable care necessary to sustain an action for negligence. Negligence does not refer to the *state of mind* of the tortfeasor, but rather focuses on his or her *conduct*. There is no requirement that the negligent tortfeasor *intend* to bring about the consequences that resulted from the action. It is only necessary that he or she fail to anticipate the risk of consequences and fail to guard against such consequences appropriately.

In 1923 a group of prominent American judges, lawyers, and legal scholars founded the American Law Institute (ALI) to combat the growing uncertainty and undue complexity of the law in several areas. The stated goal of the ALI was to produce a clear and concise statement of the existing common law, the *Restatement (Second) of Torts*, that would be considered an authority on a par with court decisions. The modern *Restatement* indicates a trend in the law, and presents a statement of what the law should be. The paralegal researcher should be familiar with the *Restatement* as a well-respected secondary authority.

In its *Restatement (Second) of Torts*, the American Law Institute defines negligence as a standard of conduct (see Figure 2-1).

Figure 2-1. Negligence

Negligence is conduct which falls below the standard established by law for the protection of others against unreasonable risk of harm.

Restatement (Second) of Torts §282

Negligence is a body of law that attempts to establish a standard for the protection of others from the unreasonable risk of harm from such careless individuals. Defining the standard for a trier of fact to determine negligent behavior, Professor Keeton states that the law must look not to the mind of the tortfeasor, but to the demands that society places on conduct (see Figure 2-2).

Figure 2-2. Standard of Conduct

The standard of conduct imposed by the law is an external one, based upon what society demands generally of its members, rather than upon the actor's personal morality or individual sense of right and wrong. A failure to conform to the standard is negligence, therefore, even if it is due to clumsiness, stupidity, forgetfulness, an excitable temperament, or even sheer ignorance. An honest blunder, or a mistaken belief that no damage will result, may absolve the actor from moral blame, but the harm to others is still as great, and the actor's individual standards must give way in this area of the law to those of the public. In other words, society may require of a person not to be awkward or a fool.

W. Page Keeton et al., *Prosser and Keeton on the Law of Torts* §31 at 169 (5th ed. 1984)

That standard of conduct demanded by society goes well beyond mere moral blamelessness. It is a standard left to be defined by the courts, and provides the fundamental element of the tort of negligence.

Elements of Negligence

Four elements are required to maintain an action for the tort of negligence. The failure of any of the elements results in a failure of the action. Since issues placed before a jury in a tort action are phrased as questions, the elements of the tort are best understood phrased in that form. The four elements required for an action for negligence are:

- Did the defendant owe a duty of reasonable care to the plaintiff?

- Did the defendant breach the duty of reasonable care?
- Was the defendant's breach the proximate cause of the plaintiff's injury?
- Did the plaintiff suffer damages?

Figure 2-3. Elements of Negligence

These elements are presented in the order submitted to a jury in order to sustain a verdict for the plaintiff. The defendant must owe a duty to the plaintiff in order to be held responsible for a breach of that duty. By the same token, before the defendant can be held responsible for any damages, those damages must be proximately caused by the defendant's breach. The defendant is not responsible for every injury to the plaintiff; he or she is responsible only for those injuries that are directly related to a breach of a duty. If the trier of fact answers any one of these questions in the negative, then the action for negligence will fail.

Duty of Reasonable Care

duty of reasonable care

duty

The first element required to sustain an action for negligence is the existence of a duty of reasonable care: Did the defendant owe a **duty of reasonable care** to the plaintiff? The duty of reasonable care is a standard of conduct that is owed by the defendant-tortfeasor to the plaintiff in an action for negligence. A **duty** within the meaning of the law is an obligation requiring an individual to do or refrain from doing something to protect others from harm.

Black's Law Dictionary offers this definition for a duty:

Figure 2-4. Duty

An obligation, recognized by the law, requiring actor to conform to certain standard of conduct for protection of others against unreasonable risks.

Black's Law Dictionary 505 (6th ed. 1990)

It requires that individuals drive their automobiles, operate their water craft, maintain their equipment, and otherwise act to avoid the risk of harm to others.

A determination as to the existence of a legal duty is a question for the court to decide, not the trier of fact. Thus it is said that the existence of a duty of reasonable care is a legal question, not an issue of fact. The court must make its determination based upon the question: Did the defendant owe an obligation to the plaintiff to act or not to act in a certain manner?

The duty of reasonable care is best understood if examined in light of the following categories:

- reasonable person standard
- scope of the duty
- source of the duty
- an act or omission
- foreseeability

An examination of each of these categories will help the paralegal student to understand the complex issue of the duty of reasonable care.

Reasonable Person Standard

The doctrine of negligence is based upon the creation in the law of a standard by which the conduct of a community's members may be measured. The courts have met this demand by the creation of an imaginary person who never actually existed, but who exemplifies the abstract ideal of the duty of reasonable care. This abstract person is called a reasonable person, and forms the basis for the **reasonable person standard**. The reasonable person standard compares the conduct of an individual to that of an imaginary person under the same or similar circumstances in avoiding harm to another. The *Restatement (Second) of Torts* defines the reasonable person standard in similar terms (see Figure 2-5).

reasonable person standard

Figure 2-5. Conduct of a Reasonable Man: The Standard

Unless the actor is a child, the standard of conduct to which he must conform to avoid being negligent is that of a reasonable man under like circumstances.

Restatement (Second) of Torts §283

Under the reasonable person standard (formerly called the reasonable man standard), an individual conducts himself or herself as an imaginary reasonable person would to avoid or prevent injury to another. Similarly, Professor Keeton informs us that the reasonable person is an ideal individual embodying all the proper qualities less some human shortcomings (see Figure 2-6).

Figure 2-6. Reasonable Person Standard

The actor is required to do what such an ideal individual would be supposed to do in his place. A model of all proper qualities, with only those human shortcomings and weaknesses which the community will tolerate on the occasion, "this excellent but odious character stands like a monument in our Courts of Justice, vainly appealing to his fellow-citizens to order their lives after his own example."

W. Page Keeton et al., *Prosser and Keeton on the Law of Torts* §32 at 174 (5th ed. 1984)

The question of the application of the standard of the reasonable person is one for the trier of fact, usually the jury, to decide. The jury must answer this question: Under the same or similar circumstances, would a reasonable person act as this individual did? The jury must recognize that the unpredictability of human behavior dictates a certain amount of latitude in defining this imaginary person. The reasonableness of the individual's conduct must be measured in light of certain characteristics:

- physical attributes
- mental condition
- age
- knowledge, skill, and intelligence

Thus, the reasonableness of the conduct becomes a subjective determination dependent upon the circumstances of the situation and certain individual traits. It is the trier of fact that determines the application of the reasonable person standard.

Physical Attributes. The general rule is that the reasonable person has the same physical attributes as the defendant-tortfeasor. A defendant who is in some way physically incapacitated cannot be held to a standard of conduct that would be impossible for him or her to meet. For instance, a deaf individual is entitled to have allowance made for his or her disability. The deaf person cannot be held to a standard that would require him or her to hear an approaching locomotive. The applicable criterion in that case requires that the person take the precautions that an ordinary reasonable deaf person would under the same circumstances (see Figure 2-7).

Figure 2-7. Case in Point: *Jakubiec v. Hasty*

Jakubiec v. Hasty
Supreme Court of Michigan
337 Mich. 205, 59 N.W.2d 385 (1953)
June 22, 1953

BUSHNELL, Justice.

Plaintiff Theresa Jakubiec was 18 years of age at the time of her injury. Her father, Joseph Jakubiec, as her next friend, instituted an action for her damages and a separate action for medical expenses and the loss of her services. These actions were combined and tried before a jury.

Defendants Arthur L. Hasty, the owner of the taxicab which struck Miss Jakubiec, and John P. Nugent, his employee driver, have appealed from judgments entered upon the jury's verdicts in the personal injury case of $6,500, and in the medical expense and loss of service case of $1,000.

It is admitted that the taxicab struck the plaintiff while she was crossing Michigan Avenue in the city of Detroit on August 4, 1948, at 3:40 p.m. She was walking from the northwest curb of the intersection of Brooklyn Avenue to the east-bound street-car safety zone on Michigan. The day was rainy and the pavement was wet.

Plaintiff suffered a compound fracture of her right leg, with cuts and bruises which required hospitalization for four days and confinement to her home for six weeks. She was unable to resume her work until about seven months after the accident. As a result of her injury, Miss Jakubiec's right leg is now shorter than her left....

Plaintiff is a deaf-mute and was examined through an interpreter. On the day of the accident she was employed at the Banner Laundry on Brooklyn Avenue, a few blocks north of Michigan, from which place she walked southerly down the west side of Brooklyn to the northwest corner of the intersection. Michigan Avenue runs almost due east and west, while Brooklyn runs about 30 degrees west of north. She testified she looked both ways, saw a truck and car coming from the east at a distance of about 300 feet, about a block away. A streetcar was approaching from the west at the same time, also about a block distant.

Plaintiff testified that the truck passed her at about 30 miles per hour and the car that followed it was moving at about the same speed. She then started across Michigan to the east-bound safety zone. When she reached the west-bound streetcar tracks, defendant's taxicab, also going west, suddenly appeared and struck her. She said she first saw the approaching taxicab when 20 feet away in the center of the street near the west-bound rails....

Another witness for the defense was Claude D. McKim, who was the motorman of the east-bound streetcar that was involved in the accident. He testified that he saw a woman run in front of a Checker cab. In answer to the question: 'Have you any estimate of the speed of the cab?' He answered: 'No, just the usual rate of speed, around twenty-five miles an hour.' Upon objection, the court ruled: 'The answer after the word no will be stricken.' McKim said that the woman left the curb at a point about 10 feet west of the west end of the safety zone; that when he first saw the taxicab it was about 15 feet away and swerving to its left after straddling the north west-bound rail. He stated that the woman did not look when she left the curb. A Checker Cab Company employee testified that he made a search for Hasty's driver, Nugent, but that he could not be found. Neither defendant testified at the trial.

The jury, in announcing its verdicts, assessed the amounts in each case against Hasty. The trial judge informed the jury that Hasty, the owner, could not be held liable unless it was found that the driver, Nugent, was guilty of negligence. After some colloquy between the court and the jury, and an indication that some of its members wanted to further discuss the matter, the jury again retired. Verdicts against both defendants were thereafter returned.

The first question in the case is whether plaintiff was guilty of contributory negligence as a matter of law. Defendants claim that the accident occurred about 50 feet west of the westerly line of Brooklyn Avenue. Their police witness said the body was lying about 20 feet west of the crosswalk. McKim testified that the woman did not look when she left the curb and that she ran directly in front of the taxicab. Plaintiff testified that she could not see the taxicab because of the large passing truck. The speed of the taxicab is a matter of dispute. In view of the conflicting testimony a question of fact was raised for the jury as to plaintiff's contributory negligence....

We are urged to grant a new trial because of the court's refusal to instruct the jury in accordance with defendants' requests Nos. 8 and 9, which read:

"The plaintiff is a deaf mute. The fact that plaintiff is a deaf mute, and has not full use of all of her senses, is a fact which she, herself, must take into consideration in essaying to cross a thoroughfare.

"You must decide this case wholly on the evidence presented to you, and keep your minds and hearts free of any question of sympathy or prejudice."

The first request, which is in conformity with that suggested in *Covert v. Randall*, supra, might well have been given.

The court in its charge did not specifically instruct the jury that sympathy should not enter into their deliberations or that a deaf-mute is not excused from using the standards of care that an ordinarily prudent person would exercise under similar circumstances, as was charged in the Covert case. However, there is no showing that the jury's verdicts were unjust or that they were reached as the result of undue sympathy for the plaintiff. They should not be set aside on this ground. *Doyle v. Dobson*, 74 Mich. 562, 567, 42 N.W. 137....

The judgments are affirmed, with costs to appellees.

Mental Condition. In contrast to the law governing the physical attributes of an imaginary reasonable person, the courts are not as tolerant concerning the defendant-tortfeasor's mental condition. The defendant is held to an objective standard of reasonableness regardless of his or her mental health. For a minor mental deficiency, bad judgment, or an excitable temperament, the law still holds the defendant to a standard of reasonable conduct. For the defendant to allege that he or she did the best that he or she knew how is never a defense.

Figure 2-8. Case in Point: *Jolley v. Powell*

Jolley v. Powell
District Court of Appeals
299 So.2d 647 (2nd DCA 1974)
Sept. 4, 1974

McNULTY, Judge.

We answer today a question certified to us by the Circuit Court for Pinellas County in this pending wrongful death action. The question certified is as follows:

IN AN ACTION FOR WRONGFUL DEATH, IS THERE AVAILABLE TO THE DEFENDANT THE AFFIRMATIVE DEFENSE OF INSANITY AT THE TIME OF THE ACT, CAUSING THE ALLEGED WRONGFUL DEATH.

The alleged facts underlying the question are that on October 28, 1972, the defendant James Powell shot and killed Karen Ann Jolley under most bizarre circumstances. He was acquitted of homicide "by reason of insanity" in a subsequent prosecution. This action followed.

At the outset, we restrict the scope of the question. We do so because, while Florida has not answered the precise question, the general rule in jurisdictions which have considered it make a distinction between insanity as a defense to an unintentional tort and as a defense to those torts requiring a specific state of mind which defendant may be incapable of forming. These latter would include, for example, actions based on deceit, malice or defamation. Therefore, since this action is based on a "wrongful act" or "negligence," as circumscribed by Florida's wrongful death act, we limit the scope of the question as relating to unintentional tort actions and answer the question in the negative.

It is surely not unusual in tort law nor indeed is it unfair that persons may be held responsible for failing to live up to a standard which, as a matter of fact, they cannot meet. As Justice Holmes observed:

> The standards of the law are standards of general application... It does not attempt to see men as God sees them, for more than one sufficient reason...[the awkward man's] slips are no less troublesome to his neighbors than if they sprang from guilty neglect.

And who would deny that the victim of a nuisance may have it abated regardless of the intent of the offending party?

So liability without subjective fault, under some circumstances, is one price men pay for membership in society. The sane and the insane, the awkward and the coordinated are equally liable for their acts or omissions. In such cases we do not decide fault, rather we determine upon whom our society imposes the burden of redress for a given injury. As Holmes implied in his "awkward man" parable, a principle at least co-equal with that of the fault principle in the law of torts is that the innocent victim should have redress....

In addition to the foregoing reasoning, we are also of the view that practical considerations in the administration of justice militate against unnecessarily injecting all of the confusion and potential for false claims inherent in the unsatisfactory tests of insanity in criminal cases into civil actions. We therefor reiterate, when the predicate for a wrongful death action is unintentional tort the standard against which such tort is measured is the objective, "reasonable man standard" and the subjective state of mind of the tortfeasor is irrelevant.

In passing, we point out that we do not mean to say here that insanity would not be a defense to a claim for punitive damages. Our rationale would seem to suggest that such a defense would indeed be available in such cases.

We need not decide the point now, however, since punitive damages are not sought herein.

MANN, C. J., and GRIMES, J., concur.

In the case of more serious mental disorders, the courts also hold the individual to a standard of reasonable conduct even though it may be a standard that he or she cannot possibly meet. The law requires severely disturbed or psychotic individuals to conform to general standards of conduct and renders them responsible for any harm caused. The *Restatement (Second) of Torts* provides that a mental illness does not relieve the actor from responsibility (see Figure 2-9).

Figure 2-9. Mental Deficiency

Unless the actor is a child, his insanity or other mental deficiency does not relieve the actor from liability for conduct which does not conform to the standard of a reasonable man under like circumstances.

Restatement (Second) of Torts §283 B

Similarly, voluntary intoxication and drug use render the defendant fully responsible for his or her actions. The drunk or drugged person is held to the same standard as a reasonable person who is sober and straight.

Age. Allowances are made for individuals of advanced age in applying the standard of a reasonable person. The courts treat similarly the elderly and individuals with limited physical capacities. The trier of fact compares the individual with a reasonable person of similar age and infirmity under the same or similar circumstances.

The rule regarding children departs from an objective standard of reasonableness. The courts view a child as a person of so few years as to be incapable of exercising the level of prudence of a reasonable adult. The law does not require children to meet the physical standards of adults or match their ability to form mature decisions. Professor Keeton provides his observation of the law regarding the standard to be applied to children in Figure 2-10.

Figure 2-10. Children

The standard which is ordinarily applied, and which is customarily given to the jury, is to measure the child's conduct against what would be reasonable to expect of a 'child of like age, intelligence and experience.' There is something of an individual standard: capacity of the particular child to appreciate the risk and form a reasonable judgment must be taken into account.

W. Page Keeton et al., *Prosser and Keeton on the Law of Torts* §32 at 179 (5th ed. 1984)

The law has also attempted to establish a minimum age below which a child cannot be held responsible for his or her actions. The age may vary from state to state, but a common minimum age for responsibility is set at seven. Above that age, the standard is that of a child of similar age and discretion, and is applied up to the age of majority. As an example, a child of five may not be held responsible for his or her actions, but at age ten, he or she will be held to a standard of conduct of a reasonable ten-year-old. Beyond the age of majority, the individual is held to the objective reasonable person standard.

Knowledge, Skill, and Intelligence. The law requires that for an act or omission to be negligence, it is necessary that an individual know that his or her act involves a risk of causing harm. Determining just *what* the defendant is required to know is a problem that has plagued the courts. **Knowledge** is defined as an awareness or understanding gained through experience or study. An individual cannot be presumed to know everything, and the law does not require such an impossibility. But the reasonable person standard does require a certain minimum level of knowledge and understanding necessary to survive. For instance, a reasonable person is aware that an object that is dropped will fall, that fire burns most things, and that water offers a potential for drowning. The *Restatement (Second) of Torts* suggests the reasonable person standard for recognizing the existence of risk (see Figure 2-11).

knowledge

Figure 2-11. Recognizing Existence of Risk

The actor is required to recognize that his conduct involves a risk of causing an invasion of another's interest if a reasonable man would do so while exercising

(a) such attention, perception of the circumstances, memory, knowledge of other pertinent matters, intelligence, and judgment as a reasonable man would have; and

(b) such superior attention, perception, memory, knowledge, intelligence, and judgment as the actor himself has.

Restatement (Second) of Torts §289

Most individuals who have led a normal life have absorbed information about such mundane matters as the weather, animals, machinery, electricity, sharp objects, and basic human behavior. A reasonable person will be presumed to possess such knowledge. By the same token, he or she will not be expected to know those things that are beyond daily experience. With society's rapid changes, individuals are assumed to possess knowledge today that would not have been required of them 25 or 50 years ago. The lack of knowledge tolerated yesterday forms the basis of liability for negligence tomorrow.

Just as the reasonable person standard requires minimum levels of knowledge for an individual, it also demands that an individual possessing superior knowledge or intelligence must act accordingly. Experts and professionals such as doctors, lawyers, dentists, and accountants are required to possess a certain minimum level of knowledge and ability beyond the exercise of reasonable care.

They are held to a higher standard than people not trained in those professions. Professional malpractice will be examined in greater detail later.

Act or Omission

act

omission

misfeasance

nonfeasance

The existence of a duty of reasonable care depends upon whether the defendant-tortfeasor acted or failed to act as a reasonable person. Conduct forming the basis of an action for negligence may be either an *act* or an *omission*. An **act** within the meaning of the law is the process of doing something. An **omission** is the failure to do something. To provide the basis of an action for negligence, the act must be a duty required of a reasonable person under the same or similar circumstances. An act of misconduct is called **misfeasance**, and may form the basis of liability for negligence if the act results in harm to another and fails to meet the reasonable person standard.

A failure to act is termed **nonfeasance**, and forms the basis of an action for negligence if a reasonable person would not have failed to act under similar circumstances. If another is harmed by the negligent nonfeasance of an individual, an action may be maintained. The key to understanding whether a court will impose liability for either misfeasance or nonfeasance lies in an application of the reasonable person standard; in other words, if a reasonable person would have acted or refrained from acting, then the tortfeasor will be held to that standard.

Source of Duty

The vast body of law concerning the duty of reasonable care is found in both federal and state case law and in federal and state statutes. The paralegal student must be familiar with these resources for the fundamental principles underlying the duty as formed by the common law, and as altered or altogether abandoned by statutory law.

Case Law. The common law of this country, embodied in its case law, forms the primary source for authority establishing the duty of reasonable care. Decisions of appellate courts determine the guidelines for negligent conduct. Those guidelines are then used by the trier of fact to determine whether conduct has conformed to those standards. The appellate courts decide the reasonableness of conduct for the community, and the juries determine whether or not those standards have been met.

The criteria established by the courts are constantly changing and reforming as our community's demands change; further, the courts continue to scrutinize the duty of reasonable care model as society evolves. This process serves to prevent inflexibility in the application of the duty of reasonable care.

Statutory Law. Certain applications of the duty of reasonable care may also be found in congressional and legislative enactments. Statutes have been enacted that are designed to protect the individual from certain harm just as the common law seeks to require ordinary care. Some statutes establish a fixed standard to be met under certain specified circumstances. For instance, statutes addressing product warranties, medical consent, and limitations of actions represent situations where a legislature has abrogated common law principles and established new standards of conduct. Worker's compensation laws and federal tort claim actions are other areas where there has been legislative modification of common law negligence principles.

Breach of the Duty of Reasonable Care

The second element required to maintain a tort action for negligence is found in the question: Did the defendant breach the duty of reasonable care? If a defendant-tortfeasor owes a duty of reasonable care, and he or she has breached that duty by failing to exercise reasonable care, then an action for negligence may be supported.

breach

A **breach** is a failure to perform a legal obligation or duty. A violation of the duty of reasonable care constitutes a breach of the duty. If the defendant-tortfeasor's conduct is unreasonable, then he or she has breached the duty. If the defendant-tortfeasor fails to perform a duty that is expected of a reasonable person, then the duty has been breached.

As seen in the discussion of the duty of reasonable care, negligence requires more than a mere state of mind of the defendant-tortfeasor; it is conduct that falls below a standard established by law. A mere failure to exercise due care is insufficient to constitute a breach of the duty. According to Professor Keeton, the breach must be more than a failure to consider another (see Figure 2-12).

Figure 2-12. Breach of Duty

The almost universal use of the phrase "due care" to describe conduct which is not negligent should not obscure the fact that the essence of negligence is not necessarily the absence of solicitude for those who may be adversely affected by one's actions but is instead behavior which should be recognized as involving unreasonable danger to others.

W. Page Keeton et al., *Prosser and Keeton on the Law of Torts*
§31 at 169 (5th ed. 1984)

Therefore, the trier of fact must focus on the conduct of the defendant rather than his or her state of mind. An individual will not be held liable for thinking negligently, but will be held liable for conduct that is unreasonable.

Proximate Cause

The third required element necessary to sustain a tort action for negligence is a proximate cause between the breach of the duty of reasonable care and the plaintiff's injury: Was the defendant's breach the proximate cause of the plaintiff's injury?

Proximate Cause Defined

The term *proximate cause* is the source of much confusion in legal writing. The paralegal student will encounter numerous attempts to clarify the term, attempts that sometimes serve only to add to the confusion and disagreement.

proximate cause

Proximate cause simply means that the defendant-tortfeasor's conduct caused a foreseeable injury to the plaintiff. It is frequently called legal cause, and refers to a conclusion by the trier of fact that the plaintiff's injuries are a natural and probable consequence of the conduct of the defendant. A defendant-tortfeasor cannot be found liable for negligence without a cause that is proximate to the harm.

cause

proximate

The term **cause** means something (an act or omission) that produces an effect, a result, or a consequence. The term **proximate** means something (an act or omission) that is closely related in space, time, or logical order. A combination of the two definitions results in a definition of proximate cause as a closely related act or omission by the defendant-tortfeasor that produces an injury to the plaintiff.

Causation

Cause in Fact. In order for a defendant-tortfeasor to be liable to an injured plaintiff, the trier of fact must decide that the conduct of the defendant has caused the harm. **Cause in fact** means the defendant's conduct was the cause of the plaintiff's injury. It is the most simple and direct way to look at causation of injury, and refers to all things that lead to the eventual injury. To illustrate cause in fact, assume that Arthur threw a banana peel on the sidewalk in front of his home. When Samantha rode by on her bicycle and struck the hazard with her front tire, she fell to the ground, injuring herself. Arthur's conduct in throwing the banana peel on the sidewalk was the cause in fact of Samantha's fall and injury.

cause in fact

But-for Rule. In a negligence action, the trier of fact must conclude not only that the conduct of the defendant-tortfeasor was a cause in fact, but that it was the legal cause of the injury. One test used by the courts for many years is called the **but-for rule.** The but-for rule states that if the harm would not have occurred without (but for) the conduct of the defendant, then the defendant-tortfeasor is liable. Professor Keeton also refers to this as the *sine qua non* rule (see Figure 2-13).

but-for rule

Figure 2-13. But-for Rule

From such cases many courts have derived a rule, commonly known as the "but-for" or "*sine qua non*" rule, which may be stated as follows: The defendant's conduct is a cause of the event if the event would not have occurred but for that conduct; conversely, the defendant's conduct is not a cause of the event, if the event would have occurred without it.

W. Page Keeton et al., *Prosser and Keeton on the Law of Torts* §41 at 266 (5th ed. 1984)

In the illustration above, but for the fact that Arthur threw his banana peel on the sidewalk, Samantha would not have been injured. The application of the but-for rule makes Arthur's conduct the proximate cause of Samantha's injury. The trier of fact could conclude that his conduct was the legal cause of the injury.

The but-for rule works well to define legal cause with one cause involved in the equation but is limited to situations where there is *only* one causative factor. When there is more than one cause leading to the injury to a plaintiff, either one of which acting alone would have been sufficient to result in harm, then another test is required.

substantial factor rule

Substantial Factor Rule. A rule of determination of proximate cause that is more widely accepted than the but-for rule is the **substantial factor rule**. The rule states quite simply that if the defendant-tortfeasor's conduct was a substantial factor in bringing about the plaintiff's injury, then proximate cause may be found. The trier of fact may find the defendant's conduct to have been a substantial factor if it was a material element in bringing about the injury. The *Restatement (Second) of Torts* provides the generally accepted rule for legal causation (see Figure 2-14).

Figure 2-14. What Constitutes Legal Cause

The actor's negligent conduct is a legal cause of harm to another if

(a) his conduct is a substantial factor in bringing about the harm, and

(b) there is no rule of law relieving the actor from liability because of the manner in which his negligence has resulted in the harm.

Restatement (Second) of Torts §431

In determining if the cause was a substantial factor in the production of the plaintiff's injury, the trier of fact must conclude that a reasonable person would regard it as a cause.

Conversely, the defendant's conduct would not be a substantial factor if the harm would have occurred anyway. Consider a situation wherein Clarence takes his friend Walter fishing on a large body of water in his canoe. Clarence has not provided a life jacket for Walter. In a storm so heavy that a life jacket would have been of no value, Walter falls overboard and drowns. Certainly, Clarence's conduct in failing to provide a life jacket for Walter is negligent. But the storm was the substantial factor in the drowning, not the lack of a life jacket. Here, the trier of fact is faced with two causes: a failure to provide a life jacket, and a violent storm. The trier of fact must choose which of the causes was a substantial factor in Walter's death. A reasonable person would conclude that the storm was the substantial factor in the death.

Scope of Liability

The determination of the defendant-tortfeasor's legal responsibility for harm to the plaintiff only begins with a finding that the conduct was one of the causes of the injury. Once causation has been established by either the but-for or the substantial factor rule, then the trier of fact must decide whether the defendant should be held to be responsible as a matter of law. To find a defendant legally responsible for an injury, the defendant's conduct must have been the proximate cause of the harm to the plaintiff. A finding of proximate cause will support a finding of liability for the injury. Liability is legal responsibility for the harm caused to another. The trier of fact must conclude that the defendant's conduct was not merely *a* cause of the injury to the plaintiff, but must conclude that it was *the* proximate cause of the harm. The confusion over the use of this term has been the subject of much debate by legal scholars, as noted by Professor Keeton (see Figure 2-15).

Figure 2-15. Proximate Cause

The term "proximate cause" is applied by the courts to those more or less undefined considerations which limit liability even where the fact of causation is clearly established. The word "proximate" is a legacy of Lord Chancellor Bacon, who in his time committed other sins. The word means nothing more than near or immediate; and when it was first taken up by the courts it had connotations of proximity in time and space which have long since disappeared. It is an unfortunate word, which places an entirely wrong emphasis upon the factor of physical or mechanical closeness. For this reason "legal cause" or perhaps even "responsible cause" would be a more appropriate term. There is, however, no present prospect that long ingrained practice will ever be altered by the substitution of either.

W. Page Keeton et al., *Prosser and Keeton on the Law of Torts* §42 at 273 (5th ed. 1984)

Foreseeability or Unforeseeability

foreseeability

An essential factor in an appreciation of proximate cause is found in the concept of **foreseeability**. Foreseeability is a reasonable anticipation that harm will occur from an act or omission. It is a question that is the sole province of the trier of fact. To make a finding of proximate cause, the trier of fact must conclude that a reasonable person would have anticipated the injury to others resulting from his or her conduct. If a reasonable person could have anticipated the harm, then the harm was foreseeable.

unforeseeability

Another way to look at the concept of foreseeability is to look at those causes that are beyond the scope of foreseeability, which means that they are viewed as to their **unforeseeability**. Unforeseeability occurs when a reasonable person could not conclude that an injury would occur from an act or omission. While it presents the converse of foreseeability, the courts frequently view liability in terms of the unforeseeability of harm as opposed to its foreseeability. If the defendant-tortfeasor could not reasonably foresee harm from his or her conduct, i.e., harm is clearly unforeseeable to a reasonable person, then no liability exists.

The paralegal student will be better able to appreciate the concept of proximate cause or legal cause by viewing it in terms of foreseeability or unforeseeability. The case of *Pitre v. Louisiana Tech University* provides a vehicle for an analysis of the issues of duty and causation (see Figure 2-16).

Figure 2-16. Case in Point: *Pitre v. Louisiana Tech University*

PITRE v. LOUISIANA TECH UNIVERSITY
655 So.2d 659, 100 Ed.Law Rep. 1214 (La. App. 1995)
May 10, 1995

BROWN, Judge.

During an unusual winter storm in 1988, Earl Garland Pitre, Jr., a 20-year-old resident student at Louisiana Tech University, joined a number of other students in sledding down a hill at the school's Assembly Center. Tragically, Pitre's sport ended when he struck a light pole in the parking lot at the bottom of the hill. He is now a paraplegic.

The trial court dismissed Pitre's lawsuit against Tech on a summary judgment motion. Because the danger was obvious, the trial court ruled that Tech owed no duty to warn or protect students engaged in this voluntary activity. On appeal this court concluded that a duty existed due to Tech's ownership or custody of the land and its special relationship to its students. The case was reversed and remanded for trial on the merits to determine outstanding issues of breach, causation, comparative fault and damages....

On remand and after trial, Pitre's claims were rejected as the trial court again found that Tech owed no duty to Pitre. On the duty issue, however, the facts at trial were substantially identical to those presented in the summary judgment motion. Thus, we reverse and render judgment for plaintiffs, allocating fault and assessing damages....

FACTS

An ice and snow storm moved through northeast Louisiana in early January 1988. Prior to the storm, the Louisiana Tech Housing Office issued a winter bulletin to all dormitory residents. The bulletin, entitled "Winter Storms and Louisiana Tech," was placed on the beds of each dorm resident by a staff member. The following is excerpted from the bulletin:

> We encourage snowmen, sledding, etc., in proper areas and using good judgment. We discourage sledding down the hills along Tech Drive into the path of oncoming cars—not good judgement [sic]—nor is being dragged behind a moving vehicle considered good judgement [sic]. Fifteen reported personal injuries were associated with such behavior during the last snow.

Earl Pitre, Jr., was a sophomore at Louisiana Tech in January 1988. Earl, who lived in a dormitory on campus, attended a Lady Techsters basketball game the evening of January 7, 1988. Classes had been canceled that day as a result of the ice storm and many students, confined to the campus by the weather, took the opportunity to enjoy the snow. After the game, Earl met with some friends who were going sledding off the hill between the Thomas

Assembly Center and the Joe Aillet Football Stadium. The hill, which was approximately 85 feet high, led to a large, open parking lot, which was illuminated by several large light posts spaced approximately 150 feet apart. On the other side of the parking lot was the football stadium.

The students at the Assembly Center used makeshift sleds, such as cardboard boxes, plastic advertising signs and serving trays. Also utilized by the sledders were part of a rocking chair and a toilet seat. The most popular sled was a large, round, plastic trash can lid, approximately five feet in diameter. Because the lid was faster, traveled further and would hold several people on one ride, students waited in line for its use. After several trips down the hill on a cardboard sled, Earl joined the line of students who were using the lid. While riding on the lid, Earl and three other students struck one of the concrete-based lights in the parking lot. Earl received head and back injuries in the accident and is paralyzed from mid-chest down.

Earl and his parents filed suit against Louisiana Tech and the Board of Trustees for State Colleges and Universities, alleging that the university was negligent in failing to prohibit sledding around the Thomas Assembly Center and in failing to warn of the hazards of sledding in that area. Plaintiffs also alleged that Louisiana Tech *was* negligent in *encouraging* sledding in areas known to be hazardous and in failing to place cushions around the bases of the light posts in the parking lot.

Plaintiffs and defendants filed motions for summary judgment. The trial court found that there were no disputed issues of material fact and that the issue was whether plaintiffs or defendants were entitled to judgment as a matter of law. The trial court denied plaintiffs' motion for summary judgment, granted defendants' motion and dismissed plaintiffs' demands. Plaintiffs appealed. This court concluded that the trial court erred in finding that no duty existed, reversed and remanded for trial. *Pitre*, supra.

Trial was held in March 1993. The trial court once again found that defendants did not have a duty to implement, disseminate or enforce a no sledding policy on campus. Judgment in defendants' favor was rendered and plaintiffs' demands were dismissed on January 14, 1994. It is from this judgment that plaintiffs appeal, arguing that the trial court erred in revisiting the duty issue and in failing to find that their injuries were caused by defendants' negligence.

APPLICABLE LEGAL PRINCIPLES

LSA-C.C. Art. 2315 provides in part that every act of man that causes damage to another obliges him by whose fault it happened to repair it. If this act involves the failure to exercise reasonable care, it is deemed negligence....

In order to prevail in a negligence action, a plaintiff must prove:

(1) the defendant had a duty to conform his or her conduct to a specific standard of care (the duty element);

(2) the defendant failed to conform his or her conduct to the appropriate standard (the breach of duty element);

(3) the defendant's substandard conduct was a cause in fact of the plaintiff's injuries (the cause in fact element);

(4) the defendant's substandard conduct was a legal cause of the plaintiff's injuries (the scope of liability or scope of protection element); and
(5) actual damages (the damages element).

Duty

Duty is defined as the obligation to conform to the standard of conduct associated with a reasonable man in like circumstances.... The question of whether a duty exists in a particular set of circumstances is a question of law for the court to decide....

The evidence introduced at trial consisted overwhelmingly of the evidence that was before the trial court in the form of depositions on the motions for summary judgment. The additional testimony elicited and depositions introduced at the trial of this matter primarily addressed the issues of causation and damages. As noted above, whether a duty is owed is a legal determination. This court's conclusion that a duty was owed by defendants is the law of the case. In light of our previous holding in this case, we conclude that the duty issue was not properly before the trial court on remand and will not be considered again by this court on appeal. That issue became final when the Supreme Court denied writs and the matter was remanded to the trial court.

Breach

Through Tech's University Police, defendants were aware that students were sledding off the hill at the Thomas Assembly Center. Additionally, defendants were aware of the danger presented by the light poles in the parking lot at the foot of the hill. Therefore, they had a duty to either correct the unreasonably dangerous condition presented by the light poles or to warn of its existence.

The test for determining whether a breach of a landowner's duty to protect or warn against an unreasonably dangerous condition is whether, in the management of his property, he has acted as a reasonable man in view of the probability of injury to others.

Generally, a party who owes a duty breaches that duty when he fails to exercise reasonable care in protecting those at risk. Factors considered in the "reasonable man" analysis include the likelihood and gravity of the harm, the burden of prevention and the social utility of defendant's conduct....

Defendants knew that the hill at the Assembly Center was utilized by sledders. They knew that the last snow resulted in fifteen personal injuries associated with student play in the snow and icy conditions. Furthermore, the danger presented by the light poles in the parking lot at the Assembly Center was such that serious injury was likely to occur should a sledder strike one of the posts. As noted above, the burden of prevention was minimal to the university; there were several inexpensive measures that could have been implemented to either warn students of the danger presented or to make the hill safe. The only positive action taken by the university was to place a bulletin on each dorm student's bed encouraging sledding. Defendants breached the duty owed to Earl by failing to correct or warn of the danger presented by the light poles at the bottom of the Assembly Center hill.

Cause in Fact

Cause in fact is a "but for" inquiry; if the plaintiff would not have sustained the injuries but for the defendant's substandard conduct, then such conduct is a cause in fact of the plaintiff's harm....

When multiple causes are present, an alternative method for determining cause in fact is the "substantial factor" test.... Under this test, if the defendant's conduct was a "substantial factor" in bringing about the plaintiff's harm, cause in fact is established. Based on its erroneous conclusion that no duty was owed, the trial court did not determine whether defendants' conduct was a cause in fact of the accident and plaintiffs' resulting injuries.

This determination is not simply whether the winter storms bulletin was the impetus that caused Earl to sled down the hill at the Assembly Center. The proper inquiry is whether or not defendants' failure to warn or correct the unreasonably dangerous condition presented by the light poles in the parking lot was a cause in fact of plaintiffs' injuries. Under the facts and circumstances of this case, we find that both defendants' and Earl's own conduct contributed to the accident and plaintiffs' resulting injuries. Defendants' conduct was a substantial factor because in spite of its knowledge of the danger, it encouraged the activity and failed to warn or protect against the unreasonably dangerous condition created by the light poles. This failure to warn or protect was a substantial factor in bringing about the accident and resulting injuries.

Earl's conduct in sledding down an icy hill into a parking lot dotted intermittently with light poles, on an over-sized garbage can lid, headfirst, lying on his back, with three other students, was also a substantial factor in causing his and his parents' injuries.

Scope of Liability or Scope of Protection

The fourth inquiry, whether defendants' conduct was a legal cause of plaintiffs' injuries, entails a determination of whether their injuries were within the contemplation of the duty set forth above. There is no rule for determining the scope of the duty; the inquiry is ultimately a question of policy as to whether the particular risk falls within the scope of the duty.... In determining legal cause, the ease of association test asks how easily the risk of harm can be associated with the duty that was breached.

We have found that one cause in fact of the accident was defendants' breach of duty by failing to warn [of] or correct the unreasonably dangerous condition presented by the light poles in the parking lot at the bottom of a hill utilized by students for sledding. It is evident that the primary purpose for imposing such a duty is the protection of students from injuries incurred as a result of sliding into the light poles or other objects at the bottom of the hill, *such as* parked or moving vehicles, trash cans or other obstacles. The risk that a student might harm himself in such a fashion was therefore clearly within the scope of protection contemplated by imposition of that duty....

CONCLUSION

For the reasons set forth above, the judgment of the trial court is REVERSED and judgment is RENDERED as follows:

(1) Plaintiff, Earl Pitre, Jr. is awarded the following damages, with legal interest from date of judicial demand, subject to reduction according to his fault (75%):

General Damages: $2,500,000.00
Special Damages: $1,292,601.87
$3,792,601.87

(2) Plaintiffs, Earl and Joan Pitre, are each awarded $35,000, together with legal interest from date of judicial demand, for loss of consortium, subject to reduction according to plaintiff's, Earl Pitre, Jr.'s, fault (75%).

(3) Costs, here and below, are taxed against defendants.

The equation displayed in Figure 2-17 helps to illustrate the requirement of proximate cause as an essential element in establishing a defendant's liability for tort. To create liability, proximate cause involves cause in fact, either but-for or a substantial factor, and a foreseeable plaintiff.

Figure 2-17. An Equation for Proximate Cause

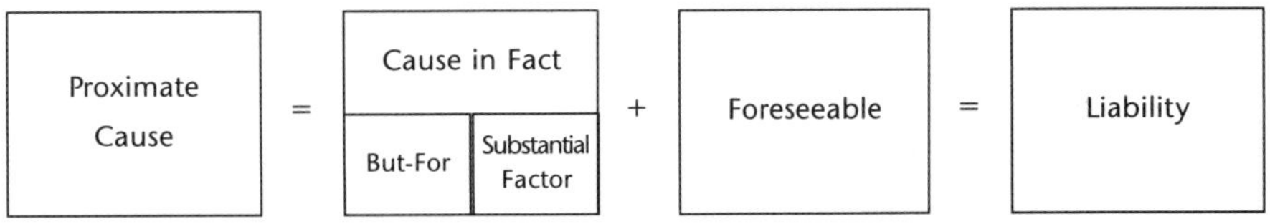

The question for the trier of fact does not depend on whether the defendant actually foresaw the injury, but on whether it was reasonable to have foreseen it. The *Restatement (Second) of Torts* supports the principle that if the conduct was a substantial factor, and a reasonable person would conclude foreseeability, then proximate cause exists (see Figure 2-18).

Figure 2-18. Foreseeability of Harm

(1) If the actor's conduct is a substantial factor in bringing about harm to another, the fact that the actor neither foresaw nor should have foreseen the extent of the harm or the manner in which it occurred does not prevent him from being liable.
(2) The actor's conduct may be held not to be a legal cause of harm to another where after the event and looking back from the harm to the actor's negligent conduct, it appears to the court highly extraordinary that it should have brought about the harm.

Restatement (Second) of Torts §435

Foreseeable Plaintiffs: The *Palsgraf* Case

In 1928 the New York Court of Appeals issued a decision in what became the most significant tort case of all time. This famous case is *Palsgraf v. Long Island*

Railroad Co., 248 N.Y. 339, 162 N.E. 99 (1928). Justice Cardozo wrote the opinion for the majority, and that opinion has been the most debated in all of tort law. Judge Cardozo held that there is no liability to a plaintiff that is not foreseeable. The principle of proximate cause was forsaken for the principle of a foreseeable plaintiff. The focus shifted from the foreseeability of the consequences to the foreseeability of the plaintiff.

The facts are these: Mrs. Palsgraf, the plaintiff, was standing on a platform of the defendant, Long Island Railroad. As a train stopped at the station, two men ran forward to board it. One of the men was carrying a package and jumped aboard the railroad car unsteadily. While two guards on the train tried to assist him, the package dropped to the tracks. Although there was nothing in its appearance to give notice of its contents, the package in fact contained fireworks, which exploded when the package fell. The shock of the explosion caused a set of scales at the other end of the platform to fall and strike Mrs. Palsgraf.

Judge Cardozo held that the defendant railroad was not liable to plaintiff Palsgraf for negligence. He found that negligence must be based upon the foreseeability of harm to the plaintiff. While the conduct of the employees of the defendant railroad may have been negligent toward someone else, it was not a foreseeable risk to the plaintiff (see Figure 2-19).

Figure 2-19. Case in Point: *Palsgraf*

PALSGRAF v. LONG ISLAND R. CO.
Court of Appeals of New York
248 N.Y. 339, 162 N.E. 99
May 29, 1928

Judgment entered on the verdict of a jury in favor of the plaintiff was affirmed by the Appellate Division by a divided court (222 App. Div. 166, 225 N.Y.S. 412), and defendant appeals.

Reversed, and complaint dismissed.

CARDOZO, C. J.

Plaintiff was standing on a platform of defendant's railroad after buying a ticket to go to Rockaway Beach. A train stopped at the station, bound for another place. Two men ran forward to catch it. One of the men reached the platform of the car without mishap, though the train was already moving. The other man, carrying a package, jumped aboard the car, but seemed unsteady as if about to fall. A guard on the car, who had held the door open, reached forward to help him in, and another guard on the platform pushed him from behind. In this act, the package was dislodged, and fell upon the rails. It was a package of small size, about fifteen inches long, and was covered by a newspaper. In fact it contained fireworks, but there was nothing in its appearance to give notice of its contents. The fireworks when they fell exploded. The shock of the explosion threw down some scales at the other end of the platform many feet away. The scales struck the plaintiff, causing injuries for which she sues.

The conduct of the defendant's guard, if wrong in its relation to the holder of the package, was not a wrong in its relation to the plaintiff, standing far away. Relatively to her it was not negligence at all. Nothing in the situation gave notice that the falling package had in it the potency of peril to persons thus removed. Negligence is not actionable unless it involves the invasion of a legally protected interest, the violation of a right. Proof of negligence in the air, so to speak, will not do... "Negligence is the absence of care, according to the circumstances."... (Citations omitted.) The plaintiff, as she stood upon the platform of the station, might claim to be protected against intentional invasion of her bodily security. Such invasion is not charged.... These, from the point of view of the law, were the bounds of her immunity, with perhaps some rare exceptions, survivors for the most part of ancient forms of liability, where conduct is held to be at the peril of the actor.... If no hazard was apparent to the eye of ordinary vigilance, an act innocent and harmless, at least to outward seeming, with reference to her, did not take to itself the quality of a tort because it happened to be a wrong, though apparently not one involving the risk of bodily insecurity, with reference to someone else. "In every instance, before negligence can be predicated of a given act, back of the act must be sought and found a duty to the individual complaining, the observance of which would have averted or avoided the injury." (Citations omitted.) "The ideas of negligence and duty are strictly correlative." The plaintiff sues in her own right for a wrong personal to her, and not as the vicarious beneficiary of a breach of duty to another.

A different conclusion will involve us, and swiftly too, in a maze of contradictions. A guard stumbles over a package which has been left upon a platform. It seems to be a bundle of newspapers. It turns out to be a can of dynamite. To the eye of ordinary vigilance, the bundle is abandoned waste, which may be kicked or trod on with impunity. Is a passenger at the other end of the platform protected by the law against the unsuspected hazard concealed beneath the waste? If not, is the result to be any different, so far as the distant passenger is concerned, when the guard stumbles over a valise which a truckman or a porter has left upon the walk? The passenger far away, if the victim of a wrong at all, has a cause of action, not derivative, but original and primary. His claim to be protected against invasion of his bodily security is neither greater nor less because the act resulting in the invasion is a wrong to another far removed. In this case, the rights that are said to have been violated, are not even of the same order. The man was not injured in his person nor even put in danger. The purpose of the act, as well as its effect, was to make his person safe. If there was a wrong to him at all, which may very well be doubted, it was a wrong to a property interest only, the safety of his package. Out of this wrong to property, which threatened injury to nothing else, there has passed, we are told, to the plaintiff by derivation or *succession* a right of action for the *invasion of an interest of* another order, the right to bodily security. The diversity of interests emphasizes the futility of the effort to build the plaintiff's right upon the basis of a wrong to someone else. The gain is one of emphasis, for a like result would follow if the interests were the same. Even then, the orbit of the danger as disclosed to the eye of reasonable vigilance would be the orbit of the duty. One who jostles one's neighbor in a crowd does not invade the rights of others standing at the outer fringe when the unintended contact casts a bomb upon the ground. The wrongdoer as to them is the man who carries the bomb, not the one who explodes it without suspicion of the danger. Life will have to be made over, and human nature transformed, before prevision so extravagant can be accepted as the norm of conduct, the customary standard to which behavior must conform....

The law of causation, remote or proximate, is thus foreign to the case before us. The question of liability is always anterior to the question of the measure of the consequences that go with liability. If there is no tort to be redressed, there is no occasion to consider what damage might be recovered if there were a finding of a tort. We may assume, without deciding, that negligence, not at large or in the abstract, but in relation to the plaintiff, would entail liability for any and all consequences, however novel or extraordinary. (Citations omitted.) There is room for argument that a distinction is to be drawn according to the diversity of interests invaded by the act, as where conduct negligent in that it threatens an insignificant invasion of an interest in property results in an unforeseeable invasion of interest of another order, as, e.g., one of bodily security. Perhaps other distinctions may be necessary. We do not go into the question now. The consequences to be followed must first be rooted in a wrong.

The judgment of the Appellate Division and that of the Trial Term should be reversed, and the complaint dismissed, with costs in all courts.

The *Palsgraf* case has been cited many times to support the principle that when an injury to an individual cannot be anticipated, then negligence does not exist. In other words, if there was no foreseeable plaintiff, then there cannot be an action for negligence. An action for negligence may be maintained only when the plaintiff is within an obvious area of danger. Thus, a defendant-tortfeasor owes a duty of reasonable care only to the foreseeable plaintiff. While the ruling in the *Palsgraf* case has received widespread acceptance in the tort law of most states, a lack of certainty as to what is foreseeable and what is unforeseeable has resulted in court decisions that seem to be in contrast to this ruling. The paralegal student must carefully research the law of his or her individual state for specific precedents.

Intervening Causes

intervening cause

There is a principle in the law of causation that is similar to proximate cause, yet it serves to relieve a defendant-tortfeasor from responsibility. That principle states that a negligent defendant-tortfeasor is relieved from liability by an **intervening cause**. An intervening cause is the act of a third person or some other force that produces injury to the plaintiff *after* the negligent act of the defendant. The intervening cause relieves the defendant from liability regardless of the fact that his or her negligence was a substantial factor in bringing about the injury.

The *Restatement (Second) of Torts* calls an intervening cause a *superseding cause,* and takes the position that it relieves the defendant from liability.

Given an unlimited number of causes that may be intervening causes, the courts apply the element of foreseeability to the intervening event. Professor Keeton takes the position that the superseding event must be foreseeable to alleviate the defendant's liability (see Figure 2-20).

Figure 2-20. Intervening Cause

The number and variety of causes which may intervene, after the negligence of the defendant is an accomplished fact, are obviously without any limit whatever. In the effort to hold the defendant's liability within some reasonable bounds, the courts have been compelled, out of sheer necessity and in default of anything better, to fall back upon the scope of the original foreseeable risk which the defendant has created. The question is always one of whether the defendant is to be relieved of responsibility, and the defendant's liability superseded, by the subsequent event. In general, this has been determined by asking whether the intervention of the later cause is a significant part of the risk involved in the defendant's conduct, or is so reasonably connected with it that the responsibility should not be terminated. It is therefore said that the defendant is to be held liable if, but only if, the intervening cause is foreseeable.

W. Page Keeton et al., *Prosser and Keeton on the Law of Torts* §44 at 302 (5th ed. 1984)

Just as the courts have diluted the rule in the *Palsgraf* case, their uneven treatment of the intervening cause principle has weakened that rule as well. For specific situations, the paralegal student must research the law of his or her particular jurisdiction.

DAMAGES

damages

The fourth essential element in an action for negligence is the question of damages: Did the plaintiff suffer damages? It is a fundamental rule in the law of negligence that the plaintiff must suffer actual harm to person or property for there to be any recovery. **Damages** consist of the recovery of money to compensate for loss or harm as a result of an unlawful act or wrong by another. In all tort actions for negligence, damages are money awarded to the plaintiff for injury resulting from the tortious conduct of another. Damages in a tort action are always monetary in nature, but the type of recovery may vary in its function. For instance, in an action for negligence, the plaintiff must have sustained some harm, loss, or injury. Actual harm is not required for some intentional torts, whereby it is sufficient merely that the tort occurred.

Types of Damages

There are three major types of damages that may be awarded in a tort action. The form of damages awarded will depend on both the tort and the presence of actual loss or injury. These are the three categories:

compensatory damages

Compensatory damages—The form of damages most frequently awarded in negligence actions, compensatory damages are to compensate the plaintiff for actual loss or injury. The elements that typically make up compensatory damages include medical expenses, property damage, lost wages, permanent loss of bodily function, and pain and suffering.

punitive damages

Punitive damages—The type of damages occasionally awarded for intentional torts or gross negligence (see Chapter 3) as punishment of the defendant, these damages are sometimes called *exemplary damages* or *treble damages*.

nominal damages

Nominal damages—The category of damages awarded when the plaintiff has sustained no actual loss or injury, they are awarded in intentional tort cases and in those involving strict liability. Nominal damages are never awarded in a negligence case because of the required element of actual harm.

The law of each individual state must be consulted to determine the types of damages that are allowed. Many states have enacted legislation that alters the availability of the common law forms of damages. Tort reform legislation in many states has altered the amounts of damages that may be awarded in particular types of tort cases, e.g., medical malpractice, and may also have placed a limitation on the amount of damages that can be awarded for pain and suffering. The paralegal student must review the statutes of his or her state on the question of damages allowed in tort actions.

Loss of Consortium

loss of consortium

A distinct type of damage awarded in some tort cases compensates the spouse of the injured party for loss of love, companionship, services, affection, and sexual relations. This form of damages is referred to as a claim for **loss of consortium**. The purpose of a claim for loss of consortium is to fully compensate the victims of negligent conduct. If one's spouse sustains injury at the hands of a defendant-tortfeasor, and that injury results in an inability to perform all that is customarily expected within the marital relationship, then there has been a loss beyond any monetary damage. The trier of fact bears the burden of making a subjective evaluation of the loss, an evaluation that is difficult and often based upon emotion rather than fact.

While the claim for loss of consortium under the old common law was available only to husbands, that gender bias was declared unconstitutional in 1950 in the matter of *Hitaffer v. Argonne Co.*, 183 F.2d 811 (1950), *certiorari* denied 340 U.S.

852, 71 S.Ct. 80, 95 L.Ed. 624. In virtually every jurisdiction, wives may now claim a loss of consortium for injuries to their husbands. Similarly, parents may claim a loss of consortium for injuries to children based upon a loss of society, companionship, and affection.

Avoidable Consequences

avoidable consequences

The doctrine of **avoidable consequences** is an important consideration for the paralegal student in reviewing the question of damages. If the plaintiff has sustained an injury, the doctrine of avoidable consequences mandates that he or she must take reasonable steps to prevent any further injury. The doctrine provides an effective limitation on damages for which the defendant-tortfeasor may be responsible. It concerns the conduct of the injured plaintiff after the initial injury at the hands of the defendant. The plaintiff's potential recovery is reduced by the amount of damage brought on by his or her own subsequent conduct. The doctrine of avoidable consequences is also sometimes called a failure to mitigate damages.

A plaintiff who fails to seek medical attention following injury typifies the doctrine of avoidable consequences. The conduct of the plaintiff has added to the damage from the original injury. The defendant is not to be held responsible for the failure of the plaintiff to seek medical attention when to do so would have been reasonable under the circumstances. This principle is different from the principle of contributory negligence, which serves as a total bar to any claim by the plaintiff. Contributory negligence is considered in detail in Chapter 4.

Collateral Source Rule

collateral source rule

Another doctrine impacting the determination of damages for which a defendant-tortfeasor may be responsible is the **collateral source rule**. It states that the defendant-tortfeasor may not benefit from the fact that the plaintiff has received compensation for his or her injuries from some other source. If the injured plaintiff receives money from a source independent of the defendant, the defendant's liability is not reduced.

Many individuals carry medical insurance or are entitled to medical benefits for injuries. These are known as collateral sources, and do not serve to reduce the amount of damages for which the defendant is responsible even though a double recovery for the plaintiff may result. To prevent the circumstance of double recovery, many collateral source providers have a contractual agreement with the plaintiff to reimburse the provider out of any recovered funds.

Summary

The issues surrounding the law of negligence are more difficult to conceptualize than any other single area of study. Individuals have a duty to avoid creating an undue risk of harm to others. This is the fundamental principle upon which the law of negligence is based. Negligence occurs when the individual's conduct falls below his or her duty to avoid creating the risk of injury. An action for negligence arises when the duty has been breached, proximately causing damages to the person harmed. The legal concepts of duty, reasonable person, breach of duty of reasonable care, proximate cause, and damages are all issues with which the paralegal student must be familiar. As these concepts are mastered, the student will have the capacity to better understand those issues that are ancillary to the central questions of a negligence action.

Review Questions

1. Provide a definition of negligence.
2. List the four elements that are essential to maintain an action for negligence.
3. What is the duty of reasonable care?
4. Describe the reasonable person standard.
5. What does the reasonable person standard require of an individual with superior knowledge and training?
6. Discuss the distinction between misfeasance and nonfeasance.
7. What constitutes a breach of the duty of reasonable care?
8. List the two forms of cause in fact.
9. What is proximate cause?
10. What are the three principal forms of damages?

Focus Your Skills

The annual January 1 celebration of the North American Free Trade Agreement was in full swing at the Cordon Sanitaire Retirement Home with its customary feast of juevos rancheros. The home was owned and operated by the American Society for the Preservation of Nearly Everything (ASPNE), a nonprofit organization dedicated to a century of tradition unfettered by progress. The society's logo consisted of a kelly-green ensign emblazoned with the motto, "You can't run, but you can hide!"

Resident Muriel Mieldhew had been confined to a wheelchair for the past two years, preferring the Easy Glider model, with outriggers, manufactured by Olds Mobile Wheel Chairs, Inc. As she exited from the festivities her Easy Glider brought her at great speed to the point outside the dining building where there should have been a barrier-free ramp to the garden level of the grounds.

Unfortunately for Muriel, the ramp was under construction by one Arnold "The Terminator" Roach, owner of Bugs 'R Us Exterminator Co. Seemingly inconsistent with the society's stated mission, at that exact moment The Terminator was actively engaged in rooting out a particularly virulent strain of termite menacing the wooden ramp.

At the precise moment that Muriel flashed by the posted "Hard Hat Zone" warning, the brakes on the Easy Glider failed, causing Muriel to make a wheels-up landing in the middle of The Terminator's back. The collision left Arnold narrowly clinging to life, never to walk again. Muriel escaped physical harm, although from a psychological standpoint, reality had become only an illusion.

The facts of the case present a unique opportunity for an analysis of the negligence issues presented. Review the case and provide your summary of these issues:

A. Duty

B. Reasonable care

C. Causation

D. Damages

3

Proof of Negligence

To hear patiently, to weigh deliberately and dispassionately, and to decide to impartially; these are the chief duties of a Judge.

Albert Pike (1809–1891)

A tort action for negligence presents unique legal issues of proof. Is there any liability if the accident was unavoidable? Are there situations in which the tortfeasor's negligence was so obvious that liability is automatic? How far must a plaintiff go to prove the tortfeasor's negligence? Who is responsible when there is more than one tortfeasor? In a death resulting from negligence, who is the plaintiff? These questions have provided legal scholars with ample opportunity for disagreement and debate for many years. A thorough knowledge of tort law requires that the paralegal student be familiar with the legal issues involved in the proof of a negligence case. This chapter does not focus on the development of the evidence necessary to prove facts. The investigation, information gathering, discovery, and trial of a negligence case are similar to any litigation, and are the proper subject of texts devoted to civil litigation. This chapter instead presents an analysis of the legal issues specific to proving an action for negligence.

Chapter Topics

1. Legal Proof
2. Unavoidable Accidents
3. Acts of God
4. Degrees of Negligence
5. Burden of Proof
6. *Res Ipsa Loquitur*
7. Joint Tortfeasors' Liability
8. Survival Actions and Wrongful Death

Objectives

After completing this chapter, you will be able to:

1. Analyze the concept of legal proof in a tort action.
2. Discuss the significance of unavoidable accidents in an attempt to prove negligence.
3. Distinguish between the degrees of negligence.
4. Evaluate the burden of proof in a negligence case.
5. Understand and apply the doctrine of *res ipsa loquitur*.
6. Profile joint tortfeasors' liability.
7. Summarize the principles of wrongful death and the survival of actions.

Legal Proof

legal proof

Establishing the elements to sustain a cause of action for negligence is a necessity for every attorney and paralegal. Rules control the types of evidence that may be presented to the trier of fact, the jury, and from which it may draw a valid inference. **Legal proof** is the result of drawing valid inferences from the available facts. Certain types of evidence are available to the jury, while others are excluded based upon the rules of legal process.

Rules of Evidence

rules of evidence

The presentation of legal proof is a process governed by the **rules of evidence**. The rules of evidence are rules of courts that govern the admissibility of evidence in a trial. Federal court rules are contained in the Federal Rules of Evidence found in Title 28 of the United States Code. Most states have modeled their respective rules of evidence after the Federal Rules.

evidence

Evidence is something that proves or disproves a fact. Evidence is presented to the trier of fact in the form of witnesses' testimony, exhibits, documents, and physical objects. The trier of fact must draw valid inferences and make its decisions from the evidence properly presented pursuant to the applicable rules.

The function of the jury as the trier of fact in a negligence case is to decide questions of fact. Questions concerning the law applicable to those facts are the judge's sole province. The general rule is that juries decide facts and judges decide the law. A **question of fact** is the resolution of an issue concerning the existence of a fact, as opposed to a question of law.

question of fact

It is sometimes difficult for the student to draw a distinction between a fact and an opinion. A **fact** is the existence of an actual occurrence or event as determined by the evidence presented. An **opinion** is what a person thinks or believes as a conclusion drawn from facts. It is an inference from facts, but is not a fact in and of itself. The jury must draw its conclusion as to the existence of facts, and is permitted to consider opinion evidence only from expert witnesses.

fact

opinion

To illustrate this concept, assume that the plaintiff in a tort action must prove that the defendant was angry at the time of the injury. The defendant's anger can be established by an expert witness qualified to render an opinion concerning human behavior. That opinion would represent the expert's inference drawn from certain facts, e.g., facial tension, redness, sweating, verbal statements, and related behavior. These observable phenomena are the facts, while the conclusion of anger would be the expert's opinion. The court would not allow a nonexpert to testify as to anything other than observable facts.

The fundamental principles of evidence common to all statutory codes of evidence may be summarized as follows:

- Evidence that is not relevant to the case cannot be received.
- With certain exceptions, hearsay evidence cannot be received.
- Opinion testimony can be received only from expert witnesses.
- The content of most writing cannot be varied by oral testimony.
- Privileged communications cannot be received.
- Evidence must be offered pursuant to the formal rules of court.

A full understanding of the concepts contained in these basic principles goes well beyond the parameters of this text. Questions concerning relevancy of evidence, hearsay testimony, the parol evidence rule, and privileged communications are subjects discussed in detail in treatises on evidence. The paralegal student should be aware that these rules are primarily designed to prevent the jury from hearing evidence that traditionally has been found to be unreliable. The function of the trier of fact is best served by reliance on evidence that is competent as opposed to reliance on facts that are not trustworthy.

Preponderance of the Evidence

Once the rules of evidence have determined the type and quantity of evidence the jury may consider, the jury weighs that evidence to form a conclusion as to

preponderance of the evidence

the existence of a fact. In a criminal case, the guilt of the defendant must be proven beyond a reasonable doubt. In civil actions for tort, the standard of proof is less stringent, requiring that the existence of a fact be proven by a **preponderance of the evidence**. This is a conclusion that a fact is more probable than not, more true than untrue. When weighing the evidence, the jury must decide the facts of the case on the basis of the greater probability of something existing. It must determine the credibility of witnesses, resolve conflicting testimony, and apply the standard of the reasonable person in making its findings. Issues such as proximate cause and the value of damages must also be resolved through the application of the same standard of proof.

Unavoidable Accident

unavoidable accident

The mere occurrence of an accident does not prove negligence as a matter of law. An action for negligence requires the plaintiff to prove that the injury was proximately caused by the breach of a duty by the defendant-tortfeasor. As discussed in Chapter 2, an essential element of proximate cause is the requirement that the injury to the plaintiff must have been clearly foreseeable. It follows that if the event or occurrence resulting in injury to the plaintiff could not have been foreseen or prevented by the exercise of reasonable care, then there can be no proximate cause. The doctrine of **unavoidable accident** states that an accident is unavoidable if it was not proximately caused by the act or omission of the defendant-tortfeasor. Unavoidable accidents lack the requisite proximate cause to sustain an action for negligence.

The rationale behind the doctrine is based upon the practical necessity of having to draw a line somewhere limiting the responsibility for human behavior. The law does not hold that every human act or omission is done at peril of facing exposure for liability. The limitation exists to prevent a defendant from being held liable for a mere accident, the result of which was clearly unforeseeable.

Act of God

act of God

Closely related to the concept of an unavoidable accident is the legal principle of an **act of God**. An act of God is a sudden, unexpected, and extraordinary demonstration of the force of nature from which humans cannot protect themselves. When harm results from an act of God, there is no liability for negligence.

The application of this principle is seen in the situation of a common carrier's liability for the safekeeping of goods placed in its possession. If the goods are destroyed through an act of God, and in no way through the negligence of the carrier, then there will be no liability for negligence. Professor Keeton supports this view (see Figure 3-1).

Figure 3-1. Unforeseeable Causes

If the defendant can foresee neither any danger of direct injury, nor any risk from an intervening cause, the defendant is simply not negligent. Negli-

> gence cannot be predicated solely upon a failure to anticipate that extraordinary and unprecedented rainfall will flood the streets, that a pedestrian will slip and fall upon an apparently safe highway, that the wind will blow a door latch against the eye of a boy, or that a ribbon held across a street to stop a wedding procession will cause one carriage to run into another. But once the defendant's negligence is established, because injury of some kind was to be anticipated, intervening causes which could not reasonably be foreseen, and which are no normal part of the risk created, may bring about results of an entirely different kind.
>
> W. Page Keeton et al., *Prosser and Keeton on the Law of Torts* § 44 at 311-312 (5th ed. 1984)

However, when an act of God combines with the negligence of the defendant-tortfeasor to produce harm or injury, then the defendant is liable for the damage. The theory is that the injury would not have occurred *but for* the negligence of the defendant. The defendant's negligence creates an element of foreseeability upon which to base a finding of liability. For instance, if the common carrier above delivered the goods to the wrong recipient, and in so doing placed the goods in the path of a sudden and unexpected force of nature, e.g., a tornado, then the carrier would still be liable. The act of God would not preclude the defendant's liability for negligence.

The application of this rule precludes any recovery for injuries caused by extreme weather conditions. No one is liable for an injury proximately caused by an act of God, which is an injury due directly and exclusively to natural causes, without human intervention, that could not have been prevented by the exercise of reasonable care and foresight. Extreme weather conditions such as excessive rains and floods have long been considered acts of God.

Degrees of Negligence

A now obsolete viewpoint in the law of negligence once imposed differing standards of conduct for different defendants or situations. The old law held that the greater the risk, the greater the care required by the defendant. It recognized three distinct degrees of negligence:

- slight negligence—the failure to use great care; still used in cases of common carrier liability;
- ordinary negligence—the failure to use ordinary care; and
- gross negligence—the failure to use slight care, falling short of willful and wanton disregard.

Attempts at the application of degrees of care to all negligence cases resulted in confusion and lack of uniformity in court decisions.

One Standard

The difficulty in classifying conduct and care required most courts to seek a single standard by which negligence can be measured. The current view in most jurisdictions is that there are no degrees of negligence, but merely one standard of care which is the same thing as ordinary negligence. (See Figure 3-2.)

Figure 3-2. Case in Point: *Massey v. Scripter*

MASSEY v. SCRIPTER
Supreme Court of Michigan
401 Mich.385, 258 N.W.2d 44
Oct. 6, 1977

MOODY, Justice.

On July 24, 1972, the plaintiffs, Lester and Wanda Massey, were riding their newly purchased tandem bicycle in an easterly direction on the shoulder of the westbound lane of Holmes Road in Ypsilanti Township, Washtenaw County, so that they were riding against the traffic. Mr. Massey was on the tandem's front seat and Mrs. Massey on the tandem's rear seat. As they approached the intersection of Ridge and Holmes Roads, Lester Massey pulled out onto Holmes Road to avoid chuckholes in the road shoulder.

A pickup truck driven by the defendant, Daniel Scripter, was legally stopped at the stop sign on southbound Ridge Road, waiting for traffic to clear on Holmes Road. As the truck started moving to enter the intersection, the tandem bicycle reached the intersection and passed slowly in front of the pickup truck. Defendant testified that as soon as he saw the bicycle he slammed on his brakes. Although the truck was traveling at a maximum speed of six miles per hour, according to a witness's testimony, an impact occurred causing both plaintiffs to sustain injuries requiring medical treatment.

The plaintiffs sued to recover for the personal injuries sustained in the accident and a jury returned a verdict of no cause of action. The plaintiffs appealed, claiming three errors in the trial court's instructions to the jury, and a fourth error in the trial judge's exclusion of testimony concerning the safety aspects of riding bicycles against the traffic. The Court of Appeals affirmed the trial court as to all four issues. This Court granted leave on November 1, 1976.

Plaintiffs claim error in the trial judqe's instructions as to the standard of care required of plaintiffs if they were riding their bicycle against the traffic in violation of M.C.L.A. § 257.660; M.S.A. § 9.2360, which provides in part:

> Sec. 660. (a) Every person operating a bicycle upon a roadway shall ride as near to the right side of the roadway as practicable, exercising due care when passing a standing vehicle or one proceeding in the same direction....

Twice during the jury charge the trial judge referred to the plaintiffs' duty to use "greater care" if they violated the statute....

Under Michigan law, while the standard of conduct required may differ depending upon the activity one is involved in, the standard of care required does not change. The standard of care required of a party is always that which a reasonably careful person would do or would refrain from doing under the circumstances....

One standard of care, that care which a reasonably prudent person would use under similar circumstances, is mandated in view of the medley of circumstances that may be presented to the trier of fact. While legal scholars and law school professors may use language intimating varying degrees of care, when charging a jury but a single standard of care is permissible.

In *Frederick v. City of Detroit*, 370 Mich. 425, 121 N.W.2d 918, we held it would have been an error to charge the jury that the defendant in a negligence case owed the plaintiff a "high degree of care." The measure of duty of a negligence-charged defendant is, as stated in *Frederick*, at page 431, 121 N.W.2d (918) at page 920, "reasonable care appropriate to the circumstances of the case, a standard of negligence which allows the fact finder to determine that some factual circumstances reasonably require greater or lesser diligence than do other circumstances in order to constitute reasonable or due care." In a legal opinion addressed to bench and bar it is not inappropriate to speak in terms of degrees of care and caution, as a form of legal shorthand; but when a jury of laymen is charged on the common law of negligence, the charge must be cast only in terms which a jury will understand impose a standard measured by that which a reasonably prudent man would regard as reasonably required by the specific factual circumstances of the case....

Therefore, we hold that the trial judge erred in instructing the jury that if plaintiffs' operation of their bicycle violated the Michigan statute, they would be required to use greater care than if they had kept the bicycle as near to the right side of the road as practicable. Viewing the instructions as a whole, this charge stands out as clear judicial usurpation of the jury's function. The necessity of greater or lesser care under the given circumstances is a question for the trier of fact. The Court of Appeals decision is reversed and this case is remanded to the trial court for a new trial.

As the court stated in *Massey*, the trier of fact should be charged with deciding the degree of care appropriate under the circumstances. Reference to degrees of care may be a legal shorthand, but is not required of the jury. To impose degrees of care would only serve to infringe on the duty of the trier of fact.

Willful, Wanton, and Reckless Conduct

willful, wanton, and reckless conduct

Modern negligence theory provides for a category of conduct that exists somewhere between ordinary negligence and purely intentional harm. It is called **willful, wanton, and reckless conduct**. The three terms are used interchangeably in the law, and almost invariably are used together to describe a form of highly unreasonable behavior, departing far beyond ordinary negligence. The courts have treated this behavior as aggravated negligence or, in some cases, gross negligence. Professor Keeton states the essence of this principle. (See Figure 3-3.)

Figure 3-3. Willful, Wanton, and Reckless Conduct

Lying between intent to do harm, which, as we have seen, includes proceeding with knowledge that the harm is substantially certain to occur, and the mere unreasonable risk of harm to another involved in ordinary negligence, there is a penumbra of what has been called "quasi-intent." To this area the words "willful," "wanton," or "reckless," are customarily applied; and sometimes, in a single sentence, all three. Although efforts have been made to distinguish them, in practice such distinctions have consistently been ignored, and the three terms have been treated as meaning the same thing, or at least as coming out at the same legal exit. They have been grouped together as an aggravated form of negligence, differing in quality rather than in degree from ordinary lack of care.

W. Page Keeton et al., *Prosser and Keeton on the Law of Torts* § 34 at 212 (5th ed. 1984)

The nature of the behavior goes well beyond ordinary negligence, but does not equal intentional conduct. It requires that the defendant-tortfeasor intend the act or omission, but need not intend the consequences. The *Restatement (Second) of Torts* treats the difference between reckless conduct and negligence in terms of the amount of risk, requiring that the defendant's behavior involve a risk substantially greater in amount than that necessary to make the conduct negligent (see Figure 3-4).

Figure 3-4. Reckless Disregard

The actor's conduct is in reckless disregard of the safety of another if he does an act or intentionally fails to do an act which it is his duty to the other to do, knowing or having reason to know of facts which would lead a reasonable man to realize, not only that his conduct creates an unreasonable risk of physical harm to another, but also that such risk is substantially greater than that which is necessary to make his conduct negligent.

Restatement (Second) of Torts § 500

The trier of fact determines whether conduct is willful, wanton, and reckless. The jury decides whether there has been a failure to exercise due care, and whether there was a great probability harm would result from the lack of care. The presence of the second element in this test allows a finding of willful, wanton, and reckless conduct.

Figure 3-5. Case in Point: *Matkovich v. Penn Central*

MATKOVICH v. PENN CENTRAL TRANSPORTATION COMPANY
Supreme Court of Ohio
69 Ohio St.2d 210, 431 N.E.2d 652
Feb. 17, 1982

CELEBREZZE, Chief Justice.

In this case, the jury found that Penn Central and Jennings were guilty of wanton misconduct. However, the Court of Appeals reversed. Therefore, we must determine whether the jury could have reasonably concluded, based on the evidence, that wanton misconduct existed. We will consider the conduct of appellees separately—first Penn Central, then Jennings.

The test for determining wanton misconduct was defined in *Hawkins v. Ivy* (1977), 50 Ohio St.2d 114, 363 N.E.2d 367. As stated by the Court of Appeals in the instant case, *Hawkins* created a two-part test for wanton misconduct. First, there is a failure to exercise any care whatsoever by those who owe a duty of care to the appellant. Secondly, this failure occurs under circumstances in which there is great probability that harm will result from the lack of care. The first prong of the test requires that we determine the duty appellees owed appellant, and also the extent of care exercised by appellees. Then, we must consider the nature of the hazard created by the circumstances....

Penn Central contends that the train in the crossing is, in itself, actual notice and an adequate warning. Because the train extended across the road, Penn Central argues that the train preempted the crossing and ordinary care did not require any additional warnings. Furthermore, it argues that the crossing was not exceptionally hazardous and no extra-statutory warnings were required....

The concept of a train serving as notice may have been reasonable decades ago when this standard was formulated. However, we must determine whether the train constituted actual notice of the hazard under the circumstances in this case. The train itself had no reflective tape, and the record reflects that the jury could have reasonably found that no warning devices were used by the railroad at the crossing. Considering the darkness of the night and of the train and the normal rate of speed of today's motor vehicles, appellant may not have had sufficient time to stop and avoid the collision after it became evident to him that the train blocked the road ahead. Therefore, we conclude that the train may not have been perceived at a sufficient distance to serve as notice. Penn Central had a duty to exercise ordinary care to protect the public safety and in this case that duty required giving additional warning of the presence of the train.

The infrequent use of the tracks is another reason for our conclusion that the railroad had an affirmative duty to warn of the train's presence. The record indicates that the tracks were a spur line and seldom used.... In the instant case, appellant lived in the area and was well aware of the crossing, but he also was cognizant that the tracks were rarely used. Penn Central should have foreseen that motorists would not expect a train to be in the crossing because it was an unusual occurrence. Therefore, ordinary care would dictate that Penn Central should have taken some affirmative precautions to warn of the hazard. The Court of Appeals concluded that there was no crossbuck sign, which the railroad is statutorily required to erect at the track, and no other device or signal to warn of the actual presence of the train in the crossing. Penn Central created the hazard by placing the train in the crossing; however, it did nothing to warn motorists of the hazard, even though any of [several] warning devices could have been easily used. This lack of care at the crossing was more than simple negligence.

Wanton misconduct is a jury question. On these facts, the jury could have reasonably concluded that Penn Central disregarded the safety of motorists and failed to exercise any care whatsoever to motorists....

The second prong of the *Hawkins* test is that the failure to exercise care occurs under circumstances in which there is a great probability that harm will result. In its previous decisions, this court has recognized that "almost every railroad grade crossing involves a substantial risk of danger to those using the highway over such crossing." ... Clearly, the dark train on a seldom used crossing at night creates a hazard and there is a great probability of collisions and injuries when no precautions are taken to warn of its presence....

Although we recognize the needs of railroads to preempt crossings to carry on their business, the primary consideration should be the public's safety, especially when the track is an infrequently used spur line. The cost is minimal, in terms of dollars and time, for a railroad to warn with flares, fuses, reflective tape and lanterns. In comparison, the probability of accidents occurring and the gravity of harm are both great. A railroad has a responsibility to exercise ordinary care to prevent accidents, a potential it creates when a train is in a crossing. A jury could have concluded, based on these circumstances, that a great probability of harm could result from the lack of care exercised. Therefore, the second prong of the *Hawkins* test for wanton misconduct is satisfied.

The behavior of the defendant-tortfeasor in a willful, wanton, and reckless situation takes two different forms. One is an act and the other is a failure to act. Either one is sufficient to impose liability, and in either case the recklessness must be unreasonable and something more than ordinary negligence.

Negligence *Per Se*

negligence *per se*

In some circumstances, state legislatures have defined a standard of conduct for a reasonable person applicable to all persons. Any deviation from that standard of conduct by a defendant-tortfeasor is presumed by statute to be negligent. Proof of negligence in such a case is met by showing that the statute has been violated. Violation of a statutory standard of conduct is termed **negligence *per se*.** In an action for negligence, once the plaintiff has shown that the defendant's conduct was in violation of a statutory standard of conduct, then the defendant's negligence is presumed. The burden of proving negligence has been met merely by establishing the statutory violation. It is then incumbent upon the defendant to provide his or her defense.

A recovery under a theory of negligence *per se* requires that the plaintiff be a part of a class of individuals the legislature sought to protect in enacting the statute. For instance, if a state statute prohibits the sale of fireworks to minors, the legislature clearly intends to protect the class of minors from the fireworks. Should a minor be injured through the use of fireworks that were purchased in violation of the statute, then he or she would be able to maintain an action based upon a theory of negligence *per se* (see Figure 3-6).

Figure 3-6. Negligence *Per Se*

Once the statute is determined to be applicable—which is to say, once it is interpreted as designed to protect the class of persons, in which the plaintiff is included, against the risk of the type of harm which has in fact occurred as a result of its violation—and once its breach has been established, probably a majority of the courts hold that the issue of negligence is thereupon conclusively determined, in the absence of sufficient excuse, and that the court must so direct the jury. The standard of conduct is taken over by the court from that fixed by the legislature, and "jurors have no dispensing power by which to relax it," except insofar as the court may recognize the possibility of a valid excuse in a tort action for damages for disobedience of a criminal law.

W. Page Keeton et al., *Prosser and Keeton on the Law of Torts* § 36 at 229-230 (5th ed. 1984)

If the injured plaintiff in this case was not a part of the protected class, such as an adult who was not involved in the purchase of the fireworks, then the theory of negligence *per se* would be unavailable.

A number of defenses are open to the defendant in an action based upon a theory of negligence *per se*. Chapter 4 addresses the traditional defenses available in any negligence action, many of which may be available in such a case.

Guest Passenger Statutes

guest passenger statute

A few states have a body of statutory law under which the distinction between negligence and reckless conduct takes on further significance. Such statutes impose liability for harm done to a guest in an automobile if the driver's conduct is in reckless disregard of the guest's safety. This is called a **guest passenger statute**, or automobile guest statute. A guest passenger statute provides that the driver of an automobile is liable to a gratuitous guest (as opposed to a paying customer) only for gross negligence or aggravated misconduct.

Many states at one time had guest passenger statutes on their books, but found that the statutes presented too many varying issues to be constitutionally enforced. Several of these statutes have been held unconstitutional as a violation of the Equal Protection Clause, and have since been repealed. The paralegal student must consult his or her state's statutes and case law to determine the status of any such legislation.

Burden of Proof

At the outset of this chapter, it was established that negligence must be proved by preponderance of the evidence. The party attempting to prove the existence

burden of proof

of negligence, as a matter of fact and law, has the **burden of proof** by a preponderance of the evidence. As a principle of the law of evidence, the burden of proof is the obligation of a party to prove a fact to the satisfaction of the jury. It has also been called the burden of persuasion and the risk of nonpersuasion. The burden of proving a defendant-tortfeasor's negligence rests squarely on the shoulders of the plaintiff (see Figure 3-7).

Figure 3-7. Burden of Proof

...the burden of proof that the tortious conduct of the defendant has caused the harm to the plaintiff is upon the plaintiff.

Restatement (Second) of Torts § 433 B

The plaintiff is required to produce evidence that more likely than not, the conduct of the defendant-tortfeasor has been a substantial factor in the plaintiff's injury.

Function of Court and Jury

Under the United States' system of jurisprudence, the existence of negligence is in part a question of fact for the jury to decide, and in part a question of law for the court to decide. Recall that courts decide questions of law and juries decide questions of fact.

Traditionally, the questions of law for the court to decide are these:

- Is there a duty—the imposition of a legal obligation on one person for the benefit of another?
- What is the general standard of conduct? Once the court has found that a duty exists, the general standard of conduct is imposed, that of a reasonable person under the same or similar circumstances.

Questions of fact for the jury to decide are these:

- Is the evidence sufficient? Have facts been proven that give rise to the existence of a duty, a breach thereof, and resulting damages?
- What is the weight of the evidence, the value of the proofs offered, and the conclusions to be drawn from it?
- What is the particular standard of conduct? What would a reasonable person have done under the circumstances?

In drawing the distinctions between what the court will decide and what matters will be left to the jury, most courts generally hold that if reasonable minds may differ as to the conclusion to be drawn, then the matter is best left to the jury.

Presumptions

presumption

A **presumption** is a rule of law stating that the jury may assume the existence of a fact. It requires the jury to make a finding of fact absent any proof as to the existence of that fact. For instance, in a negligence action, a frequent presumption is that a person is presumed to possess normal mental faculties and reasoning powers. As a matter of law, the jury must make such a finding unless there has been evidence presented to rebut the presumption. Once persuasive rebuttal evidence is produced, then the presumption ceases to exist.

Courts and legal scholars continue to debate the role of presumptions in the trial of civil cases. The paralegal student should carefully consult the laws of his or her state for the current status of any presumption.

Prima Facie Case

prima facie

Once the plaintiff in a negligence action has met the burden of proving the necessary elements of the case (duty, breach of duty, proximate cause, and damages), the plaintiff has proven a ***prima facie*** case of liability. *Prima facie* literally means "on the face of it," and shifts the burden of proof to the defendant to rebut the plaintiff's case. The term means the plaintiff's proofs are sufficient to establish the claim. A *prima facie* case has been established if the proofs would support a verdict for the plaintiff were the defendant to fail to present any rebuttal evidence. In actual trial of such a case a judge would deny a motion for a directed verdict or a motion to dismiss by the defendant.

RES IPSA LOQUITUR

doctrine of *res ipsa loquitur*

In the law of negligence, a unique doctrine of proof is available under certain circumstances to assist the plaintiff in establishing the negligence of the defendant-tortfeasor. Normally, the mere occurrence of an injury will not give rise to an inference that it was due to negligence on the part of the defendant. While the law of every jurisdiction quite clearly states that negligence must be proved and will never be presumed, the **doctrine of *res ipsa loquitur*** provides an exception. *Res ipsa loquitur* permits an inference of negligence on the part of the defendant under certain circumstances.

When the instrumentality that caused the injury is under the defendant's control, and when in the ordinary course of things the injury would not have occurred if the defendant used proper care, there is an inference that the injury arose from the defendant's lack of care. The term *res ipsa loquitur* literally means "the thing speaks for itself," and represents a fusion of the concept of circumstantial evidence, which indirectly proves the existence of a fact, with the plaintiff's burden of proof.

The concept of *res ipsa loquitur* arose from the comments of Baron Pollock in the matter of *Byrne v. Boadle* in England in 1863. In that case, a barrel of flour rolled from a warehouse window and struck a pedestrian. It was argued that it was a reasonable conclusion from the unusual circumstances of the accident that the defendant was at fault since the injury would not have occurred if the defendant had used proper care.

Most jurisdictions require that the following conditions are necessary to the application of the doctrine:

- The event must be of the type that would ordinarily not occur without the defendant's negligence; in the light of ordinary experience, there must have been negligence on someone's part.
- The accident must be caused by some instrumentality in the exclusive control of the defendant. The purpose of this requirement is to link the defendant with the presumed negligent act.
- The accident must not be due to any contribution on the part of the plaintiff; this prevents the application of the principle if the plaintiff contributed to the event, a defense that is considered in Chapter 4.

While these are the traditional elements of *res ipsa loquitur*, individual states have substantially modified the doctrine. For instance, many courts have added a requirement that the doctrine cannot be applied unless the evidence of the true explanation of the accident is more accessible to the defendant than to the plaintiff. Some jurisdictions take a procedural approach to the doctrine, serving only to remove the causation question from the hands of the court and place it in the hands of the jury. Other jurisdictions have taken the position that the doctrine exists to shift the burden of proof to the defendant. This is another instance where the paralegal student should consult individual state case law to determine the status of the doctrine.

Figure 3-8. Case in Point: *Hake v. George Wiedemann Brewing Co.*

HAKE v. GEORGE WIEDEMANN BREWING CO.
23 Ohio St.2d 65, 262 N.E.2d 703
Supreme Court of Ohio
Sept. 23, 1970

LEACH, Judge.

The question presented is whether the trial court erred in refusing to apply the rule of *res ipsa loquitur* at the close of plaintiff's case.

It is well established by earlier decisions of this court that *res ipsa loquitur* is a rule of evidence which permits the trier of fact to infer negligence on the part of the defendant from the circumstances surrounding the injury to plaintiff....

To warrant application of the rule a plaintiff must adduce evidence in support of two conclusions: (1) That the instrumentality causing the injury was, at the time of the injury, or at the time of the creation of the condition causing the injury, under the exclusive management and control of the defendant; and (2) that the injury occurred under such circumstances that in the ordinary course of events it would not have occurred if ordinary care had been observed.... Whether sufficient evidence has been adduced at trial to warrant application of the rule is a question of law to be determined initially by the trial court, subject to review upon appeal. It is prejudicial error for the trial court to direct a verdict for defendant at the close of plaintiff's evidence where the evidence presented warrants the application of the rule....

In the instant case, plaintiff presented two witnesses who testified that, on October 11, 1962, they saw a beer keg roll off and fall from an exterior second story stairway platform at premises owned by the Cincinnati Gas & Electric Company. They also saw plaintiff in a contracted position underneath the platform immediately thereafter, and the beer keg lying on the ground nearby. One of those witnesses saw two Wiedemann employees descend the staircase shortly after the barrel rolled off the platform, and both that witness and plaintiff testified that they saw the two Wiedemann employees at the bottom of the staircase shortly thereafter. Plaintiff testified that he was hit by a metal beer keg as he walked out a doorway and underneath the platform. There was extensive testimony with respect to the seriousness of plaintiff's injury. Defendant admitted ownership of the metal beer keg and the presence of its employees on the premises who were there for the purpose of removing several empty beer kegs from the second story, which kegs were left from a gas company employees' party the night before. However, no witness actually saw the keg being handled by a Wiedemann employee, and defendant argues that proof of this fact is critical to plaintiff's case.

In other words, defendant insists that plaintiff should be required to show exclusive management and control by the defendant of the particular beer keg which struck plaintiff during the period immediately prior to the time plaintiff was struck in order to warrant application of the rule of *res ipsa loquitur* to this case. Plaintiff argues that no such showing is necessary since defense counsel admitted the fact of exclusive management and control during his opening statement to the jury.

During his opening statement counsel for the defense revealed:

> The evidence will disclose that Mr. Griese and his helper were up on the second floor of the party room at the Cincinnati Gas & Electric Company, where they, the gas company employees, had apparently had a party, and had had some beer. The (sic) went to get the empty beer barrel. The evidence will disclose that accidentally Mr. Griese in some manner stubbed his toe, and he accidentally let the thing slip. He didn't toss it, and he didn't kick it. The evidence will show that it accidentally slipped out of his hands and came down.

We agree with plaintiff that defense counsel's opening statement constitutes a judicial admission sufficient to establish exclusive management and control on the part of the defendant at the time of the occurrence of the injury to plaintiff.

This being so, does the evidence adduced by plaintiff lead to the conclusion that the injury occurred under such circumstances that in the ordinary course of events it would not have occurred if ordinary care had been observed? We believe that it does.

The evidence presented in this case bears a remarkable similarity to that presented in the leading English case with respect to *res ipsa loquitur*. In *Byrne v. Boadle* (1863), 2 H. & C. 722, 728, 159 Eng. Rep. R. 299, Pollock, C. B., stated:

> The present case upon the evidence comes to this, a man is passing in front of the premises of a dealer in flour, and there falls down upon him a barrel of flour. I think it apparent that the barrel was in the custody of the defendant who occupied the premises, and who is responsible for the acts of his servants and the control of it; and in my opinion the fact of its falling is *prima facie* evidence of negligence, and the plaintiff who was injured by it is not bound to shew that it could not fall without negligence, but if there are any facts inconsistent with negligence it is for the defendant to prove them.

We are convinced that the rule of *res ipsa loquitur* applies in the instant case and that the trial court erred in directing a verdict for the defendant at the close of plaintiff's evidence. Therefore, the judgment of the Court of Appeals, affirming the judgment of the trial court, should be, and hereby is, reversed.

JOINT TORTFEASORS' LIABILITY

Not all harm as a result of negligence involves merely one defendant. In many situations an injured party has a claim against multiple defendant-tortfeasors. While a defendant cannot be held liable in tort for an injury that he or she did not cause, liability for injury does attach to each defendant involved in the injury to the plaintiff. If two or more defendant-tortfeasors were negligent, whether they acted in concert or alone, and each was the cause of a single harm to the plaintiff, then both are liable to that plaintiff. The term for the liability of two or more persons together is **joint liability**.

joint liability

Concerted Action

In its earliest form, joint liability arose when two individuals acted in concert to commit a tort by common design. When there was a common design and joint enterprise involved in the act, it was found that the act of one was the act of all. Therefore, each individual was liable for the damage done. These original actions were primarily criminal in nature and involved a conspiracy between the two individuals to harm the plaintiff. It is in concerted intentional action that today's conspiratorial crimes originated. Two negligent defendant-tortfeasors will rarely be liable for concerted action because of the lack of intent. While they may be liable for one or more intentional torts, concerted action is not frequently found in negligence cases.

Joint and Several Liability

A defendant-tortfeasor is liable for the entire harm sustained by the plaintiff even if his or her negligence combined with that of another defendant-tortfeasor to produce the ultimate injury. If the acts or omissions of two or more individuals, acting simultaneously or in sequence, were the proximate cause of the injury to the plaintiff, then they are both liable for the entire result. This is called **joint and several liability**. Each defendant-tortfeasor is individually liable for the full extent of the harm proximately caused to the plaintiff.

joint and several liability

As an example, assume that Winston was a passenger in an automobile driven by Carlisle which collided with a truck driven by Morton. Both Carlisle and Morton were negligent in their driving and the negligence of both contributed to the collision. As a result of the collision, Winston sustained serious injuries. The theory of joint and several liability would find both drivers, Carlisle and Morton, liable to Winston for the full extent of the injury.

Contribution and Indemnity

A common issue facing joint tortfeasors in a negligence action is the sharing of the payment of any award to the plaintiff. Most states have statutory provisions for **contribution** among joint tortfeasors. Contribution is the ability of one joint tortfeasor to recover a share of the judgment from the remaining joint tortfeasor(s). The principle of contribution allows a defendant-tortfeasor against whom a judgment has been entered to recoup a proportionate share of the judgment from any other tortfeasors who contributed to the injury.

contribution

A related concept is the principle of **indemnification**, which calls for a full reimbursement of the party paying a judgment to the plaintiff. Indemnification differs from contribution in that it involves reimbursement for the *entire* amount of the award instead of a proportionate *share* of the award. Indemnification is frequently seen in situations involving vicarious liability (discussed in detail in Chapter 10), and is often a matter of contract between parties.

indemnification

Survival Actions and Wrongful Death

The English common law contained three principles that materially affected the ability to maintain an action for negligence involving a death. Those rules provided the following:

- A defendant-tortfeasor's death terminated the right of the plaintiff to proceed.
- The plaintiff's death before any recovery terminated the cause of action.
- Relatives of a deceased plaintiff-victim of a tort had no cause of action for loss of support and affection.

The principles terminating the right of recovery with the death of either the plaintiff or the defendant were termed **survival** rules because the action could not be maintained after the death of either party. The rule prohibiting family

survival

wrongful death action

survival statutes

members from pursuing a negligence action against the defendant-tortfeasor responsible for the death was termed a **wrongful death action**.

Today, most jurisdictions have enacted **survival statutes** that allow for the survival of a negligence action after the death of either party to the case. Also, every jurisdiction has enacted a wrongful death statute allowing a cause of action for a deceased plaintiff's personal representative or beneficiaries. These statutes are compensatory in nature for the loss of support and affection, creating a cause of action that did not exist at common law. Both types of statutes vary greatly as to the torts covered and the parties affected. The paralegal student must carefully review applicable state statutes to determine the extent of coverage.

SUMMARY

The issues related to the proof of a claim for negligence arise once the necessary elements exist: duty, breach, proximate cause, and damages. The paralegal student must be aware that certain rules govern the presentation of the evidence necessary to prove the case by a preponderance of the evidence. While the standard of the ordinary reasonable person remains unchanged as the fundamental fact to be proven by competent evidence, it must be remembered that not every injury is going to result in an action for negligence. The paralegal must respond to statutory changes to that standard, the function of the court as opposed to the jury, the doctrine of *res ipsa loquitur*, the issues related to multiple tortfeasors, and the survivability of actions involving a death. These issues must be addressed even before considering the potential defenses available to the defendant.

REVIEW QUESTIONS

1. What is legal proof?
2. Discuss the distinction between fact and opinion.
3. Distinguish the standard of proof in a civil case from that in a criminal case.
4. What is the doctrine of unavoidable accident?
5. Discuss the degree of negligence that must be proven by a preponderance of the evidence in an action for negligence.
6. What are the functions of the court and the jury in an action for negligence?
7. Define *res ipsa loquitur*.
8. What is the principle underlying joint and several liability?
9. Discuss the distinction between contribution and indemnification.
10. What is the purpose of a wrongful death statute?

Focus Your Skills

When Hurricane Rip slammed into the West Coast of Florida from the Gulf of Mexico with dinosaur-eliminating force, the Nu-Cache Trash Company's failure to meet state-required landfill safety regulations became immediately apparent. All landfill sites must be constructed with a "vortex velocity reduction tract" designed to take the punch out of Nature's dark side. Orville Cull, sole owner of Nu-Cache and singularly committed to turning cache to cash, was not above sidestepping costly safety regulations to fatten up his bottom line. The fact that Orville had not seen his lap since the early 70s attested to his penchant for excess.

Nu-Cache's regulatory disregard caused J. Burlington Zephyr, attorney-at-law (retired), to be struck on the occipital region of his skull by the flying front bumper from a 1959 Edsel sedan. The 150-mph winds from Hurricane Rip (or Hurricane R.I.P. as dubbed by the press), the most devastating hurricane of the century, sent the bumper from the Nu-Cache site some 700 meters through the air straight into the middle of the Tenth Annual Advocates' Cheese Ball. The ball was being held at the neighboring Solicitors' Sundown, a retirement community dedicated to the final spittin' 'n whittlin' days of many of this country's finest legal eagles.

Since the injury, J. Burlington spends his final days in quiet contemplation of the concept of life on Mars, wondering if they, too, would hate lawyers. The only physical evidence of his injury consists of a permanent expression of befuddlement on his face. His *vivre* had permanently lost its *joie*.

As a potential tort action for negligence, the case of J. Burlington Zephyr presents several problems of proof. Analyze these facts in light of the principles of proving a negligence case as discussed in this chapter.

4 Defenses to Negligence

No man's error becomes his own Law; nor obliges him to persist in it.

Thomas Hobbes, *Leviathan* (1650)

The plaintiff has the burden of proving entitlement to compensation for harm resulting from the negligence of another. The mere negligence of the defendant is not alone sufficient to entitle the plaintiff to a judgment for damages. Once the defendant's negligence is established, the defendant's burden is to offer a legal excuse sufficient to diminish or deny recovery by the plaintiff. The law allows the defendant to prove the extent of the plaintiff's contribution to the eventual injury. Depending on the nature and extent of that contribution, the plaintiff's claim may be defeated entirely. Previous chapters focused on the defendant's role in an action for negligence. This chapter addresses the acts or omissions of the plaintiff that may provide a defense to the action.

Chapter Topics

1. Contributory Negligence
2. Last Clear Chance
3. Comparative Negligence
4. Assumption of Risk

Objectives

After completing this chapter, you will be able to:

1. Understand the defense of contributory negligence.
2. Evaluate the concept of last clear chance as a negligence defense.
3. Discuss comparative negligence as a defense to a negligence action.
4. Distinguish assumption of risk from the other negligence defenses.

Contributory Negligence

The plaintiff's conduct may form the basis for a defense to an action for negligence. If his or her conduct falls below a standard to which the plaintiff should conform for his or her own protection, the defendant may have a defense to the action. When the plaintiff's conduct has a tendency to increase exposure to risk, but is not necessarily criminal in nature, the defendant has an opportunity to offer proof of such conduct as a defense.

Defined

contributory negligence

Contributory negligence is conduct on the part of the plaintiff that falls below the standard to which he or she is required to conform for his or her own protection. The plaintiff's conduct combines with the acts or omissions of the defendant to cause the injury. Contributory negligence focuses on the plaintiff's acts or omissions and imposes a duty to care for one's own safety. The *Restatement (Second) of Torts* similarly defines contributory negligence (see Figure 4-1).

Figure 4-1. Contributory Negligence Defined

Contributory negligence is conduct on the part of the plaintiff which falls below the standard to which he should conform for his own protection, and which is a legally contributing cause co-operating with the negligence of the defendant in bringing about the plaintiff's harm.

Restatement (Second) of Torts § 463

This definition has been uniformly adopted by the courts in allowing the use of contributory negligence as a defense. The issue presented in all cases employing this defense is whether the plaintiff's conduct conformed to that of an ordinarily reasonable person under the same or similar circumstances.

Bar to Action

bar to action

A defense of contributory negligence operates as a complete **bar to action** by the plaintiff. A bar to action ends the plaintiff's claim. Once a *prima facie* case has been proven by the plaintiff and the defense of contributory negligence has been established, the plaintiff's case is defeated. Consider the use of the defense in the case of *Brown v. Piggly-Wiggly* (see Figure 4-2).

Figure 4-2. Case in Point: *Brown v. Piggly-Wiggly*

Frank C. BROWN v. PIGGLY-WIGGLY STORES
Supreme Court of Alabama
454 So.2d 1370
July 27, 1984

FAULKNER, Justice.

The plaintiff, Frank C. Brown, appeals from a summary judgment entered against him in favor of Piggly-Wiggly Stores and Kenny Poffenbarger in a personal injury suit. We affirm.

The facts are as follows: On February 10, 1983, Brown went shopping at the Piggly-Wiggly store located in Citronelle, Alabama. After purchasing his groceries and placing them in his pickup truck, Brown proceeded to return his shopping cart to the area designated for cart returns. En route, Brown bumped a motorcycle which had been parked on the sidewalk approximately thirty-two feet from the store entrance. The motorcycle fell on Brown and broke his leg.

The motorcycle was owned by one of the defendants, Kenny Poffenbarger, who was employed by the Piggly-Wiggly store as a second assistant manager. The store's manager, Craig McLendon, had authorized Poffenbarger to park his motorcycle on the sidewalk in front of the store.

Brown filed suit in Mobile County Circuit Court, alleging that Poffenbarger, with Piggly-Wiggly's authorization, had negligently parked his vehicle so as to create an unsafe and dangerous condition which caused Brown's injury. After allowing Brown several opportunities to amend his complaint, the trial court entered summary judgment against him....

The second issue raised by Brown concerns whether the trial court properly entered summary judgment in favor of Piggly-Wiggly and Poffenbarger. Our review must consider whether the moving parties have shown that there is no genuine issue of material fact and that they are entitled to a judgment as a matter of law.... After reviewing the record in its entirety, we conclude that the defendants have met their burden.

Under the laws of Alabama, a plaintiff cannot recover in a negligence suit where plaintiff's own negligence is shown to have proximately contributed to his damage, notwithstanding a showing of negligence on the part of the defendant. Of course, this principle applies only where contributory negligence has been raised as an affirmative defense....

In order to prove contributory negligence, the defendant must show that the party charged: (1) had knowledge of the condition; (2) had an appreciation of the danger under the surrounding circumstances; and (3) failed to exercise reasonable care, by placing himself in the way of danger....

The question of contributory negligence is normally one for the jury. However, where the facts are such that all reasonable men must reach the same conclusion, contributory negligence may be found as a matter of law.... This is such a case.

By all accounts, the motorcycle in question was in plain view, both from within and without the store. It was parked approximately two feet from the store front on a sidewalk which was nine feet wide. Brown had already walked past the vehicle once, moments before the accident. By his own admission, the motorcycle fell on him only after he had bumped it. The record is devoid of any evidence indicating that Brown bumped the motorcycle for any reason other than his own inattention. We find that reasonable men could reach no other conclusion than that: (1) Brown knew the motorcycle was parked by the wall; (2) Brown appreciated the danger inherent in a two-wheeled vehicle resting on a kickstand, specifically, that it may fall if disturbed; and (3) Brown nevertheless put himself in the way of the danger by carelessly bumping the motorcycle. Therefore, without regard to the negligence *vel non* of the defendants, we hold that Brown's injuries were the proximate result of his failure to exercise reasonable care when he bumped a parked motorcycle. It follows that there was no genuine issue as to a material fact and summary judgment was properly entered against Brown.... Accordingly, the judgment of the trial court is due to be, and it is hereby, affirmed.

Now consider the following example in which the principle of contributory negligence bars an action. One evening Prudence bicycles without lights into a busy intersection and fails to stop at the red Stop sign. She is struck and injured by an automobile driven by Dusty. Dusty had been driving his automobile without lights on and at an excessive rate of speed. A court may find that Dusty was negligent in the operation of his automobile, but may bar any recovery by Prudence because of her negligence in bicycling at night without lights and failing to stop when required. In such a case, Prudence would recover nothing for personal injury from Dusty.

Appellate courts justify this doctrine as a bar to action in various ways. The most reasonable argument presented is that the courts use it to prevent recoveries when the circumstances of the case would render them unwarranted or unconscionable. The paralegal student must be familiar with the rationale for retaining the principle of contributory negligence. Local state law must be researched for that rationale in those jurisdictions still adhering to the principle.

Distinguished from Negligence

As Professor Keeton points out, it is unfortunate that contributory negligence uses the term *negligence* at all. A more accurate phrasing would be to refer to the defense as contributory *fault*. Negligence involves a duty toward another person, while contributory negligence involves the conduct of the plaintiff creating an undue risk of harm to self.

Figure 4-3. Contributory Fault

Negligence as it is commonly understood is conduct which creates an undue risk of harm to others. Contributory negligence is conduct which involves an undue risk of harm to the actor himself. Negligence requires a duty, an obligation of conduct to another person. Contributory negligence involves no duty, unless we are to be so ingenious as to say that the plaintiff is under an obligation to protect the defendant against liability for the consequences of the plaintiff's own negligence.

W. Page Keeton et al., *Prosser and Keeton on the Law of Torts* § 65 at 453 (5th ed. 1984)

Yet, contributory negligence continues to be measured in exactly the same terms as ordinary negligence. A plaintiff is required to act as an ordinary reasonable person under the same or similar circumstances. Failing in that duty, a plaintiff may not then complain of the negligence of an otherwise negligent defendant. The theory and the formula placed before the trier of fact are the same in determining the negligence of either the defendant or the plaintiff.

Role of Causation

The trier of fact must apply the principles of ordinary negligence to make a finding of contributory negligence by applying the rules of causation. The rules regarding cause in fact and proximate cause apply to the defense of contributory negligence. Appellate court opinions frequently state that a plaintiff is barred from any recovery whose own negligence contributed to the injury "in any manner." It might appear that any contribution, no matter how slight, would bar the plaintiff's action, but this is not the case. Most appellate courts hold that the plaintiff's negligence must have been a substantial factor in causing the injury, otherwise the action is not barred.

Further, the injury to the plaintiff must have been clearly foreseeable for the defense of contributory negligence to operate. This involves the application of the principles of the doctrine of proximate cause discussed in Chapter 2. The plaintiff's action is not barred when failure to exercise reasonable care for his or her own safety creates a foreseeable risk. Consider the facts of *Garreans* in applying the principles of proximate cause, when 12-year-old boys dropped lit firecrackers into a drum of flammable liquid (Figure 4-4).

Figure 4-4. Case in Point: *Garreans v. City of Omaha*

GARREANS v. CITY OF OMAHA
Supreme Court of Nebraska
216 Neb. 487, 345 N.W.2d 309
Feb. 17, 1984

BOSLAUGH, Justice.

This is an action under the Nebraska Political Subdivisions Tort Claims Act against the City of Omaha, Nebraska, to recover damages for the injuries sustained by the plaintiffs, John Garreans, Jr. and Vince Hartline, in an explosion which occurred at N.P. Dodge Park on July 5, 1980, while the plaintiffs were visiting with their grandparents, Ray and Evelyn Stoops, at the park. The petition included a second cause of action for the medical expenses incurred by the parents of the plaintiffs as a result of the explosion. At the time of the accident both plaintiffs were 12 years of age. The action was brought by their fathers as the next friends of the plaintiffs. The defendant has raised no issue in this court concerning joinder.

The evidence shows that on July 3, 1980, Ray and Evelyn Stoops entered N.P. Dodge Park in Omaha, Nebraska, with their camper, intending to camp in the park over the 3-day holiday. Evelyn Stoops paid a $10.50 fee at the concessionaire's office for the use of camper pad No. 25 for the 3-day period. Electrical service was provided at that pad. While they were setting up camp, the Stoopses noticed a black, 55-gallon drum nearby. The black drum was in addition to a trash barrel at the pad, which was a 55-gallon drum from which the top had been removed. Trash barrels, which consisted of 55-gallon drums from which the tops or lids had been removed, were distributed throughout the park, including the camping area. These drums were painted various colors and were labeled "TRASH" on the side.

Printing or lettering on the side of the black drum indicated that it had contained an antifreeze compound. A red or orange label, approximately 4 inches square, was affixed to the top of the drum. The label bore the legend "Flammable Liquid" printed below a representation of a fire or flames.

The lid or top of the black drum was intact, and the drum was closed except for a small opening, approximately 1 inch in diameter, from which a plug had been removed. There is no evidence that the city placed the black drum in the park, and a search of city records showed that the city had not purchased the black drum. The plaintiffs contended that the city was negligent in failing to remove the drum from the park.

On July 5, 1980, the plaintiffs entered the park to visit with their grandparents at camper pad No. 25. In accordance with park policy, no admission fee was charged them. Both boys had been given firecrackers by their fathers. The boys used a cigarette lighter to light the firecrackers, and used the black drum as a shelf for their activities. The explosion occurred when they dropped a lighted firecracker into the black drum through the 1-inch hole in the lid. The drum exploded, spraying flammable liquid on the boys. John received severe burns on his lower extremities. Vince suffered injuries to his nose and arm, and was also burned.

The trial court found that the city had failed to properly supervise the area around camper pad No. 25; had failed to observe, inspect, and remove the 55-gallon drum; had failed to warn the public of the dangerous nature of the drum; was guilty of willful negligence; and that the plaintiffs were not contributorily negligent.

The city has also assigned as error the finding of the trial court that the plaintiffs were not guilty of contributory negligence. An actor is contributorily negligent if he breaches the duty imposed upon him by law to protect himself from injury; if his actions concur and cooperate with actionable negligence of the defendant; and if his actions contribute to his injuries as a proximate cause.... A child is required to exercise that degree of care which a person of that age would naturally and ordinarily use in the same situation under the same circumstances....

Although we have concluded that no "willful or malicious" negligence existed on the part of the city, we believe the evidence in this case shows that the plaintiffs were contributorily negligent sufficient to bar their recovery as a matter of law. The finding of the trial court to the contrary was clearly wrong.

The use of firecrackers in the city of Omaha and within the park was prohibited by ordinance, as well as by park regulation. The plaintiffs had been warned by their parents that fireworks were dangerous and that they should be careful when using them. The plaintiffs testified that they were aware of the danger involved in using fireworks. The degree of care required increases when an actor is dealing with a dangerous activity such as exploding firecrackers. Despite these warnings, the evidence is that the plaintiffs were lighting firecrackers above the opening in the drum and dropping lighted firecrackers into the drum.

Although there is conflicting testimony with regard to whether the boys noticed the "flammable" marking on the drum, the label was plainly visible, and the plaintiffs testified that they understood what the term "flammable" meant. In the exercise of proper care the boys should have seen the warning label on the top of the drum upon which they were lighting firecrackers. Moreover, they should have known that dropping lighted firecrackers into the drum created an unreasonable risk of explosion.

The judgment of the district court is reversed and the cause remanded with directions to dismiss the petition.

Avoidable Consequences

The doctrine of avoidable consequences (see Chapter 2) is closely related to the issue of contributory negligence. This rule of law denies recovery for any damages that could have been averted by the plaintiff's exercise of reasonable conduct. It often occurs when an injured plaintiff who would reasonably require medical attention fails to obtain proper medical treatment. Any consequences attributable to the failure to obtain medical care could not form the basis of a claim for damages.

The principle behind the doctrine of avoidable consequences is that the plaintiff must take proper care to protect his or her own interests. The concept is closely related to contributory negligence in the plaintiff's failure to exercise reasonable conduct for his or her own welfare. However, the doctrine of contributory negligence applies to acts or omissions *before* the injury, while the doctrine of avoidable consequences applies *after* any injury.

Knowledge of Peril

The doctrine of contributory negligence requires that the plaintiff should have known of the danger to which he or she was exposed, and failed to prevent injury. Conversely, the plaintiff will not be barred from maintaining an action by the doctrine of contributory negligence if he or she had no knowledge of the danger and could not anticipate the hazard that caused the injury. Knowledge on the plaintiff's part is required to maintain a defense of contributory negligence.

If a sudden emergency affords the plaintiff no opportunity to evaluate the peril, the law will not hold him or her to a strict ordinary reasonable person standard. If there is no time for deliberation, a plaintiff will not be penalized for failing to take the safest course of action; therefore, most jurisdictions will not apply the doctrine of contributory negligence.

Momentary Forgetfulness

Any individual may have a moment of temporary forgetfulness that may place him or her in a position of peril. Forgetfulness is not considered contributory negligence unless it constitutes a failure to exercise due care. The doctrine of momentary forgetfulness states that forgetfulness is not necessarily negligence, but is one factor in determining the plaintiff's own negligence.

The trier of fact must decide whether the plaintiff's own peril was due to mere momentary forgetfulness or to a breach of his or her own duty to avoid peril. The standard to be applied is that of the ordinary reasonable person. Consider the contributorily negligent conduct of the professional exterminator who fell down stairs that he had traversed on many occasions (see Figure 4-5).

Figure 4-5. Case in Point: *Hundt v. LaCrosse Grain Co.*

HUNDT v. LA CROSSE GRAIN CO., INC.
Supreme Court of Indiana
446 N.E.2d 327
March 15, 1983

HUNTER, Justice.

This case began when Everett Hundt, a professional exterminator, filed a complaint for damages as a result of a fall down the basement stairs in the office building of LaCrosse Grain Company in LaCrosse, Indiana....

The underlying facts of this action are not in dispute. Mr. Hundt and his son went to LaCrosse Grain Company on March 9, 1976, to do pest control work which involved spreading a chemical on rafters in a storage shed to discourage birds from being present and damaging the grain. After finishing this work, Hundt and his son went into the office building to wash up. Mr. Hundt had done pest extermination work for LaCrosse since 1955, and was thoroughly familiar with the office building and its facilities. On this occasion, Hundt entered the back door of the office building and then mistakenly opened the door leading to the basement rather than the washroom door. He stepped through the doorway and fell down the basement stairs through his own momentum. It was uncontradicted that the basement door was closed, the hallway was well lighted, and there were signs above two doors indicating the men's and ladies' washrooms. It was also uncontradicted that the basement door opened inward, there was no landing inside the door, and there was no handrail or bracing device beside the stairs. Hundt acknowledged at the trial that he knew where both the washroom and the basement were located and had been in these areas about 100 times during the twenty years he had visited the LaCrosse buildings. He also admitted that he was familiar with the fact that the basement door opened inward while the washroom door opened outward, and that the basement stairway had no landing or handrails. He also testified that he had never entered the building from the rear door before, but had previously always entered from the front....

This Court has consistently held that the basis for contributory negligence is conduct on the part of the plaintiff which falls below the standard to which he should conform for his own protection and safety. Lack of reasonable care that an ordinary man would exercise in like or similar circumstances is the factor upon which the presence or absence of negligence depends.... Further, it must be shown that the plaintiff's negligent act was a proximate cause of his injury and that he was actually aware of or should have appreciated the risks involved....

Accordingly, Indiana courts have found contributory negligence as a matter of law in cases in which the voluntary conduct of the plaintiff exposed him to imminent and obvious dangers which a reasonable man exercising due care for his own safety would have avoided....

Here, the fact is undisputed that the door to the stairway was closed, thus guarding that area.... Hundt was an adult and did not have any disability or limitation of perception. The hallway area where the basement and washroom doors were located was well lighted and the washroom doors were clearly marked. Hundt had been in the building and in both the washroom and basement on numerous prior occasions. He acknowledged that he was familiar with the fact that the basement door opened inward while the washroom door opened outward. In this case, the plaintiff was thoroughly familiar with the hallway area of the building and with the types of rooms and areas that were protected by the closed doors. The only conclusion which can be drawn from the facts in this case is that Hundt was disregarding an obviously known and appreciated danger by opening the closed door in such a manner as to preclude any opportunity to observe what was on the other side.

We find that the undisputed evidence establishes that Hundt was guilty of contributory negligence which was the proximate cause of his injury. Such negligence is contributory negligence as a matter of law under the circumstances of this case and for this reason the verdict of the jury is contrary to law.

The doctrine ameliorates the "all or nothing" aspect of the contributory negligence principle. The doctrine of momentary forgetfulness gives the trier of fact the option to place the plaintiff's conduct in perspective within the test of reasonable care.

Last Clear Chance

last clear chance

A mitigation of the doctrine of contributory negligence is found in the doctrine of **last clear chance**. This doctrine allows a plaintiff in a negligence action to recover regardless of his or her own negligence if the defendant had the last clear chance to avoid the injury. It has been called the discovered peril doctrine because it refers to a situation wherein the defendant had the last opportunity to discover the plaintiff's peril and avoid injury through reasonable care. This doctrine counteracts the defense of contributory negligence by providing the plaintiff with a response to that defense.

The doctrine arose in England in 1842 with the case of *Davies v. Mann*. In that case, the defendant's carriage struck an animal left tied in the highway by the plaintiff. The court found that the plaintiff could recover notwithstanding his own negligent act of leaving of the animal tied in the street. The defendant, by exercising reasonable care, could have avoided striking the animal. While the doctrine provides justice in some cases, the net result has been substantial confusion and lack of conformity in its application.

There are two situations that allow the uniform application of the doctrine of last clear chance:

- when the plaintiff is helpless; or
- when the plaintiff is inattentive of the peril.

Plaintiff Helpless

The rule of law for a plaintiff in helpless peril is that, if the defendant had a reasonable opportunity to avoid the injury, then the plaintiff's contributory negligence will not bar a recovery for damages due to the defendant's negligence. A greater degree of fault attaches to a negligent defendant after discovering the plaintiff's peril. For its application, the doctrine requires that the defendant discovered the peril, had an opportunity to avoid the injury, then failed to exercise reasonable care to avoid harm to the plaintiff (see Figure 4-6).

Figure 4-6. Last Clear Chance: Helpless Plaintiff

A plaintiff who has negligently subjected himself to a risk of harm from the defendant's subsequent negligence may recover for harm caused thereby if, immediately preceding the harm,

(a) the plaintiff is unable to avoid it by the exercise of reasonable vigilance and care, and
(b) the defendant is negligent in failing to utilize with reasonable care and competence his then existing opportunity to avoid the harm, when he
  (i) knows of the plaintiff's situation and realizes or has reason to realize the peril involved in it or
  (ii) would discover the situation and thus have reason to realize the peril, if he were to exercise the vigilance which it is then his duty to the plaintiff to exercise.

Restatement (Second) of Torts § 479

The justification provided is that the defendant's negligence is the proximate cause of the injury to the plaintiff.

Plaintiff Inattentive

There is also a body of case law concerning the plaintiff's failure to notice the peril of his or her surroundings. When the defendant encounters an inattentive plaintiff and has an opportunity to avoid an injury, the plaintiff's own contributory negligence will not bar a recovery. In such a situation, the defendant is said to have had the last clear chance to avoid the injury. The situation is similar to that of the helpless plaintiff (see Figure 4-7).

Figure 4-7. Last Clear Chance: Inattentive Plaintiff

A plaintiff who, by the exercise of reasonable vigilance, could discover the danger created by the defendant's negligence in time to avoid the harm to him, can recover if, but only if, the defendant
  (a) knows of the plaintiff's situation, and
  (b) realizes or has reason to realize that the plaintiff is inattentive and therefore unlikely to discover his peril in time to avoid the harm, and
  (c) thereafter is negligent in failing to utilize with reasonable care and competence his then existing opportunity to avoid harm.

Restatement (Second) of Torts § 480

The circumstances must be such that the defendant *saw* the plaintiff and *knew* that the plaintiff was inattentive. If he or she did not possess such knowledge, then there can be no presumption of any last clear chance to avoid the injury. No recovery would be available to the plaintiff under such circumstances.

The courts' application of the last clear chance doctrine has been confusing. Professor Keeton criticizes the doctrine for its substantial lack of any rational fundamental theory to support it, and blames the confusion on that deficiency (see Figure 4-8).

Figure 4-8. Criticism

This variety of irreconcilable rules, all purporting to be the same, and the lack of any rational fundamental theory to support them, suggest that the "last clear chance" doctrine is more a matter of dissatisfaction with the defense of contributory negligence than anything else. In its application, it is not infrequent that the greater the defendant's negligence, the less likely it is that he will be held liable for the resulting harm.... Nor is it easy to defend a rule which absolves the plaintiff entirely of his own negligence, and places the whole loss upon the defendant, whose fault may be the lesser of the two. The doctrine thus appears to be a dying one, particularly in many of the jurisdictions which have adopted a system of comparative fault.

W. Page Keeton et al., *Prosser and Keeton on the Law of Torts* § 66 at 468 (5th ed. 1984)

COMPARATIVE NEGLIGENCE

Critics of the doctrine of contributory negligence have long argued that it imposes undue hardship by absolutely barring the plaintiff's claim. The last clear chance doctrine had been adopted by most jurisdictions to limit the rigidity of contributory negligence. But the last clear chance doctrine presented more problems than it solved. Many states' dissatisfaction with contributory negligence led them to replace the doctrine with a statutory apportionment of damages between the parties. Comparative negligence shifts the focus of the trier of fact from liability to the division of damages between those at fault.

Nature of Comparative Negligence

comparative negligence

Comparative negligence is a statutory system of apportioning damages between the parties to a negligence action, reducing the recovery by the percentage of negligence attributed to the plaintiff. Many states have replaced the contributory negligence defense with statutory systems requiring an apportionment of damages whereby both the plaintiff and the defendant share some measure of fault.

A comparative negligence defense requires the following elements:

1. actionable negligence by the defendant causing harm or injury to the plaintiff;
2. a negligent act by the plaintiff that contributed to his or her injury;
3. a measurement of the percentage of the relative contribution of the negligence of both plaintiff and defendant; and
4. an award of damages to the plaintiff reduced by the percentage of his or her own negligence.

Under comparative negligence statutes, the plaintiff's recovery is not absolutely barred by his or her own negligence. Instead, the trier of fact measures the negligence of the plaintiff and reduces the amount of any damages to be awarded by the percentage that his or her negligence contributed to the total injury.

Assume for example that Parker negligently left his automobile partially blocking a lane of traffic on the street in front of his house. Further assume that Race, driving his car in excess of the speed limit, noticed Parker's automobile but was unable to stop before colliding with its rear bumper. Parker then sued Race for damages to his automobile totaling $20,000. The trier of fact made a finding that Parker was 25 percent negligent and Race was 75 percent negligent. A system of pure comparative negligence would reduce the award to Parker by the amount of his negligence, 25 percent, and award the remainder to him. Therefore, under a system of pure comparative negligence, Parker would recover $15,000.

Comparative negligence statutes did not appear until early in the twentieth century. The state of Mississippi enacted the first general comparative negligence statute in 1910. Slowly, reform-minded legislatures conformed to the recommendations of jurists and legal scholars so that by the early 1990s, most jurisdictions in the United States had adopted some form of a comparative negligence system.

Systems of Comparative Negligence

Comparative negligence systems vary between states, and the paralegal student should consult local state statutes to determine the exact nature of the statutory system. There are three principal types of comparative negligence systems:

- Pure comparative negligence—A plaintiff's negligence does not serve to bar a claim, but does reduce damages in proportion to fault; this system forms the basis of the Uniform Comparative Fault Act.
- Modified comparative negligence—Sometimes called the 50 percent system; a plaintiff's contributory fault does not bar a recovery under this system so long as it remains below a specified level of contribution, usually 50 percent.
- Slight-gross system—A plaintiff's contributory negligence is not a bar to his or her claim as long as his or her negligence is slight and the negligence of the defendant is gross.

The modified comparative negligence system is the most common. Each system offers an opportunity for the trier of fact to apportion fault, although limiting the scope of apportionment in all but pure comparative negligence.

Joint Tortfeasors

When a negligence action involves more than one defendant-tortfeasor, most jurisdictions enacting a system of comparative negligence have maintained the common law rule of joint and several liability (see Chapter 3). Under that rule, the plaintiff is entitled to recover whatever judgment may be awarded from any defendant found to be liable.

Once the liabilities of the plaintiff and the defendants have been measured by the trier of fact, the issue of contribution between the joint tortfeasors arises. Some states allow the apportioning of the damages equally among the defendants according to what is called the **equality rule**. Under this rule, all defendants share equally in their respective liability to the plaintiff. Other states have adopted a system of apportionment of damages between defendants based upon their respective fault. This system is called **comparative contribution**, and involves an assessment by the trier of fact of the degree of fault of each defendant. Once the measurement of the comparative share of fault among the defendants has been made, damages are awarded accordingly. State laws differ greatly regarding joint and several liability as well as on the issues of contribution and indemnification. These laws must be consulted for the application of these principles.

equality rule

comparative contribution

Assumption of Risk

assumption of risk

Another major defense to a claim of negligence is the doctrine of **assumption of risk**. Assumption of risk provides a defense to a claim of negligence in cases where the plaintiff knowingly exposes himself or herself to danger and assumes responsibility for any harm. If the plaintiff voluntarily assumes a certain risk, then he or she may not recover for any injuries sustained. It finds its rationale in the Latin phrase *violenti non fit injuria*, which means "that to which a person assents is not deemed an injury at law."

The doctrine of assumption of risk became established as a legal principle in the late nineteenth century. It is based upon the premise that an individual is responsible for the consequences of choice. This defense is an absolute bar to an action for damages similar to the defense of contributory negligence. It requires two basic elements:

- voluntary assumption of a known risk by the plaintiff; and
- full knowledge of the danger inherent in the risk.

The presence of these elements relieves the defendant from an obligation to the plaintiff which he or she might otherwise have borne.

Assumption of risk differs slightly from the defense of contributory negligence. It involves the knowing acceptance of a danger and the voluntary assent to exposure. Contributory negligence, on the other hand, involves a departure from the standard of care of an ordinary reasonable person. The two defenses may exist in the same case, or they may be available independently of each other. Consider the case of the student teacher injured while participating in a donkey baseball game (see Figure 4-9).

Figure 4-9. Case in Point: *Arbegast v. Board of Education*

ARBEGAST v. BOARD OF EDUCATION
OF SOUTH NEW BERLIN CENTRAL SCHOOL
Court of Appeals of New York
480 N.E.2d 365
June 6, 1985

MEYER, Judge.

Plaintiff, a student teacher at the South New Berlin Central School, was injured during a donkey basketball game when the donkey she was riding put its head down and she fell off. The game, sponsored as a fund raising event for the senior class, was staged under contract by the defendant Buckeye Donkey Ball Company, which provided the donkeys, helmets for each of the players, and an employee who transported and handled the animals, gave instructions to the participants, and acted as referee of the games, in return for which the company received a percentage of the receipts. Two games were played; the first pitted the faculty team against the fire department team and was won by the faculty team; the faculty team then opposed the senior class team in the second game. Plaintiff participated in the first game without mishap, but had a different, larger donkey for the second game than she had had for the first. She spent a good deal of the game walking the donkey around but, at the urging of another faculty member, mounted. Soon thereafter she was thrown over the donkey's head when it put its head down as it stopped, with resultant permanent injury to her left arm....

A

Until the enactment in 1975 of CPLR article 14-A, it was, except in an action for wrongful death, a substantive part of the plaintiff's right to recover in a negligence action that plaintiff prove himself or herself free from negligence contributing in the slightest degree to the occurrence.... The theory was that plaintiff's negligence was an intervening cause, which broke the causal connection between the defendant's negligent act and plaintiff's injury....

B

It is against this background that CPLR article 14-A was enacted in 1975, providing that as to all causes of action accruing on or after September 1, 1975, "the culpable conduct attributable to the claimant or to the decedent, including contributory negligence or assumption of risk, shall not bar recovery, but the amount of damages otherwise recoverable shall be diminished in the proportion which the culpable conduct attributable to the claimant or decedent bears to the culpable conduct which caused the damages," and "shall be an affirmative defense to be pleaded and proved by the party asserting the defense."...

Because the Legislature contemplated that article 14-A would "apply to cases where the conduct of one or more of the parties will be found not negligent" and "in which the plaintiff's negligences may be the only negligence," but also that defendant's culpable conduct would include "conduct giving rise to liability upon a theory of strict liability," it is clear that both the basis of liability asserted against the present defendant and the plaintiff's acts may constitute "culpable conduct" within the meaning of the statute.

Thus, what the statute requires comparison of is not negligence but conduct which, for whatever reason, the law deems blameworthy, in order to fix the relationship of each party's conduct to the injury sustained and the damages to be paid by the one and received by the other as recompense for that injury. Comparative causation is, therefore, the more accurate description of the process, ... as is evident both from the wording of CPLR 1411 ("shall be diminished in the proportion which the culpable conduct attributable to the claimant or decedent bears to the culpable conduct which caused the damages" [emphasis supplied]) and from the section of the Judicial Conference Report entitled "Causal Culpability": "Only culpable conduct which was a substantial factor in causing the harm for which recovery is sought is to be considered in determining the amount by which damages are to be diminished. For example, if P accepts a ride in an automobile driven by A, with knowledge that A is intoxicated, and P is injured when B negligently drives his vehicle into the rear of A's vehicle which is properly stopped for a red traffic signal, in P's action against B, there will be no diminution of damages. While P may have engaged in culpable conduct in accepting a ride with A, that conduct was not a substantial factor in causing the damage suffered by P." As that example makes clear, for the statute to operate, plaintiff's conduct must be a cause in fact of his or her injury. When it is, the statute "requires that the culpable conduct attributable to the decedent or claimant be compared with the total culpable conduct which caused the damages."

Neither article 14-A nor its legislative history defines "assumption of risk." The common law distinguished between express and implied assumption of risk. Express assumption, which was held to preclude any recovery, resulted from agreement in advance that defendant need not use reasonable care for the benefit of plaintiff and would not be liable for the consequence of conduct that would otherwise be negligent.... Implied assumption was founded not on express contract, but on plaintiff's voluntarily encountering the risk of harm from defendant's conduct with full understanding of the possible harm to himself or herself....

Here there is evidence from which the jury could have concluded that plaintiff had knowledge of the risk and by participating in the games voluntarily assumed it, and no question that plaintiff's conduct in mounting the donkey from which she was thrown was a cause in fact of her injuries. She would, therefore, have been entitled to a comparative causation charge on implied assumption of the risk had she not conceded that she was told before the games began that "participants are at their own risk." In light of that concession, however, the Trial Judge should have directed a verdict for defendant.

The defense of assumption of risk applies under two basic circumstances. Those situations are when the plaintiff:

- expressly consented to the risk; or

- impliedly consented to the risk.

Both situations involve conduct by the plaintiff that may be considered to be reasonable and non-negligent, and thus do not give rise to a defense of contributory negligence.

Express Consent

The clearest application of the defense of assumption of risk occurs when the plaintiff expressly agrees not to hold the defendant liable for any injury. The courts do not find any violation of public policy in allowing an individual to look out for his or her own welfare before entering into a contract. Limitations on the defense apply in cases where there is an obvious disadvantage in bargaining power between the parties. For instance, an employer may not require employees to enter into a contract limiting the employer's exposure to liability for injury.

For the assumption of risk defense to apply, two basic express consent elements are required. It is essential that:

- the assent to the risk be freely given; and
- the assent be for the particular risk that led to the injury.

Professor Keeton states that if both conditions are present, the courts are going to apply the doctrine and exempt the defendant from liability (see Figure 4-10).

Figure 4-10. Express Consent

If an express agreement exempting the defendant from liability for his negligence is to be sustained, it must appear that its terms were brought home to the plaintiff; and if he did not know of the provision in his contract, and a reasonable person in his position would not have known of it, it is not binding upon him, and the agreement fails for want of mutual assent. It is also necessary that the expressed terms of the agreement be applicable to the particular misconduct of the defendant, and the courts have strictly construed the terms of exculpatory clauses against the defendant who is usually the draftsman.

W. Page Keeton et al., *Prosser and Keeton on the Law of Torts* § 68 at 483-484 (5th ed. 1984)

It is clear that the principles of strict construction of contracts apply to the express consent for assumption of risk.

The plaintiff in the *Meier* case consented to ride a mechanical bull installed as an amusement. The New York state legislature had limited the application of express consent, further restricting the ability of a defendant to avoid responsibility (see Figure 4-11).

Figure 4-11. Case in Point: *Meier v. Ma-Do Bars, Inc.*

MEIER v. MA-DO BARS, INC.
Supreme Court, Appellate Division
484 N.Y.S.2d 719
Jan. 31, 1985

HARVEY, Justice.

This is an action for serious personal injuries sustained by plaintiff while attempting to ride a "mechanical bull" owned and operated by defendant Clean Snow Corporation. There appears to be no significant issue on this appeal as to the respective liabilities and duties of defendants Paul Solodar and Clean Snow Corporation. It is presumed that Paul Solodar was the owner and in complete control of Clean Snow Corporation. Because their interests are identical insofar as the issue on this appeal is concerned, we shall refer to both defendants collectively as "Solodar."

Solodar obtained permission from defendant Ma-Do Bars, Inc. to install and operate a mechanical amusement device in Hunter Village Inn, a tavern owned by Ma-Do Bars, Inc. The device simulated the spinning and bucking of actual bulls as they perform when ridden in rodeos. The participants attempted to ride the device in the same manner as animals are ridden. It must be assumed that when the device was ridden by patrons of the bar, a rodeo atmosphere was created in which satisfaction was derived from being able to stay on the bull for the predetermined period of time. That it was anticipated that some riders would be unable to stay on the bull was indicated by the fact that air mattresses were spread on the floor surrounding the device.

After observing the mechanical bull being ridden by other patrons, plaintiff talked to the operator and was informed that he could ride the bull upon payment of a $2 fee and execution of a "Liability, Release, Indemnification and Authorization" agreement. He complied with both conditions. He mounted the device and was thrown from it under circumstances not material to the issue before us now.

After commencement of this action and the completion of certain discovery procedures, Solodar moved for summary judgment contending that the agreement was a complete bar to plaintiff's recovery of damages. Special Term granted the motion and plaintiff now appeals. For the purposes of this appeal, we assume that the agreement, if valid and enforceable, was completely exculpatory of any liability on the part of Solodar.

The main thrust of plaintiff's argument is that the exculpatory agreement must be deemed to be void as against public policy and wholly unenforceable because of section 5-326 of the General Obligations Law, which provides:

> Every covenant, agreement or understanding in or in connection with, or collateral to, any contract, membership application, ticket of admission or similar writing, entered into between the owner or operator of any pool, gymnasium, place of amusement or recreation, or similar establishment and the user of such facilities, pursuant to which such owner or operator receives a fee or other compensation for the use of such facilities, which exempts the said owner or operator from liability for damages caused by

> or resulting from the negligence of the owner, operator or person in charge of such establishment, or their agents, servants or employees, shall be deemed to be void as against public policy and wholly unenforceable.
>
> This appears to be a case of first impression involving circumstances such as these. The Legislature's intent in enacting such a statute is the determinative factor in deciding the limits of its application.... It is for the courts to definitively resolve the legal question of the applicability of a statutory enactment to a particular situation....
>
> In our view, the instant case is a classic example of those situations which the Legislature had in mind when it extended the declaration of public policy in the General Obligations Law to apply to places of amusement and similar establishments. The mechanical bull was an amusement device for which plaintiff paid a fee to use and enjoy. That a potential danger existed is exemplified by the owner and operator's requirement that an exculpatory agreement be signed by a user. Defendant created a place of amusement or recreation by the installation of the device.... We conclude from the facts before us that section 5-326 of the General Obligations Law is controlling and that the agreement is null and void.

Implied Consent

In most cases involving the assumption of risk defense, there is no express consent. The consent is usually implied from the plaintiff's conduct. The plaintiff accepts potential consequences by engaging in conduct that entails risk, and proceeds even though injury may result.

The defense arises in cases when the defendant offers an activity to the plaintiff without any obligation to accept the offer. The activity carries certain unavoidable danger. The plaintiff, aware of the risks, agrees to participate in the activity, considering the risk worthwhile. For example, assume that Rappel owns an indoor rock-climbing training facility that is open to the public. Climber attempts to scale the wall one afternoon, and is struck and injured by a rock dislodged by another patron. In Climber's lawsuit for damages, Rappel would have the defense of an implied assumption of the risk even though there was no express contract between the two parties.

Knowledge of Risk

As noted above, the defense of assumption of risk requires two elements: that the assent to the risk be freely given, and that the assent must be for the particular risk that led to the injury. Professor Keeton stresses that knowledge of the risk is the watchword for assumption of risk (see Figure 4-12).

Figure 4-12. Knowledge of Risk

> 'Knowledge of the risk is the watchword of assumption of risk.' Under ordinary circumstances the plaintiff will not be taken to assume any risk of either

activities or conditions of which he has no knowledge. Moreover, he must not only know of the facts which create the danger, but he must comprehend and appreciate the nature of the danger he confronts.

W. Page Keeton et al., *Prosser and Keeton on the Law of Torts* § 68 at 487 (5th ed. 1984)

The purely subjective standard to be applied is based on the particular plaintiff and his or her ability to understand the danger. If the danger cannot be comprehended by the plaintiff, then the defense is not available to the defendant. Consider the following case of a health club patron overcome by fumes (see Figure 4-13).

Figure 4-13. Case in Point: *Larsen v. Vic Tanny International*

LARSEN v. VIC TANNY INTERNATIONAL
Appellate Court of Illinois
474 N.E.2d 729
Nov. 28, 1984

HARRISON, Justice:

Defendant Vic Tanny International, a corporation, appeals the denial of its motion for summary judgment against plaintiff Gregory N. Larsen. The issue upon which defendant's motion hinges is the validity of an exculpatory clause in a contract between plaintiff and defendant. Upon denying defendant's motion, the circuit court of St. Clair County certified the question for interlocutory appeal pursuant to Supreme Court Rule 308. (87 Ill.2d R. 308.) We granted the appeal.

Plaintiff, a member of defendant's organization, alleged that he was injured while utilizing defendant's health club facilities. Plaintiff's complaint stated that plaintiff sustained serious internal injuries as a result of inhaling gaseous vapors.... Plaintiff's membership contract contained the following provisions:

> "By the use of the facilities of Seller and/or by the attendance at any of the gymnasiums owned by Seller, the Member expressly agrees that Seller shall not be liable for any damages arising from personal injury sustained by the Member or his guest in, on or about the premises of the said gymnasiums or as a result of their using the facilities and the equipment therein....

The courts of Illinois have long held that, under appropriate circumstances, a person may by contract avoid liability for his or her negligence.... In the absence of fraud or willful and wanton negligence, exculpatory contracts will be enforced unless "(1) it would be against the settled public policy of the State to do so, or (2) there is something in the social relationship of the parties militating against upholding the agreement."

The obvious rationale behind this rule is that a plaintiff who expressly consents to relieve a defendant of an obligation of conduct toward the plaintiff assumes the risk of injury as a result of the defendant's failure.... The doctrine of assumption of risk presupposes, however, that the danger which causes the injury is such that it ordinarily accompanies the activities of the plaintiff, and that the plaintiff knows or should know both the danger and the possibility of injury prior to its occurrence.... The standard to be applied is a subjective one geared to a particular plaintiff and her situation, and the determination ordinarily will be made by a jury....

Foreseeability of a specific danger is thus an important element of the risk which a party assumes, and, for this reason, serves to define the scope of an exculpatory clause. This is but another way of stating that, although the type of negligent acts from which a person expressly agrees to excuse another need not be foreseen with absolute clarity, such acts cannot lie beyond the reasonable contemplation of the parties; or, as stated in a comment to the section of the *Restatement of Torts (Second)* recognizing the validity of express assumptions of risk: "In order for the agreement to assume the risk to be effective, it must also appear that its terms were intended by both parties to apply to the particular conduct of the defendant which caused the harm." (*Restatement of Torts (Second)* Sec. 496 B comment d (1977).) No agreement to assume unknown risks shall be inferred.

Plaintiff in the instant action claims injury resulting from defendant's act of mixing chemical compounds in a manner which produced an explosion of harmful vapors. The question upon which the enforceability of the exculpatory clause hinges is whether defendant's conduct and the risk of injury inherent in this conduct was of a type intended by the parties to fall within the scope of exculpation....

A plaintiff's decision to assume the risk of injury resulting from a defendant's conduct attains efficacy only in a context in which the plaintiff may foresee the range of possible dangers to which he subjects himself, thus enabling the plaintiff to minimize the risk by altering his conduct in order to employ a proportionately higher degree of caution. A plaintiff agreeing to assume a risk of injury in partial exchange for the right to use gymnasium facilities could reasonably contemplate the possibility of injury resulting from slippery surfaces in or around a swimming pool...or a steam room...and could, upon reflection, exercise increased care while utilizing these facilities. The assertion that such a plaintiff would necessarily contemplate the danger of combustible cleaning compounds being mixed in such a manner as to injure the plaintiff's respiratory system, and that the plaintiff could accordingly exercise a more rigid standard of caution either by avoiding certain areas of the gymnasium or by altering his breathing habits while present in those areas is untenable according to the standards of common experience.

Moreover, noting that "the American public is obsessed with health and physical fitness," and that "we as a society benefit from a healthy, fit populace," two justices of the Supreme Court of Minnesota recently have taken the position that gymnasiums in fact offer the type of public service properly characterized as "essential," necessarily investing the owner with a decisive advantage of bargaining strength over any member of the public seeking her services....

The order of the circuit court denying defendant's motion for summary judgment is affirmed.

Contrasted with Comparative Negligence

Legal scholars have debated whether an assumption of risk defense is needed in light of comparative negligence statutes. Other than in cases of express consent, the defense has been criticized as of little value. Opponents of assumption of risk argue that the legislature intends to eliminate harsh rules absolutely barring recovery. They argue that it is in the public interest to apportion fault rather than preclude recovery in situations involving an implied voluntary assumption of a known risk. In fact, the comparative negligence statutes of some states have specifically abolished assumption of risk as a defense (see Figure 4-14).

Figure 4-14. Comparative Negligence Statute: New York

§ 1411 Damages recoverable when contributory negligence or assumption of risk is established

In an action to recover damages for personal injury, injury to property, or wrongful death, the culpable conduct attributable to the claimant or to the decedent, including contributory negligence or assumption of risk, shall not bar recovery, but the amount of damages otherwise recoverable shall be diminished in the proportion which the culpable conduct attributable to the claimant or decedent bears to the culpable conduct which caused the damages.

New York Civil Practice Law and Rules, Article 14-A

Proponents of assumption of risk contend that the defense is still applicable because it is based upon consent to encounter risk rather than a measure of fault.

To fully appreciate the impact of a comparative negligence statute on assumption of risk, the risk assumed must be separated into three classes. This will help the paralegal student to understand how the courts have handled the question. The classes are:

- Express assumption of risk—This continues to serve as a total bar to the plaintiff's claim.
- Unreasonable assumption of risk—The assumption appears to be similar to contributory negligence, and therefore should be absorbed by the comparative negligence statute.
- Reasonable assumption of risk—This is treated the same as an unreasonable assumption; the plaintiff's assumption is similar to negligence and should fall within the scope of a comparative negligence statute.

The paralegal student should carefully review individual state statutes to discover the treatment of assumption of risk and comparative negligence. If the statutes are silent, then the student must review the state's case law.

Summary

The law continues to follow the time-honored principle that a defendant whose conduct would otherwise be negligent toward another may not be liable to the plaintiff for the harm caused by the consent or fault of that plaintiff. The plaintiff's contributory negligence absolutely bars an action for negligence in those jurisdictions that adhere to that principle. The comparative negligence of the plaintiff diminishes his or her recovery in the many jurisdictions that have enacted a comparative negligence law. The doctrines of last clear chance and assumption of risk continue to conflict among the various jurisdictions; this makes it necessary for the paralegal student to conduct legal research. The defenses to negligence actions will continue to receive attention as the various state legislatures further define the public welfare.

Review Questions

1. Define *contributory negligence.*
2. Describe the effect of a defense of contributory negligence on a plaintiff's claim.
3. In what way is contributory negligence not really negligence at all?
4. Discuss the doctrine of avoidable consequences.
5. How would a lack of knowledge of a peril on the part of the plaintiff affect a contributory negligence defense?
6. Explain why the last clear chance doctrine has been called the discovered peril doctrine.
7. Define *comparative negligence.*
8. List the elements of a comparative negligence defense.
9. What are the circumstances under which the doctrine of assumption of risk applies?
10. What are the elements of a defense of assumption of risk?

Focus Your Skills

The Order of By Jove! found inspiration in the recent discovery of the existence of the chemical building blocks of life on Jove, one of Jupiter's nine moons. Made up of a group of dedicated astronomy students at the Alpha Centauri College of Space Studies, the Order was headed by world-renowned exobiologist, Dr. Celeste Teal.

Ever hopeful of legitimizing their existence, the By Jovians gathered one quiet August evening for an astro-critical view of the surface of Jove. The meeting was held at the college's Whanna Peak Observatory, which housed its 120-inch Newtonian reflector telescope. The occasion provided an opportunity that the Upsilon Nu Fraternity found irresistible. Led by their resident wag, Horton Blemish, the U Nus decided to assist the By Jovian quest for credibility with a cosmic thumb in the eye. Horton and his fellow nonbelievers smeared the face of the telescope's lens with a particularly virulent penicillin culture stolen from the college's Biology lab. Focusing the big Newtonian scope on Jove, Dr. Teal discovered it alive with cellular life forms. She quite understandably became very animated, leading to a disastrous headlong fall down the steps of the observatory. She sustained a serious cranial injury as a result of the fall, and will spend the rest of her life trying to eat with only one chopstick.

Dr. Celeste Teal has sued Horton Blemish for the seemingly harmless prank that precipitated her permanent injury. Horton must now assert a defense to the negligence action. Analyze the facts of this case to determine the applicability of the following defenses:

- contributory negligence,
- last clear chance, and
- assumption of risk.

5 Intentional Torts

Slander, Whose sting is sharper than the sword's.

William Shakespeare, *The Winter's Tale*

Tort law is divided into two classes of liability—negligence and intentional torts. Both involve the invasion of the interests of another. The distinction between the two classes rests with the state of the mind of the actor. As defined in Chapter 2, negligence is based upon a breach of a standard of reasonable care and does not require that the defendant intended the consequences of his or her actions. Intentional torts like assault, false imprisonment, or defamation require an intentional state of mind on the part of the actor to cause a harmful result from his or her actions. The defendant's state of mind provides the basis for the classification, and this chapter considers the nature and elements of those intentional actions that the law deems tortious conduct.

Chapter Topics

1. Intent
2. Harm to Persons
3. Harm to Property

Objectives

After completing this chapter, you will be able to:

1. Distinguish between negligence and intentional torts.
2. Discuss the legal effect of intent.
3. Describe the intentional torts that involve an injury or harm to persons.
4. Illustrate each of the intentional torts.
5. Summarize the intentional torts involving an injury to property.

Intent

intentional tort

An intentional invasion of another's personal or property interest, regardless of fault or harm, exposes the actor to liability in tort. This is called an **intentional tort**, and it imposes liability on a defendant-tortfeasor for any intentional interference with another person's body, reputation, or financial interests. Liability results from the defendant's attempt to harm the plaintiff in some manner otherwise excused by law. The legal excuses, or defenses, to intentional torts are discussed in Chapter 6.

Intent is the desire to bring about a particular result. The term is derived from the Latin word *intendere*, meaning "to form a plan or purpose." The plan or purpose refers to the actor's state of mind. Thus, intent begins with a state of mind on the part of the actor. In its tort application, an intentional state of mind combines with an act designed to bring about harm, resulting in liability.

The *Restatement (Second) of Torts* defines intent as a desire to cause certain consequences (see Figure 5-1).

Figure 5-1. Intent

The word "intent" is used throughout the Restatement of this Subject to denote that the actor desires to cause consequences of his act, or that he believes that the consequences are substantially certain to result from it.

Restatement (Second) of Torts § 8A

The *Restatement* emphasizes the consequences of the act rather than the act itself. All of the consequences that the defendant-tortfeasor desires to bring about are the intended consequences.

Most jurisdictions traditionally require three basic elements for intentional torts. Those elements are:

- a state of mind;
- an intentional act; and
- substantially certain consequences.

Thus, when the defendant-tortfeasor has the requisite state of mind (intent), accompanied by some act or omission, liability may be imposed for those consequences. For example, assume that Candace, oblivious to the actions of her fellow students, was ready to take her seat in the classroom before a lecture. Just as she was about to sit down, Clement quickly jerked her chair out from underneath her, causing her to fall and injure herself. Clement intended to and did commit an act, the consequences of which were reasonably certain. Although the extent of the injury could not be accurately predicted, some harm was sure to result.

The law of intentional torts concerns acts directed at an individual and those directed at property. Intentional torts involving harm to persons generally consist of the following:

- assault and battery,
- false imprisonment and arrest,
- infliction of emotional distress,
- misrepresentation and fraud,
- invasion of privacy,
- defamation, and
- misuse of legal procedure.

The intentional torts involving harm to property are:

- trespass to land and chattels, and
- conversion.

Whether the intentional tort is directed at persons or at property, it still violates an individual's freedom from harm as a result of the intentional acts of others. The same intentional act may form the basis for both a civil action and a criminal action. The crime is considered a wrong against society as a whole. The tort is considered an accountable wrong against an individual or his or her property, and for that reason remains actionable.

Harm to Person

Chapter 2 discussed the action for negligence originating from the common law action of trespass on the case. Other common law actions were addressed through the writ of trespass, which provided a remedy for harm caused by acts intended to invade some interest of another. Intentional torts involving harm to persons thus began with the common law writ of trespass. Today, the law of every jurisdiction provides an action in tort for the harm to an individual caused by the intentional acts or omissions of the defendant-tortfeasor, regardless of the old common law distinctions of direct or indirect injury.

Assault and Battery

assault

The freedom from harmful contact or the apprehension thereof is the essence of the law of assault and battery in tort. The intentional tort of **assault** provides a remedy for an individual who has been placed in apprehension of harmful or offensive physical contact. Assault does not require actual physical contact, but only that the plaintiff be placed in apprehension of harm. It is a form of mental injury as opposed to physical, and the resulting damages are based upon an emotional response rather than actual physical injury.

The elements of the tort of assault are:

- an act,
- intent to cause either actual physical harm or the apprehension of it, and
- apprehension of imminent harm.

The *Restatement (Second) of Torts* defines assault as an act that causes apprehension of immediate contact without requiring any tangible material harm to the other (see Figure 5-2).

Figure 5-2. Assault

(1) An actor is subject to liability to another for assault if

(a) he acts intending to cause a harmful or offensive contact with the person of the other or a third person, or an imminent apprehension of such a contact, and

(b) the other is thereby put in such imminent apprehension.

(2) An action which is not done with the intention stated in Subsection (1, a) does not make the actor liable to the other for an apprehension caused thereby although the act involves an unreasonable risk of causing it and, therefor, would be negligent or reckless if the risk threatened bodily harm.

Restatement (Second) of Torts § 21

The defendant's act must create an apprehension of physical harm. The fear must be reasonable, and the threat must be immediate. An assault may consist of a weapon aimed or directed at an individual in a threatening manner. The plaintiff must be aware of the threat in order to be placed in apprehension of harm. For instance, it is an actionable assault to point a gun at a person in a threatening manner, but not to point it at the same person behind his or her back while he or she is unaware of the gesture.

Additionally, most jurisdictions hold that words alone do not constitute an assault unless accompanied by the means to carry them out. This is because mere words are insufficient to place one in the imminent apprehension of bodily contact. For instance, assume that Butch shouts at Manfred, "If you go out with my girlfriend again, I will take a baseball bat to your head!" The anger and raised voice are still mere words, and alone, are insufficient to sustain a finding of assault.

Suppose, though, that Butch waved a 36-inch Louiseville Slugger while threatening Manfred. Would such an act place Manfred in apprehension of imminent physical contact? The answer lies in a determination of whether the threat was imminent. Since Butch would not strike Manfred unless he dated his girlfriend again, it is doubtful that there was any immediate danger. But, if Butch had raised the baseball bat and said, "Manfred, since you dated my girlfriend, you are going to suffer the consequences," then Manfred would be in imminent apprehension of physical contact. A finding of assault would be justified.

battery

A **battery** is the actual harmful physical contact resulting from an intentional act on the part of another. Where assault is the apprehension of imminent contact, battery is the contact itself. It is sometimes said that a battery is a completed assault. This is not entirely accurate in light of the fact that harmful physical contact may occur without the threat associated with an assault.

The elements of the intentional tort of battery are:

- an intentional act by the defendant,
- harmful physical contact, and
- the contact unpermitted by the plaintiff.

As with assault, the tort of battery is directed at the freedom from intentional and unpermitted physical contact extending to any part of the body or anything associated with it. Thus, a battery occurs with the intentional and unpermitted touching of another's clothing, the chair upon which he or she sits, or the automobile in which the plaintiff is riding. In addition, the act of the defendant-tortfeasor must have been intended to cause harm to the plaintiff. Professor Keeton notes that the mere negligence or even recklessness of the defendant would be insufficient to sustain a finding of battery (see Figure 5-3).

Figure 5-3. Battery

The act must cause, and must be intended to cause, an unpermitted contact. Mere negligence, or even recklessness, which creates only a risk that the contact will result, may afford a distinct cause of action in itself, but under modern usage of the term it is not enough for battery.

W. Page Keeton et al., *Prosser and Keeton on the Law of Torts* § 9 at 41 (5th ed. 1984)

Most jurisdictions will not allow a finding of battery in situations that customarily involve only social touching. Consent is presumed to exist in those ordinary circumstances surrounding daily living whereby an individual is sure to be exposed to some physical contact. For instance, in a crowded store or narrow passageway, one is presumed to have consented to some physical contact that customarily occurs. The time and place of the circumstances will control a court's finding of battery, and the law may vary from jurisdiction to jurisdiction.

False Imprisonment

false imprisonment

Freedom from restraint of movement is the basis of the intentional tort of **false imprisonment**. Also called false arrest, false imprisonment is an intentional confinement without consent or legal right. The restraint must be such that the plaintiff is totally without a reasonable means of escape in any manner. Since the restraint involves the plaintiff's mental perception, as in assault situations, the plaintiff must have been aware of the confinement. The confinement is not sufficiently restrictive if the plaintiff has some reasonable means of escape, although not one of his or her choosing. The *Restatement (Second) of Torts* also adds the requirement that the confinement cause some form of harm or damage (see Figure 5-4).

Figure 5-4. False Imprisonment

(1) An actor is subject to liability to another for false imprisonment if
   (a) he acts intending to confine the other or a third person within boundaries fixed by the actor, and
   (b) his act directly or indirectly results in such a confinement of the other, and
   (c) the other is conscious of the confinement or is harmed by it.

(2) An act which is not done with the intention stated in Subsection (1, a) does not make the actor liable to the other for a merely transitory or otherwise harmless confinement, although the act involves an unreasonable risk of imposing it and therefore would be negligent or reckless if the risk threatened bodily harm.

Restatement (Second) of Torts § 35

A mere threat of restraint or confinement is insufficient to support an action for false imprisonment. Confinement must be perceived by the plaintiff to be real, and must in fact be actual and total. It may take place by physical restraint or confinement to a limited area such as a room or vehicle. The restriction may be limited to the grounds of a particular establishment such as a home or institution. Threats of physical harm or violence are sufficient to constitute a restraint or confinement. The law does not require that the plaintiff actually incur the violence by resisting to sustain the action.

In many jurisdictions, the question of false imprisonment arises with the assertion of a legal right to confine someone. Taking the plaintiff into custody without the legal right to do so is a false arrest and will sustain an action for false imprisonment. So long as the plaintiff believes the defendant had the authority, and the defendant was without legal authority, the elements of the tort are met. The *Restatement* defines confinement as complete restraint without means of escape (see Figure 5-5).

Figure 5-5. Confinement

(1) To make the actor liable for false imprisonment, the other's confinement within the boundaries fixed by the actor must be complete.
(2) The confinement is complete although there is a reasonable means of escape, unless the other knows of it.
(3) The actor does not become liable for false imprisonment by intentionally preventing another from going in a particular direction in which he has a right or privilege to go.

Restatement (Second) of Torts § 36

Circumstances surrounding the detention of an individual suspected of shoplifting have resulted in a variety of decisions. Consider the *Burrow* case, wherein the court declares that restraint means any confinement, no matter how slight (see Figure 5-6).

Figure 5-6. Case in Point: *Burrow v. K-Mart Corporation*

BURROW v. K-MART CORPORATION
Court of Appeals of Georgia
304 S.E.2d 460
April 15, 1983

Store customer brought action for slander and false imprisonment against store, and customer's husband joined in suit seeking damages for loss of consortium. The Superior Court, Fulton County, Fryer, J., directed a verdict for store on husband's claim, and entered judgment for customer on false imprisonment claim while granting judgment n.o.v. against customer as to slander issue. Customer and husband appealed from judgments dealing with slander and loss of consortium, and store appealed from trial court's denial of a new trial on the verdict and judgment for damages for false imprisonment....

In an action to recover damages for false imprisonment, the only essential elements of the action are the detention, and the unlawfulness of the detention.... The cases have emphasized two points: "Any restraint, however slight upon another's liberty to come and go as he pleases, constitutes an arrest. There is an illegal arrest and false imprisonment of another where he is detained for any length of time against his will."

"The restraint constituting a false imprisonment may arise out of words, acts, gestures or the like, which induce a reasonable apprehension that force will be used if plaintiff does not submit; and it is sufficient if they operate upon the will of the person threatened, and result in a reasonable fear of personal difficulty or personal injuries...." Prosser explains that "imprisonment" was originally intended to have meant stone walls and iron bars, but under modern tort law an individual may be imprisoned "when his movements are restrained in the open street, or in a traveling automobile ... or is compelled to go along with the defendant." Prosser, *Law of Torts* (4th ed.) 42, § 11. The only Georgia case presented with a problem similar to the instant case is *F.W. Woolworth Co. v. Loggins*, 115 Ga.App. 557, 155 S.E.2d 462, supra. In that case the plaintiff brought a lamp she had purchased in another store into defendant's store, ate lunch and left. An employee of the defendant followed the plaintiff out of the defendant's store, ran up behind the plaintiff as she was crossing a street, took the lamp and ran back in the store. The plaintiff followed the employee back in the store and after the manager asked plaintiff if she had taken the lamp from the store, he returned it to her.

The opinion, without discussion, found no false imprisonment, citing *Abner v. W.T. Grant Co.*, 110 Ga.App. 592, 594, 139 S.E.2d 408, supra. That case involved a situation where a customer, again outside a store, when asked by an employee if a handbag was purchased in the store, replied "This is mine," and showed the employee "my usual things in it." There, the handbag was not taken from the customer who voluntarily showed its contents and the only similarity was that both events occurred outside the store. Since that is the only similar feature we must assume that was the basis of the *Loggins* decision ... that is, there is no false imprisonment for an occurrence outside the bounds of the store....

Although the Georgia cases have not addressed the problem where one is detained by the act of another exercising dominion over one's personal possessions, other jurisdictions have confronted such issue. As Prosser points out: "A substantial number of cases in recent years have found false imprisonment where the plaintiff surrendered his freedom of motion because of force directed against his valuable property." Prosser, *Law of Torts* (4th ed.) 45, § 11.

The common thread ... is that where one is deprived of one's property he (or she) need not supinely surrender such possession but is in fact entitled (if not compelled) to remain until repossession is effectuated. Of course, one might always abandon such property but the need to protect one's own property acts as a coercive force in restraining one from leaving. The exercise of dominion over the property serves also to exercise dominion over the person owning such property. We think the rationale of these cases comports with the fundamental purpose and concept of Georgia law which finds false imprisonment in acts which operate upon the will of the person threatened and may result in a reasonable fear of personal difficulty. How stand the facts of our present case under the rules we have enunciated? Here, according to the plaintiff's testimony she was told the boxes had to be searched and they were "snatched" from her hands. Furthermore, at the conclusion of the search the plaintiff was told "she could go" by the store employee. Is this not evidence from which the jury as trier of fact might ascertain that the plaintiff, as a result of the actions and language used by the defendant's employee ("I got to search your boxes") and the act of seizing her property, was intimidated into remaining a captive of the store until she was released? The plaintiff did not actually have the choice of leaving since to do so would abandon her property, and in fact concede that it was not hers. Surely the store employee recognized that plaintiff would not leave without the boxes containing valuable merchandise and it may be inferred that the employee intended to restrain and control both the property and the person of the plaintiff until the search was completed. This is further evidenced by the concluding statement addressed to the plaintiff that she "could go" indicating that the plaintiff was now released from custody.

A jury question was presented on the facts before us as to whether the words and acts by the defendant's employee operated upon the plaintiff's will so as to restrain her. Thus, the trial judge did not err in refusing to grant the defendant a new trial as to the false imprisonment. The defendant's exception to the charge involved the slander issue which we have already decided in defendant's favor.

The paralegal student should review the statutory law of his or her state, along with the cases interpreting that statute, to become familiar with the legislative treatment of the question.

Emotional Distress

Recovery for mental distress is a relatively recent development in the law. Only in the last few decades have state courts begun to recognize the interest in peace of mind as an independent cause of action. Previously, the intentional infliction of emotional or mental distress was regarded as too difficult to measure in terms of damages, and precluded recovery for mental suffering unaccompanied by some physical injury. Denial of such claims was based upon the belief that the floodgates of litigation would be opened to fictitious claims and trivial interests.

emotional distress

Now, virtually all jurisdictions allow a recovery for the intentional infliction of **emotional distress**. Emotional distress is a state of mind characterized by fear, anxiety, horror, grief, shock, humiliation, or embarrassment. Mental anguish and psychological harm, distinguished from actual physical injury, form the basis for the cause of action for intentional infliction of emotional distress.

There is no recovery for mere insult, obscenity, or indignity. The law does not provide recovery for boorish behavior, and will not attempt to redress every trivial indignity. The First Amendment of the United States Constitution guarantees freedom of speech, and the courts will not sanction the exercise of that liberty regardless of how offensive the speech may be to another.

A cause of action for intentional infliction of emotional distress must contain the following three elements:

- outrageous conduct by the defendant,
- intent to cause mental distress, and
- actual emotional distress suffered by the plaintiff.

outrageous conduct

Outrageous conduct is conduct on the part of the defendant-tortfeasor that is beyond decency. The actual interpretation of *outrageous* varies with the circumstances as well as with any special relationship that exists between the parties. Professor Keeton has summarized the nature of outrageous conduct, but the student is advised to consult individual state law (see Figure 5-7).

Figure 5-7. Outrageous Conduct

So far as it is possible to generalize from the cases, the rule which seems to have emerged is that there is liability for conduct exceeding all bounds usually tolerated by decent society, of a nature which is especially calculated to cause, and does cause, mental distress of a very serious kind. The requirements of the rule are rigorous, and difficult to satisfy.

W. Page Keeton et al., *Prosser and Keeton on the Law of Torts* § 12 at 60-61 (5th ed. 1984)

Conduct that shocks ordinary sensibilities and exceeds the bounds of decency forms the basis for the tort, excluding all but the most extreme forms of conduct. For example, outrageous conduct may exist in the insanity of maliciously and intentionally telling a man that his children and wife have been killed in an accident, or by threatening a young woman with disclosure of promiscuity.

The *Restatement (Second) of Torts* establishes liability for emotional distress arising from intentional or reckless outrageous conduct. It also stresses the fact that liability may arise when the outrageous conduct was directed at an individual other than the one distressed. In the example above, had the mother of the woman falsely accused of promiscuity been the one who suffered the emotional distress, then the one intentionally spreading the falsehood would still face liability (see Figure 5-8).

Figure 5-8. Conduct Directed at Third Person

(2) Where such conduct is directed at a third person, the actor is subject to liability if he intentionally or recklessly causes severe emotional distress

(a) to a member of such person's immediate family who is present at the time, whether or not such distress results in bodily harm, or

(b) to any other person who is present at the time, if such distress results in bodily harm.

Restatement (Second) of Torts § 46

Right of Privacy

The right of privacy did not exist in legal literature until the notable *Harvard Law Review* article by Samuel D. Warren and Louis D. Brandeis, entitled "The Right of Privacy," was published in 1890. As a reaction to the growing excesses of the press in overstepping bounds of propriety and decency, Warren and Brandeis advocated the protection of private individuals from unjustifiable infliction of emotional distress. Today, the right of privacy is guaranteed in most jurisdictions as an actionable tort.

right of privacy

The **right of privacy** is the right of an individual to be free from an unwarranted intrusion into matters with which the public is not necessarily concerned. As reflected by the *Restatement (Second) of Torts*, an action for the invasion of the right of privacy takes one of four distinct forms, protecting four different interests of the plaintiff (see Figure 5-9).

Figure 5-9. Right of Privacy

(1) One who invades the right of privacy of another is subject to liability for the resulting harm to the interests of the other.
(2) The right of privacy is invaded by
 (a) unreasonable intrusion upon the seclusion of another ... or
 (b) appropriation of the other's name or likeness ... or
 (c) unreasonable publicity given to the other's private life ... or
 (d) publicity that unreasonably places the other in a false light before the public.

Restatement (Second) of Torts § 652A

The four tort actions based upon a right of privacy are:

appropriation

unreasonable intrusion

public disclosure

false light

- **appropriation**—the unauthorized use of the plaintiff's name or likeness for economic gain;
- **unreasonable intrusion**—an excessive and highly offensive intentional interference with another's interest in solitude or seclusion as to his or her person or private affairs;
- **public disclosure** of private facts—an intentional, unauthorized, and offensive disclosure of purely private information without any legitimate public interest; and
- **false light** in the public eye—the defendant-tortfeasor publicly and offensively attributing statements, opinions, or a likeness of the plaintiff.

The outrageous character of any published account of an individual arises when it is intentionally reported and knowingly false. The United States Supreme Court in the case of *New York Times v. Sullivan*, 376 U.S. 254, 84 S.Ct. 710, 11 L.Ed.2d 686 (1964), held that the press has a privilege from liability for false statements regarding public figures unless made with knowledge of their falsity and with reckless disregard of the truth. The burden is on the plaintiff to prove the falsity of the statement. The case law since *Sullivan* has evolved to the point that the defendant-tortfeasor cannot be held liable unless he or she has serious doubts about the truth of a statement. The courts now distinguish between public figures and private figures in terms of the test to be applied. If the maligned plaintiff is a public figure, he or she must prove a knowing falsehood. If the plaintiff is a private figure, he or she may recover merely by proving the falsity without the necessity of proving that the defendant knowingly published it. In cases in which the false statement is defamatory, the plaintiff will have a better chance of succeeding under a theory of defamation than under a theory of privacy (see Figure 5-10).

Figure 5-10. Privacy versus Defamation

If the false statement is defamatory, the plaintiff will usually have a better chance of recovery on a defamation theory than on a privacy theory, especially if the plaintiff is a private person because negligence with respect to truth or falsity will satisfy both the constitutional and common law requirement for recovery. This is not likely to be the case as regards this tort. The outrageous nature of the defendant's conduct arises in large part from the fact that the account about the plaintiff was deliberately falsified in order to enhance the sensational character of the story.... All of this being true, it appears likely that a prerequisite to recovery by anyone on this false light basis will be the requirement that the defendant publish the false statements with knowledge of the falsity or recklessly.

W. Page Keeton et al., *Prosser and Keeton on the Law of Torts* § 117 at 866 (5th ed. 1984)

Defamation

defamation

The law of defamation is inextricably linked with the First Amendment freedom of speech as reflected by state statutes and court decisions. Found originally in principles of the common law aimed at punishing seditious publications, a situation our nation's founders sought to rectify, the tort of **defamation** is aimed at the freedom from harm to an individual's reputation and good name. Defamation is any false and intentional oral or written communication injurious to another's reputation and good name. That reputation and good name exist in the minds of others in the community, thus requiring that the statement be communicated to a third person to support an action.

defamatory statement

Defamatory Statements. While an injurious statement may cause emotional distress to the one at whom it was directed, if it is not communicated to a third person it is not a **defamatory statement**. A defamatory statement is one that harms the plaintiff's reputation and good name in the eyes of another, causes the plaintiff to fall in esteem, or makes others cease associating with him or her. It is a statement to a third person of some fact that holds the plaintiff up to contempt or ridicule. The *Restatement* bases an action for defamation on the harm to reputation resulting from the tort (see Figure 5-11).

Figure 5-11. Defamatory Communication

A communication is defamatory if it tends so to harm the reputation of another as to lower him in the estimation of the community or to deter third persons from associating or dealing with him.

Restatement (Second) of Torts § 559

The communication may reflect adversely on one's moral integrity or injure an individual's financial standing. Living persons, corporations, businesses, partnerships, and those considered persons in the eyes of the law may be defamed, but it is not possible to defame a person who is already deceased.

publication

Publication of the defamatory statement is the key element in the tort. The law refers to the communication of a defamatory statement to a third person as publication.

The elements required to maintain a cause of action for defamation are:

- a defamatory statement *by* the defendant-tortfeasor,
- false defamatory communication *about* the plaintiff,
- publication of the defamatory statement to a third person,
- harm to the plaintiff's reputation and good name, and
- a causal relationship between the defamatory statement and the damages.

To maintain an action for defamation, each of these elements must be present.

libel

Libel and Slander. The law of defamation consists of the dual action in tort for libel and slander. **Libel** is a written defamatory statement communicated to a third person. Commonly, libelous defamatory statements are made by newspapers, books, magazines, letters, or other publications. The written statement may be made by pen, press, typewriter, computer, or any form of electronic publication. Broadcasting by radio or television is considered to be a form of libel. The courts are concerned with the following factors in making a determination of libel:

- wide area of dissemination,
- record of the publication with some degree of permanence, and
- deliberation and premeditation of the defendant-tortfeasor.

The tort of defamation by libel does not require any actual damage to the plaintiff in order to be actionable. Consider the *Kimmerle* case and the court's consideration of the elements necessary to maintain an action for libel (see Figure 5-12).

Figure 5-12. Case in Point: *Kimmerle v. New York Evening Journal*

KIMMERLE v. NEW YORK EVENING JOURNAL
Court of Appeals of New York
186 N.E. 217
May 23, 1933

CROUCH, Judge.

The action is for libel. The first cause of action as stated in the complaint has been held sufficient. The question of its sufficiency has been certified to this court. The answer depends solely upon whether the following words which 'on the 2d day of September, 1931, the defendant in its newspaper republished of and concerning the plaintiff,' are libelous *per se:*

> 'Weds Sister-in-Law.
>
> She accepted him and on January 16, 1905, they were married. Five days later Hoch was courting Mrs. Catherine Kimmerle in New York, in a rooming house she conducted, in 47th Street at Tenth Avenue.
>
> Mrs. Fisher complained to Chicago police about the disappearance of her husband. This report called attention to his previous marriage and his wife's death. Police exhumed the body. Poison was found. The dirty blood-smeared record he'd left behind came quickly to light.
>
> The alarm went out for Hoch as a murderer.
>
> Detective James J. O'Neill, a rookie of the W. 47th St. police station, turned Hoch in. It was chance that led him to the rooming house. He noticed two new trunks being taken in. He inquired about their ownership. He learned they belonged to a man after the description of Hoch. He won Mrs. Kimmerle's confidence. He went to the house one night when Hoch was downstairs. He stumbled, purposely entering the parlor. He fell against the wily German, stripped him of the pistol he had in a dressing gown pocket.
>
> The arch fiend was trapped.
>
> Hoch was strung from the gallows in Chicago, February 23, 1906.'

We must take this somewhat cryptic narrative as it appears in the complaint, disregarding the explanatory matter in the briefs. We may infer that the alleged libel is a republication of part of an old news article at some time appearing in defendant's newspaper. We may also infer that the entire article described the criminal career of one Hoch. It has been held that the pleading was sufficient because the purport of the whole article was such as to disgrace the plaintiff and to cause her shame among those who knew her.

The law of defamation is concerned only with injuries to one's reputation.... Written words, the effect of which is to invade privacy and to bring undesired notoriety, are without remedy, unless they also appreciably affect reputation. This is the domain, not of positive law, but of obedience to the unenforceable. From such harms one is protected only by the code of common decency.

Reputation is said in a general way to be injured by words which tend to expose one to public hatred, shame, obloquy, contumely, odium, contempt, ridicule, aversion, ostracism, degradation, or disgrace, or to induce an evil opinion of one in the minds of right-thinking persons, and to deprive one of their confidence and friendly intercourse in society....

We shall assume, although it is not alleged, that widespread notoriety came to the plaintiff from the publication in question and that she suffered greatly as a result. But there must be something more than that to make it libelous. Considered and weighed 'in the minds of right-thinking persons' or as elsewhere expressed, do the words published by defendant tend to expose plaintiff to any of the evil results catalogued in the general statement above? All that the article says about the plaintiff is that she conducted a rooming house in New York and was there courted by Hoch five days after he had married another woman in Chicago. Hoch is described, in current journalese, as a 'murderer' and 'an arch fiend,' who had 'left a dirty, bloodstained record behind' him in Chicago, where later he 'was strung from the gallows,' after being captured at plaintiff's rooming house, where he was staying, by a 'rookie' detective, who had won plaintiff's confidence. 'Courting' is a word of vague content and may include varied conduct. But it does not imply immoral relations, nor did its use in the article impute such relations to plaintiff.... There is not even an insinuation that plaintiff knew, or had reason to know, anything wrong about the man who was courting her, much less that she was an accessory to his crimes. The other reference to plaintiff is that the detective, on the track of Hoch, won her confidence. What that means is obscure, unless the text following permits an inference that she cooperated with the detective in the identification and capture of Hoch.

Without a suggestion in the article to the discredit of plaintiff, how could any just and right-thinking person reading it entertain any feelings except regret and sympathy for plaintiff? Embarrassment and discomfort no doubt came to her from the publication, as they would to any decent woman under like circumstances. Her own reaction, however, has no bearing upon her reputation. That rests entirely upon the reactions of others. We are unable to find anything in this article which could appreciably injure plaintiff's reputation.

slander

Slander is an oral defamatory communication to another, and in most situations requires proof of actual damages. A concise formal distinction between the dual torts is offered by the *Restatement* (see Figure 5-13).

Figure 5-13. Libel and Slander Distinguished

(1) Libel consists of the publication of defamatory matter by written or printed words, by its embodiment in physical form or by any other form of communication that has the potentially harmful qualities characteristic of written or printed words.
(2) Slander consists of the publication of defamatory matter by spoken words, transitory gestures or by any form of communication other than those stated in Subsection (1).
(3) The area of dissemination, the deliberate and premeditated character of its publication and the persistence of the defamation are factors to be considered in determining whether a publication is a libel rather than a slander.

Restatement (Second) of Torts § 568

A generalization may be made that while libel is communicated by a sense of sight or touch, slander is communicated through the sense of hearing. This distinction certainly does not cover all situations; for example, the reading aloud of a defamatory writing is still considered by most courts to be a libel.

slander *per se*

The common law rule that slander requires proof of actual damages also offered specific exceptions. For four types of slander, known as **slander *per se*,** no proof of actual harm to reputation or good name is required to maintain the action. Slander *per se* consists of the following types:

- Accusation of a crime—The slander must involve the suggestion of a crime that involves moral turpitude, which is an inherent baseness or corruption of the human soul.
- Accusation of a loathsome disease—Originally intended to refer to venereal disease, this is intended to cover those conditions that involve a certain social stigma.
- Statements affecting one's reputation in business or profession—The law protects individuals involved in a legitimate profession or calling and seeks to protect the professional from an accusation of the improper conduct of business.
- Accusation of unchastity—Statements alleging a failure of the moral character of either sex form the basis for this type of slander.

These forms of slander do not require actual harm, and are grounds for an award of nominal damages in the absence of proof of any actual loss. Any other forms of slander require proof of actual harm or damages.

Defamation by Computer. The recent growth in the use of computers in both private and commercial settings has given rise to exposure for defamation. The likelihood of mistake, the ease of publication, and the potential for widespread dissemination create fertile ground for an intentional tort of **defamation by computer**. The tort consists of the communication of intentionally false statements affecting the reputation and standing of another in the community via computer. The use of the Internet to publish statements concerning another will be the source of much litigation. All of the issues associated with the law of libel apply to actions for computer defamation. This new area of tort law will bear close scrutiny by the paralegal student in the near future.

defamation by computer

Truth. The basis of the tort of defamation is the publication of a defamatory statement that is false. Under the common law, if the statement was true, then there was no liability. The truth of an otherwise defamatory statement is an affirmative defense that must be pled by the defendant and then proved. The *Restatement* confirms the rule that if the statement is true, there is no liability (see Figure 5-14).

Difficulties arise regarding statements that are substantially true. If a reasonable person would decide that the accusation was justified, then the truth will operate as a defense. Regarding a publication made with the most vile motives, yet which remains true, the legislatures of some states have intervened by requiring that the publication must have been made without malice. The statutes and case law of an individual's state must be carefully reviewed.

Figure 5-14. True Statements

One who publishes a defamatory statement of fact is not subject to liability for defamation if the statement is true.

Restatement (Second) of Torts § 581A

Similar in function to the truth defense, the law of privilege also completely bars an action for defamation. Members of Congress, legislators, and judges and attorneys in a courtroom all have an absolute privilege concerning defamatory statements. The law of privilege as a defense is considered in greater detail in Chapter 7.

Misuse of Legal Procedure

The intentional use of legal process or procedure to harm another forms the basis for three actions: malicious prosecution, wrongful civil proceedings, and abuse of process. Malicious prosecution involves the use of the criminal process to harm one; wrongful civil proceeding provides a remedy for malicious civil claims; and abuse of process involves the use of the civil process beyond its intended purpose. The freedom to be protected is the same: the interest in freedom from unjustifiable litigation.

malicious prosecution

Malicious Prosecution. An individual wrongfully prosecuted for a criminal act suffers both by reputation and by confinement, forming the basis for damages for the tort of **malicious prosecution**. Malicious prosecution is the unjustified use of the criminal process against another person. The tort requires these elements:

- criminal proceeding instituted against the plaintiff—issuance of a complaint or continuation of a proceeding;
- termination of the proceeding in favor of the plaintiff—acquittal or dismissal of charges;
- absence of probable cause for the proceeding—absence of a reasonable belief that the accused committed the crime;
- malice on the part of the defendant-tortfeasor—can be inferred from the circumstances and need not be proven directly.

Actual harm to the plaintiff must be shown through a loss of reputation, mental distress, legal expenses, or loss of a job. The harm is usually a combination of these types of damages, permitting a single award.

Wrongful Civil Proceedings. A tort action for the commencement of wrongful civil proceedings is based upon the same elements and theory as malicious prosecution. Most jurisdictions impose liability for the commencement of a civil action without probable cause, although it is sometimes erroneously still referred to as malicious prosecution.

The basis for the action is a lack of probable cause for the commencement of the civil action. The lack of probable cause must be very clearly proven, and must be more than a mere uncertainty as to how a court may rule. In addition, this tort demands that the defendant must have a motive of ill will toward the plaintiff and have no belief in the success of the action.

abuse of process

Abuse of Process. The tort of **abuse of process** is the improper use of legal proceedings that may have been properly initiated. If the proceedings have been properly started, no wrongful action can be maintained because of the lack of malice in the suit's commencement. But when civil litigation is used for an improper goal, then a cause of action for abuse of process exists. The tort focuses on the motive of the defendant in the use of civil process.

The elements of a cause of action for abuse of process are:

- an ulterior purpose in the use of civil process,
- a willful act in the use of the process, and
- harm to the plaintiff.

The tort requires some definite use of the process beyond what it was intended for. It usually involves coercion to obtain an advantage. In that sense, the tort is similar to the crime of extortion in that the civil process is used to gain something not otherwise lawfully obtainable.

Damages

The defendant-tortfeasor faces liability for all damages resulting from his or her intentional conduct in each of these torts involving harm to person. The torts of assault, intentional infliction of emotional distress, invasion of privacy, defamation, and misuse of legal procedure all share mental distress as a significant component of the harm suffered by the plaintiff. While the mental distress may result in physical illness, it is primarily the mental suffering that is the focus of the tort. The plaintiff is entitled to recover for embarrassment, humiliation, anxiety, depression, or an aggravation of many underlying emotional conditions. The recovery is for any damages related to the illness. In those situations where the defendant-tortfeasor acted with malice, punitive damages may also be available. In situations where more than one tort is involved, there will be only one recovery.

Harm to Property

Exclusive use of property is a right guaranteed to an owner of both personal and real property. Interference with the right of possession and enjoyment of property has been the basis for the tort action of trespass since the early common law. Its two basic forms are trespass to land and trespass to chattels.

Trespass to Land

An action for harm to land occurs when there has been an entry on another's real property without consent. The defendant's intentional entry violates the owner's right of enjoyment of the property. In most jurisdictions a trespass to land requires three elements:

- an entry upon the land of another without consent,
- an intentional entry, and
- an interference with the use and enjoyment of the land.

An unauthorized intentional invasion of another's real property is actionable at law regardless of actual harm to the property.

entry

Entry. The first requirement of an intentional **entry** on the land of another is invasion without consent that interferes with the plaintiff's exclusive right of use and enjoyment of the property. Entry occurs by a personal invasion, by causing another to invade, or by causing some tangible thing to invade the property. It is an invasion to physically walk upon another's land as well as to throw some object onto his or her property. No entry occurs without some tangible interference, which means that noise or light cannot form the basis for an action for trespass.

Intent. The second requirement of an intentional entry is that the defendant-tortfeasor intended the invasion of the property interest of another. The intrusion must be the inevitable consequence of the defendant's act. If the invasion was negligent, then the theory of the tort is different and the law of negligence applies. Under the law of trespass, as opposed to the law of negligence, the defendant is liable even if he or she acted in good faith and an honest belief that no wrong was committed.

Damages. The intended invasion need not cause any actual harm to the property, but only an interference with its use and enjoyment. The invasion alone is sufficient to maintain an action. This technical trespass may entitle the plaintiff only to nominal damages instead of compensatory or punitive damages, but it still provides sufficient grounds for action.

Possession. The tort also requires the element of possession. Possession refers to actual and exclusive possession of the property, and does not necessarily refer to the interest of an owner. The occupier of the land, e.g., a tenant, has the right of enjoyment that is protected by the tort. Thus, an owner of land who does not have the right of possession, such as a landlord, may not maintain an action for trespass because that right of enjoyment was given to the tenant by the lease contract.

Vertical Possession. The protection of the interest of use and enjoyment of land is not limited to the mere surface of the land. The possessor of land has a property interest that extends above and below the surface of the land. Theoretically, one owns the sky above his or her property. Any interference with that air space is a trespass. As a practical matter, owners of land have had to yield to the demands of modern society to allow for such things as aircraft flying over property and the use of overhead and underground utility lines. Statutes and contractual arrangements have limited the right to maintain a trespass action for the use of air space. Similarly, the land beneath the surface belongs to the owner of property, and includes all of the water and mineral rights attached to the land. The difficulty arises with a subsurface invasion beneath the land of another as in the case of the construction of a tunnel. Such a technical trespass may not support an action unless there has been some actual interference with the use of the property.

Toxic Torts. Our modern industrial society has produced numerous toxic substances as by-products of the manufacturing process. For years, these substances, many of which remain undetected, were merely released into the air or dumped into the soil or waters. Improper disposal of toxic wastes has contaminated surrounding property through airborne pollution or seepage through underground water sources.

toxic torts

Actions for trespass to land for these toxic invasions have been called **toxic torts**, meaning an action in tort for toxic interference with one's ownership and enjoyment of property. Toxic tort litigation has been maintained under a theory of intentional trespass to land, negligence, absolute liability, and the law of nuisance. Individual state case law must be reviewed to determine the status of a particular theory in support of a toxic tort action. As an example, consider the case of the airborne pollutants in *Bradley* (see Figure 5-15).

Figure 5-15. Case in Point: *Bradley v. American Smelting and Refining Company*

BRADLEY v. AMERICAN SMELTING AND REFINING COMPANY
Supreme Court of Washington
709 P.2d 782
Nov. 14, 1985

CALLOW, Justice.

This comes before us on a certification from the United States District Court for the Western District of Washington. Plaintiffs, landowners on Vashon Island, had sued for damages in trespass and nuisance from the deposit on their property of microscopic, airborne particles of heavy metals which came from the American Smelting and Refining Company (ASARCO) copper smelter at Rushton, Washington....

The parties have stipulated to the facts as follows: Plaintiffs Michael O. Bradley and Marie A. Bradley, husband and wife, are owners and occupiers of real property on the southern end of Vashon Island in King County, Washington. The Bradleys purchased their property in 1978. Defendant ASARCO, a New Jersey corporation doing business in Washington, operates a primary copper smelter on real property it owns in Rushton, which is an incorporated municipality surrounded by the city of Tacoma, Washington.

On October 3, 1983, plaintiffs brought this action against defendant alleging a cause of action for intentional trespass and for nuisance. Plaintiffs' property is located some 4 miles north of defendant's smelter. Defendant's primary copper smelter (also referred to as the Tacoma smelter), has operated in its present location since 1890. It has operated as a copper smelter since 1902, and in 1905 it was purchased and operated by a corporate entity which is now ASARCO. As a part of the industrial process of smelting copper at the Tacoma smelter, various gases such as sulfur dioxide and particulate matter, including arsenic, cadmium and other metals, are emitted. Particulate matter is composed of distinct particles of matter other than water, which cannot be detected by the human senses....

As a part of defendant's smelting process, the Tacoma smelter emits into the atmosphere gases and particulate matter. For the purposes of resolving the certified questions, the parties stipulate that some particulate emissions of both cadmium and arsenic from the Tacoma smelter have been and are continuing to be deposited on plaintiffs' land....

Does an intentional deposit of microscopic particulates, undetectable by the human senses, upon a person's property give rise to a cause of action for trespassory invasion of the person's right to exclusive possession of property as well as a claim of nuisance?

The courts have been groping for a reconciliation of the doctrines of trespass and nuisance over a long period of time and, to a great extent, have concluded that little of substance remains to any distinction between the two when air pollution is involved.... We agree with the observations on the inconsequential nature of the efforts to reconcile the trappings of the concepts of trespass and nuisance in the face of industrial airborne pollution when Professor Rodgers states:

> Trespass is a theory closely related to nuisance and occasionally invoked in environmental cases. The distinction between the two originally was the difference between the old action of trespass and the action on the case: if there was a direct and immediate physical invasion of plaintiff's property, as by casting stones or water on it, it was a trespass; if the invasion was indirect, as by the seepage of water, it was a nuisance.

Today, with the abandonment of the old procedural forms, the line between trespass and nuisance has become "wavering and uncertain." The basic distinction is that trespass can be defined as any intentional invasion of the plaintiff's interest in the exclusive possession of property, whereas a nuisance requires a substantial and unreasonable interference with his use and enjoyment of it. That is to say, in trespass cases defendant's conduct typically results in an encroachment by "something" upon plaintiff's exclusive rights of possession.

The first and most important proposition about trespass and nuisance principles is that they are largely coextensive. Both concepts are often discussed in the same cases without differentiation between the elements of recovery....

Both of these concepts are nonsensical barriers, although the courts are slow to admit it. The requirement that the invasion be "direct" is a holdover from the forms of action, and is repudiated by contemporary science of causation. Atmospheric or hydrologic systems assure that pollutants deposited in one place will end up somewhere else, with no less assurance of causation than the blaster who watches the debris rise from his property and settle on his neighbor's land. Trespassory consequences today may be no less "direct" even if the mechanism of delivery is viewed as more complex....

The view recognizing a trespassory invasion where there is no "thing" which can be seen with the naked eye undoubtedly runs counter to the definition of trespass expressed in some quarters. [Citing the *Restatement (First), Torts* and *Prosser*]. It is quite possible that in an earlier day when science had not yet peered into the molecular and atomic world of small particles, the courts could not fit an invasion through unseen physical instrumentalities into the requirement that a trespass can result only from a direct invasion. But in this atomic age even the uneducated know the great and awful force contained in the atom and what it can do to a man's property if it is released. In fact, the now famous equation $E=MC^2$ has taught us that mass and energy are equivalents and that our concept of "things" must be reframed. If these observations on science in relation to the law of trespass should appear theoretical and unreal in the abstract, they become very practical and real to the possessor of land when the unseen force cracks the foundation of his house. The force is just as real if it is chemical in nature and must be awakened by the intervention of another agency before it does harm....

The measure of damages for a permanent trespass, like a nuisance, is depreciation of market value....

We hold that the defendant's conduct in causing chemical substances to be deposited upon the plaintiffs' land fulfilled all of the requirements under the law of trespass.... We hold that theories of trespass and nuisance are not inconsistent, that the theories may apply concurrently, and that the injured party may proceed under both theories when the elements of both actions are present.

Trespass to Chattels

trespass to chattels

chattel

Any intentional interference with another's personal property is considered a **trespass to chattels**. Another term for personal property is a **chattel**, separate and distinct from real property. The tort action is based upon an intentional interference with the property interest of possession. The plaintiff must have had a legal right of possession that was intentionally interfered with by the defendant-tortfeasor. The defendant must intend to deprive the plaintiff of the use and enjoyment of the property. Recovery is limited to the damages sustained to the chattel.

Conversion

conversion

Conversion is a tort action for harm to property and is similar to trespass to chattels. The theory behind an action for trespass was that the owner of the property had his or her property interest interrupted, yet the plaintiff remained the owner. In conversion, the defendant-tortfeasor deprives the owner of possession and puts the chattel to his or her own use. Such an act also deprives the plaintiff of his or her ownership interest. The defendant is then said to have converted the property. Conversion originates from the common law writ of trover, which concerned itself with a finder of lost goods putting the goods to his or her own use.

The modern distinction between trespass and conversion lies in the seriousness of the interference. For interferences resulting in relatively minor damage, the action of trespass is relied upon. In more serious interferences, an action for conversion is used to have the defendant pay full value for the goods. If the defendant's interference has been of such an extent and duration, and is inconsistent with the plaintiff's rights, then an action for conversion will be proper. The tort requires three elements:

- interference with possession of a chattel,
- intent to convert the chattel to one's own use, and
- lack of consent on the part of the owner.

The circumstances that support an action for conversion vary greatly from one jurisdiction to the next. In most states, the act of conversion is not only the basis for an action in tort, it is also a criminal offense. The paralegal student must consult his or her individual state statutes and case law to determine the character of the tort.

Injurious Falsehood

injurious falsehood

Injurious falsehood is a body of tort law that has evolved to address interference with economic relations. It began with an action for written aspersion to title to property, called slander of title, and was then extended to include disparagement of the quality of property, called commercial disparagement. The title to property, its quality, and the possible effect on the sale of that property are the interests to be protected by an action for injurious falsehood. The tort requires the following elements:

- publication of a false statement regarding the plaintiff's property, title, or affairs;
- intent on the part of the defendant-tortfeasor to prevent others from dealing with the plaintiff;
- communication of the falsehood to another; and
- actual damages.

While the tort of injurious falsehood appears similar to defamation, note its direction at a property interest and the effect on the value of that property interest as opposed to a false statement directed at a person and his or her reputation. The First Amendment freedom of speech protection applies to the tort of injurious falsehood in the same manner as it does to defamation. Thus, the principles enunciated by the United States Supreme Court in the case of *New York Times v. Sullivan*, and subsequent decisions further interpreting the question, apply here.

Deceit

deceit

The tort action for **deceit** is used to cover many differing types of action for misrepresentation, fraud, and nondisclosure. Deceit is a cause of action for monetary loss as a result of intentionally false statements. It is based upon the existence of the following elements:

- false representation by the defendant-tortfeasor,
- knowledge by the defendant-tortfeasor that the representation is false,
- an intent to induce the plaintiff to act or refrain from acting,
- reliance upon the misrepresentation by the plaintiff, and
- damage to the plaintiff.

Much confusion exists between jurisdictions over the name given to the tort. States using the term *fraud* define it as deceit intended to induce another to part with something of value. States relying on the term *misrepresentation* define it as any false statement intending to deceive. Some states use the terms interchangeably. The paralegal student must consult individual state case law for any particular situation.

Summary

Intentional torts are distinguished by the state of mind of the defendant-tortfeasor. In cases where he or she intended actions or omissions, and the result was harmful to another, liability will attach to such intent. The defendant is subject to liability when there has been an intentional invasion of another's interests, reputation, person, property, or business interest. The defendant faces liability in such cases regardless of any concept of fault that forms the basis of a claim for negligence. Intentional torts, unlike negligence, require only the intent to invade another's interests.

Review Questions

1. Discuss the role of intent in an intentional tort.
2. Describe the difference between an assault and a battery.

3. What is the extent of confinement required for liability for false imprisonment?
4. What is the state of mind of the plaintiff necessary to sustain a finding of intentional infliction of emotional distress?
5. Discuss outrageous conduct and its relationship to the tort of infliction of emotional distress.
6. List the four tort actions based upon the right of privacy.
7. Describe the interest that is to be protected by the torts of defamation.
8. What is the key element in all defamation?
9. List the elements necessary to maintain an action for trespass to land in most jurisdictions.
10. Discuss the distinction between a trespass to a chattel and the tort of conversion.

Focus Your Skills

Inspired by the research of Albert Einstein, Hope Springs was certain that she had found a simple mathematical formula that would prove the relativity of time as well as providing a formulaic equivalent of the Fountain of Youth. Her solution was the simple use of a 26-hour day instead of the usual 24, allowing for the gain of 1 day out of every 12. By the time of her death from the natural aging process at 73, it was apparent that her theory was dimmed by the realities of the mortal body's tendency to deteriorate with age, regardless of how one counts.

Rusty Springs, Hope's devoted husband of more than 50 years, lovingly respected her testamentary wishes by sending her body to the Eternal Voyage Stellar Mausoleum for cremation. Eternal Voyage offered a package deal for orbital eternity providing for cremation of the beloved deceased, stowage of the remains in a capsule, and launch and orbit of the cremonaut for only $11,000. Rusty delivered Hope's body to Eternal Voyage on May 15 for cremation and encapsulation. On May 20, Hope's capsule, along with several thousand other cremonauts, was placed in a geophysical orbit for eternity.

The Reverend Early Light is a self-proclaimed protector of fundamental religious values and founder of an evangelical haven known as The Dawn. The Reverend, known affectionately as The Dawn's Early Light, considered the quest for immortality by the cremonauts to be the most heinous form of blasphemy. He decided it was time to present his views publicly and seek vengeance through the Fourth Estate. His vitriolic attack on the cremonauts was published by a muckraking journal called *The Malevolent Tattler*. On May 30, a headline in *The Tattler* read, "Hope Springs Eternal?" The essence of the article was a malicious attack on the launching of the cremonauts as a sacrilegious act of satanic proportions. He was quoted as saying, "Rusty Springs, Hope Springs, and her fellow cremonauts are a bunch of nut cases, and Eternal Voyage is a fraud for preying on the weakness of individuals who are obviously mentally ill and possessed by the Devil."

Rusty Springs and Eternal Voyage Stellar Mausoleum, Inc. have decided to sue the Reverend Early Light, The Dawn, and *The Malevolent Tattler* for defamation. Analyze the issues presented in light of the opinion of the United States Supreme Court in the case of *New York Times v. Sullivan*.

6

DEFENSES TO INTENTIONAL TORTS

We judge ourselves by what we feel capable of doing, while others judge us by what we have already done.

Henry Wadsworth Longfellow

In a tort action the burden rests with the plaintiff to prove a *prima facie* case of liability against the defendant-tortfeasor. Once the plaintiff has met this burden, then responsibility shifts to the defendant to excuse or justify his or her conduct by way of certain traditional defenses. Only the law of sovereign immunity, considered in Chapter 7, will relieve the defendant-tortfeasor from liability in all situations. But one or more of the traditional defenses may be available for each of the intentional torts. This chapter reviews the traditional defenses to intentional torts, analyzes the elements of each, and illustrates their application. Figure 6-1 indicates which defenses are available for each of the intentional torts.

Chapter Topics

1. Consent
2. Defense of Self, Persons, and Property
3. Legal Process
4. Mistake
5. Necessity
6. Privilege
7. Reasonable Discipline
8. Recapture of Land and Chattels
9. Statute of Limitations
10. Warrantless Arrest

Objectives

After completing this chapter, you will be able to:

1. Demonstrate the concept of defense to intentional tort.
2. Classify the traditional defenses available in an action for intentional tort.
3. Summarize the elements of each defense to an intentional tort.
4. Illustrate the defenses that are applicable to each of the intentional torts.

Figure 6-1. Available Defenses

Tort	Available Defenses
Assault	Consent, Defense, Immunity, Mistake, Necessity, Privilege, Statute of Limitations, Warrantless Arrest
Battery	Consent, Defense, Immunity, Mistake, Necessity, Privilege, Recapture of Chattel, Statute of Limitations, Warrantless Arrest
Conversion	Consent, Defense of Property, Immunity, Mistake, Recapture of Chattel, Statute of Limitations
Deceit	Consent, Immunity, Mistake, Statute of Limitations
Defamation	Consent, Immunity, Mistake, Privilege, Statute of Limitations, Truth
Emotional Distress	Consent, Immunity, Mistake, Privilege, Reasonable Discipline, Recapture of Chattel, Rightful Possession, Statute of Limitations
False Imprisonment	Consent, Defense, Immunity, Privilege, Reasonable Discipline, Statute of Limitations
Injurious Falsehood	Consent, Defense, Immunity, Privilege, Reasonable Discipline, Statute of Limitations

Tort	Available Defenses
Misuse of Legal Procedure	Consent, Immunity, Mistake, Privilege, Statute of Limitations
Privacy	Consent, Immunity, Mistake, Necessity, Privilege, Reasonable Discipline, Recapture of Chattel, Rightful Possession, Statute of Limitations
Toxic Torts	Consent, Defense of Property, Immunity, Mistake, Privilege, Rightful Possession, Statute of Limitations
Trespass to Chattels	Consent, Defense, Immunity, Mistake, Necessity, Privilege, Recapture of Chattel, Statute of Limitations
Trespass to Land	Consent, Defense, Immunity, Mistake, Necessity, Privilege, Rightful Possession, Statute of Limitations

Consent

consent

An individual with full mental capacity and complete knowledge of all relevant facts may freely grant consent to another. If such consent is granted, then he or she may not recover for harm to his or her interests by such conduct. Often called the doctrine of informed choice, **consent** is a defense to every form of action for intentional tort. Consent is defined as an act of agreement to accept the intentional acts or omissions of another by a person of sufficient mental capacity to make an intelligent, informed choice. Technically, consent is not a defense at all. The rationale is that when consent has been given, there can be no intentional tort. Consent negates any wrongful act and results in the failure of any tort at all. The common law contained a fundamental principle that stated *violenti non fit injuria*, which means that to one who is willing, there can be no injury. The *Restatement (Second) of Torts* expresses it as a willingness on the part of the plaintiff to an invasion of an interest (see Figure 6-2).

Figure 6-2. Consent

The word "consent" is used ... to denote willingness in fact that an act or invasion of an interest shall take place.

Restatement (Second) of Torts § 10A

Consent requires the existence of the following elements:

- willingness to accept an invasion of an interest, and
- full understanding of the consequences of the invasion.

Both of these elements must be present or there can be no effective defense of consent. Consent is considered ineffective under any of the following conditions:

- The plaintiff lacked capacity to consent.

- The consent was coerced.
- The plaintiff did not understand the nature and quality of the invasion of interest.
- The conduct was of such a nature that no plaintiff could consent.

Thus, when the plaintiff lacks capacity because of age or mental infirmity, or does not have legal authority to act (no principal–agent relationship), there is no capacity to consent. If the consent was given under conditions of coercion, mistake, fraud, or duress, then the consent cannot be said to have been given willingly. In such cases, the defense will be unavailable.

The plaintiff's consent extends to the *nature* of the conduct of the defendant, not its *consequences*. Because of this, the law states that when the invasion exceeds the consent, the defense fails. For instance, consent to enter a wrestling match does not include consent to have one's ear bitten off. In such a case, the consequences (the loss of an ear) exceeded the consent (to enter a wrestling match). Also, if the conduct was of such a nature that the plaintiff could not consent, e.g., criminal behavior, then the defense also fails. Consider the plight of the acting students in the Case in Point (see Fig 6-3).

Figure 6-3. Case in Point: *Micari v. Mann*

MICARI, et al. v. MANN
Supreme Court, New York County
481 N.Y.S.2d 967
Nov. 13, 1984

EDWARD H. LEHNER, Justice

Plaintiffs, students in defendant's acting school, instituted this action to recover damages based on allegations of sexual abuse and harassment. At trial the moving plaintiffs (all of whom were in their early twenties at the time of the incidents complained of) testified that defendant (who was then in his mid sixties) caused them to perform at school various sexual acts with him or in his presence, including fellatio upon him and masturbating and engaging in lesbian acts in his presence. Plaintiffs acknowledged that no physical force was employed or threatened by defendant to cause them to perform these acts. They asserted, however, that defendant individually told them that this sexual activity was intended to release their inhibitions and thus improve their acting skills. They indicated that, in light of defendant's outstanding reputation as an acting teacher who had taught many famous members of the profession, they trusted him, although they each professed doing so with a certain amount of trepidation.

Defendant denied that any of the alleged sexual activity occurred except for one instance of fellatio which he stated was initiated by one of the plaintiffs....

Claims based on three common law causes of action were submitted to the jury, to wit: 1) assault, 2) battery, and 3) intentional infliction of mental distress. With respect to the claims of assault and battery, the court

> charged that the consent of the plaintiffs to the performance of the sexual acts complained of would be a complete defense unless i) the defendant falsely represented to the plaintiffs that their performance of such acts was related to their training as actresses, and ii) plaintiffs relied upon such misrepresentation.... With regard to the claim of intentional infliction of mental distress, the jury was advised that in order for plaintiffs to recover it must find that defendant's conduct was so outrageous and shocking that it exceeded all reasonable bounds of decency. The court further informed the jury that plaintiffs, in addition to demanding compensatory damages, were seeking an award of punitive damages on each of the three causes of action, and instructions were given with respect to the jury's authority with regard thereto....
>
> Here the wrongs which the jury found defendant to have committed are most reprehensible. The jury, by rendering a verdict for plaintiffs on each of the three causes of action submitted to it, determined that defendant misrepresented the reason he requested the performance of the sexual acts about which the plaintiffs testified. Thus, defendant, a person with a distinguished reputation as an acting teacher, abused the relationship which he, as a teacher with overpowering influence over his students, possessed....
>
> Here the testimony indicated that defendant, playing upon the emotional needs of his insecure students, actively sought to be ensconced as their trusted father figure—indeed, one of the plaintiffs described defendant's behavior after a sexual experience as "fatherly." It is this studied effort at domination under the guise of acting *in loco parentis*, coupled with both his actual and apparent ability to affect plaintiffs' dearest aspirations, that renders defendant's actions so heinous. This gross violation was not merely of their bodies but of their trust as well, an invasion so reprehensible as to cry out for the imposition of a sanction expressing the moral outrage of society....
>
> Thus, considering the deplorable and outrageous conduct which the jury found was committed by defendant upon these young women under his tutelage, the court believes that the foregoing discretion should be exercised in the case at bar. Accordingly, the court hereby orders a new trial solely on the issue of punitive damages unless defendant shall, within 30 days from the date hereof, stipulate to an award of $5,000 punitive damages for each movant.

The willing consent of the plaintiff bars action for all of the intentional torts (see Figure 6-1). The consent may be either express or implied by the conduct of the parties. Yet, that consent extends only to the conduct of the defendant-tortfeasor, and not the consequences that were not contemplated by the consent. Public policy dictates that no consent is operative to include an illegal act on the part of the defendant-tortfeasor.

Defense of Self, Persons, and Property

self-defense

Since the 1400s, the law has recognized **self-defense** as a privilege based upon the necessity to take reasonable steps to prevent harm to oneself, another, or property, by taking reasonable steps to defend oneself. All reasonable force may be used to prevent any threatened bodily harm or damage to property. Reasonable force may be used either when the threat is real or when there is a reasonable belief that the threat is real. The burden rests with the defendant-tortfeasor to prove the necessity of defending oneself, another, or one's property.

The *Restatement (Second) of Torts* notes that the force must match the threat. The force is limited to that which appears necessary for protection against the threat. If the defense of one's self or of another person is not against a threat of death or serious bodily harm, then the actor's use of force is limited to that not intended to cause death or bodily harm (see Figure 6-4).

Figure 6-4. Force Not Threatening Death or Bodily Harm

(1) An actor is privileged to use reasonable force, not intended or likely to cause death or serious bodily harm, to defend himself against unprivileged harmful or offensive contact or other bodily harm which he reasonably believes that another is about to inflict intentionally upon him.
(2) Self-defense is privileged under the conditions stated in Subsection (1), although the actor correctly or reasonably believes that he can avoid the necessity of so defending himself,
- (a) by retreating or otherwise giving up a right or privilege, or
- (b) by complying with a command with which the actor is under no duty to comply or which the other is not privileged to enforce by the means threatened.

Restatement (Second) of Torts § 63

On the other hand, the actor may defend himself, herself, or another person against a force likely to cause death or bodily harm by the use of similar force (see Figure 6-5).

Figure 6-5. Force Threatening Death or Bodily Harm

(1) Subject to the statement in Subsection (3), an actor is privileged to defend himself against another by force intended or likely to cause death or serious bodily harm, when he reasonably believes that
- (a) the other is about to inflict upon him an intentional contact or other bodily harm, and that
- (b) he is thereby put in peril of death or serious bodily harm or ravishment, which can safely be prevented only by the immediate use of such force.

(2) The privilege stated in Subsection (1) exists although the actor correctly or reasonably believes that he can safely avoid the necessity of so defending himself by
- (a) retreating if he is attacked within his dwelling place, which is not also the dwelling place of the other, or

(b) permitting the other to intrude upon or dispossess him of his dwelling place, or
(c) abandoning an attempt to effect a lawful arrest.

(3) The privilege stated in Section (1) does not exist if the actor correctly or reasonably believes that he can with complete safety avoid the necessity of so defending himself by

(a) retreating if attacked in any place other than his dwelling place, or in a place which is also the dwelling of the other, or
(b) relinquishing the exercise of any right or privilege other than his privilege to prevent intrusion upon or dispossession of his dwelling place or to effect a lawful arrest.

Restatement (Second) of Torts § 65

This approach of matching the allowable defense to the degree of the force is codified in the penal laws of most states. Some jurisdictions impose a duty to retreat if an avenue of escape is available. Yet even those jurisdictions hold that one is not obligated to retreat from one's own home.

Defense of another person, as opposed to one's self, involves the same test. If the actor believes that the third person had a privilege of self-defense and the intervention was necessary to protect the third person, then the actor is entitled to use the same force as allowed in the defense of self. As an example, assume that Fred and Felicia were taking a romantic stroll through a city park on a warm summer's eve. While in a deserted area of the park, they were approached by a sinister-looking individual keeping one hand in his jacket pocket, who then demanded Felicia's purse. Fred, ready to protect a female in distress, struck the hapless would-be robber and knocked him to the ground. In an action against Fred for battery, he could assert his defense of another person threatened with bodily harm.

Protection of one's property, either land or chattel, is subject to the same rules as the protection of oneself or another. The property owner has an interest in protecting his or her property and its peaceful use and enjoyment. When that peace and enjoyment are threatened by an intrusion that is likely to cause death or serious bodily harm to the owner or another, then the owner may respond in kind. Professor Keeton refers to this as "protection by self-help," and limits its application to situations where there is no time to resort to the law (see Figure 6-6).

Figure 6-6. Defense of Property

The interest in peaceful possession and enjoyment justifies protection by self-help, in situations where there is usually no time to resort to the law. The limitations upon the privilege are much the same as in the case of self-defense: the force must be, or reasonably appear to be, necessary, and not excessive in view of the interest involved.

W. Page Keeton et al., *Prosser and Keeton on the Law of Torts* § 21 at 131 (5th ed. 1984)

Defense of self, another person, and one's property is available for the following intentional tort actions:

- assault
- battery
- conversion
- false imprisonment
- infliction of emotional distress
- toxic torts
- trespass to land and chattels

The assertion of the defense is the defendant's burden in the tort action. Once the plaintiff has proven a *prima facie* case of liability for any of the above actions, then it is incumbent upon the defendant to prove the defense.

Legal Process

A principle of law well settled in American jurisprudence is the concept that a public officer cannot be held liable for an action authorized by law or taken at the direction of proper legal authority. When this principle is applied to an intentional tort against a person or property, it provides a defense for the public officer acting within authority. A problem frequently arises in situations involving an arrest pursuant to a warrant or the seizure of property under a writ of attachment or execution. The public officer is merely carrying out duties as directed by law, and has the defense of legal process available so long as he or she remains within that authority.

The defense of legal process is available when the following conditions exist:

- The actor is engaged in the service of process or execution of an order of a court or other public authority.
- The process is valid.
- The force is reasonably necessary for the service of process or execution of the order.

The law requires that in order for the privilege to exist, there must be a valid court order, meaning that the order or process must be "fair on its face." If the order is obviously defective in some way and the officer attempts to serve it anyway, then the defense is not available. Also, if the officer exceeds the force necessary to carry out the execution, the defense is unavailable. While Chapter 7 addresses the subject of immunity in greater detail, questions concerning the constitutionality of an arrest are best left to criminal law texts.

Mistake

mistake

Mistake is an available legal defense to many of the intentional torts when the defendant-tortfeasor has acted upon incorrect information or an erroneous belief as to certain facts. It is an act or omission by the defendant based upon a genuine belief that circumstances exist that justify his or her conduct. The defense is based upon the principle that individuals must be free to defend themselves if they believe that they are under attack, that they have the right to possession of land or chattels, or that they have the authority to make an arrest. In each case, the defendant-tortfeasor is operating out of a genuine belief that the otherwise tortious conduct is justified.

The elements that must exist to allow the defense of mistake for an intentional tort are:

- a genuine belief in the existence of some fact or circumstance,
- an act or omission based upon that belief, and
- a tortious interference with the interests of another.

A mistake differs from the accidental injury that forms the basis of a negligence action. Negligence is an unintentional act by the defendant, while mistake is an intentional act that is based upon an erroneous belief.

Mistake is not an absolute defense in cases involving intentional torts. When the defendant intended an act leading to harm, he or she cannot claim mere mistake. Mistake as a defense must be subjected to the reasonable person test. If a reasonable person would have acted in the same way based upon a mistaken belief, then the defense may give rise to a privilege (see Figure 6-7).

Figure 6-7. Mistake

The law is, then, that if the defendant entertained the intent necessary for the particular tort, such as trespass to land, battery, or false imprisonment, it will be no excuse, ordinarily, that he was mistaken as to something justifying his conduct. But this generality does not apply when the defendant is regarded as having a justifiable reason for the exercise of a privilege. If, in other words, the defendant's motive or purpose is that of self-defense, or defense of another, then even though he may be acting under an erroneous belief as to the necessity for the exercise of this defense, he may be justified.

W. Page Keeton et al., *Prosser and Keeton on the Law of Torts* § 17 at 111 (5th ed. 1984)

The paralegal student should consult the laws of his or her individual state to determine the legal status of the defense of mistake.

NECESSITY

necessity

The defense of **necessity** has received only infrequent application in the law. The defense is used in a situation when the defendant-tortfeasor is acting to prevent a threatened injury from some force of nature. In that sense, it is closely related to self-defense, except that the threat does not come from the plaintiff. For necessity to arise, the threat must come from some natural force such as a storm, flood, or fire.

The elements required for the defense of necessity to arise are:

- an intentional tort by the defendant directed at the property or person of the plaintiff,
- the threat of a more serious injury to the defendant or some third person(s),
- the threat originating from some source other than the plaintiff,
- avoidance of a greater harm than that which resulted to the plaintiff.

The essence of the defense is the avoidance of a greater harm by choosing a lesser injury; in other words, choosing the lesser of two evils.

The defense of necessity has found minor application in the law, stemming from early cases involving such acts as jettisoning goods from a boat during a storm in order to save the passengers. Over the years, the defense has divided into two lines of cases: *public* necessity and *private* necessity. Public necessity arises when the threat is directed at protecting some public interest. For instance, in time of war, the destruction of private property to keep it from falling into the hands of the enemy would occasion the defense. In that situation, the goods of the plaintiff would be necessarily destroyed to protect a public interest. The law would not require that such a heroic act result in personal liability.

Private necessity arises with even greater infrequency. In situations when the emergency is sufficiently great, the defendant-tortfeasor may be excused from some intentional tort on the basis of necessity. By way of an example, assume that Walker was strolling through wooded terrain on a summer hike and came upon a bear feeding in a meadow. Feeling apprehension and choosing flight as a reasonable course of action, Walker fled the scene at a dead run that took him across the private property of Farmer. The law may very well hold that Walker's intentional trespass to the land of Farmer was allowed out of necessity.

So long as the defendant believes that the threat is greater than the interest of the plaintiff to be protected, the defense may be available (see Figure 6-8).

Figure 6-8. Necessity

So far as the decisions indicate, the privilege of necessity resembles those of self-defense and defense of property, in that, assuming the reasonable appearance of necessity, an honest mistake as to its existence will not destroy the privilege.

W. Page Keeton et al., *Prosser and Keeton on the Law of Torts* § 24 at 148 (5th ed. 1984)

As with the defense of self, the defense of necessity is available for the intentional torts of assault, battery, and trespass. It has not been applied extensively and would not hold in those tort actions involving substantial personal harm to the plaintiff.

PRIVILEGE

privilege

Confusion frequently arises over the use of **privilege** as a defense to a tort action, in that many of the traditional defenses to intentional torts are merely another form of privilege. It is a circumstance that justifies or excuses intentionally tortious conduct, allowing the defendant to commit an act that is contrary to another's interests without facing liability. The application of privilege as a defense finds justification based upon an interest of some social importance that the defendant is entitled to protect at the expense of the plaintiff. Social policy allows the defendant freedom guaranteed by the law of privilege (see Figure 6-9).

Figure 6-9. Privilege

[Privilege] is applied to any circumstance justifying or excusing a *prima facie* tort, such as a battery, assault, or trespass; it signifies that the defendant has acted to further an interest of such social importance that it is entitled to protection, even at the expense of damage to the plaintiff. The defendant is allowed freedom of action because his own interests, or those of the public, require it, and because social policy will best be served in permitting it. The privilege is bounded by current ideas of what will most effectively promote the general welfare.

W. Page Keeton et al., *Prosser and Keeton on the Law of Torts* § 16 at 109 (5th ed. 1984)

The law of privilege as a defense to intentional torts parallels the principles behind defense of self, third persons, and property, recapture of property, warrantless arrest, and reasonable discipline. Each of these traditional defenses involves a form of conditional privilege applicable to the intentional torts of assault, battery, and trespass.

Privilege can take two distinct forms in the law of torts. The first form, considered in this chapter as a defense to intentional torts, is its application to cir-

motive

cumstances when the defendant's behavior is conditioned upon a proper **motive**. Motive is the mental state of the defendant compelling him or her to act in a certain manner. When the defendant's behavior is conditioned upon a proper motive, he or she is said to be exercising a privilege. To illustrate a conditional privilege based upon the motive of the defendant, consider a hypothetical situation wherein Starr is walking toward Natalie on a neighborhood sidewalk. He sees that she is about to be struck from behind by a junior moto-cross rider on a bicycle. He violently pushes Natalie out of the path of the crazed rider into a roadside ditch where she is humiliatingly and irrevocably soiled. While Starr may be *prima facie* liable for the intentional tort of battery, he has a defense of privilege available to him on the basis of his heroic motive.

The second form of privilege recognized by the law is that type of intentional behavior not permitting an inquiry into the defendant's motive. This privilege is considered absolute, as in the case of a doctor–patient relationship, and is referred to as an immunity. Chapter 7 considers this second type of privilege in greater detail.

Privilege is a limited defense based upon the motive of the defendant-tortfeasor. Courts attempt to balance the interests of the defendant in the exercise of his or her privilege with the interests of the plaintiff based upon an inquiry into these questions:

- Is the defendant's motive sufficient justification for interference with the interests of the plaintiff?
- Assuming the defendant's motive is valid, is the defendant's conduct justified?
- Is the defendant allowed to be mistaken on the basis of fact or law in the exercise of the privilege?

The courts of each jurisdiction may approach the question of privilege as a defense in their own way in an attempt to balance the interests of the parties. The paralegal student should carefully review the case law of his or her jurisdiction to determine how the courts apply the defense. The cases will vary significantly based upon differences in individual situations.

Reasonable Discipline

reasonable discipline

Maintenance of order and child discipline give rise to a privilege to use some degree of force and restraint so long as the individual acts in good faith and in a reasonable manner. This is called the doctrine of **reasonable discipline**. It originates from the common law whereby the head of the household was recognized as having authority to discipline members of his family. That privilege no longer extends to the exercise of discipline toward wives, but in most jurisdictions a child has no civil action against a parent for personal injury.

in loco parentis

One who stands in the position of a parent, ***in loco parentis,*** has the same rights and liabilities a parent has. The term means literally "in place of a parent," and means that those standing in place of a parent assume a parent's rights and responsibilities. Those rights include the use of reasonable force and corporal punishment for discipline and control. Parents and those standing in the place of parents are assumed to have the welfare of the child at heart in rendering discipline (see Figure 6-10).

Figure 6-10. Reasonable Discipline

(1) A parent is privileged to apply such reasonable force or to impose such reasonable confinement upon his child as he reasonably believes to be necessary for its proper control, training, or education.
(2) One other than a parent who has been given by law or has voluntarily assumed in whole or in part the function of controlling, training, or educating a child, is privileged to apply such reasonable force or to impose such reasonable confinement as he reasonably believes to be necessary for its proper control, training, or education, except in so far as the parent has restricted the privilege of one to whom he has entrusted the child.

Restatement (Second) of Torts § 147

The elements traditionally associated with a defense of reasonable discipline include:

- The force is necessary to further the education of the child or maintain reasonable discipline.
- The force is not designed to create a substantial risk of death, serious physical injury, disfigurement, extreme pain, or extreme mental distress.

These elements apply to a parent, guardian, teacher, or another person to whom the education and welfare of the child have been entrusted.

Most jurisdictions today discourage the use of corporal punishment by teachers toward students. Such acts have been the subject of legislative attention by most states, resulting in statutory regulation of the use of force by teachers and a movement away from the doctrine of *in loco parentis.* Consider the statutory treatment of the use of force by a teacher as found in the Kentucky Revised Statutes (see Figure 6-11).

Figure 6-11. Kentucky Revised Statutes

503.110 USE OF FORCE BY PERSON WITH RESPONSIBILITY FOR CARE; DISCIPLINE OR SAFETY OF OTHERS

(1) The use of physical force by a defendant upon another person is justifiable when the defendant is a parent, guardian or other person entrusted with

the care and supervision of a minor or an incompetent person or when the defendant is a teacher or other person entrusted with the care and supervision of a minor, for a special purpose, and:

(a) The defendant believes that the force used is necessary to promote the welfare of a minor or mentally disabled person or, if the defendant's responsibility for the minor or mentally disabled person is for a special purpose, to further that special purpose or maintain reasonable discipline in a school, class or other group; and

(b) The force that is used is not designed to cause or known to create a substantial risk of causing death, serious physical injury, disfigurement, extreme pain, or extreme mental distress.

The Kentucky statute on the use of force was considered by the court in the *Holbrook* case in applying the statutory principles to an *in loco parentis* situation (see Figure 6-12).

Figure 6-12. Case in Point: *Holbrook v. Commonwealth*

HOLBROOK v. COMMONWEALTH
925 S.W.2d 191
Court of Appeals of Kentucky
November 10, 1995

HUDDLESTON, Judge.

Anita Holbrook, a fourth grade teacher, was convicted in Carter District Court of fourth-degree assault on one of her students. The conviction resulted from the paddling of the student for failure to complete an in-class assignment. Holbrook appealed to Carter Circuit Court which affirmed her conviction. We granted discretionary review to determine whether the district court erred when it failed to grant Holbrook's motion for a directed verdict.

A directed verdict of acquittal should be granted when, viewing the evidence in the light most favorable to the Commonwealth, it would be unreasonable for a jury to find guilt.... In cases where a defendant is relying upon a defense of justification, a directed verdict should be granted when the evidence conclusively establishes justification. *Townsend v. Commonwealth*, Ky., 474 S.W.2d 352 (1971). Where all the elements of justification are proven and the justification has not been lost, it would be unreasonable for a jury to find guilt....

A teacher is justified in the use of physical force within certain bounds. Force is permissible if (1) the teacher believes that the force is necessary to further the education of the child or "maintain reasonable discipline," and (2) the force is not "designed to cause or known to create a substantial risk of causing death, serious physical injury, disfigurement, extreme pain, or extreme mental distress." KRS 503.110. The privilege to use force is unavailable as a defense if the teacher is "wanton or reckless in believing the use of any force, or the degree of force used, to be necessary." In its response to Holbrook's motion for discretionary review, the Commonwealth concedes that Holbrook was not wanton or reckless in deciding to paddle the student. Absent a wanton or reckless belief that force is necessary, the teacher is privileged to use whatever force is necessary so long as that force is not "designed to cause or known to create a substantial risk of causing death, serious physical injury, disfigurement, extreme pain, or extreme mental distress...."

The evidence at trial established that in paddling the student Holbrook did not use force in excess of that permitted by the teacher justification statute. At most, the student received bruises on her buttocks from three strokes of the paddle. The paddling certainly did not create a substantial risk of causing death. Bruises of the nature sustained by the student do not constitute serious physical injury, which is defined as a "physical injury which creates a substantial risk of death, or which causes serious and prolonged disfigurement, prolonged impairment of health, or prolonged loss or impairment of the function of any bodily organ...." Neither did the student suffer disfigurement, extreme pain or extreme mental distress. The child did not require medical care and she testified that, by the next morning, her buttocks "didn't sting bad or hurt." Furthermore, considering the child's testimony that she got along well with Holbrook after the paddling and even took several of her classes the following year, evidence of extreme mental distress was lacking. In sum, there was no evidence that Holbrook exceeded the permissible degree of force.

Since Holbrook did not exceed the degree of force permitted, the only possible question for the jury was whether the teacher was reckless or wanton in her belief that physical force was necessary. Inasmuch as the Commonwealth has conceded that Holbrook was not wanton or reckless in deciding to paddle her student, the evidence conclusively established all of [the] elements of justification. Thus, no reasonable jury could have found Holbrook guilty of fourth-degree assault, and the district court should have directed a verdict of acquittal.

In view of our decision that Holbrook was entitled to a directed verdict of acquittal, it is unnecessary that we address her contention that the jury instruction containing the wanton or reckless belief qualification was incorrect. In any event, we agree with the Commonwealth that the issue was not preserved for appellate review.

The opinion and order from which this appeal is prosecuted is reversed and this case is remanded to Carter Circuit Court. The circuit court shall remand this case to Carter District Court with directions to vacate the judgment convicting Anita Holbrook of fourth-degree assault and to enter a judgment of acquittal.

The privilege does not extend to conduct that is considered unreasonable under the circumstances. Those circumstances may vary greatly depending upon the age and size of the child and his or her past behavioral tendencies. The circumstances also vary based upon the type of control or restraint employed. Established statutory procedures, combined with the common law remedy for excessive and unreasonable force, ensure that the child is not left without safeguards. Local state law must be reviewed to determine statutory treatment and interpretation.

Recapture of Land and Chattels

recapture

A defense of a privilege is available, in actions for intentional trespass, to use force against another to retake possession of land or chattels. The conduct of the defendant-tortfeasor may be excused for the use of force to dispossess another or to regain possession. The privilege is almost identical in its application concerning **recapture** of land or of chattels. Recapture refers to the taking of possession of property in the custody of another.

The common law held that an individual is entitled to possession of property that another is wrongfully holding, and that one is entitled to use force to recapture that property so long as the force did not threaten death or serious bodily harm (see Figure 6-13).

Figure 6-13. Recapture

The privilege does not exist unless possession is taken wrongfully from the defendant. Any wrongful taking without a claim of right, such as theft, will suffice. Any wrongful and forcible taking, even under claim of right, will also suffice. But the courts have extended the privilege beyond this, and have recognized it where the goods were obtained by fraud.

W. Page Keeton et al., *Prosser and Keeton on the Law of Torts* § 22 at 138-139 (5th ed. 1984)

The English common law principles, codified in the ancient Statutes of Forcible Entry and Detainer, have received legislative treatment by every state. Each jurisdiction has its own statutory procedure established for the peaceful repossession of both land and chattels. Generally, most jurisdictions require certain conditions for the use of force for the purpose of recapture. Those conditions are:

- Tortious dispossession—The defendant must have been dispossessed without a claim of right, by force or fraud.
- Immediate possession—The defendant must be entitled to immediate possession.
- Prompt recapture—Recapture is made promptly after the defendant knows of the dispossession.
- Demand—A request to give up the property peacefully must have been made.

The summary procedure required in each state provides legal process by which an owner may recover possession after a brief delay. The rationale behind the establishment of legal process is that the public interest in preserving the peace takes precedence over the temporary inconvenience to the owner.

Statute of Limitations

statute of limitations

bar

toll

All litigation for intentional torts must comply with the **statute of limitations** imposed on such actions by the legislatures of the individual states. Also referred to as limitation of actions, a statute of limitations is a legislative enactment establishing maximum time periods during which certain types of actions at law may be brought. After the time period has expired, no lawsuit may be brought for that particular type of action regardless of its merit. A statute of limitations is a **bar** to an action, that is, it prohibits an action once the statutory time limit has been reached. For instance, assume that a particular state has a three-year statute of limitations for the filing of an action for battery. Once the three-year period has expired from the date of the battery, the action cannot be filed regardless of the merit of the plaintiff's claim. The action is barred by the statute of limitations.

The laws of most states also establish circumstances whereby the limitation period of a statute of limitations does not run, referred to as a **toll** of the statute. The term *toll* means that the statute of limitations is temporarily suspended until some event occurs. Typically, statutes of limitation are tolled when the defendant is (a) absent from the jurisdiction, (b) avoiding service of process, or (c) suffering from a lack of competency. During the existence of those circumstances, the statutory period does not run.

The period provided by a statute of limitations begins the day following the act or omission that gives rise to the cause of action. For instance, if a battery were to occur on the fourteenth day of the month, then the statute of limitation would begin running on the fifteenth day of the month, which would be counted as day number one. Statutes of limitation are generally expressed in terms of years, and the number of days in the period is computed simply by attributing 365 days for each year allowed. If expiration of the statutory period occurs on a weekend or holiday when a lawsuit cannot be filed with the court, the statute is briefly tolled until the next business day.

Warrantless Arrest

warrantless arrest

The subject of arrest without a warrant by an officer of the law is a topic more properly considered in a treatise on criminal law. The rules vary depending upon whether the arrest is made by an officer of the law or a private citizen, and are dependent upon the seriousness of the crime. As a defense to an action for intentional tort, the subject of **warrantless arrest** is concerned with the occurrence of some tort during an arrest by a private citizen. For tort law purposes, a warrantless arrest is any detention or taking into custody by a private citizen of a suspect in a felony or breach of the peace. A warrantless arrest is sometimes referred to colloquially as a citizen's arrest.

Once the crime has been committed, the constitutional safeguards guaranteed to the accused take precedence. The *Restatement (Second) of Torts* clearly sets forth the law of most jurisdictions concerning warrantless arrest (see Figure 6-14).

Figure 6-14. Warrantless Arrest

... a private person is privileged to arrest another without a warrant for a criminal offense
(a) if the other has committed the felony for which he is arrested, or
(b) if an act or omission constituting a felony has been committed and the actor reasonably suspects that the other has committed such act or omission, or
(c) if the other, in the presence of the actor, is committing a breach of the peace or, having so committed a breach of the peace, he is reasonably believed by the actor to be about to renew it, or
(d) if the other has attempted to commit a felony in the actor's presence and the arrest is made at once or upon fresh pursuit, or
(e) if the other knowingly causes the actor to believe that facts exist which would create in him a privilege to arrest under the statement in Clauses (a) to (d).

Restatement (Second) of Torts § 119

A crucial point in the law of warrantless arrest is the risk taken by the individual making the arrest. A private citizen bears the risk that there is actual authority for the arrest. He or she may arrest an individual if a felony has in fact been committed, and so long as there are reasonable grounds to suspect the person arrested. A mistake on the part of the private citizen will not excuse his or her actions. Also, mere misdemeanors are not the subject of this type of defense in most jurisdictions.

The defense is available for intentional torts involving assault, battery, false imprisonment, infliction of emotional distress, and trespass. The common law rules regarding warrantless arrest have received statutory treatment in most states. The paralegal student should consult his or her individual state's statutes to determine the availability of the defense for intentional tort actions.

Summary

It is the burden of the plaintiff to prove a *prima facie* case of liability for an intentional tort. Once that burden has been met, the burden of proof shifts to the defendant to establish a legal excuse or privilege for his or her conduct as a defense to the tort action. The traditional common law defenses to intentional torts involve a legal excuse or justification for the acts or omissions of the defendant that injure the plaintiff. They are each a form of privilege allowing the defendant an excuse based upon an interest of social importance outweighing the interests of the injured plaintiff. Social policy mandates that a defendant be excused from liability when the plaintiff has provided consent; the defendant is protecting self, another person, or property; or when any one of several privileges exist. Privilege takes the form of mistake, necessity, reasonable discipline, recapture of land and chattels, and warrantless arrests. Any liability for an intentional tort may be avoided by the statutory limitations of time for filing an action. The defenses to intentional tort are based upon a social policy encouraging activity that promotes the general welfare and maintains peace.

Review Questions

1. Describe the doctrine of informed choice.
2. List the circumstances under which consent is ineffective.
3. Discuss the use of reasonable force in the defense of self, another person, or property.
4. What is the defense of legal process?
5. List the elements of the defense of mistake.
6. Distinguish between public necessity and private necessity.
7. What is the rationale behind the defense of privilege?
8. Define the concept of *in loco parentis*.
9. List the conditions under which force may be used for the recapture of property.
10. What is the general rule regarding warrantless arrest by a private citizen?

Focus Your Skills

Patterned after the Parris Island Marine Corps training facility, the mission of Camp D-Day was to retrofit a basic sense of values into the minds of today's youthful paradigms. Founded by Colonel Colt Ruger, the camp relied upon a program of reform directed at the single most powerful drug available in the United States today, testosterone. Unregulated, universally available, and believed to be behind more criminal behavior than all other street drugs combined, Colonel Ruger hypothesized that testosterone properly channeled could be used as a path to rehabilitation rather than destruction. This unique theory of behavioral reform was presented recently to the American Academy of Juvenile Detention in a paper by Col. Ruger entitled, *Testosterone: Every Man's Drug of Choice*.

After the publication of the Colonel's thesis, Camp D-Day experienced a surge in enrollment. Parents who had previously lost all hope for their little delinquents were now all too happy to sign the Camp's Release and Waiver which stated in part, "The above named parent(s) hereby relinquish all parental control, authority, and influence over said detainee for the period of enrollment."

Difficulties immediately became apparent in the real-time application of the Camp's premise. Cadet Harley "Snake" Pipes, enjoying his natural high after a vigorous day of training, kidnapped the camp mascot. The mascot happened to be the product of an unfortunate union between a Dall Ram and a Bichon Frise, aptly named Mutant, and was the apple of Colonel Ruger's eye. Snake and three other members of his squad held Mutant hostage in their barracks, demanding a ransom of pizza and beer. Predictably true to form, Colonel Ruger responded by firing tear-gas grenades into the building and then destroying its second floor with a round from a 90-millimeter cannon. The effect on the recalcitrant youths was immediate and profound. They burst from the building and immediately demanded an attorney.

Snake's parents have filed an action against Colonel Colt Ruger and Camp D-Day for various intentional torts ranging from assault and battery to infliction of emotional distress. Colonel Colt Ruger has retained your firm for advice regarding possible defenses.

7

Immunity from Tort Liability

Any law that takes hold of a man's daily life cannot prevail in a community, unless the vast majority of the community are actively in favor of it. The laws that are the most operative are the laws which protect life.

Henry Ward Beecher

Defendant-tortfeasors enjoying special status as governmental bodies, public officers, or family members may be free from tort liability based upon the doctrine of immunity. The status of the defendant-tortfeasor, for reasons of public policy or interest of social importance, determines the potential use of the immunity defense. Whether the tort action is based upon a claim of negligence or one of intentional tort, the defendant may be entitled to immunity from suit. We have previously discussed defenses to tort actions that involved situations justifying or excusing the conduct of the defendant. Immunity frees the defendant from having to justify or excuse the behavior. This chapter analyzes the concepts behind the doctrine of immunity and the classes of defendants entitled to an immunity defense.

Chapter Topics

1. Public Policy
2. Intra-Family Immunity
3. Charitable Immunity
4. Governmental Immunity
5. Immunity of Infants and Minors
6. Immunity of Mental Incompetents
7. Privileged Communication

Objectives

After completing this chapter, you will be able to:

1. Define the doctrine of immunity from tort liability.
2. Examine the rationale behind the concept of immunity from tort liability.
3. Understand the nature of immunity within a family structure.
4. Discuss the modern view of the defense of charitable immunity.
5. Analyze the doctrine of governmental immunity.
6. Determine the extent of immunity from tort liability for minors and incompetents.
7. Understand the concept of immunity for public officers.
8. Discuss the concept of privilege within the rules of evidence.

Public Policy

immunity

In the law of torts, **immunity** is a freedom from liability or action, and provides an absolute defense to an action for negligence or intentional tort. Historically, immunity provided the defendant with an absolute defense in a broad range of situations regardless of his or her tortious conduct. The common law protection of particular defendants depended totally upon their status, conferring almost absolute freedom from liability on governments and their agents. The passage of time has limited the broad application of the doctrine with limitations and statutory exceptions. Over the course of time, limitations and statutory exceptions have narrowed the doctrine's application. Contemporary courts and legislatures view the doctrine of immunity with disapproval and require justification for its continued existence.

In feudal England, the doctrine of immunity arose from the concept of the divine right of Kings, the notion that "the King can do no wrong." The courts of England were the King's courts, and maintenance of a suit against the King in the monarch's own court defied reason. The extension of immunity was also applied to ministers serving at the King's behest. This expansion to include the King's ministers led to a broader application to modern forms of government.

Today, state legislatures consider the doctrine of immunity in purely practical terms. An attempt is made to achieve a balance between the interests of the injured party and the potential financial cost to the state. The trend has been to restrict immunity in favor of the rights of injured plaintiffs, with taxpayers bearing the cost. The wide divergence in treatment of the doctrine of immunity between the various states is beyond the scope of this text. Individual state laws must be consulted to determine the conditions and extent of any immunity.

The common law application of the doctrine of immunity to family situations was based upon the traditional concept of the family as one person in the eyes of the law; one cannot be liable to oneself. The separate legal identity of a spouse was suspended for the duration of the marriage. In the United States, the application of Married Women's Property Acts in the nineteenth century changed the old common law concepts regarding the rights of women, allowing women to own property and to sue and be sued in their own right. Subsequent legislative treatment has removed many of the previous barriers to tort actions within the family.

Intra-Family Immunity

interspousal immunity

The old common law doctrine of **interspousal immunity** held that one spouse was immune from tort liability to the other spouse. The doctrine was founded on the idea that the rights of a husband and wife merged at the time of marriage. This merger prevented a wife from owning property, entering into contracts, or maintaining an action against her husband for tort. While the Married Women's Property Acts greatly eased the situation, they still did not allow intra-family actions for tort. In the latter half of the twentieth century, courts began to realize that domestic harmony could not be maintained by preventing redress for a grievous wrong caused by negligent or intentional conduct. Gradually, most courts have abandoned the concept of interspousal immunity for tort actions and now allow either spouse to pursue these matters. The *Restatement (Second) of Torts* conforms with the majority of courts in the United States in repudiating the doctrine of interspousal immunity (see Figure 7-1).

Figure 7-1. Interspousal Immunity

(1) A husband or wife is not immune from tort liability to the other solely by reason of that relationship.
(2) Repudiation of general tort immunity does not establish liability for an act or omission that, because of the marital relationship, is other wise privileged or is not tortious.

Restatement (Second) of Torts § 895F

Husband and Wife

Most states' courts have abrogated the doctrine of interspousal immunity. Although some states continue to recognize the doctrine's existence, or allow some exceptions to remain, most have rejected any form of immunity between spouses. The courts do recognize that the mere proximity of the two marriage partners will give rise to some technical application of tort principles that would normally be actionable were it not for the marital relationship. In such instances, the court will not allow an action in tort.

As an example, assume that Arliss and Henry are husband and wife, and that neither has particularly tidy personal habits. Arliss continually leaves her shoes throughout the house. Henry constantly leaves articles of discarded clothing and laundry on the floor. One accidentally tripping over the mere peccadilloes of the other will not result in an actionable tort in most states. Yet, in contrast, consider the action maintained by one spouse against another for contraction of a venereal disease in the matter of *S.A.V. v. K.G.V.* (see Figure 7-2).

Figure 7-2. Case in Point: *S.A.V. v. K.G.V.*

S.A.V. v. K.G.V.
708 S.W.2d 651
Supreme Court of Missouri
April 15, 1986

RENDLEN, Judge.

This appeal concerns Missouri's longstanding rule of interspousal immunity for tort actions.... We now decide if spousal immunity should continue as a bar to negligence actions or whether it too should be removed as we have done for the intentional tort.... For reasons hereinafter discussed we hold that the archaic doctrine of spousal immunity is no longer available as a bar to negligence actions and the cause is remanded for reinstatement of plaintiff's (appellant's) petition.

The trial court dismissed appellant's petition against respondent in which it was alleged that during the marriage, respondent contracted *herpes praeputialis* and transmitted the disease to appellant. Appellant's three-count petition alleges that respondent willfully, recklessly and negligently transmitted the disease to appellant without informing her of his infection. Count III concludes with the allegation "[t]hat [d]efendant's negligence ... is the proximate and direct cause of [p]laintiff's contracting this disease, herpes, and thereby suffering injury and damage...."

The trial court ruled that the action was barred by the doctrine of interspousal immunity and the Court of Appeals–Eastern District transferred the cause after opinion to this Court for reexamination of existing law....

It is generally argued that total abolishment of interspousal immunity will clog courts with trivial suits, disrupt family harmony and result in collusive claims. Respondent in the present case is particularly concerned that tort claims will be duplicative of property settlements and judgment obtained in dissolution of marriage proceedings.

The "flooding" of the courts argument collides with the requirement that courts must provide a forum to redress legitimate and compensable injuries. Further, that argument has been tested and apparently found wanting in thirty jurisdictions which have totally abolished the doctrine of interspousal immunity....

A similar argument is made that removal of the bar will lead to a rash of claims of the "unwanted kiss" and "rolling pin" variety.... It cannot be said it is beyond the capacity of our courts to examine and on a case-by-case basis define or adjust the duty of care required between married persons to accommodate the "give-and-take" of married life. It seems remarkably inconsistent to argue that connubial bliss will be disrupted to the breaking point by a spouse filing a tort action and in the same breath argue against removing the spousal immunity doctrine because such couples might unite for purposes of collusive claims....

In conclusion, we join the majority of our sister states who have taken this step before us....

The judgment is reversed and the cause remanded to the trial court with direction to reinstate plaintiff's petition.

The case law of each state must be consulted to determine when the courts will allow actions between spouses.

Parent and Child

The English common law did not extend the concept of the unity of the family to the relationship between a parent and a child. Children remained separate legal entities in the eyes of the law at that time, and the common law never assumed any immunity between the two. The first extension of immunity within the parent–child relationship did not occur in the United States until the Mississippi case of *Hewellette v. George*, 68 Miss. 703, 9 So. 885 (1881). In considering a false imprisonment action against a parent, the court refused to allow claims for personal torts between a parent and a minor child. Immunity between parent and child was considered almost absolute. While there was no common law precedent for the rule, the courts seemed to justify the rule on the basis of the maintenance of intra-family harmony. While some courts held the parent–child relationship analogous to that of husband and wife, this appears invalid because of the common law merger of the rights of spouses. Professor Keeton notes that the best rationale for the rule relied upon domestic tranquility and parental discipline (see Figure 7-3).

Figure 7-3. Parental Immunity

...[A]s in the case of husband and wife, the chief reason offered is that domestic tranquility and parental discipline and control would be disturbed by the action and again on the theory that an uncompensated tort makes for peace in the family and respect for the parent, even though it be rape or a brutal beating, and even though the relation itself has been terminated by death before the suit.

W. Page Keeton et al., *Prosser and Keeton on the Law of Torts* § 122 at 905 (5th ed. 1984)

Numerous exceptions to the rule began to develop, eroding the absolute immunity enjoyed within the relationship. For instance, immunity did not extend to torts against property, nor did it apply to adult children. In addition, the death of either the parent or child terminated the immunity. Finally, the immunity did not extend to one standing *in loco parentis*, that is, performing the functions of parent.

Today, most jurisdictions in the United States have rejected the concept of absolute tort immunity within the parent–child relationship except in matters of parental control and discretion in providing food and care. The *Restatement (Second) of Torts* makes clear that a parent or child is not immune from tort liability solely because of that relationship (see Figure 7-4).

Figure 7-4. Parent and Child

(1) A parent or child is not immune from tort liability to the other solely by reason of that relationship.
(2) Repudiation of general tort immunity does not establish liability for an act or omission that, because of the parent–child relationship, is otherwise privileged or is not tortious.

Restatement (Second) of Torts § 895G

Otherwise, actions for either negligence or intentional tort between child and parent may be maintained. Consider the 1985 New York case of *Grivas* involving a mother's negligent use of a lawn mower and the resulting injury to her child (see Figure 7-5).

Figure 7-5. Case in Point: *Grivas v. Grivas*

GRIVAS v. GRIVAS
Supreme Court, Appellate Division
496 N.Y.S.2d 757
Dec. 16, 1985

RUBIN, Justice.

On May 9, 1981, the infant plaintiff (who was approximately two and a half years old) and her younger brother were playing with a ball in the backyard of their parents' house. The defendant, the children's mother, was mowing the lawn in the yard with an electric powered lawn mower. Upon hearing the telephone ring, the defendant left the lawn mower still running when she went inside the house; the defendant did not instruct her children to stay away from the lawn mower. While the defendant was talking on the telephone, the infant plaintiff went to retrieve her ball, which had rolled in close proximity to the lawn mower. The infant plaintiff was severely injured when her left hand came into contact with the rotating blades of the unattended lawn mower. Thereafter, the infant plaintiff, by her father, commenced this negligence action against her mother to recover damages for personal injuries sustained in the accident. The complaint also asserted a derivative action on behalf of the father against the defendant to recover damages for medical expenses. In paragraph Ninth of the complaint, the plaintiffs alleged that the defendant was negligent in the supervision, management and control of the infant plaintiff. In paragraph Tenth, plaintiffs additionally alleged that defendant was negligent in the operation, management and control of the lawn mower....

Within the context of this case, the mother, Georgia Grivas, would not be liable to her daughter for injuries caused by her failure to instruct the child to stay away from the lawn mower, nor for permitting the child to play in a yard where an unattended, running lawn mower was located. Both the omission to give instructions and the affirmative act of permitting the child to play in proximity to a potentially dangerous condition would merely constitute negligent parental supervision.... However, the duty to exercise reasonable care in the operation of a lawn mower is a duty owed to all. Viewed in the light most favorable to plaintiff..., the facts alleged in the complaint, if proven, would establish that the defendant mother, as the operator of the lawn mower, breached the operator's duty of care by the negligent act of leaving the lawn mower unattended, with the motor running and the rotary blades turning, in an area accessible to children. The two-and-a-half-year-old plaintiff, who went to retrieve her ball which had rolled in close proximity to the lawn mower, occupied the same position as any neighborhood child with respect to the operator's duty of care. There would have been no basis to dismiss the subject complaint against the operator of the lawn mower had the injured plaintiff been the child of a neighbor retrieving a ball that had rolled into the yard and in close proximity to the unattended, running lawn mower. With respect to the operator's duty of care, the family relationship between the infant plaintiff and defendant was purely incidental. Consequently, paragraph Tenth of the complaint states a viable cause of action and should not have been dismissed. Here, a question of fact exists as to whether negligent supervision or the breach of a duty to exercise reasonable care in the operation of a lawn mower, a duty owed apart from the family relationship, was the proximate cause of the infant plaintiff's injuries. The determination as to the proximate cause or causes of the infant's injuries must await the trial of the action.

The question of parent–child immunity may vary from state to state. The paralegal student should carefully review relevant statutes and case law to determine the current status of the doctrine.

Charitable Immunity

charitable institution

For many years American jurisprudence provided charitable institutions with immunity from tort liability. A **charitable institution** is an organization that provides charity without profit or gain for itself or its owners. The justification for charitable immunity from tort liability was based upon several theories: (a) that donations to charities would be discouraged if immunity was not available; (b) that *respondeat superior* did not apply to charities; and (c) that an imposition of liability would divert funds from the donor's intended purpose.

Today, most jurisdictions have rejected the doctrine of charitable immunity as reflected in the *Restatement (Second) of Torts* (see Figure 7-6).

Figure 7-6. Charitable Immunity

One engaged in a charitable, educational, religious or benevolent enterprise or activity is not for that reason immune from tort liability.

Restatement (Second) of Torts § 895E

Virtually every state has modified traditional tort immunity by case law, either through total rejection of the principle or through some statutory modification. As an example, consider the New Jersey case of *Kasten v. Y.M.C.A.* involving a tort action for injuries sustained at a ski resort owned and operated by the charitable institution. The court based its decision on a New Jersey statute that rejects the concept of charitable immunity when the charity is engaged in a proprietary activity (see Figure 7-7).

Figure 7-7. Case in Point: *Kasten v. Y.M.C.A.*

KASTEN v. Y.M.C.A.
Superior Court of New Jersey, Appellate Division
412 A.2d 1346
March 19, 1980

KING, J. A. D.

Plaintiff brought this action for personal injuries allegedly suffered on December 26, 1976 at the Arrowhead Ski Resort located in Marlboro, Monmouth County, and allegedly operated by defendant "Y.M.C.A. of Shrewsbury." She claimed her injuries from a downhill fall were caused by "defendant's negligence in renting (her) skiing equipment, including skis, boots, poles and bindings, which were in a state of disrepair and not properly fitted." Plaintiff claimed that she was a business invitee on defendant's premises. Defendant moved for summary judgment, claiming charitable immunity....

Here the record is productive of the inference that plaintiff, a non-Y.M.C.A. member, was a paying customer, at a higher charge than members, of a ski operation which was commercially promoted and which produced an overall profit. Plaintiff made an economic contribution to the organization....

The result we reach here is consistent with the general common law rule that when an otherwise charitable or educational organization engages in commercial activities bearing no substantial and direct relationship to its general purpose, the organization loses the immunity it would customarily enjoy even though the derived profits are used for charitable purposes.

One authority has stated the common-law rule as follows:

> If, however, the corporate activities are primarily commercial in character, carried on to obtain revenue to be used for charitable purposes, a charitable corporation is subject to the ordinary rules of liability. In other words, the test of immunity is not the use to which the income is put but the nature of the source from which the income is derived, including income producing or rental real estate of a charitable corporation not used directly in its charitable activities. (10 Fletcher, Cyclopedia of Private Corporations, § 4937 at 604 (1978).

...On the record before us defendant was not entitled to summary judgment as a matter of law. We therefore reverse and remand for further proceedings. If the proofs disclosed that plaintiff was, as alleged, a non-Y.M.C.A. member and a patron of defendant's commercially promoted ski area operated for profit used for defendant's general charitable purposes, and that she paid a higher tow or lift fee than defendant's user-members, she is not barred....

Because various states take different approaches regarding the doctrine of charitable immunity, the paralegal student must consult both the statutory treatment and its judicial interpretation. Some courts have adopted the position that any statutes retaining the doctrine of charitable immunity create a protected class with special privileges. That position may involve a violation of the equal protection clause of the United States Constitution.

Governmental Immunity

sovereign immunity

The doctrine of **sovereign immunity**, or governmental immunity, protects all levels of government against legal action. Sovereign immunity is a doctrine providing exemption from tort action for governments and their agents, officers, and employees, except in areas where that government has allowed actions. The doctrine arose from the common law concept that "the King can do no wrong." While the United States had no monarchy, its modern state replaced the King in the application of the doctrine. Sovereign immunity has survived as a sound legal principle on the basis of the preservation of the doctrine of separation of powers inherent in our constitutions. In theory, judicial review of the activities and conduct of the executive branch would impose on that separation.

United States Government

The doctrine of sovereign immunity has been applied to the federal government since the formation of the federal court system. For many years, all suits based upon tort against the federal government were prohibited on the basis of immunity. Pressured for legislation providing for some tort relief, Congress passed the Federal Tort Claims Act in 1946, providing for consent by the federal government to be sued under restricted circumstances. Under the act, the United States government is to be held liable to the same extent as a private citizen. The action must be brought in federal court, but the tort law of the state in which the injury took place applies. Questions of contributory negligence, *res ipsa loquitur*, proximate cause, and assumption of risk are to be determined by the law of that particular state. The Federal Tort Claims Act provides three procedural requirements for the maintenance of an action in tort:

- Jurisdiction rests solely in the federal district courts.
- Only non-jury trials are permitted.
- A two-year statute of limitations to bring a claim applies.

The statute of limitations requirement obliges the plaintiff to make a claim in writing to the agency involved within two years of the injury, and upon denial of the claim, to file suit within six months.

The *Restatement (Second) of Torts* states clearly that unless the United States government consents to a particular type of action, it is immune (see Figure 7-8).

Figure 7-8. United States Government

(1) Except to the extent that the United States consents to suit and to tort liability, it and its agencies are immune to the liability.
(2) Statutory provisions give the requisite consent to suit and liability for many types of tortious conduct.

Restatement (Second) of Torts § 895A

One area in which the Federal government does not consent regards actions maintained by United States servicemen and women. The failure to allow such action provides a substantive exception to the allowance of Federal tort claims (see Figure 7-9).

Figure 7-9. Case in Point: *United States v. Shearer*

UNITED STATES v. SHEARER
Supreme Court of the United States
473 U.S. 52, 105 S.Ct. 3039, 87 L.Ed.2d 38
Decided June 27, 1985

Chief Justice BURGER delivered the opinion of the Court.

We granted certiorari to decide whether the survivor of a serviceman, who was murdered by another serviceman, may recover from the Government under the Federal Tort Claims Act for negligently failing to prevent the murder....

Respondent is the mother and administratrix of Army Private Vernon Shearer. While Private Shearer was off duty at Fort Bliss and away from the base, he was kidnaped and murdered by another serviceman, Private Andrew Heard. A New Mexico court convicted Private Heard of Shearer's murder and sentenced him to a term of 15 to 55 years' imprisonment.

Respondent brought this action under the Federal Tort Claims Act, 28 U.S.C. 1346(b) and 2671 et seq., claiming that the Army's negligence caused Private Shearer's death. Respondent alleged that Private Heard, while assigned to an Army base in Germany in 1977, was convicted by a German court of manslaughter and sentenced to a 4-year prison term. Upon his discharge from that confinement in Germany, the Army transferred Private Heard to Fort Bliss. Respondent alleged that, although the Army knew that Private Heard was dangerous, it "negligently and carelessly failed to exert a reasonably sufficient control over" him and "failed to warn other persons that he was at large."

...The Federal Tort Claims Act's waiver of sovereign immunity does not apply to "[a]ny claim arising out of assault [or] battery," 28 U.S.C. § 2680(h), and it is clear that respondent's claim arises out of the battery committed by Private Heard. No semantical recasting of events can alter the fact that the battery was the immediate cause of Private Shearer's death and, consequently, the basis of respondent's claim.

Respondent cannot avoid the reach of a 2680(h) by framing her complaint in terms of negligent failure to prevent the assault and battery. Section 2680(h) does not merely bar claims for assault or battery; in sweeping language it excludes any claim arising out of assault or battery. We read this provision to cover claims like respondent's that sound in negligence but stem from a battery committed by a Government employee. Thus "the express words of the statute" bar respondent's claim against the Government.... There is no indication that Congress distinguished between "negligent supervision" claims and respondeat superior claims, with only the latter excluded under the Act. Instead it appears that Congress believed that § 2680(h) would bar claims arising out of a certain type of factual situation ... deliberate attacks by Government employees....

It is clear that Congress passed the Tort Claims Act on the straightforward assurance that the United States would not be financially responsible for the assaults and batteries of its employees....

To permit this type of suit would mean that commanding officers would have to stand prepared to convince a civilian court of the wisdom of a wide range of military and disciplinary decisions; for example, whether to overlook a particular incident or episode, whether to discharge a serviceman, and whether and how to place restraints on a soldier's off-base conduct.

We hold that Congress has not undertaken to allow a serviceman or his representative to recover from the Government for negligently failing to prevent another serviceman's assault and battery.

The main limitation on the types of suits that may be brought is provided by an exception in the Act retaining immunity for all governmental conduct concerning "discretionary functions or duties." The entire question of the theory and policy behind the Federal Tort Claims Act is reviewed by the United States Supreme Court in *Dalehite v. United States*. *Dalehite* involved multiple actions filed against the Federal government for an explosion of a fertilizer compound used in a government project (see Figure 7-10).

Figure 7-10. *Dalehite v. United States*

DALEHITE v. UNITED STATES
Supreme Court of the United States
346 U.S. 15, 73 S.Ct. 956, 97 L.Ed. 1427
June 8, 1953

Mr. Justice REED delivered the opinion of the Court.

Petitioners seek damages from the United States for the death of Henry G. Dalehite in explosions of fertilizer with an ammonium nitrate base, at Texas City, Texas, on April 16 and 17, 1947. This is a test case, representing some 300 separate personal and property claims in the aggregate amount of two hundred million dollars. Consolidated trial was had in the District Court for the Southern District of Texas on the facts and the crucial question of federal liability generally. This was done under an arrangement that the result would be accepted as to those matters in the other suits. Judgment was rendered following separate proof of damages for these individual plaintiffs in the sum of $75,000. Damages in the other claims remain to be determined. The Court of Appeals for the Fifth Circuit unanimously reversed, however, *In re Texas City Disaster*, Litigation, 197 F.2d 771, and we granted certiorari, *Dalehite v. U. S.*, 344 U.S. 873, 73 S.Ct. 166, because the case presented an important problem of federal statutory interpretation.

The suits were filed under the Federal Tort Claims Act, 28 U.S.C. §§ 1346, 2671-2678, 2680, 28 U.S.C.A. §§ 1346, 2671-2678, 2680. That Act waived sovereign immunity from suit for certain specified torts of federal employees. It did not assure injured persons damages for all injuries caused by such employees....

Suing under this grant of jurisdiction, the plaintiffs claimed negligence, substantially on the part of the entire body of federal officials and employees involved in a program of production of the material—Fertilizer Grade Ammonium Nitrate (FGAN hereafter)—in which the original fire occurred and which exploded. This fertilizer had been produced and distributed at the instance, according to the specifications and under the control of the United States. The adaptability of the material for use in agriculture had been recognized long prior to 1947....

Since no individual acts of negligence could be shown, the suits for damages that resulted necessarily predicated government liability on the participation of the United States in the manufacture and the transportation of FGAN. Following the disaster of course, no one could fail to be impressed with the blunt fact that FGAN would explode. In sum petitioners charged that the Federal Government had brought liability on itself for the catastrophe by using a material in fertilizer which had been used as an ingredient of explosives for so long that industry knowledge gave notice that other combinations of ammonium nitrate with other material might explode. The negligence charged was that the United States, without definitive investigation of FGAN properties, shipped or permitted shipment to a congested area without warning of the possibility of explosion under certain conditions. The District Court accepted this theory. His judgment was based on a series of findings of causal negligence which, for our purposes, can be roughly divided into three kinds—those which held that the Government had been careless in drafting and adopting the fertilizer export plan as a whole, those which found specific negligence in various phases of the manufacturing process and those which emphasized official dereliction of duty in failing to police the shipboard loading. The Court of Appeals en banc unanimously reversed, but since only three of the six judges explicitly rejected the bulk of these findings, we shall consider the case as one in which they come to us unimpaired. Even assuming their correctness arguendo, though, it is our judgment that they do not establish a case within the Act. This is for the reason that as a matter of law the facts found cannot give the District Court jurisdiction of the cause under the Tort Claims Act....

The Federal Tort Claims Act was passed by the Seventy-ninth Congress in 1946 as Title IV of the Legislative Reorganization Act, 60 Stat. 842, after nearly thirty years of congressional consideration. It was the offspring of a feeling that the Government should assume the obligation to pay damages for the misfeasance of employees in carrying out its work. And the private bill device was notoriously clumsy. Some simplified recovery procedure for the mass of claims was imperative. This Act was Congress' solution, affording instead easy and simple access to the federal courts for torts within its scope....

One only need read § 2680 in its entirety to conclude that Congress exercised care to protect the Government from claims, however negligently caused, that affected the governmental functions. Negligence in administering the Alien Property Act, or establishing a quarantine, assault, libel, fiscal operations, etc., were barred. An analysis of § 2680(a), the exception with which we are concerned, emphasizes the congressional purpose to except the acts here charged as negligence from the authorization to sue. It will be noted from the form of the section,... that there are two phrases describing the excepted acts of government employees. The first deals with acts or omissions of government employees, exercising due care in carrying out statutes or regulations whether valid or not. It bars tests by tort action of the legality of statutes and regulations. The second is applicable in this case. It excepts acts of discretion in the performance of governmental functions or duty whether or not the discretion involved be abused. "Not only agencies of government are covered but all employees exercising discretion." It is clear that the just-quoted clause as to abuse connotes both negligence and wrongful acts in the exercise of the discretion because the Act itself covers only "negligent or wrongful act or omission of any employee, within the scope of his office where the United States, if a private person, would be liable...."

Though the findings of specific and general negligence do not support a judgment of government liability, there is yet to be disposed of some slight residue of theory of absolute liability without fault. This is reflected both in the District Court's finding that the FGAN constituted a nuisance, and in the contention of petitioner here. We agree with the six judges of the Court of Appeals, 197 F.2d 771, 776, 781, 786, that the Act does not extend to such situations, though of course well known in tort law generally. It is to be invoked only on a "negligent or wrongful act or omission" of an employee. Absolute liability, of course, arises irrespective of how the tortfeasor conducts himself; it is imposed automatically when any damages are sustained as a result of the decision to engage in the dangerous activity. The degree of care used in performing the activity is irrelevant to the application of that doctrine. But the statute requires a negligent act. So it is our judgment that liability does not arise by virtue either of United States ownership of an "inherently dangerous commodity" or property, or of engaging in an "extra hazardous" activity.... Affirmed.

The Court refused to allow an action in tort in situations calling for policy judgment and discretion. Since the Court's decision in *Dalehite*, "discretionary" immunity has been applied to many governmental planning activities.

State Government

Similar to the federal government, state governments and their agencies enjoy sovereign immunity in the absence of consent (see Figure 7-11).

Figure 7-11. State Governmental Immunity

(1) A State and its governmental agencies are not subject to suit without the consent of the State.
(2) Except to the extent that a State declines to give consent to tort liability, it and its governmental agencies are subject to the liability.
(3) Even when a State is subject to tort liability, it and its governmental agencies are immune to the liability for acts and omissions constituting
  (a) the exercise of a judicial or legislative function, or
  (b) the exercise of an administrative function involving the determination of fundamental governmental policy.
(4) Consent to suit and repudiation of general tort immunity do not establish liability for an act or omission that is otherwise privileged or is not tortious.

Restatement (Second) of Torts § 895B

eminent domain

By right of **eminent domain**, state and federal governments may take property from private individuals for public purposes. Governments must justly compensate the owners of the property and are immune from negligent or tort actions for this process, commonly referred to as condemnation. The Eleventh Amendment to the United States Constitution provides a procedural immunity from suit in federal court by private citizens, but does not prohibit suits by other states (see Figure 7-12).

Figure 7-12. Eleventh Amendment

The Judicial power of the United States shall not be construed to extend to any suit in law or equity, commenced or prosecuted against one of the United States by Citizens of another State, or by Citizens or Subjects of any Foreign State.

U.S. Constitution amend. XI

Suits against a state in its own courts require the consent of the state.

The majority of state legislatures have exercised the right of consent to suits for torts, retaining some limited immunity for discretionary decisions. The form of consent adopted by the various states can be categorized as follows:

- Administrative claims agency—Several states have retained technical immunity from an action at law, but have created state agencies to hear and decide claims against the state.
- Classified waiver of immunity—For certain types of cases, immunity is abolished; similar to municipal bodies, the states will allow suits that involve a proprietary function, retaining immunity for those activities that are governmental in nature.
- Abrogation of immunity—A large number of states have expanded their consent to suit in tort similar to claims under the Federal Tort Claims Act, retaining immunity for discretionary decisions.

The trend among state legislatures is toward expansion of tort liability and away from an assertion of immunity. Actions of the state legislatures and state courts do not subject them to tort liability. For instance, if the Court of Appeals of a given state were to render a decision that caused some injury to one of the parties (as with most lawsuits), the injured party has remedies available other than an action in tort. The losing party may exercise its right of appeal, but may not file an action in tort against the state. By the same theory, the members of state legislatures are immune from liability.

discretionary function

Reference has been made to the term **discretionary function**. Under the Federal Tort Claims Act and in virtually every state, immunity continues for those functions that are considered to be discretionary. Discretionary function refers to the exercise of a basic policy evaluation, judgment, and expertise by a state. The rationale behind the continuation of immunity for discretionary functions is based upon the refusal of the courts to involve themselves in those functions that are better left to administrative officials developing and evaluating public policy. The distinction lies in allowing immunity for the establishment of policy rather than its administration. Immunity will allow the state governments to continue to evaluate and develop state policies without judicial interference.

Municipal Government

proprietary function

governmental function

The traditional rule applied to municipal governments is to impose liability for proprietary functions and to retain immunity for governmental functions. A **proprietary function** is a service provided by the municipality for the comfort, convenience, and safety of its citizens. A **governmental function** is the administration of some phase of government that is essential to its existence in serving the public at large. Purely governmental functions continue to enjoy sovereign immunity (see Figure 7-13).

Figure 7-13. Municipal Government

(1) Except as stated in Subsection (2), a local government entity is not immune from tort liability.
(2) A local government entity is immune from tort liability for acts and omissions constituting
(a) the exercise of a legislative or judicial function, and
(b) the exercise of an administrative function involving the determination of fundamental governmental policy.
(3) Repudiation of general tort immunity does not establish liability for an act or omission that is otherwise privileged or is not tortious.

Restatement (Second) of Torts § 895C

government entity

A municipal government, or **government entity**, is traditionally the government of a county, city, town, or village, and its agencies. Figure 7-14 illustrates some functions that are considered governmental and those that are considered proprietary.

Figure 7-14. Governmental and Proprietary Functions

GOVERNMENTAL FUNCTIONS—IMMUNITY
Municipal Courts
Municipal Council/Commission/Mayor
Police/Sheriff
Fire/Rescue

PROPRIETARY FUNCTIONS—NO IMMUNITY
Electrical/Power
Water
Gas
Waste Removal
Hospital/Medical Services
Housing
Parks/Recreation

The functions listed as either proprietary or governmental will vary greatly from state to state. Some functions may retain characteristics of both, preventing categorization. The paralegal student must consult individual state statutory and case law to determine questions of immunity.

Public Officers' Immunity

Historically, any immunity for public officers was based upon the immunity of the monarch and its extension to agents carrying out its commands. Today, the complexity of governmental function requires officers and employees to make decisions and act in accordance with their offices. Tort liability could impose too harsh a burden on public officers, effectively hampering governmental function. An extension of immunity to public officers recognizes the need for freedom of action in pursuit of the discharge of their duties. Thus, the general rule of tort liability for public officers is that tort liability will not be imposed for conduct of a type that would substantially impair the individual's effective performance of a discretionary function (see Figure 7-15).

Figure 7-15. Public Officers

(1) Except as provided in this Section a public officer is not immune from tort liability.
(2) A public officer acting within the general scope of his authority is immune from tort liability for an act or omission involving the exercise of a judicial or legislative function.
(3) A public officer acting within the general scope of his authority is not subject to tort liability for an administrative act or omission if
- (a) he is immune because engaged in the exercise of a discretionary function,
- (b) he is privileged and does not exceed or abuse the privilege, or
- (c) his conduct was not tortious because he was not negligent in the performance of his responsibility.

Restatement (Second) of Torts § 895D

A question between the imposition of liability for tortious conduct and the grant of immunity is not easily resolved. The legislatures and courts of the individual states have wrestled with the division of liability for public officers for many years. The Supreme Court of the State of Michigan issued a landmark decision in the voluminous case of *Ross v. Consumers Power Company*. The *Ross* case involved the consolidation of nine separate actions involving questions of immunity from tort liability for public officers, and resulted in the court's definitive holding, only a portion of which is offered in this text (see Figure 7-16).

Figure 7-16. Case in Point: *Ross v. Consumers Power Company*

ROSS v. CONSUMERS POWER COMPANY
Supreme Court of Michigan
420 Mich. 567, 363 N.W.2d 641
January 22, 1985

PER CURIAM.

These nine cases require us to reexamine the extent of immunity from tort liability which the governmental tort liability act..., and the common law provide to the state and its agencies, non-sovereign governmental agencies, and the officers, agents and employees of these state and local governmental agencies. We hold:

1) All governmental agencies (state and local) are statutorily liable for injuries arising out of the failure to keep highways in reasonable repair...; negligent operation of a government-owned motor vehicle by an officer, agent, or employee...; and dangerous or defective conditions in public buildings under the agency's control....

2) All governmental agencies (state and local) have tort liability for injuries arising out of the performance of a proprietary function. "Proprietary function" is defined as any activity conducted primarily for pecuniary profit, excluding activities normally supported by taxes or fees.

3) All governmental agencies (state and local) are immune from tort liability for injuries arising out of the exercise or discharge of a non-proprietary, governmental function. "Governmental function" is defined as any activity which is expressly or impliedly mandated or authorized by constitution, statute, or other law. An agency's *ultra vires* activities are therefore not entitled to immunity.

4) All governmental agencies (state and local) are vicariously liable for the negligent operation of government-owned motor vehicles by their officers, employees, and agents.... Vicarious liability for all other torts may be imposed on a governmental agency only when its officer, employee or agent, acting during the course of his employment and within the scope of his authority, commits a tort while engaged in an activity which is non-governmental or proprietary, or which falls within a statutory exception.

5) Judges, legislators, and the highest executive officials of all levels of government are absolutely immune from all tort liability whenever they are acting within their respective judicial, legislative, and executive authority. Lower level officers, employees, and agents are immune from tort liability only when they are

a) acting during the course of their employment and are acting, or reasonably believe they are acting, within the scope of their authority;
b) acting in good faith; and
c) performing discretionary-decisional, as opposed to ministerial-operational, acts.

"Discretionary-decisional" acts are those which involve significant decision making that entails personal deliberation, decision and judgment.

"Ministerial-operational" acts involve the execution or implementation of a decision and entail only minor decision making.

Any system of official accountability will necessarily involve political as well as legal considerations. Review of the particular statutory and case law of an individual state is essential to an application of the concept of immunity for public officers.

Immunity of Infants and Minors

A common misconception regards immunity from tort liability for infants and minors. Contrary to some opinion, infants and minors are not immune from tort liability. Infants and minors are subject to tort liability for both intentional torts and negligence. Recovery may occur against an infant or minor for assault and battery, false imprisonment, trespass, or negligent conduct.

However, their inherent lack of mental capacity to commit a tort restricts infants' and minors' tort liability. The child's limited intelligence and experience prevent him or her from forming the necessary intent to commit certain torts (see Figure 7-17).

Figure 7-17. Minors and Infants

...[I]nfants may escape liability for certain intentional torts, not because of immunity in itself but because they lack the mental capacity to commit a tort in the first place.

W. Page Keeton et al., *Prosser and Keeton on the Law of Torts* § 134 at 1071 (5th ed. 1984)

As an example, the tort of battery requires an intent to cause harmful bodily contact. Assume that four-year-old Paulette was playing peacefully in her day care center when she was struck violently from the rear with a plastic baseball bat by five-year-old Timothy. The law would hold that Timothy did not have the requisite intent to harm because of his limited experience and intelligence. The ruling would have the same effect as immunity, but it does not truly apply the immunity doctrine. In this case, the principles of tort law are operating and not those of immunity.

A similar result is found in the application of the principles of the law of negligence to the torts of minors and infants. Minors and infants are not immune from tort liability for negligent conduct. The law does, however, take into account the age and experience of the child in determining liability. Many courts have held that a child of tender years may not be found negligent, and have placed the threshold age at seven. Those courts have held that a child under the age of seven cannot be found liable for tortious conduct because he or she lacks sufficient experience regarding behavior. Again, the effect is similar to immunity, but is solely a function of the application of the principles of negligence.

Immunity of Mental Incompetents

Mentally incompetent persons are not immune from tort liability solely because of their condition. As with infants and minors, the principles governing tort law for both intentional torts and negligence apply to the conduct of mentally incapacitated individuals. (see Figure 7-18).

The rule has resulted in many harsh decisions and has been criticized by legal scholars as unjust to those handicapped by some mental incompetence. Yet the law continues to hold an insane person liable for assault and battery, false imprisonment, trespass, conversion, and negligence.

Figure 7-18. Deficient Mental Capacity

One who has deficient mental capacity is not immune from tort liability solely for that reason.

Restatement (Second) of Torts § 895J

Traditionally, the courts have ruled that the mentally incompetent individual may be capable of forming sufficient intent to bring about a certain result even though he or she is under some delusion (see Figure 7-19).

Figure 7-19. Case in Point: *Goff v. Taylor*

GOFF v. TAYLOR
Court of Appeals of Kentucky
708 S.W.2d 113
May 13, 1986

HAYES, Chief Judge.

At issue in this appeal is the appropriate standard by which to judge the conduct of one suffering from a mental disability or defect in a civil action. Appellant submits that the liability of an alleged tortfeasor should be measured by a subjective standard, whether he possessed the ability to distinguish right from wrong and could conform his conduct to the law. The trial judge ruled that insanity is not a defense to civil liability in this Commonwealth. We agree with the decision of the trial judge on this and the other issues advanced by appellant and accordingly we affirm the judgment below.

This is a wrongful death action. Appellant, while apparently suffering from a brain disease or disorder, shot and killed Randall Taylor without provocation. The case was tried before a jury which awarded appellee $3,510.00 funeral expenses and $700,000.00 for destruction of earning power. In this appeal appellant attempts to persuade us that we should depart from the standard applied in the majority of jurisdictions and relieve appellant from liability for his actions on the basis of his mental disability. We decline to do so primarily because we believe the policy considerations supporting the current standard outweigh the reasons advanced by appellant for discarding it: that it is simply unfair to hold a person responsible for a wrong he is incapable of avoiding.

Appealing an argument as that may be, it falls short when balanced against the long-accepted doctrine that where one of two innocent persons must suffer a loss, it should be borne by the one who occasioned it.... Appellant cites us to recent law review articles...which criticize, in view of modern scientific advances in the area of mental illness, the long-standing approach to this problem manifested in the case law and in the *Restatement of the Law of Torts*. The basic premise in each article is that a subjective standard would at least provide a mentally disabled defendant the opportunity to present evidence of his inability to avoid the alleged wrong and thus assert the defense of insanity. That the subjective standard would afford fairer treatment of a defendant afflicted with a mental disability cannot be disputed. The question the commentators do not attempt to reach is the fairness to the victim of the wrongful conduct. Is a victim any less entitled to compensation for his loss because of the mental deficiencies of his tortfeasor? We believe that the answer is no and the tort law as it stands has long served to accommodate that principle. This view does not penalize the mentally incompetent, it merely places them on a par with the rest of society in terms of responsibility for their wrongful acts. The mentally deficient are insulated from punitive damages, reinforcing our belief that tort law has kept faith with its duty to balance the protection of society at large with compassion for those unable to conform their conduct to the expected standard.

Next, appellant contends the trial court erred in refusing his instruction on unavoidable accident due to sudden or physical illness. We are convinced that such an instruction has no application to the facts of this case. There is nothing in the evidence from which one could conclude that this death was accidental. The only fair interpretation of the evidence leads to the conclusion that the shooting was an intentional act.

Thirdly, appellant assigns as error the granting of a directed verdict on the issue of liability for compensatory damages. We agree with appellee that given the undisputed evidence regarding the shooting and the fact that no defense or legal excuse was put forth, a directed verdict was entirely appropriate.

Furthermore, we are convinced that the damages awarded for the destruction of Randall Taylor's earning capacity were not at all excessive and are fully supported by evidence of his youth, health, educational pursuits and industrious character prior to this death.

Finally, appellant complains that it was error to submit the question of punitive damages to the jury. As the jury found for appellant under this instruction, his claim of prejudice must be directly related to the charge that the award of compensatory damages was excessive. We have already determined that the evidence amply supported the amount of compensatory damages and thus we are unable to discern any possible prejudice suffered by appellant from the instruction on punitive damages.

The judgment of the Pike Circuit Court is affirmed

However, if an individual's insanity reaches such proportions that he or she is incapable of forming the specific intent necessary for a particular tort, e.g., defamation, then no liability will be imposed.

Questions of negligent behavior of mental incompetents receive the strict application of tort law, holding the insane person to the standard of conduct of a reasonable person. Failure to meet the standard may impose liability. Thus, the mental incompetence of the defendant in a negligence action offers no immunity, and in most cases will not provide the individual with a defense. Criticism of the rule has resulted in efforts in many states to find solutions to the questions posed (see Figure 7-20).

Figure 7-20. Mental Incompetents

Against the liability of mentally disabled it has been said that the rule of liability is a product of an era when confinement of the mentally limited was the accepted social goal, as it no longer is, that it is unjust to impose responsibility without fault upon the disabled when fault is the standard of liability to others, and that at the very least the incompetent should be relieved of any duty of reasonable care toward those who know of his disability and can protect themselves from it.

W. Page Keeton et al., *Prosser and Keeton on the Law of Torts* § 135 at 1073 (5th ed. 1984)

The paralegal student should consult his or her local state law regarding the liability of mental incompetents in tort actions.

Privileged Communication

privileged communication

Concerns of fairness in trial practice require that the plaintiff meet the burden of proof as a prerequisite to the defendant proceeding. The rules of evidence control the quantity and character of the evidence presented for consideration by the trier of fact. Contained within those rules of evidence is the concept of **privileged communication**. Privileged communications are statements made by persons within a protected relationship that the law protects from disclosure in court. In its application, the concept of a privileged communication operates similarly to a privilege or immunity from tort liability. Within a protected relationship, the defendant has the right to decline to testify regarding any statements.

Traditionally, there are six relationships within which a privileged communication is recognized by most jurisdictions. Those relationships are:

- Self-incrimination—The Fifth Amendment to the United States Constitution upholds the right of an accused person to decline to testify in a criminal proceeding.
- Attorney–client privilege—A client may refuse to disclose any confidential communication made to his or her attorney, and may prevent the attorney from disclosing such communications.
- Physician–patient—A patient may refuse to disclose any confidential communication made to a doctor relating to his or her medical care, allowing the physician to be fully advised of the patient's medical condition without concerns of legal disclosure, and may prevent the doctor from disclosing such communications.
- Clergy–penitent—A penitent may refuse to disclose any confidential communication made to a priest, minister, rabbi, or other clergy member relating to religious or spiritual counseling, and may prevent the clergy from disclosing such communications.

- Intra-marital—A spouse may refuse to disclose any confidential communication made to the other spouse during the marriage, and may prevent the other from disclosure.
- Governmental information—Some limited forms of governmental information collected by the government is confidential, e.g., tax records, and an individual may prevent disclosure to third persons.

The protected relationships provide the individuals within those relationships with a form of immunity from disclosure that may operate in many circumstances to create an immunity from tort liability. For instance, suppose that Quincy is represented by attorney Garfield regarding a potential litigation matter against Martin. During private conversations between Quincy and Garfield, Quincy makes defamatory statements about Martin alleging that he is a crook and a thief. If those comments were not made within the protection of the attorney–client relationship, the statements may be actionable in tort. The effect is that the rules of evidence pertaining to privileged communications create a form of immunity within a protected relationship.

Summary

Public policy and concerns of social import have created a freedom from tort liability based on the doctrine of immunity. The status of the defendant-tortfeasor as a governmental officer, family member, or charitable organization may provide an immunity from tort liability depending upon the status of the doctrine of immunity in a particular jurisdiction. The effect of the principle is to protect certain classes, allowing the performance of mandated functions without fear of interference for otherwise tortious conduct. Public policy dictates that some forms of tortious conduct be excused from liability under defined circumstances. The doctrine of immunity is constantly evolving because of state legislative actions and appellate court decisions. The paralegal student should review the status of immunity in his or her individual state to determine the viability of a particular tort action for either intentional tort or negligence.

Review Questions

1. Define the concept of immunity.
2. Discuss the origins of the doctrine of immunity.
3. Describe the status of interspousal immunity in most jurisdictions today.
4. Discuss the current status of parental immunity that exists in most jurisdictions today.
5. What is the status of charitable immunity in most states today?
6. What is sovereign immunity?

7. Discuss the principle limitation imposed upon the general tort liability of the United States government under the Federal Tort Claims Act.
8. What is the general rule regarding the immunity of infants and minors from tort liability?
9. What is the general rule regarding the immunity from tort liability for mental incompetents?
10. List the six types of privileged communication generally recognized by the rules of evidence.

Focus Your Skills

Lionel Gillbreath had spent his entire life in preparation for his position as Chief Ranger with the State Department of Recreation. Lionel was a loner almost from birth, having suffered the trauma of his parents' changing their names and moving without leaving a forwarding address, twice. Assigned to the Two Cheeks State Park, 875 acres of forest and meadow with 3.5 miles of pristine oceanfront beach, he saw himself as protector of our natural resources and family values. His vehicle bore a bumper sticker that read, "Those Who Live by the Sword Get Shot by Those Who Don't."

When the county passed an ordinance prohibiting lewd and lascivious conduct and nude sunbathing on its beaches, Lionel was ready to show the flag, protect the American way of life, and enforce the letter of the law. The opportunity soon presented itself when seven members of the Coalition for the Naked, Unclad, Disrobed, and Exempt (NUDE) formed a protest demonstration in front of the Two Cheeks headquarters building. The protest was led by the founder of NUDE, Buff Creetin, a self-styled activist determined to make up for being born too late to participate in the protests of the Sixties. Marching naked and carrying banners reading, "Save the Whales; Collect the Whole Set" and "Clothing Is Un-Bareable," NUDE posed a threat to everything good and true in the eyes of Chief Ranger Lionel Gillbreath. He waded into the breach of naked bodies with truncheon held high, leveling a blow at anything not covered with cloth. In less than three minutes, he had subdued Buff and his followers and had them lined up against the wall of his office wearing only handcuffs.

Buff Creetin and the other members of NUDE's protest march at Two Cheeks State Park have started a tort action against the State Department of Recreation and its loyal servant, Chief Ranger Lionel Gillbreath. Advise as to the defense of immunity from tort liability for Lionel.

8

PREMISES LIABILITY

Private property was the original source of freedom. It still is its main bulwark.

Walter Lippman (1889–1974)

Protection of personal interests having a definite social value is the principle underlying tort law. Historically, possessors of property have enjoyed the protection of their individual interests under the law. Along with the legal protection of the property owners comes a responsibility to others that attends that possessory interest. Yet, mere ownership or possession of land alone cannot create tort liability; some legal duty toward others must be created. This chapter views the possessor of land as a potential defendant-tortfeasor whose liability depends upon the *use* of the land and the *relationship* between that use and the plaintiff. Once the general nature of the landholder's duty to others is understood, the paralegal student will be able to determine questions of liability based upon the relationship of the landholder to the injured party. Tort law does not impose on a landholder the same duty toward a trespasser as toward an invited guest. The degree of tort liability will vary depending both on the injured party's particular purpose and on whether he or she has been invited to enter the property.

Chapter Topics

1. General Duty of a Landholder
2. Entry upon Land
3. Lessor and Lessee
4. Vendor and Vendee

Objectives

After completing this chapter, you will be able to:

1. Describe the duties of a landholder to all persons entering the property.
2. Discuss the role of natural conditions in the duty of landholders.
3. Examine the liability of a landholder toward trespassers.
4. Understand the concept of licensee in relation to liability to persons entering property.
5. Analyze the liability of a landholder toward an invitee.
6. Examine the liability of lessors and lessees toward persons entering the property.
7. Understand the liability of landholders toward vendors and vendees.

General Duty of a Landholder

landholder

premises

premises liability

A **landholder** is any person who has rightful possession of land. The term includes not only those individuals owning land, but also those persons who have a lawful right to possession of the premises. **Premises** refers to real property, its attached buildings, grounds, facilities, and structures, and those things attached to the land or growing from it. Thus, when defining premises liability, the paralegal student must consider the exposure faced by a landholder in the use and enjoyment of real property stemming from a possessory interest. **Premises liability** is the liability of a landholder for the use and enjoyment of real property and its attachments.

The general duty of a possessor of property that is not in its natural state is one of due care to prevent harm to another person. When a landholder fails to reasonably care for property and harm results from that failure, the landholder may face tort liability to the injured party.

Reasonable Care

Landholders have the privilege of use and enjoyment of property but are responsible for the condition of that property. The possessor of property is in the best position to know its condition and to discover any danger. The privilege of use and enjoyment is not absolute, but is limited by the interests of other individuals potentially affected by that use. The landholder's privilege is limited by the reasonableness of the care provided to the property. For example, suppose Coldwell erected a large flagpole on his property. In his haste to observe a national holiday by hoisting the colors, he neglected to secure the pole sufficiently to support the weight of his 10-foot by 20-foot flag. When he raised the flag, the entire pole fell onto his neighbor's property, crushing the family cat. Coldwell's failure to exercise reasonable care in the use of his property caused harm to another. Unreasonably risking harm to others may result in tort liability.

The duty of reasonable care is defined in Chapter 2 as the requirement that an individual conduct himself or herself as an imaginary reasonable person would to avoid or prevent injury to another. A determination of the existence of the duty of reasonable care is based upon an analysis of the scope of the duty, the source of the duty, an act or omission, and the foreseeability of the injury. Reasonable care requires the landholder to conduct any activities on land in a manner to protect persons on or near the premises. Consider the *Boudreaux* case wherein the injury occurred as a result of the placing of a sign too close to the highway and obstructing the view of traffic (see Figure 8-1).

Figure 8-1. Case in Point: *Boudreaux v. Sonic Industries, Inc.*

BOUDREAUX v. SONIC INDUSTRIES, INC.
Court of Appeals of Oklahoma
729 P.2d 514
June 24, 1986

HANSEN, Judge:

This appeal by Plaintiff below arises out of the trial court's order granting Defendant's motion for summary judgment. Plaintiff, Joann Boudreaux, filed suit against Sonic Industries, Inc., Sonic Drive In (Sonic), and Stephanie Cobb for the wrongful death of her husband Kenneth Boudreaux. At the time of the accident Miss Cobb was attempting to exit the Sonic Drive-In Restaurant on N.E. 23rd, east of Oklahoma City, Okla. When she pulled to the curb line, the view to the east was obstructed by a large, permanent Sonic sign. As she made a left turn onto 23rd Street she struck a motorcycle coming from the east driven by decedent Kenneth Boudreaux. He was thrown from his motorcycle, suffered a head injury and subsequently died.

After filing this action, Plaintiff settled with the driver of the car, Ms. Cobb. Plaintiff alleged in her petition Sonic was negligent in placing its sign too close to the highway so that it obstructed the view of traffic. She further alleged this negligence caused the death of decedent. Sonic moved for summary judgment arguing statements in Ms. Cobb's deposition clearly indicated the sign was not the cause of the accident. In response Plaintiff submitted an affidavit of the police officer who had investigated and photographed the accident scene. These pictures appeared to support allegations the view of the road was obstructed by the sign. The officer stated his investigation disclosed that because of the sign, a vehicle 200 feet down the highway could not be seen by a driver exiting Sonic without her pulling into the roadway. Nevertheless, the trial court granted Sonic's motion and Plaintiff appeals....

The questions of whether Sonic created a dangerous situation by placing the sign so close to the highway and whether such action was the proximate cause of decedent's death are for the jury. In addition whether Sonic could have reasonably foreseen or anticipated injurious consequences from a hazardous placement of its sign is also a jury question.

The trial court did not address the threshold issue of a landowner's duty to travelers on a public highway. Its ruling was based solely on lack of causation. It is axiomatic Sonic owes a duty of care toward Ms. Cobb as its customer and invitee. But under Oklahoma law if Sonic's duty of care does not extend, through Ms. Cobb to lawful travelers on the public highway, then this court may affirm, even though the trial court did not rule on that issue. A trial court will be affirmed if its judgment reaches a legally correct result. For this reason this court requested and received briefs by the parties addressing the issue of whether a landowner whose property abuts a highway owes a duty of care to the traveling public.

Oklahoma has long recognized an owner has the right to construct anything he chooses on his land, even in close proximity to a public roadway. But that right must be exercised with due regard to coexisting rights of its invitees. Our historic and fundamental right to use our property in any legal manner we so choose collides head-on with our classic duty to refrain from creating a hazard with the potential to harm a member of the public. Does not Sonic owe some special duty to Ms. Cobb, inherent in its description as a "drive in," to provide a safe entrance and exit or at least not to create a hazardous one? Under these circumstances we hold that it does.

We now must decide whether this duty extends to travelers on the highway. The right of Sonic to erect a sign is undeniable, but Sonic has a duty to exercise that right with due regard to the right of the public to use the roadway. A property owner thus owes a duty to maintain his property in such a manner that when it is put to its normal business use, it does not create an unreasonable hazard to travelers upon the abutting roadway. This has long been the law in Oklahoma as well as in other jurisdictions when that duty is applied to the use of property that permits obstructions or hazards actually to intrude on the roadway. However the test for liability should not be some mechanistic rationale based on actual physical contact with the premises hazard. If a landowner uses his property without regard to the traveling public, it is immaterial whether the injury is caused by physical contact or by another means such as here....

One must use his own rights so as not to infringe upon rights of another. How far this obligation extends depends on the foreseeability that a particular plaintiff might be injured by a defendant's conduct. Foreseeability is not only involved in a determination of proximate cause, it is one of the yardsticks by which duty is measured. Even under the historic *Palsgraf* limitation of liability, decedent was a foreseeable plaintiff to whom Sonic owed a duty to refrain from acts which would threaten his safety. If Sonic owes a duty to Ms. Cobb to refrain from creating a hazardous exit, then that duty extends to a motorist placed in jeopardy by any breach of that duty. It is foreseeable that any injury to Ms. Cobb would also cause an injury to the traveler upon the highway with whom she collides. It would be patently unjust to require an innocent plaintiff in that situation to bear the burden of her loss because of a technicality relieving a defendant of liability for proven negligence. If Sonic is negligent as to Ms. Cobb, it is negligent as to Decedent....

We limit our holding today to acts of "misfeasance." We do not tamper with the traditional rule that a landowner is under no affirmative duty to remedy view obstructions of purely natural origin upon his land. We leave that distinction to another day....

Accordingly, we hold the public's right of passage imposes an obligation upon the owners and occupiers of abutting commercial property to use reasonable care to refrain from creating a view obstruction which might cause foreseeable harm to the users of the highway. Under the facts and circumstances of this case, any liability of Sonic to Plaintiff is derivative from its potential liability to Ms. Cobb. It is not within our realm to impose a universal duty of care upon a landowner to all the world, limited only by the foreseeability of injury. But there is no reason in modern-day life to insulate a landowner, under the circumstances of this case, from entirely foreseeable consequences.

The Sonic sign was either the proximate cause of the injuries or it was not. A jury must decide.

In affirming the general duty of a landholder, the court held that the landholder has an obligation to use reasonable care to refrain from creating an obstruction that might cause foreseeable harm to the users of the highway.

Natural Conditions

Historically, the law has always permitted an exception to the general duty of the landholder. An exception to the general duty of any possessor of land arises concerning conditions on the land that are purely natural in origin. When the economy of colonial America was agrarian and undeveloped, any requirement of a landholder to inspect property and make it safe would have been a significant burden. The exception that a landholder cannot be held liable for conditions that exist naturally on the land became recognized at that time. This view is supported by the *Restatement (Second) of Torts* which requires a landholder to exercise reasonable care, but does not create liability for natural conditions (see Figure 8-2).

Figure 8-2. Natural Conditions

(1) Except as stated in Subsection (2), neither a possessor of land, nor a vendor, lessor, or other transferor, is liable for physical harm caused to others outside of the land by a natural condition of the land.
(2) A possessor of land in an urban area is subject to liability to persons using a public highway for physical harm resulting from his failure to exercise reasonable care to prevent an unreasonable risk of harm arising from the condition of trees on the land near the highway.

Restatement (Second) of Torts § 329

---

natural conditions

Natural conditions refer to the state of land unaltered by human act. This includes the natural occurrence of trees and vegetation of any kind, along with rock and mineral formations. If the landholder erects a structure on the land or changes its natural condition, tort liability may accompany any such artificial alteration.

The applicability of the rule for natural conditions is limited in urban settings. Formulated originally to address rural area liability issues, the rule has undergone some modification in its application to populated areas. Dead limbs that might fall from a tree and cause injury illustrate the distinction. In a rural area, a landholder is under no obligation to remove the dangerous tree limbs. But in an urban location, the landholder has a duty of reasonable care to make sure that the tree does not cause injury to persons on the land or on adjacent property. This trend to limit the exception for natural conditions is discussed in the *McGarr* case (see Figure 8-3).

Figure 8-3. Case in Point: *McGarr v. United States*

McGARR v. UNITED STATES
United States Court of Appeals
Third Circuit
736 F.2d 912
June 15, 1984

GIBBONS, Circuit Judge

McGarr alleges that his son, Edward Christopher McGarr, was seriously injured when on April 3, 1982, McGarr's automobile went out of control on County Line Road and struck a tree. The road is owned by the Commonwealth of Pennsylvania, but traverses the Valley Forge National Historical Park, which is owned by the United States. The amended complaint alleges: The aforesaid accident was caused by the negligence, carelessness and recklessness of the United States of America in creating or permitting to remain on its property a condition which involved an unreasonable risk to those traveling on the highway adjacent thereto....

It is the plaintiff's position that the muddy, slippery and dangerous condition[s] upon the roadway and bridge were caused by runoff and other material from the land adjacent to the highway which is sloped on the highway and bridge. Plaintiff's position is that it was the Defendant's responsibility not to permit a dangerous condition to exist upon its land which would create, permit, or cause a dangerous condition upon the adjacent highway.

The dangers of a flooded or washed out or muddy road and bridge are evident and certainly foreseeable where proper runoff and drainage are not secured.... McGarr also made clear to the court that he pleaded alternatively the maintenance of a dangerous natural condition and a dangerous artificial condition, asserting that discovery may yet reveal the existence of an artificial condition such as grading, drainage course or shoring excavation so as to cause the muddy, slippery and dangerous conditions Plaintiff encountered while crossing County Line Road Bridge....

Assuming that the appeal is properly before us, an issue we address in Part III infra, we must therefore consider whether under Pennsylvania law McGarr could recover against an owner of land abutting a highway for the maintenance on the land of an artificial or natural condition causing an unreasonable risk to travelers on the highway....

The Federal Tort Claims Act provides that the United States shall be liable "in the same manner and to the same extent as a private individual, under like circumstances." 28 U.S.C. a 2674 (1982). The United States relies heavily on section 363 of the *Restatement (Second) of Torts* (1965), which provides:

> Natural Conditions
> (1) Except as stated in Subsection (2), neither a possessor of land, nor a vendor, lessor, or other transferor, is liable for physical harm caused to others outside of the land by a natural condition of the land.
> (2) A possessor of land in an urban area is subject to liability to persons using a public highway for physical harm resulting from his failure to exercise reasonable care to prevent an unreasonable risk of harm arising from the condition of trees on the land near the highway. *Restatement (Second) of Torts* § 363 (1965).

Comment b to that section provides that the phrase "natural condition of the land" is used to indicate that the condition of land has not been changed by any act of a human being, whether the possessor or any of his predecessors in possession, or a third person dealing with the land either with or without the consent of the then possessor. It is also used to include the natural growth of trees, weeds, and other vegetation upon land not artificially made receptive to them. On the other hand, a structure erected upon land is a non-natural or artificial condition as are trees or plants planted or preserved, irrespective of whether they are harmful in themselves or become so only because of the subsequent operation of natural forces....

The "natural condition" standard for imposing or not imposing liability creates the anomalous situation of imposing liability on a landowner who improves and maintains his property while precluding liability of a neighboring landowner who allows the "natural condition" of his property to run wild. Under this analysis, landowner A may plant hedges or bushes around the perimeter of his property and if they are allowed to become too thick or too tall so as to obstruct a motorist's vision of an intersection, he will be held liable. Landowner B, on the other hand, may neglect his property, allowing it to be overrun and overgrown with weeds, plants, grasses and other natural foliage, to an equal or greater detriment to passing motorists, but with no liability to himself. The distinction appears to be arbitrary at best....

The trend in the law is in the direction of imposing a duty of reasonable care upon the possessor of land with regard to natural conditions of land. The erosion of the doctrinal underpinning of the rule of nonliability is evident from even a cursory review of the case law. Also evident is the lack of congruence between the old common law rule of nonliability and the relevant factors which should determine whether a duty exists. All this leads to but one conclusion. The distinction between artificial and natural conditions should be rejected. "A [person's] life or limb [or property] does not become less worthy of protection by the law nor a loss less worthy of compensation under the law" because that person has been injured by a natural, as opposed to an artificial condition.

It seems evident, therefore, that if McGarr proves either an artificial or a natural condition on land owned by the United States which caused the allegedly dangerous condition he encountered on County Line Road, he may be able to recover from the United States as a landowner.

Thus, for most urban settings, the landholder must exercise reasonable care in the inspection and maintenance of property and may not invoke the defense of natural conditions.

Entry upon Land

In cases of injury to one person on the land of another, the law has established arbitrary categories of liability based upon the duty owed to that individual. The categories of liability are:

trespasser

licensee

invitee

- **trespasser**—one who enters upon the land of another without permission, privilege, or consent;
- **licensee**—one who is privileged to enter the land of another by consent;
- **invitee**—members of the public on public land, or business visitors.

The three categories of liability support separate degrees of duty to those entering land based upon their status. As the status of the person entering the land improves in the eyes of the law, he or she enjoys greater protection from the negligence of the landholder. This arbitrary categorization has been criticized by the courts and legal scholars but remains a part of American jurisprudence (see Figure 8-4).

Figure 8-4. Entry upon Land

Those who enter upon land are divided unto three fixed categories: trespassers, licensees, and invitees, and there are subdivided duties as to each. They make out, as a general pattern, a rough sliding scale, by which, as the legal status of the visitor improves, the possessor of the land owes him more of an obligation of protection. This system has long made many legal writers, and some of the courts, quite unhappy because of its arbitrary and sometimes unreasonable character; and there has been some recent movement toward abolishing the distinctions, at least between invitees and licensees. But the traditional entrant classification scheme is well entrenched in the great majority of jurisdictions, and so the categories must be carefully considered one by one.

W. Page Keeton et al., *Prosser and Keeton on the Law of Torts* § 58 at 393 (5th ed. 1984)

Trespassers

As already noted, a trespasser is one who has entered upon the land of another without the permission or consent of the landholder and has no privilege that excuses his or her presence. To such intruders, the landholder is not liable for injury caused by a failure to exercise reasonable care. Thus, the general rule is that a possessor of property is under no obligation to keep that property safe for trespassers (see Figure 8-5).

Figure 8-5. Liability to Trespassers

...[A] possessor of land is not liable to trespassers for physical harm caused by his failure to exercise reasonable care
(a) to put the land in a condition reasonably safe for their reception, or
(b) to carry on his activities so as not to endanger them.

Restatement (Second) of Torts § 333

The general rule is subject to many exceptions that may vary from state to state. Consider the *Mendoza* case, which contains a discussion of the distinctions (see Figure 8-6).

Figure 8-6. Case in Point: *Mendoza v. City of Corpus Christi*

MENDOZA v. CITY OF CORPUS CHRISTI
700 S.W.2d 652
Court of Appeals of Texas
Oct. 31, 1985

NYE, Chief Justice.

At the time of his death, Hector Mendoza was working for Lanphier Construction Company, removing debris from Lanphier's land which adjoined Lake Corpus Christi. On August 31, 1982, Mendoza told a co-worker he was going swimming. His co-workers later became concerned when he failed to return to work after a lunch break. His body was found about ten yards off Lanphier's pier in about two and a half feet of water. His neck was broken and the cause of death was drowning....

The City's duty to Mendoza in this instance is directly related to his status at the time of the accident. Was he a trespasser, a licensee or an invitee in this situation? A trespasser is one who enters upon the property of another without any right, lawful authority, or express or implied invitation, permission, or license, not in performance of any duties to the owner, but merely for his own purpose, pleasure or convenience....

The legal duty the landowner owes a trespasser is only not to injure him willfully, wantonly or through gross negligence.... A licensee's presence on the premises is for his own convenience or on business for someone other than the owner. The duty owed a licensee is not to injure willfully, wantonly, or through gross negligence and to warn of or make safe dangerous conditions actually known.... The standard of conduct required of a premises occupier toward his invitees is the ordinary care that a reasonably prudent person would exercise under all pertinent circumstances.... The test to determine if an individual is upon the land as an invitee is whether the injured person has business relations with the owner at the time of the injury which would render his presence of mutual aid to both....

Liability depends on whether the owner acted reasonably in light of what he knew or should have known about the risks accompanying a premises condition....

The evidence in this case shows that Hector Mendoza was on Lanphier's property for the purpose of removing trash and debris. After eating lunch he decided to go swimming. He did not have permission from the landowner, his supervisor, or the City to swim or dive off the pier. He left the area around which he had been conducting business for Mr. Lanphier and proceeded on a venture of his own choosing.

The permit that was issued by the City to construct the pier was limited to fishing or loading purposes only. It was not a diving or swimming pier, nor was it open to the public for any purpose. Mendoza had no business relationship with the City, and there was nothing about his venture off the pier that was for the mutual benefit or aid to both himself and the City. It is clear from the undisputed evidence, therefore, that Mendoza was not an invitee. He was never given permission by the City to swim or dive into the waters at Lanphier's pier.

It is apparent that Mendoza was either a trespasser or, at most, a licensee. Actually, it is unnecessary for us to determine in this instance which status he carried because, under either theory, the evidence does not bear out the jury's finding that the City had actual notice of the shallow condition of the water in the particular area where Mendoza dove. There is no contention by the appellants, nor was there any evidence presented, that the City's conduct was willful, wanton or constituted gross negligence. Appellants did not plead nor did they prove any grossly negligent conduct on the City's part. If, indeed, Mendoza was a trespasser as to the City, which unquestionably he was, it is clear that the City was not liable because they committed no grossly negligent acts or omissions toward Mendoza.

In order for the City to be held liable under the best possible status (the licensee theory), Mendoza's survivors were required to prove that: 1) the City had actual knowledge that the Lake waters were shallow at Lanphier Pier; 2) they knew that Mendoza or someone of the same status would dive off the Lanphier pier; and 3) the City failed to warn Mendoza and/or make safe this allegedly dangerous condition.

The paralegal student should always consult local statutory and case law on such questions.

Adults. The general rule of a lack of liability to trespassers is intended to apply to trespassing adults. The justification for this form of limited immunity is that a landholder should not be expected to anticipate trespassers, and therefore should not be held accountable.

An exception arises in situations when the landholder has knowledge of frequent trespassers on an area of the land. Most jurisdictions hold a landholder legally responsible for injuries when there is frequent trespass and require a higher degree of reasonable care to protect the trespassers in the conduct of certain activities. The *Restatement (Second) of Torts* confirms the landholder's responsibility to frequent trespassers when the landholer engages in activities that pose a threat of great bodily harm or death (see Figure 8-7).

Figure 8-7. Constant Trespassers

A possessor of land who knows, or from facts within his knowledge should know, that trespassers constantly intrude upon a limited area thereof, is subject to liability for bodily harm there caused to them by his failure to carry on an activity involving a risk of death or serious bodily harm with reasonable care for their safety.

Restatement (Second) of Torts § 334

A frequently cited example of this situation involves railroad tracks adjacent to a factory parking lot. At the end of their shift, the workers cross the tracks to get to the parking lot. The railroad should be aware of the situation, and is under a duty of reasonable care to prevent injury to the workers by passing trains. The railroad would therefore face tort liability for an injury sustained by a worker conducting business on the premises.

A further exception to the general rule occurs when the landholder discovers a trespasser on the property. Once a trespasser is found the landholder has a duty to exercise reasonable care to provide for the safety of the trespasser. The landholder must refrain from intentionally injuring trespassers once their presence is revealed. Thus, the general rule is that a landholder is under no duty to protect a trespasser whose existence is unknown, but once the presence is known, the landholder must refrain from willful or wanton conduct designed to injure.

Children. Because of their inherent lack of maturity and judgment, children are excepted from the general nonliability rule for trespassers. In the landmark case of *Sioux City & Pacific Railroad Co. v. Stout*, 84 U.S. 657 (1873), recovery was allowed for a child trespassing on railroad property and injured while playing on a turntable. From this decision and cases following, the courts developed the **doctrine of attractive nuisance**. This doctrine holds a landholder liable for injuries to children when an artificial condition exists on his or her land that may be expected to attract children (see Figure 8-8).

doctrine of attractive nuisance

Figure 8-8. Case in Point: *Barnhizer v. Paradise Valley*

BARNHIZER v. PARADISE VALLEY UNIFIED SCHOOL DISTRICT
599 P.2d 209
Supreme Court of Arizona
July 23, 1979

STRUCKMEYER, Vice Chief Justice.

This is a wrongful death action brought by William D. and Georgia B. Barnhizer to recover damages for the death of their son, Steven A. Barnhizer....

The facts of this case are not in dispute. On the evening of May 2, 1975, Steven Barnhizer, then thirteen years old, and two companions went to the Desert Shadows School in Scottsdale where a school sponsored dance was in progress. After telling a teacher chaperone that they were not going to the dance, they were told to leave the area. They left, but later returned to the school from a different direction. Steven suggested to his companions that they climb to the roof of the school building. One of his companions, John Hert, then 15 years old, expressed opposition because he had seen other boys being told by teachers and janitors not to climb onto the roof. However, Steven's suggestion prevailed. Steven fell from the roof, incurring injuries which resulted in his death....

Ordinarily, the duty of a landowner to a trespasser is not to willfully or wantonly injure him.... Or, as the *Restatement of Torts (Second)* § 333 puts it, a possessor of land is not liable to trespassers for physical harm caused by failure to exercise reasonable care to put land in a condition reasonably safe for their reception. Where children are concerned, an exception to this rule has developed, commonly known as the doctrine of attractive nuisance.

The *Restatement of Torts (Second)* recognizes that a possessor of land may be liable to a child trespasser if certain conditions concur.

Section 339 of the *Restatement* provides:

> A possessor of land is subject to liability for physical harm to children trespassing thereon caused by an artificial condition upon the land if (c) the children because of their youth do not discover the condition or realize the risk involved in intermeddling with it or in coming within the area made dangerous by it....

In *McHugh v. Reading Co.*, 346 Pa. 266, 30 A.2d 122 (1943), the Pennsylvania Supreme Court considered the application of § 339 to a case involving a fatal fall. Plaintiffs' decedent, a six-year-old girl, climbed onto a bridge abutment, 24 feet above the street, to play on an ornamental cornice dubbed the "king's throne." Attempting to descend from the "throne" she lost her footing and fell to her death. The Court first set out the purpose of the duty of the landowner to trespassing children:

> "The purpose of the Duty is to protect children from dangers which they are unlikely to appreciate and not to protect them against harm resulting from their own immature recklessness in the case of known danger."

Then it said:

> "No danger is more commonly realized or risk appreciated, even by children, than that of falling; consciousness of the force of gravity is almost from animal instinct. Certainly a normal child nearly seven years of age indeed any child old enough to be allowed at large knows that if it steps or slips from a tree, a fence, or other elevated structure, it will fall to the ground and be hurt. It may be that some children, while realizing the danger, will disregard it out of the spirit of bravado, or because, to use the language of the *Restatement*, of their 'immature recklessness,' but the possessor of land is not to be visited with the responsibility for accidents

due to this trait of children of the more venturesome type."... Other courts have adopted the same or similar reasoning....

We are persuaded, as was the trial court, that, as a matter of law, plaintiffs failed to meet the condition set forth in part (c) of § 339 of the Restatement, supra, a condition which must exist before a duty arose to protect the decedent against his own folly. Steven was just eight weeks short of his fourteenth birthday and was of the age and intelligence to appreciate the clear danger of falling. The doctrine of attractive nuisance did not, therefore, have application.

Appellants argue that even assuming that Steven was trespassing at the time of his death and that he recognized the danger of falling, because the School District knew that school children could climb to the roof, it had a duty to eliminate or reduce the risk. The problem with this argument is that Steven on this occasion was not an invited school child but a trespasser for whom the School District had no duty except not to willfully or wantonly injure him. The possessor of property is not under a duty to prevent every possibility of harm.

The doctrine is accepted in most jurisdictions, although it has been modified to include general negligence theory. The *Restatement* expresses the doctrine creating liability toward trespassing children in pure negligence terms (see Figure 8-9).

Figure 8-9. Trespassing Children

A possessor of land is subject to liability for physical harm to children trespassing thereon caused by an artificial condition upon the land if
(a) the place where the condition exists is one upon which the possessor knows or has reason to know that children are likely to trespass, and
(b) the condition is one of which the possessor knows or has reason to know and which he realizes or should realize will involve an unreasonable risk of death or serious bodily harm to such children, and
(c) the children because of their youth do not discover the condition or realize the risk involved in intermeddling with it or in coming within the area made dangerous by it, and
(d) the utility to the possessor of maintaining the condition and the burden of eliminating the danger are slight as compared with the risk to children involved, and
(e) the possessor fails to exercise reasonable care to eliminate the danger or otherwise to protect the children.

Restatement (Second) of Torts § 339

For example, assume that the Dingle family had just recently installed an inground swimming pool in their backyard for their children and friends. The little Dingles were encouraged to invite their friends to supervised swimming activities when the senior Dingles were present. The Dingles did not erect a fence around the pool. Further, assume that nine-year-old Butch, a friend of the little Dingles and a frequent guest, decided to go for a dip in the pool after the Dingles had retired for the evening. In the dark, Butch tripped over the protruding diving board and fell into the water, severely injuring his head as it struck the side of the pool. In this situation, the Dingles may be held responsible for the injury to a trespassing child because they failed to exercise reasonable care in erecting a fence around the pool. The case law of individual states varies regarding the limitations on the doctrine and should be consulted whenever applicable.

Licensees

As noted above, a licensee is anyone who has consent, or license, to enter land. The element of consent refers to the willingness of the landholder to have the licensee enter the property. Individuals typically considered licensees are:

- persons entering for the benefit of the licensee—persons entering the property solely for their own interest;
- household members—persons considered as family members, but not paying guests or servants;
- social guests—persons to whom the use of the premises is a personal favor; not to be confused with invitees simply because they are invited on the premises.

The courts often examine custom and usage in a geographic area to determine the existence of the relationship with the landholder. If the visitor fits any of the above categories, he or she will be considered a licensee. As an example, assume that Pushman was soliciting campaign contributions door-to-door for a local judicial candidate. Upon entering the property of Landman, he tripped over a skateboard left on the front walk, seriously injuring himself. Pushman would fit the first category of a person entering the property solely for his own interests with the tacit consent of Landman.

The general rule of a landholder's liability toward a licensee is similar to that of the responsibility toward trespassers. The landholder has been held liable only for intentional, willful, or wanton conduct. In the example above, Landman would be liable only for willful and wanton disregard for the safety of others. The decision in the *Hundt* case hinged upon whether the visitor was a licensee or an invitee (see Figure 8-10).

Figure 8-10. Case in Point: *Hundt v. LaCrosse Grain Co.*

HUNDT v. LACROSSE GRAIN CO., INC.
425 N.E.2d 687
Court of Appeals of Indiana
September 21, 1981

MILLER, Judge.

This appeal is from a negligence action brought by appellant and cross-appellee Everett Hundt against the LaCrosse Grain Co., Inc., appellee and cross-appellant, following a fall by Hundt down a flight of stairs on property owned by LaCrosse. Hundt had been employed by LaCrosse for a number of years through an oral agreement to exterminate pests from various buildings located near the company's grain elevator in LaCrosse, Indiana....

We initially relate the facts upon which Hundt based his claim for damages. One morning in March 1976, Hundt and his son Brad visited the LaCrosse Grain Company for the purpose of applying bird exterminating substances to the rafters of a storage shed on the premises pursuant to their agreement with LaCrosse. When the two arrived, they first went into a small building where the company had an office (and where the misadventure later occurred) and made their presence known to the company's manager, Jim Anderson. They entered the office through the front door, as they always had done in the past. After a few minutes, the Hundts left the building and proceeded to the storage shed located about 180 yards to the rear of the office. The evidence also revealed it was the first time the Hundts had done bird exterminating work on the premises, although the elder Hundt had visited the LaCrosse buildings approximately once a month since 1955 for the purpose of exterminating various other pests. Hundt stated the LaCrosse facility was one of 127 grain elevators (along with various restaurants, farms, stores, and taverns) where he regularly did exterminating.

The particular work they were doing that day required the use of highly toxic chemicals, and after one and one-half to two hours of working with the substance, when the job was complete, Hundt and his son returned to the office building to wash up. This time, however, they entered through the back door of the office building, which was the closest door to the shed where they had been working. Hundt's fall occurred in the building housing the company's office. In this regard, he stated he opened the back door of the building, walked forward a few feet, and then mistakenly opened the door to the basement instead of the washroom door, and his momentum from these actions caused him to fall down the basement stairs. Significantly, the uncontradicted evidence was that the basement door opened inward, there was no landing inside the door, and there was no handrail or other bracive device alongside the stairs....

In ascertaining the duty which a landowner owes to one who comes upon his land, Indiana law has long recognized the relationship between them is determinative of such duty. One who enters at the owner's express or implied invitation to transact business of mutual benefit to both is an invitee to whom the landowner owes a duty of reasonable care to protect against dangers, while one who enters for his own convenience, curiosity, or entertainment is a licensee by permission, or a mere licensee, who (with certain exceptions) must take the premises as he finds them.... As a general rule, however, in cases where the evidence of material facts is in conflict, it is a matter for the jury to determine under appropriate instructions by the court whether a status of invitee or licensee is presented, and the question becomes one for the court only where the controlling facts are undisputed.

LaCrosse contends Hundt was a licensee as a matter of law to whom no duty was breached because, on cross-examination, he acknowledged no one had forced or induced him to open the basement door and that "(t)he washing up would only help me." Even assuming this were the only evidence in the case, we do not believe Hundt must be viewed as a licensee as a matter of law....

In the case at bar, we believe similar reasoning may be applied to conclude Hundt was not necessarily acting as a licensee when he went looking for a washroom on the premises of LaCrosse. Moreover, the record also reveals there was additional testimony, not acknowledged by LaCrosse, creating an inference that Hundt's activity in looking for a place to wash his hands may legally be viewed as a necessary part of the job he was doing for LaCrosse. In this regard, Hundt's son stated the chemicals they were using were "very toxic" and "we had that chemical on us," and thus it was necessary to wash it off "because the chemical burns and if you get enough on you it would permeate your skin and could make you very deathly ill or could kill you." Similarly, Hundt himself testified "(t)here is no way you can keep from getting it (the chemical) on you" despite protective gloves and face shields, and that washing up "is just taken for granted" as "part of the job" and that "(m)y convenience has nothing to do with it." Under these facts, the jury was not required to conclude that Hundt was a mere licensee when he fell.

Making a further distinction, the *Armstrong* decision states that a licensee relationship is formed when one who is an invitee exceeds the bounds of that relationship. At that point, the relationship between the parties has changed, and the resulting duty of care has also changed (see Figure 8-11).

Figure 8-11. Case in Point: *Armstrong v. Sundance Entertainment, Inc.*

ARMSTRONG v. SUNDANCE ENTERTAINMENT, INC.
347 S.E.2d 292
Court of Appeals of Georgia
June 20, 1986

BENHAM, Judge.

Appellant brought suit against appellee to recover damages for injuries suffered when appellant was shot outside appellee's nightclub. Asserting that there are genuine issues of material fact, appellant brings this appeal from the grant of summary judgment to appellee. We affirm.

"The liability of [appellee] depends upon whether [appellant], at the time he suffered his ... injury, was ... a licensee or an invitee...." Under OCGA § 51-3-2, the owner or proprietor of the premises is liable only for wilful or wanton injury to a licensee, whereas under OCGA § 51-3-1 the landowner or occupier owes an invitee the duty to exercise ordinary care in keeping the premises safe....

To determine whether a person is an invitee or a mere licensee, the nature of his relation or contact with the owner or occupier of the premises must be determined. The test is whether the injured person at the time of the injury had present business relations with the owner of the premises which would render his presence of mutual aid to both, or whether his presence on the premises was for his own convenience....

> If an invitee does not go beyond that part of the premises to which, as it reasonably appears to him the invitation extends, he does not become a licensee. If, however, he does go beyond that part to which he is invited, he becomes a mere licensee....
>
> It is apparent to us ... that the requirement that an invitee not go beyond the limits of his invitation extends to the temporal dimension as well as the spatial: one who uses the premises of a merchant at a time beyond that to which an implied invitation extends is a mere licensee....
>
> The uncontradicted evidence in the record shows that appellee's business had closed for the night prior to the occurrence of appellant's injury. Affidavits by appellee's employees established that the nightclub had closed its doors for the night before appellant was accosted and shot. Appellant's affidavit and that of a companion indicated that appellant had departed the club and had sat for some time in his car before the events which led to his injury.
>
> Under those circumstances, we find that there are no questions of fact regarding appellant's status at the time of his injury: he was a licensee.

Invitees

The term *invitee* is of particular importance in the law of premises liability. The term generally refers to visitors for the economic benefit of the landholder or for both parties. Visitors may be considered invitees if:

- they enter by the expressed or implied invitation of the landholder,
- the entry is concerned with the nature of the landholder's business,
- there is a mutual benefit for both the visitor and the landholder.

Social guests are licensees and are not considered invitees, even though they have been invited onto the premises. The *Restatement (Second) of Torts* defines an invitee as either a business visitor or a public invitee (see Figure 8-12).

Figure 8-12. Invitee

(1) An invitee is either a public invitee or a business visitor.
(2) A public invitee is a person who is invited to enter or remain on land as a member of the public for a purpose for which the land is held open to the public.
(3) A business visitor is a person who is invited to enter or remain on land for a purpose directly or indirectly connected with business dealings with the possessor of the land.

Restatement (Second) of Torts § 332

The invitee is an individual who has entered land with the assurance that he or she has an invitation to enter, and has an understanding that reasonable care has been exercised in maintaining the property.

invitation

Invitation. An element essential to invitee status is the express or implied invitation to enter the premises. An **invitation** is conduct on the part of the landholder or possessor of the premises that justifies the visitor's belief that his or her entry is sought. The invitation includes the entrance to the premises, the exit, and all parts of the premises that the visitor may be expected to visit. Thus, a visitor may be considered an invitee in using rest rooms provided on the premises, but may not keep that status if he or she were to sneak into a storeroom or locked closet.

Standard of Care. A landholder or possessor of property is under a legal obligation to exercise reasonable care for the safety and protection of an invitee. The landholder is not obligated to protect an invitee against his or her own negligence, but is under an obligation not to act negligently toward the invitee and to warn the invitee of any known dangers. The *Restatement* adopts this approach, and is supported by the case law of most jurisdictions unless there has been some statutory modification (see Figure 8-13).

Figure 8-13. Standard of Care Owed to Invitees

A possessor of land is subject to liability for physical harm caused to his invitees by a condition on the land if, but only if, he
(a) knows or by the exercise of reasonable care would discover the condition, and should realize that it involves an unreasonable risk of harm to such invitees, and
(b) should expect that they will not discover or realize the danger, or will fail to protect themselves against it, and
(c) fails to exercise reasonable care to protect them against the danger.

Restatement (Second) of Torts § 343

As an example, assume that Bulldog Bus Lines regularly discharges its passengers at a designated gate on its premises, allowing the passengers to enter the terminal. To enter the terminal, passengers must alight from the bus, traverse three feet of roadway, and step onto a curb. Assume that recent weather conditions had buckled the curb and roadway, leaving a hazardous path to the terminal. Bulldog would be liable to any passenger who sustained an injury because of the unsafe entrance to its terminal.

business visitors

Business Visitors. **Business visitors** are those who enter the premises of the business for the purpose for which it is open to the public. Business visitors are invitees to whom the landholder owes a duty of reasonable care. Reasonable care must be taken to protect shoppers, restaurant patrons, theatergoers, office patrons, and any other individuals invited onto premises for the purpose of conducting business. This duty extends to protect the visitor from employees of the landholder as well as from other invitees.

Public Invitees. The issue of public employees required to enter premises for the purpose of conducting some public function unrelated to the business of the landholder has caused difficulty in the courts. Meter readers, postal workers, fire inspectors, and garbage collectors may be found in this category. They are not truly invitees because they are not on the landholder's premises as clients or customers. Nor are they trespassers, in that they are lawfully allowed to enter the property. Most jurisdictions have held that the landholder has some obligation of reasonable care to make the premises safe for such visitors. The rationale may be that they are incidental to the conduct of business.

Fireman's Rule. In direct distinction to public invitees, firefighters and police officers have been held by most jurisdictions to be mere licensees. Such persons enter the premises under authority of law, not by any implied invitation of the landholder, and do not fit any classification of invitee. The landholder has the same obligation toward such individuals as toward any licensee: not to intentionally, willfully, or wantonly cause harm or injury.

Elimination of Traditional Distinctions

The vast majority of jurisdictions continue to distinguish the duty owed a visitor to premises on the basis of the status of that individual—trespasser, licensee, or invitee. Several notable court decisions have eliminated the distinction, holding that the landholder has a duty of reasonable care to all persons entering the premises. Those courts have found that such arbitrary classifications have created more dilemmas than they have solved, and that it is time to scrap the entire system. The paralegal student should consult local state statutory and case law treatment of the issue to determine whether the traditional paradigm has begun to change.

Lessor and Lessee

The lessor–lessee relationship involves a legal status between the parties affecting premises liability. In a traditional lease situation, the lessor–owner of property transfers a possessory interest to the tenant–lessee, and in so doing, surrenders control over the property. The traditional common law rule is that the landlord is no longer responsible for the property and is under no duty of reasonable care to keep the premises safe for visitors. Regardless of the status of the visitor—trespasser, licensee, or invitee—the lessor owes no duty of reasonable care.

A number of exceptions have arisen to mitigate the legal effect of the common law rule in light of modern commercial practices (see Figure 8-14).

Figure 8-14. Lessor/lessee

Modern ideas of social policy have given rise to a number of exceptions to these general rules of nonliability of the lessor, which to a large extent swallow up the general no-duty rule. There is increasing recognition of the fact that the tenant who leases defective premises is likely to be impecunious and unable to make the necessary repairs, and that sometimes the financial burden is best placed upon the landlord, who receives a benefit from the transaction in the form of rent.

W. Page Keeton et al., *Prosser and Keeton on the Law of Torts* § 63 at 435 (5th ed. 1984)

The exceptions to the common law rule that have evolved by statute and court decision concern the following situations:

- Concealed dangerous conditions—Landlord is under an obligation to disclose.
- Conditions dangerous to third persons—Landlord has an ongoing liability for dangerous conditions.
- Premises leased for public benefit—Landlord has a duty to exercise reasonable care when the premises are leased for public use.
- Common areas under landlord's control—Landlord has an obligation of reasonable care.
- Landlord's agreement to repair—The majority of jurisdictions hold landlord responsible for repairs not made within a reasonable time.

In all such cases, the landlord will be held to a duty of reasonable care to keep the premises safe for visitors to the premises. For example, assume that Baldwin leased a duplex apartment to Tingle. Upon signing the lease, Baldwin told Tingle to be careful on the front staircase because the top step was loose. The first time Tingle climbed the stairs, he fell on the loose step and was injured. Without an agreement to repair, and assuming that the stairs were not under Baldwin's care, the disclosure of the defect would give rise to the general rule, eliminating any liability on Baldwin's part. In contrast, consider the liability imposed on the landlord in the *Strunk* case (see Figure 8-15).

Figure 8-15. Case in Point: *Strunk v. Zoltanski*

STRUNK v. ZOLTANSKI
479 N.Y.S.2d 175
Court of Appeals of New York
July 3, 1984

JONES, Judge.

A landlord who, with knowledge that a prospective tenant has a vicious dog which will be kept on the premises, nonetheless leases the premises to such tenant without taking reasonable measures, by pertinent provisions in the lease or otherwise, to protect persons who might be on the premises from being attacked by the dog may be held liable to a person who while thereafter on the premises is bitten by the dog.

Plaintiff here seeks to recover damages from the landlord for injuries suffered when he was bitten by a dog owned by the tenant. After the landlord had filed an answer denying liability, plaintiff and his mother and defendant Sophie Zoltanski were examined before trial. Defendants then moved for summary judgment dismissing the complaint. Supreme Court granted the motion as to Joseph Zoltanski, the husband, who had no interest in the property on which the dog bite occurred. The court denied the motion as to Sophie Zoltanski, however, concluding that there were issues of fact as to her knowledge of the presence of the dog and of its vicious nature. The Appellate Division affirmed and granted Mrs. Zoltanski leave to appeal to our court on a certified question. We conclude that there should be an affirmance.

It appears from the papers submitted on the motion for summary judgment that, about five years prior to plaintiff's being bitten, Sophie Zoltanski inherited from her sister a six-acre parcel of land on which two residences were located. She did not live in either house but rented both. Plaintiff tendered proof in admissible form from which a jury could find that one Carl Kenyon, operator of a gas station, was occupying one of the two houses in April, 1979; that on one occasion during that month Mrs. Zoltanski was on the premises later leased to Kenyon where the German Shepherd dog which subsequently bit plaintiff was tied in her full view; that at the time the dog was "barking very loudly, jumping up and down, growling and acting ferocious." Mrs. Zoltanski stated on her examination before trial that she leased the premises to Kenyon on an oral basis in May.

On May 8, 1979 plaintiff, then a boy of 14, encountered Kenyon at his gas station and the latter asked him if he wanted the dog. Plaintiff replied that he would have to check with his mother. His mother wanted to see the dog and went with plaintiff to the Kenyon premises. She waited at the residence next door while plaintiff went to get the dog. The boy walked toward the dog to untie it, and it was then that the dog jumped up and bit him on the mouth and later on his arm as he sought to defend himself.

The general rule is that, in conventional settings in which premises are rented by a tenant who acquires exclusive possession and control, the landlord is not liable for attacks by animals kept by the tenant on those premises where the landlord had no knowledge of the animal or its dangerous proclivities at the time of the initial letting of the premises.... The aspect peculiar to the present case is the circumstance that here the jury might find, although she herself denies it, that at the time she leased the premises to Carl Kenyon, Mrs. Zoltanski knew that her prospective tenant had a 'vicious' German Shepherd dog which he intended to keep on the leased premises. Notwithstanding this prior knowledge, at a time when she had complete control of the premises she leased them to the tenant, permitted him to keep the dog on the premises, and, so far as appears on this motion, took no measures by pertinent provisions in the lease or otherwise to protect third persons who might be on the premises from being attacked by the dog.

The principle with respect to the liability of a landlord whose tenant comes into possession of the animal after the premises have been leased (that to establish liability it must be shown that the landlord had knowledge of the vicious propensities of the dog and had control of the premises or other capability to remove or confine the animal [id.]) likewise is not determinative here. The present is a situation in which the landlord, by leasing the premises to the owner of the dog, could be found affirmatively to have created the very risk which was reasonably foreseeable and which operated to injure plaintiff. On the basis of the evidence tendered on the motion for summary judgment, the jury could find that, having created this risk, Mrs. Zoltanski took no steps reasonably calculated to protect this plaintiff from the injuries which he suffered. We do not intend to suggest that the landlord would be subject to the same strict liability to which a tenant as harborer of the dog would be subject (see *Restatement, Torts 2d,* § 509), but landlords as others must exercise reasonable care not to expose third persons to an unreasonable risk of harm....

Considerations of public policy, the appropriate frame of reference for determination of tort liability in situations newly confronted by the courts, require that a landlord who, prior to leasing the premises, has knowledge that the tenant may be expected to carry on activities on the premises in such a manner as unreasonably to expose third persons to risk of physical injury has a duty to take such precautions as lie within the control of the landlord reasonably to protect such third persons from the injuries to be foreseen if such precautions are taken. In the present case, no evidence was tendered on the motion for summary judgment that this landlord, aware of the danger of the situation, took any steps to protect this plaintiff.... The parties have not called our attention to any authority in case law or legal writings which addresses the question of liability of a landlord who has knowledge of a tenant's ownership of a vicious dog prior to the initial letting, and our research has disclosed none.

We recognize that in today's world there may be tenants whose interest in keeping a watch or guard dog for protection of person or property, in consequence of the character of the neighborhood in which the leased premises are located or by virtue of the peculiar circumstances of the individual tenant, is legitimate and not necessarily to be discouraged. Nevertheless, the tenant who harbors the dog and derives protective benefit from its presence on the premises will be held strictly liable to third persons for injuries inflicted by the dog.... In such situations, however, it would defeat what may properly be accepted as a socially useful purpose, namely, provision of housing for persons who may legitimately keep watch or guard dogs, to announce a rule of law which would have the practical effect of discouraging all landlords (who themselves derive no benefit, or at most only an incidental benefit, from the dog's presence) from ever leasing to any tenant who seeks to keep such a dog. The proper accommodation of these interests calls for the imposition on the landlord of a duty, at the inception of the lease when it is known that the tenant will keep a watch or guard dog, to take reasonable precautions for the protection of third persons, by provisions in the lease with respect to confinement or control of the dog or otherwise.

The circumstance, to which the dissent draws attention, that the dog here was tied up both when observed by the landlord prior to the letting of the premises and at the time of the attack on plaintiff is not conclusive on the present motion for summary judgment. Liability, if any, of the landlord will depend on whether at trial the jury finds, on evidence sufficient to warrant such a finding, that, knowing of the tenant's ownership of a vicious dog, she took reasonable care in her arrangements with the tenant to protect third persons from injury. In the record before us there is no tender of evidence of her having taken any care. Whether the exercise of reasonable care in the circumstances would have called for a requirement that the dog be tied, or be otherwise confined so as both to restrain the dog and to exclude third persons, and also a requirement that warnings be posted, as well as whether the landlord's failure to take any care, if such be the proof on trial, was the proximate cause of plaintiff's injuries, both present factual issues to be resolved by the triers of the facts. We do not intend to imply that there must be a finding that this landlord is liable for the injuries suffered by this plaintiff; we do no more than conclude that there are factual questions which foreclose dismissal based on the submissions on the motion for summary judgment.

Statutory provisions regarding the liability of landlords toward tenants have been enacted in many states. The paralegal student should consult local statutes and case law to determine questions of landlord responsibility.

Vendor and Vendee

caveat emptor

The vendor, or seller, of real property transfers all responsibility for the property to the vendee, or purchaser, as a general rule. The common law doctrine of ***caveat emptor***, or "Let the buyer beware," provided that the vendor of real property was not liable to the vendee for any condition of the land existing at the time of the sale. As a result of an increased regard for personal safety, this general rule has been eroded through the application of the principle of implied warranties accompanying the purchase of chattels. The vendor of property is now under a duty to disclose defects in the property to the vendee, and failure to disclose any hidden defects will result in liability.

The *Restatement* places responsibility on the vendor for defects, whether natural or artificial, if the vendee has no reason to know of the defect (hidden) and the vendor fails to disclose the condition (see Figure 8-16).

Figure 8-16. Vendor's Liability

(1) A vendor of land who conceals or fails to disclose to his vendee any condition, whether natural or artificial, which involves unreasonable risk to persons on the land, is subject to liability to the vendee and others upon the land with the consent of the vendee or his subvendee for physical harm caused by the condition after the vendee has taken possession, if

(a) the vendee does not know or have reason to know of the condition or the risk involved, and

(b) the vendor knows or has reason to know of the condition, and realizes or should realize the risk involved, and has reason to believe that the vendee will not discover the condition or realize the risk.

(2) If the vendor actively conceals the condition, the liability stated in Subsection (1) continues until the vendee discovers it and has reasonable opportunity to take effective precautions against it. Otherwise the liability continues only until the vendee has had reasonable opportunity to discover the condition and to take such precautions.

Restatement (Second) of Torts § 353

Continuing with our example, assume that Baldwin had sold the property to Tingle rather than leasing the premises. If Tingle had then fallen, Baldwin would continue to be without liability. As a further illustration, consider the *Preston* case concerning a vendor's liability after a sale (see Figure 8-17).

Figure 8-17. Case in Point: *Preston v. Goldman*

PRESTON v. GOLDMAN
720 P.2d 416
Supreme Court of California
July 14, 1986

LUCAS, Justice.

Should former owners, allegedly negligent in constructing an improvement on their property, be subject to liability for injuries sustained on that property long after they have relinquished all ownership and control? The *Restatement Second of Torts* proposes that liability is terminated upon termination of ownership and control except under specified exceptions, and we agree....

Defendants Jon and Marion Kubichan bought the subject property in 1968. Around January 1972, over the course of a weekend, they designed and built a pond with a fountain in their backyard for a total cost of approximately $130. The pond was built by excavating the ground to a disputed depth and putting a wall approximately 12 inches above ground around the pond.

In October 1973, Alan Goldman bought the property from the Kubichans. Goldman made no alterations to the pond and maintained water in it. In November 1974, Goldman entered into a lease-option to buy agreement with the Reids who took possession. The Reids, who had two small children, put a new brick facing around the pool's exterior, bricked the patio surrounding it, replaced the flagstone coping with brick, and put a layer of brick around the top of the pool walls. The Reids had emptied the pond and were aware of its depth and configurations.

On May 7, 1976, plaintiff Clinton Preston and his siblings were brought to the property by their parents, Cynthia and Stephen Preston, to visit their aunt and uncle, the Reids. Plaintiff was then 22 months of age. The Prestons had been at the house before and were aware of the pond. At some point Mr. Reid and Mr. Preston went out to the garage, accompanied by the children. The men later returned to the house without them. After some time, the parents looked for the children and found Clinton immersed in the pond. As a result of the accident, plaintiff suffered severe permanent brain damage and quadriplegia....

The jury rendered special verdicts in favor of all defendants. It specifically determined that Goldman and the Kubichans were not negligent and that while the Reids were negligent, their negligence was not a legal cause of plaintiff's injury....

The development of the law of predecessor landowners' liability has been, in fact, somewhat murky. Three separate approaches have arisen regarding damages sustained by persons on private property due to artificial or natural conditions existing on the land when the present owner or possessor assumed control. "[T]he ancient doctrine of caveat emptor has lingered on to a very large extent" in this area, albeit with some recent exceptions. (*Prosser & Keeton on Torts* (5th ed. 1984) @ 64, pp. 446-447, fn. omitted.) In the *Restatement* view, described above, termination of liability occurs upon transfer of control except under specified circumstances. (*Rest. 2d Torts*, supra, §§ 352, 353.) Comment a to section 352 observes that the reliance on the doctrine of caveat emptor may well have developed and persisted "because great importance always has been attached to the deed of conveyance, which is taken to represent the full agreement of the parties, and to exclude all other terms and liabilities. The vendee is required to make his own inspection of the premises, and the vendor is not responsible to him for their defective condition, existing at the time of transfer." Prosser and Keeton take a more expansive view than simple application of the doctrine of "caveat emptor." They acknowledge the general rule, but observe that two exceptions have developed. "The first ... is that the vendor is under a duty to disclose to the vendee any hidden defects which he knows or should know may present an unreasonable risk of harm to persons on the premises, and which he may anticipate that the vendee will not discover." (*Prosser & Keeton*, supra, a 64 at p. 447, fns. omitted.) This exception echoes those in *Restatement* section 353. In addition, a second exception "is found in a number of cases where the land, when it is transferred, is in such condition that it involves an unreasonable risk of harm to those outside of the premises." (Id. at p. 448; see *Rest.2d Torts*, § 385.) The treatise concludes that even where liability continues after divestiture of possession, "it seems obvious that there must be some time limit upon the duration of the potential liability.... The emerging view is that the vendor is no longer liable once the vendee has had a reasonable time to discover and remedy the condition, unless the vendor has actively concealed it.... (*Prosser & Keeton*, supra, a 64 at pp. 448-449,...)...

After consideration of the relevant variables reviewed above, we have concluded that we should not depart from the existing rules restricting liability of predecessor landowners.... The injury here was in a strict sense foreseeable, but at the time the Kubichans built the pool for their own use the prospect that a future landowner who would allow children on the premises would not take appropriate precautions was a tenuous proposition. Unquestionably, plaintiff suffered injury. The closeness of the defendant's conduct and plaintiff's injuries, is, as mentioned in regard to foreseeability, not very great. The Kubichans had no control over the backyard or access to it at the time the injury occurred; nor could they affect the degree of supervision exercised over persons on the premises. They played no direct role in the circumstances of this particular accident, nor would they have been able at the time to take additional precautions to prevent its occurrence. Moreover, as to moral blame, such a concept is difficult to apply to anyone involved in this case. Arguably, however, the greater "blame" should be placed on those in present control of the circumstances who have the power to make changes, take needed precautions, and control the entry of persons on the land.

As to the burden to the defendant and consequences to the community, as we have discussed, given the importance usually placed on control before liability is ascribed, we believe that the weight of this factor tends towards absolving the Kubichans and other homeowners who make similar improvements to their property. Our belief is strengthened by consideration of statutory limitations placed on the liability of professional builders and contractors. The liability of the homeowner as urged by plaintiff here would be temporally unlimited. So long as the improvement existed, the landowner could be held liable no matter how much time had elapsed since he had done the work and transferred the property; the potential cloud of liability over the head of any do-it-yourself owner would be far-reaching. The landowner who made an improvement which, in terms of the needs and status of his family and situation, was adequate and safe, and who sold the property to another who was made aware of the condition, could be held liable despite use of the improvement by persons over whom he has no control.

Once the transfer of property pursuant to a sale has taken place, the vendee becomes the insurer of the safety of visitors pursuant to traditional tort principles.

Summary

Since the early common law, the possessor of property has had a social interest that received the protection and favor of the tort law. Questions of liability have traditionally been resolved by determining the relationship between the possessor of the property and the visitor. Trespassers received little or no protection under the tort law unless the owner was guilty of willful or wanton disregard for the safety of others. Licensees received similar treatment and were afforded protection only from a willful disregard for their safety. Invitees have received the greatest protection under the tort law, and the possessor of property has been held to a duty of reasonable care for the safety of invitees. The modern trend has been to hold all occupiers of land to the same standard, one of reasonable care, for the protection of visitors to the property. State statutes and court decisions have done much to erode the traditional common law principles. Local law must be consulted carefully.

Review Questions

1. Define premises liability.
2. State the general duty of a possessor of land.

3. Describe the factors used to determine the existence of reasonable care.
4. What is the general rule of liability of a landholder for natural conditions on the land?
5. State the traditional rule of liability of a landholder owed to a trespasser.
6. What is the traditional liability of a landholder toward licensees?
7. Define the duty of a possessor of land owed to an invitee.
8. What is the Fireman's Rule?
9. Discuss the general liability of a lessor owed to a lessee.
10. What duty does a vendor owe to a vendee of real property?

Focus Your Skills

Elmer Hilton dwelled in a constant state of confusion caused by the strenuous mental effort required to contain his body's primal urge to choke the living daylights out of anyone who desperately deserved it. His shrink diagnosed this confusion as nothing more than stress, and recommended that Elmer engage in a business venture that would relieve his anxiety. Seizing the entrepreneurial opportunity, he decided to open a small saloon catering to the modern soldier of fortune. He named his enterprise Suds-N-Studs, and in addition to offering a full line of American beers, he also featured T-shirts and bumper stickers appealing to right-wing military misanthropes. His best-selling shirt displayed a buxom, scantily dressed young lady holding a sniper rifle and proclaimed, "Those who live by the sword get shot by those who don't." His hottest bumper sticker declared, "Gun control is a steady hand."

Each evening, after the last would-be mercenary had gone, Elmer closed up his establishment and set his home-made alarm. The system consisted of a latticework of acid-coated punji sticks and bungee cords fixed to the ceiling above the doors and windows. Anyone foolish enough to attempt an unauthorized entry to the premises would certainly get Elmer's point.

Inevitably, such an illegal entry was attempted one night after hours by one George "Knuckles" Furbush. After an evening spent downing a case of St. Louis' finest, Knuckles had fallen asleep in the parking lot. Awakened by one of nature's own alarms, Knuckles decided that the closest facility was inside the Suds-N-Studs saloon. Forgetting about the booby traps, Knuckles punched in the rear door and was immediately peppered by 14 foot-long, razor-sharp, acid-dipped punji sticks. His hospital bill ran to the high six figures.

Mr. Furbush has contacted your office for advice concerning a possible action against Suds-N-Studs and Mr. Elmer Hilton for premises liability. Prepare a memorandum regarding the law that would apply to this case. Emphasis should be placed on the traditional liability of a landholder toward a trespasser, licensee, and invitee.

9
Doctrine of Nuisance

It is from the level of calamities, not that of every day life, that we learn impressive and useful lessons.

Thackeray (1811–1863)

The doctrine of nuisance occupies a unique place in the law of torts. Virtually *any* interference with an individual's interests has been termed a nuisance by the courts at one time or another. Such generalization and lack of clear definition has resulted in a tangled web of fact and principle that makes the doctrine of nuisance difficult to grasp. Technically, the doctrine of nuisance does not offer a specific cause of action but rather refers to the harm caused by the use of one's property that interferes with the interests of another. This chapter deals with the origins and fundamental principles of the nuisance doctrine, the distinction between a private and a public nuisance, and the interests to be protected.

Chapter Topics

1. Doctrine of Nuisance
2. Private Nuisance
3. Substantial and Unreasonable Interference
4. Absolute Nuisance
5. Public Nuisance
6. Remedies
7. Negligence and Strict Liability

Objectives

After completing this chapter, you will be able to:

1. Discuss the nature and history of the concept of nuisance.
2. Analyze the interests and requirements of a private nuisance.
3. Define the invasion of rights involved in a nuisance.
4. Discuss the interference with the use and enjoyment of land from a nuisance.
5. Identify the nature of a public nuisance.
6. Discuss the remedies available for a nuisance.

Doctrine of Nuisance

The doctrine of nuisance has continued to defy explanation in the law. It is a term used to describe, rather than define, the problem. The courts have been content to call almost any interference with another's interests a nuisance. Thus, its meaning must come from its usage rather than from any limited definition.

History

In feudal England, a lord granted a servant or vassal land to use and enjoy. Interference with the use and enjoyment of property became the subject of a criminal writ known as an Assize of Nuisance. Its purpose was to remedy interference with the plaintiff's land by a defendant's activity. Following its thirteenth-century origin as a criminal action, a civil action directed at the interference with one's use and enjoyment of property formed the basis for the modern concept of a private nuisance.

Concurrent with the development of the private nuisance, the common or public nuisance concept became recognized. Invasions of the right of way for a public highway in ancient England became a criminal action by the crown against the individual responsible for the encroachment. In ancient England, an individual invading a public highway's right of way was subject to criminal prosecution by the crown for the encroachment. From the mere blocking of a public access, the concept expanded to include any inconvenience to the exercise of rights common to all persons. From its criminal origin, the doctrine of public nuisance soon evolved into a civil action available to private individuals who had been similarly harmed by the invasion of a public right.

Concept of Nuisance

nuisance

The term **nuisance** originates from the French word for harm, and applies to any activity arising from the uses of one's property producing substantial and unreasonable interference with another's interests. Any activity that causes annoyance, inconvenience, and discomfort to another can be classified as a nuisance. Activities endangering life, health, decency, or the senses, or affecting the use and enjoyment of property, also constitute nuisances and may be the subject of legal action.

While the courts have loosely termed a nuisance anything that is harmful, annoying, offensive, or inconvenient, the word should be thought of in its narrower legal context. This can be done by considering a nuisance in one of three ways:

- an activity—human conduct or condition that is harmful or annoying to others;
- a harm—the effect produced by the conduct or condition; or
- a liability—a combination of the conduct and the harm producing legal responsibility.

Whether one regards a nuisance as the activity, the effect, or the legal responsibility, the tortious conduct has been divided into two separate categories: private nuisance and public nuisance. Civil liability remedies the former; criminal penalties attach to the latter. Confusion results when one particular activity creates both civil and criminal liability, occurring when a public nuisance also interferes with the private use and enjoyment of one's property. Consider the court's decision in *City of Virginia Beach v. Murphy*, involving an attempt to distinguish between a public and a private nuisance (see Figure 9-1).

Figure 9-1. Case in Point: *City of Virginia Beach v. Murphy*

CITY OF VIRGINIA BEACH v. MURPHY
389 S.E.2d 462
Supreme Court of Virginia
March 2, 1990

WHITING, Justice.

This case involves the validity of a city's noise ordinance. Maureen Murphy was prosecuted for violating Virginia Beach City Code

§ 2347 because she permitted loud music to emanate from her restaurant in the City of Virginia Beach (the city). As pertinent, that code section provides:

> (a) It shall be unlawful for any person to create, or allow to be created any unreasonably loud, disturbing and unnecessary noise in the city or any noise of such character, intensity and duration as to be detrimental to the life or health of any person or persons or to unreasonably disturb or annoy the quiet, comfort or repose of any person or persons. The following acts, among others, are declared to be loud, disturbing and unnecessary noise in violation of this section, but such enumeration shall not be deemed to be exclusive:
>
> > (1) The playing of any television set, radio, tape player, phonograph or any musical instrument in such a manner or with such volume as to annoy or disturb the quiet, comfort or repose of any person or persons....

On October 24, 1988, at the conclusion of the city's case in a non-jury trial, the trial court took Murphy's motion to strike the city's evidence under advisement. On December 13, 1988, it sustained the motion on the ground that the city "may not under its general police power undertake to make conduct which affects only one person (any person) a public nuisance." The city appeals.

If an ordinance makes criminal that conduct which is a public nuisance, it is a presumptively valid exercise of the locality's police power.... On the other hand, if the prohibited conduct is merely a private nuisance, it cannot be made criminal because a municipality has no authority under its police power to punish conduct which is a private nuisance.... Thus, this decision turns on whether the forbidden conduct can be classified as a public nuisance or only a private nuisance.... [W]e described the difference between the two concepts as follows:

Nuisances are of two kinds—public or common nuisances, which affect people generally, and private nuisances which may be defined as anything done to the hurt of the lands, tenements, or hereditaments of another....

We have described a private nuisance as "an activity which unreasonably interferes with the use and enjoyment of another's property...." In other words, a private nuisance is one which implicates or interferes with a right or interest that is unique to an individual, such as an interest in land. *Restatement (Second) of Torts* §§ 8215 comment h, 821D (1977).

In a case involving a noisy business, Judge Cardozo pointed out that a public nuisance may arise in two situations:

Public is the nuisance "whereby a public right or privilege common to every person in the community is interrupted or interfered with," as by the obstruction of a public way. Public also is the nuisance committed "in such place and in such manner that the aggregation of private injuries becomes so great and extensive as to constitute a public annoyance and inconvenience, and a wrong against the community, which may be properly the subject of a public prosecution."

Thus, the distinction between a public and a private nuisance does not depend solely upon the number of people who are actually affected, as the trial court held....

The right not to be subjected to "unreasonably loud, disturbing and unnecessary noise," as provided in Virginia Beach Code § 23-47, is "common to all members of the general public," *Restatement (Second) of Torts* § 821B comment g (1977), and not particular to individuals in the enjoyment of their property. In that sense, this ordinance differs from that in White, which attempted to control door-to-door solicitation and affected only the individual property rights of householders.

For these reasons, we are of opinion that the trial court erroneously concluded that the activity proscribed in the ordinance could only be a private nuisance. Therefore, the trial court erred in declaring the ordinance facially unconstitutional on that ground. Accordingly, we will reverse the judgment of the trial court and enter final judgment on that ground.

Reversed and final judgment.

This chapter examines the distinction between private and public nuisances.

Private Nuisance

private nuisance

A **private nuisance** is an interference with an individual's use and enjoyment of land. It forms the basis for a cause of action in tort for an invasion of an individual's use and enjoyment of a possessory interest in land based upon interference by the conduct or activities of another. The *Restatement (Second) of Torts* defines a private nuisance in the same manner but adds to the requirement that the interference be nontrespassory (see Figure 9-2).

Figure 9-2. Private Nuisance

A private nuisance is a nontrespassory invasion of another's interest in the private use and enjoyment of land.

Restatement (Second) of Torts § 821D

Thus, the term private nuisance is applied to a tort action for an interference with an individual's interest in land and the use and enjoyment thereof that is short of a trespass.

Interest Protected

Historically, an individual's right to the use and enjoyment of property with some reasonable degree of comfort and convenience was the interest protected by civil liability for private nuisance. The protection continues today, with the tort action for nuisance providing a remedy for invading that interest.

Residence, agriculture, and commercial ventures are purposes for which land may be used and enjoyed. Use and enjoyment may consist of any of the following:

- physical condition
- comfort and convenience
- peace of mind
- tranquility
- freedom from threat of future injury

The freedom from annoyance in the enjoyment of one's property can be as important a legal right as freedom from changes in the physical condition of the land itself. In the case of *Page County Appliance Center, Inc. v. Honeywell, Inc.*, the Supreme Court of Iowa considered an invasion of the use and enjoyment of property by computer transmissions (see Figure 9-3).

Figure 9-3. Case in Point: *Page County Appliance Center, Inc. v. Honeywell, Inc.*

PAGE COUNTY APPLIANCE CENTER, INC. v. HONEYWELL, INC.
347 N.W.2d 171
Supreme Court of Iowa
March 14, 1984

REYNOLDSON, Chief Justice.

Plaintiff Page County Appliance Center, Inc. (Appliance Center), sued Honeywell, Inc. (Honeywell), and ITT Electronic Travel Services, Inc. (ITT), for nuisance and tortious interference with business relations. Defendants appeal from judgment entered on jury verdicts awarding compensatory and punitive damages. Honeywell appeals from a judgment rendered against it on ITT's cross-claim for indemnification. We reverse and remand for new trial. Appliance Center has owned and operated an appliance store in Shenandoah, Iowa, since 1953.

In 1975 the store was acquired from his father by John Pearson, who sold televisions, stereos, and a variety of appliances. Before 1980 Pearson had no reception trouble with his display televisions. In early January 1980, however, ITT placed one of its computers with Central Travel Service in Shenandoah as part of a nationwide plan to lease computers to retail travel agents. Central Travel was separated by only one other business from the Appliance Center. This ITT computer was manufactured, installed, and maintained by Honeywell.

Thereafter many of Pearson's customers told him his display television pictures were bad; on two of the three channels available in Shenandoah he had a difficult time "getting a picture that was fit to watch." After unsuccessfully attempting several remedial measures, in late January 1980, he finally traced the interference to the operations of Central Travel's computer. Both defendants concede Pearson's problems were caused by radiation leaking from the Honeywell computer.

Pearson discussed the problem with Kay Crowell, owner of Central Travel. She placed a call to ITT's president in New York. Although he was unavailable, ITT personnel apparently notified Honeywell. ITT's only contact with Pearson was through a telephone call some ten months later. At that time Pearson told ITT's sales representative that Honeywell was working on the problem; he made no effort to follow up on ITT's interest in the problem.

Honeywell indeed was working to correct the situation, and had been since February 1980. Honeywell technicians made repeated trips to make various unsuccessful adjustments to the computer. They found the computer was operating properly; the interference-causing radiation was a design and not a service problem. Pearson then telephoned Armando Benitez, the technicians' supervisor. Pearson testified Benitez told him Honeywell was "way over budget" on the Central Travel computer and that "if you don't like it, you can move." Nonetheless, in early fall of 1980 Honeywell sent out Phil Brzozoski, one of its engineers from Boston. According to Pearson, when he asked Brzozoski why it had taken him so long to come, the latter replied he would not have been there at all had Pearson not instituted suit; that was the way big business worked. Kay Crowell, admittedly Pearson's friend, testified Brzozoski told her the delay was "good business." Pearson in fact did not bring suit until December 22, 1980, although his counsel sent demand letters to Honeywell and ITT in October 1980. At trial a top Honeywell employee testified it was not company policy to await lawsuits before taking remedial action.

The Honeywell engineers effected a 70 percent improvement in the television reception by certain modifications of the computer in the fall of 1980. Pearson, still dissatisfied, started this action in December. While the suit was pending, Honeywell further modified the computer, finally alleviating Pearson's problems in May 1982.

At trial a Honeywell senior staff engineer admitted the technology to manufacture a non-radiation-emitting computer was available long before it developed this computer, but opined it would have been neither cost nor consumer effective to utilize that technology. He testified Honeywell believed it had corrected Pearson's problems in the fall of 1980.

The Appliance Center's case against Honeywell and ITT finally was submitted to the jury on the theories of nuisance and tortious interference with prospective business relations. It asked for only injunctive relief against Kay Crowell, doing business as Central Travel Service. The latter's motion for summary judgment was sustained. The jury found for the Appliance Center against the remaining defendants on both theories, and further found the Appliance Center should recover $71,000 in compensatory damages and $150,000 in exemplary damages. Following jury trial, Kay Crowell's cross-claim against Honeywell and ITT's cross-claim against Honeywell were submitted to the court. Crowell's cross-claim was dismissed. She did not appeal and is not involved in this proceeding. Trial court awarded ITT full indemnity against Honeywell, in the amount of $221,000, together with attorney fees and costs. Both defendants appeal from the judgment in favor of Appliance Center; Honeywell additionally appeals from the judgment awarding ITT indemnity....

Narrowing our focus, we note the Appliance Center is alleging a "private nuisance," that is, an actionable interference with a person's interest in the private use and enjoyment of his or her property.... It also is apparent that if Central Travel's computer emissions constitute a nuisance it is a "nuisance per accidens, or in fact"—a lawful activity conducted in such a manner as to be a nuisance....

Principles governing our consideration of nuisance claims are well established. One's use of property should not unreasonably interfere with or disturb a neighbor's comfortable and reasonable use and enjoyment of his or her estate. A fair test of whether the operation of a lawful trade or industry constitutes a nuisance is the reasonableness of conducting it in the manner, at the place, and under the circumstances shown by the evidence. Each case turns on its own facts and ordinarily the ultimate issue is one of fact, not law.

The existence of a nuisance is not affected by the intention of its creator not to injure anyone. Priority of occupation and location—"who was there first"—is a circumstance of considerable weight....

When the alleged nuisance is claimed to be offensive to the person, courts apply the standard of "normal persons in a particular locality" to measure the existence of a nuisance.... This normalcy standard also is applied where the use of property is claimed to be affected. "The plaintiff cannot, by devoting his own land to an unusually sensitive use, ... make a nuisance out of conduct of the adjoining defendant which would otherwise be harmless." W. Prosser, *The Law of Torts* s 87, at 579 (4th ed. 1971)....

In the case before us, ITT asserts the Appliance Center's display televisions constituted a hypersensitive use of its premises as a matter of law, and equates this situation to cases involving light thrown on outdoor theater screens in which light-throwing defendants have carried the day.... Several of those cases are distinguishable both on facts and by the way the issue was raised.

We cannot equate the rare outdoor theater screen with the ubiquitous television that exists, in various numbers, in almost every home. Clearly, the presence of televisions on any premises is not such an abnormal condition that we can say, as a matter of law, that the owner has engaged in a peculiarly sensitive use of the property. This consideration, as well as related considerations of unreasonableness, gravity of harm, utility of conduct, and priority of occupation, are factual determinations that should have been submitted to the jury in this case. We find no trial court error in refusing to direct a verdict on this ground....

A nuisance action differs from an action based upon a trespass. The distinction lies in the nature of the interest protected by the action. Trespass involves an invasion of the plaintiff's interest in exclusive possession of the land by a defendant's physical entry; the interest protected is exclusive possession. Nuisance is an interference with the plaintiff's interest in the use and enjoyment of property by the defendant's conduct; the interest protected is the use and enjoyment.

Figure 9-4. Significant Harm

There is liability for a nuisance only to those to whom it causes significant harm, of a kind that would be suffered by a normal person in the community or by property in normal condition and used for a normal purpose.

Restatement (Second) of Torts § 821F

In the case of a nuisance, there must have been some actual harm to the plaintiff, whereas trespass does not require harm to be actionable. The *Restatement (Second) of Torts* takes the position that liability for nuisance exists only if there has been some significant harm to the plaintiff. It defines harm as that suffered by a normal person in the community (see Figure 9-4).

The normalcy test has been widely accepted by courts in most states, but the paralegal student should consult local statutory and case law on the point. The harm must be of some importance and involve more than slight annoyance. If the harm involves some detrimental change to the land itself, there can be little doubt that an action may be maintained. When the invasion involves only personal discomfort, then it becomes more difficult to determine whether an action for nuisance can be maintained. The standard to be applied is that of how a normal person is impacted by the invasion and is similar to the reasonable person standard applied in negligence cases. As an example, assume that Alphonse celebrated Independence Day with a fireworks display for his family and friends. The fireworks display lasted two hours and produced brilliant colors and loud noise that could be seen and heard by his neighbor, Semple. In fact, Semple was deprived of several hours of sleep while the display lasted. While Semple may have been annoyed, absent a local statute governing such displays, an action for nuisance would be unlikely. But, if Alphonse had repeated the display for the next four days, well beyond the holiday period, then Semple may have maintained an action for nuisance.

Requirements for Recovery

An action in tort for damages for nuisance may be maintained in those cases meeting certain requirements to protect the possessor of land from conduct that intentionally interferes with the plaintiff's property interest. The requirements for a recovery are:

- Intentional act—The defendant must have committed some intentional act.
- Interference with use and enjoyment—The amount and extent of the interference need not have been anticipated.
- Substantial harm—This element forms the basis for the damages claim based upon a reduction in value of the property.
- Unreasonableness of the invasion—The nature, duration, and amount of the interference were such as to be considered unreasonable.

These four requirements form the basis for an action for nuisance. It is an action based on the effect upon the plaintiff's interest, not on the defendant's conduct, as seen in an action for negligence. Nuisance law focuses on the effect on the land and its possessor's rights that subjects the defendant to liability. In the *Padilla* case, the decision of the New Mexico court centered on the impact on the plaintiffs and their property (see Figure 9-5).

Figure 9-5. Case in Point: *Padilla v. Lawrence*

PADILLA v. LAWRENCE
685 P.2d 964
Court of Appeals of New Mexico
June 7, 1984

MINZNER, Judge.

Atanacio Padilla, Juanita Padilla, and their son, Johnny E. Padilla ("plaintiffs"), long-term residents of Bernalillo, New Mexico, filed a class action complaint against defendant Amy Lawrence and defendant Sun Country Garden Products, a corporation ("the plant"). Lawrence is the owner of the plant, also located in Bernalillo, which processes bark and manure for the purpose of packaging soil conditioner for sale. Plaintiffs requested an injunction against the plant and sought money damages based upon theories of trespass, public nuisance, private nuisance, negligence, and personal injury....

Plaintiffs Atanacio and Juanita Padilla own real property on which their residence is located, which is approximately 600 feet from the nearest boundary of the plant. They have resided in the house for over twenty-five years. The plant has been in operation for approximately five years. It is located in the industrial park of Bernalillo and covers over nine acres. Plaintiffs' house is among several residences near the plant. The record indicates that these residences are outside the industrial park.

The trial court heard testimony from the plaintiffs, from several of their neighbors, from plaintiffs' expert witness, and from a realtor as to the negative physical and aesthetic impact of the plant's operation on plaintiffs' enjoyment of their property. The witnesses testified that the plant's operation has resulted in plaintiffs' exposure to odors, dust, noise, and flies, which were not in evidence prior to construction and operation. The witnesses testified that an odor, variously described as that of a dead animal, of a pig pen, and of rotten fish, permeated the air, and that dust, noise, and flies were also a problem. The odor prohibited cooking in the summer, prevented use of evaporative cooling, and generally interfered with normal residential activities. Plaintiff Atanacio Padilla testified that the odor and dust caused him to have nosebleeds and fits of choking.

Mr. Padilla also testified that he and his wife finally moved from the residence in 1982 because of the problems associated with the plant's operation and that the nosebleeds and choking have stopped. Plaintiff Johnny E. Padilla testified that he began renting the residence at that time and that the problems continue. The realtor testified that the plant's operation caused problems that affected the property's value as a residence....

A private nuisance has been defined as a non-trespassory invasion of another's interest in the private use and enjoyment of land.... It is a civil wrong based on a disturbance of rights in land.... The elements of proof depend on whether the conduct is intentional or unintentional. Liability for intentional conduct requires that the conduct be unreasonable....

We must sustain the trial court's findings and conclusions if they are supported by substantial evidence, and we must review the facts and evidence in the light most favorable to the prevailing party.... Viewed in this light, the evidence would support a finding that the invasion was intentional because defendants knew or should have known that their conduct in operating the plant interfered with plaintiffs' use and enjoyment of their land. See *Restatement* § 825(b). Evidence also supports the finding that the operation of the plant was unreasonable.

Defendants have argued that the trial court's finding of unreasonableness lacks substantial evidence, but they have analyzed "unreasonableness" as if the issue were negligence. Although defendants offered testimony that steps were taken to reduce the plant's negative impact on the area and that they had complied with City Council and Environmental Improvement Division requests and requirements, liability for nuisance, unlike liability for negligence, exists regardless of the degree of care exercised to avoid injury.... In the nuisance context, an intentional invasion is unreasonable if the gravity of the harm outweighs the utility of the actor's conduct, ... or if the harm caused by the conduct is serious and the financial burden of compensating for the harm would not make continuing the conduct unfeasible....

The trial court found that the operation of the plant deprived plaintiffs from enjoying the use of their property and caused plaintiffs Atanacio and Juanita Padilla to move away from their residence of twenty-five years. Further, there was evidence that the property would be difficult to sell for residential purposes and the court found that the value of the residence has been diminished. Plaintiffs Atanacio and Juanita Padilla established their home long before defendants began operating the plant, and priority of occupation is a circumstance of considerable weight in determining unreasonableness.... There was substantial evidence to support the trial court's finding of unreasonableness. The finding of a private nuisance is affirmed.

The types of losses occurring in a nuisance action will vary greatly depending upon the nature of the invasion and the extent of the interference with the land's use and enjoyment, and may take any of the following forms:

- harm to the property—actual physical damage to the land, crops, soil, or water;
- physical harm—personal injury to those using the land;
- emotional harm—mental disturbance and annoyance to those using the land, and not uniformly protected by a tort action; or
- economic loss—depreciation in value of the property as a result of the nuisance.

These types of loss may exist alone or in combination with another to form the basis of an action in tort for nuisance. Individual state laws may vary on the extent of recovery for a particular form of loss.

Substantial and Unreasonable Interference

As noted by Professor Keeton, the "law does not concern itself with trifles." The doctrine of nuisance is not designed to remedy every ill that may arise from contemporary life, but to remedy an interference that is *substantial* and *unreasonable.* The harm is considered substantial if the damages to the plaintiff are significant, that is, greater than a mere triviality. The harm is unreasonable if the court is of the opinion that it would be unreasonable to avoid compensating the plaintiff for it.

Unreasonable Interference

The interference that is the subject of a claim for nuisance must not only be substantial, it must also meet the test of unreasonableness. Liability is imposed by the doctrine of nuisance when the interference to the plaintiff is greater than a person ought to bear in a contemporary metropolitan environment. A conflict arises when the conduct of the defendant is reasonable, yet the interference with the plaintiff's use and enjoyment of property is unreasonable. The issue must ultimately be decided by the trier of fact in such an action.

There are several factors the jury may examine in determining the unreasonable nature of the interference. Those factors are:

- The amount of harm—The harm must be substantial.
- The relative capacity of the defendant to bear the loss—The defendant may pass the cost to consumers or carry insurance to cover it.
- The nature of the defendant's use of his or her property—The activity must be consistent with that use.
- The nature of the locality—The defendant's conduct must be consistent with the area.
- The chronology of the defendant's activities and the plaintiff's interests—Which interest arose first?

These factors require the defendant to avoid an interference with property based upon the reasonableness of that invasion. See the *Rodrigue* case, in which the Louisiana Supreme Court determined the unreasonable interference of a large Christmas display in a noncommercial neighborhood (see Figure 9-6).

Figure 9-6. Case in Point: *Rodrigue v. Copeland*

RODRIGUE v. COPELAND
475 So.2d 1071
Supreme Court of Louisiana
Sept. 10, 1985

DIXON, Chief Justice

Plaintiffs, three residents of the Pontchartrain Shores Subdivision in Jefferson Parish, instituted this action to enjoin defendant, Alvin C. Copeland, from erecting and operating his annual Christmas display. The plaintiffs sought injunctive relief ... due to problems associated with an enormous influx of visitors to their limited access, residential neighborhood....

Since 1977 defendant has annually maintained a Christmas display on his premises at 5001 Folse Drive. The display has grown in size and popularity since the year of its inception. The display consists of an extravagant array of lights and lighted figures accompanied by traditional Christmas music. The neighborhood is a limited access area which is zoned solely for single-family residences....

Since 1982 defendant's exhibition has drawn numerous spectators to the neighborhood during the hours while the display is in operation. The spectators view the display either from their automobiles or on foot after parking their vehicles in the surrounding neighborhood. The increased congestion in the neighborhood has created numerous problems for some of the defendant's neighbors such as restricted access to their homes, noise, public urination, property damage and a lack of on-street parking....

These obligations of vicinage are legal servitudes imposed on the owner of property. These provisions embody a balancing of rights and obligations associated with the ownership of immovables. As a general rule, the landowner is free to exercise his rights of ownership in any manner he sees fit. He may even use his property in ways which "... occasion some inconvenience to his neighbor." However, his extensive rights do not allow him to do "real damage" to his neighbor....

At issue in this case is whether Copeland's light and sound display has caused a mere inconvenience or real damage to his neighbors and their right to enjoy their own premises.

In determining whether an activity or work occasions real damage or mere inconvenience, a court is required to determine the reasonableness of the conduct in light of the circumstances. This analysis requires consideration of factors such as the character of the neighborhood, the degree of the intrusion and the effect of the activity on the health and safety of the neighbors. In the past, this court has borrowed from the common law of nuisance in describing the type of conduct which violates the pronouncements embodied in C.C. 667-669. In *Robichaux v. Huppenbauer*, 258 La. 139, 150, 245 So.2d 385, 389 (1971), we considered whether a horse stable located in the City of New Orleans could be abated under C.C. 669. We stated the following test:

> "Thus noxious smells, rats, flies and noise may constitute an actionable nuisance although produced and carried on by a lawful business, where they result in material injury to neighboring property or interfere with its comfortable use and enjoyment by persons of ordinary sensibilities."...

Although the common law of nuisance has no binding, precedential value in the courts of this state, that body of law does correspond to some extent with the obligations of neighborhood established by C.C. 667-669. Therefore, the analysis employed by the courts of our sister states has been useful as persuasive authority regarding the application of our law.

Applying the foregoing principles to this case, we conclude that defendant's display has occasioned real damage, not mere inconvenience, upon plaintiffs. Likewise, we conclude that plaintiffs will be irreparably harmed unless injunctive relief is granted.

Defendant's exhibition constitutes an unreasonable intrusion into the lives of his neighbors when considered in light of the character of the neighborhood, the degree of the intrusion and its effect on the use and enjoyment of their properties by his neighbors.

The record demonstrates that the affected area is a single-family residential neighborhood. Access to the neighborhood is restricted to residential streets and Transcontinental Drive, a divided paved thoroughfare which ends at Folse Drive, just to the east of defendant's residence. There is no access to and from defendant's premises from the north since the Lake Pontchartrain levee is located immediately to the rear of the lots fronting on Folse Drive.

The damage suffered by plaintiffs during the operation of defendant's display is extensive, both in terms of its duration and its size. Defendant's display becomes operative in early December and remains in operation until January 5. During this period, plaintiffs are forced to contend with a flow of bumper to bumper traffic through their limited access neighborhood. In addition, they must endure the noise and property abuse associated with the crowd of visitors who congregate near the display.

The display begins operation at dusk each evening and continues until 11:00 p.m. on weekdays and 12:00 midnight on weekends. The display is occasionally operational beyond midnight. While in operation, it features an extravagant display of lights which are located across the front of defendant's residence, on the roof and in the enclosed yard to the west of the residence. Some of the lights comprising the display are shaped into figures such as a star, a reindeer, a snowman, three angels and a depiction of Santa and his reindeer. Lights are also located in the trees and shrubs. In addition to the lights, the display features a tapestry proclaiming "Glory to God in the Highest" and a creche.

Noise emanates from the display and from the visitors. The display is accompanied by traditional Christmas music which is amplified through loudspeakers located on the second floor of defendant's residence. The music is audible inside the home of Mary Borrell. The plaintiffs also complain of noise emanating from car engines, car horns, the slamming of car doors and police whistles.

The record clearly indicates that traffic in the neighborhood is congested due to the slow progress of vehicles carrying spectators by the display. The traffic has seriously impaired the ability of plaintiffs to gain access to and from their premises. Furthermore, on-street parking for plaintiffs or their guests becomes virtually nonexistent. As a result of the traffic congestion and lack of parking, plaintiffs and children of defendant's neighbors cannot have their own Christmas celebrations and gatherings....

Plaintiffs' injury stems from the nature and size of the display which render it incompatible with a restricted access, residential neighborhood. Defendant is enjoined from erecting and operating a Christmas exhibition which is calculated to and does attract an unusually large number of visitors to the neighborhood.

Conduct of Others

The ability of the plaintiff to maintain an action for nuisance against one particular defendant can be diluted by the conduct of others. If other individuals in the same area are contributing to the interference with the plaintiff's use and enjoyment, that fact becomes important in determining the reasonableness of the defendant's behavior. For instance, a plaintiff residing adjacent to an industrial park will have less opportunity to complain of industrial noise than a plaintiff residing in a predominantly residential area.

However, the courts will apportion liability among multiple defendants so long as the contribution of each is definable. In some cases, joint and several liability may be established when the responsibility is not able to be apportioned (see Figure 9-7).

Figure 9-7. Conduct of Others

A dozen nuisances do not each obtain immunity because they all interfere with the plaintiff's use of his land. Where the damage done is incapable of any practical division, as where a river polluted with oil burns a barn, or poisons cattle, each will be liable for the entire loss.

W. Page Keeton et al., *Prosser and Keeton on the Law of Torts*
§ 88B at 634 (5th ed. 1984)

There are cases in many jurisdictions wherein the conduct of the plaintiff may affect his or her right to bring an action. As in the case of a negligence action, the contributory negligence of the plaintiff may prevent any recovery. Also, if the plaintiff moves into an area where an invasive condition exists, he or she may not be able to maintain an action. This is referred to as "coming to a nuisance," and may serve to bar a recovery in some jurisdictions. Individual statutory and case law must be consulted.

Absolute Nuisance

Absolute nuisance as used in tort law refers to one of three types of interference with a landholder's use and enjoyment of the property. The term defies generalization because of its varied usage by the appellate courts of individual states. Appellate courts have varied widely in applying this concept. The three separate conditions under which an absolute nuisance has been found are:

- Riparian nuisance—Landholders of property with a stream or percolating waters have rights that are fixed and invariable as a natural condition, rendering tortious any interference.
- Unlawful conduct—If the conduct has been declared unlawful by statute or ordinance, any interference caused by that conduct is unreasonable

and a nuisance under any circumstances. This concept is often confused with public nuisance (see the following section).

- Strict liability—The type of interference or harm that comes from abnormally dangerous conduct, this is similar to the absolute or strict liability discussed in Chapter 12.

Since the courts have also chosen to use the term absolute nuisance for conduct usually associated with other areas of tort law (strict liability, public nuisance, riparian rights), confusion over its meaning may develop. The paralegal student must consult local state case law to determine how the term is used in a particular state.

Public Nuisance

public nuisance

Contrasted with the private nuisance, a nuisance may also be classified as a **public nuisance**. A public nuisance is an intentional act, or failure to perform a legal duty, that harms or endangers the public health, safety, and welfare. It injures the public at large as opposed to harming a particular individual. A specific nuisance may constitute both a private and a public nuisance depending upon the extent of the harm (see Figure 9-8).

Figure 9-8. Public Nuisance

No better definition of a public nuisance has been suggested than that of an act or omission "which obstructs or causes inconvenience or damage to the public in the exercise of rights common to all Her Majesty's subjects." The term comprehends a miscellaneous and diversified group of minor criminal offenses, based on some interference with the interests of the community, or the comfort or convenience of the general public.

W. Page Keeton et al., *Prosser and Keeton on the Law of Torts* § 90 at 643 (5th ed. 1984)

Under English common law, public nuisances were considered to be invasions of the interests of the King. The earliest cases involved encroachments on the public highways and were the subject of action by the Crown. This was eventually extended to include all invasions of the interest of the public, yet without any definite meaning. The penalty was initially only criminal in nature, but public nuisances later became the subject of private redress. Private redress was originally allowed only to cover actions by individuals seeking to have the nuisance stopped. It later came to include damages for harm to individuals who were able to show harm over and above that sustained by the general public. The public interest continued to be protected by criminal penalties. Today, most states continue the common law tradition.

To constitute a public nuisance, the invasion must be an unreasonable interference with a common public right. The unreasonableness of the interference is determined in many cases by statute, but is also subject to the test of its effect on the public comfort and convenience (see Figure 9-9).

Figure 9-9. Public Nuisance

(1) A public nuisance is an unreasonable interference with a right common to the general public.
(2) Circumstances that may sustain a holding that an interference with a public right is unreasonable include the following:
 (a) Whether the conduct involves a significant interference with the public health, the public safety, the public peace, the public comfort or the public convenience, or
 (b) whether the conduct is proscribed by a statute, ordinance or administrative regulation, or
 (c) whether the conduct is of a continuing nature or has produced a permanent or long-lasting effect, and, as the actor knows or has reason to know, has a significant effect upon the public right.

Restatement (Second) of Torts § 821B

For example, assume that the Sunny Shores residential retirement community has enacted an ordinance declaring illegal the failure to control the breeding of mosquitoes in a pond, pool, or lake on private property. Further, assume that the swimming pool of Mr. Foster Gore was so rarely cleaned that it allowed encephalitis mosquitoes to proliferate and endanger the local populace. The failure of Mr. Gore to clean the pool, and thus eliminate the hazard caused by the breeding insects, would constitute a public nuisance. His violation of the local ordinance would subject him to criminal prosecution. He could also be the subject of a tort action for public nuisance whereby the plaintiffs would request that the court order the pool cleaned and the nuisance terminated. If one of Mr. Gore's neighbors should contract encephalitis from a mosquito bred in the pool, then Gore could face a tort action for damages for a public nuisance.

Remedies

The remedies that are available as a result of a nuisance depend upon both the nature of the nuisance and the interest invaded. Conduct constituting a public nuisance is redressed by the criminal statutes and ordinances of the local community, and both must be consulted to determine the extent of any sanction for criminal activity. Individual liability in tort for a public nuisance exists only if there is some individual interest that has been invaded. Individual tort liability for private nuisance is dependent upon the extent of the invasion. Consider the *Baldwin* case involving the odor from a hog-raising venture (see Figure 9-10).

Figure 9-10. Case in Point: *Baldwin v. McClendon*

BALDWIN v. McCLENDON
288 So.2d 761
Supreme Court of Alabama
January 24, 1974

McCALL, Justice.

The respondents, Robert Baldwin and W. J. Bottcher, appeal from an adverse final decree in equity. The appellees, James E. McClendon and Ethel McClendon, are husband and wife. Their home, for some fifteen years, has been a forty-seven acre farm, located in a rural agricultural area of Blount County, about seven miles southeast of Oneonta on the road to Springville. In early 1970, the appellants commenced hog production on a large commercial scale on the appellant Baldwin's property which adjoins the appellees. In their business, the appellants operate two hog parlors each with a separate connecting lagoon. One hog parlor will house something over a thousand hogs and a second smaller one will accommodate approximately four hundred. There is also a third servicing lagoon. The hog parlor is a covered shelter with a concrete floor, laid on a plane, slightly declining toward the adjoining lagoon. The hogs are fed and watered in the parlors, and there they live, sleep and grow to a desired weight, when they are topped out. The lagoons which adjoin the hog parlors are related facilities, designed for the purpose of retaining the disposing of the waste material excreted by the hogs on the floor in their parlors. These lagoons are entrenched bodies of water into which the hog waste is flushed down with water in cleaning the parlor floors. In the lagoons, the waste material, commingling with the water, creates a chemical reaction resulting in a disintegration of the waste. This causes the emission of offensive odors. During the trial, the extent and intensity of the odor was the subject of much conflicting testimony. The appellees and witnesses offered by them, in general, said that the odor was so bad that they had to keep the doors and windows in the house closed, that it sickened them at the stomach, caused loss of appetite and practically ruined all outdoor recreation about the homeplace. The appellees' residence was said to be at distances varying from two hundred to a thousand feet from the nearest hog parlor and adjoining lagoon. Witnesses testified that these facilities adjoined the appellees' land near the division line between the parties.

While much of the evidence conflicts, the appellants admit in their brief that there was an odor which arose from the operation of the hog parlor and that the evidence was in conflict as to how far it could be detected. After stating that he visited the appellees' premises and inspected the stream in their pasture, the rock formation from which part of it flowed, the hog parlors and lagoons operated by the appellants, and the poultry houses and hog pasture of an adjacent neighbor, the trial judge found 'with no doubt about it' that the appellants' operations emitted foul odors which had a detrimental effect on the appellees' enjoyment of their home and the value of their property....

The court further found that the operation of the hog parlors and lagoons was an obnoxious nuisance subject to abatement by a court of equity, and that the appellees suffered damages from the nuisance because of its proximity to their home, one of the lagoons being about as close to the appellees' property line as it could be built. The court also observed that the appellants had spent some $31,300 in creating the hog parlors and lagoons, and that an injunction would bring a severe blow to them. The court concluded that the appellees were entitled to have the nuisance abated, or else, be compensated in damages, if the nuisance is allowed to continue.

Accordingly, the court ordered and decreed that the appellants be enjoined, prohibited and restrained from operating the hog parlors and lagoons, provided that, if the appellants paid into the court the sum of $3,000 as damages for the use of the appellees, the injunction would not go into effect, and the appellees' only relief would be compensation for damages, but, if not paid within thirty days, the injunction would go into full force and effect without further orders of the court.

The appellants argue that their operation is carried on in a rural community given over almost entirely to agricultural pursuits, such as the growing of farm produce, the raising of turkeys and chickens, the dairy business, and hog and cattle production, and that it follows that fowl and animal odors will permeate the area to some degree. They assert that the appellees should endure some unpleasantness and not be permitted to enjoin a lawful business, the facilities for which were constructed according to approved plans and specifications, and the operation of which is conducted in a reasonable manner.

While these contentions must be considered in deciding the case, we think the decision also hinges on other factors, such as the location and proximity of the operation to the appellees' home, the intensity and volume of the odors, their interference, if any, with the appellees' own well-being and the enjoyment of their home, and any consequential depreciation in value of their home. It appears that the trial judge considered these matters....

On several occasions, we have defined a private nuisance as "any establishment, erected on the premises of one, though for the purposes of trade or business, lawful in itself, which, from the situation, the inherent qualities of the business, or the manner in which it is conducted, directly causes substantial injury to the property of another, or produces material annoyance and inconvenience to the occupants of adjacent dwellings, rendering them physically uncomfortable, is a nuisance. In applying this principle, it has been repeatedly held that smoke, offensive odors, noise, or vibrations, when of such degree or extent as to materially interfere with the ordinary comfort of human existence, will constitute a nuisance...."

We have read the evidence in the record, as well as the condensed recital of the testimony in the appellants' brief. We allude to this only to say that ample legal evidence appears to support the trial judge's finding and conclusion that a private nuisance did in fact exist....

In the prayer of their bill of complaint, the appellees specifically pray for a writ of injunction to enjoin the nuisance, and also, for monetary damages. In addition, the appellees pray for general relief. The court decreed an injunction to issue, conditioned, however, on the failure of the appellants to pay into court within thirty days from the date of the decree the sum of $3,000, as damages, for the use of appellees. The appellants have not contended that the court lacked power to enter such a decree, granting, in the alternative, the relief awarded to the appellees. The objection is that the court committed manifest error, because the decree is contrary to the great weight and preponderance of the evidence, and that there is a lack of evidence to support it. As we have already pointed out, we are unable to agree with these contentions.

Here the object of the bill is to abate a nuisance and to recover attendant damages....

Prosser on Torts, 4th ed. (1971), p. 603, 604, states: "Furthermore, even where there is an existing nuisance and present harm, the equity court may in its discretion deny the injunction where the balance of the equities involved is in favor of the defendant. It may take into consideration the relative economic hardship which will result to the parties from the granting or denial of the injunction, the good faith or intentional misconduct of each, and the interest of the general public in the continuation of the defendant's enterprise. Where liability for damages is concerned, the defendant's conduct may be found to be so unreasonable that he should pay for the harm that his factory is causing, but where an injunction is in question, it may be found to be still so far reasonable that he should be allowed to continue it if payment is made...."

Here, the trial court decreed that the appellees were entitled to have the nuisance abated, or else be compensated in damages, if the nuisance is to continue. No doubt the court deemed such relief appropriate under the facts. We will not undertake to surmise the court's reasons for so decreeing....

The effect of the decree is clear. If the appellants do not pay the $3,000, the nuisance will be abated, and no damages will then be forthcoming, because the court did not award any damages other than to realty. On the other hand, if the appellants pay the damages, they may continue their operation, and this will continue indefinitely the depreciated value of the appellees' property. The damages awarded are measurable for all time, because if paid, the nuisance may be expected to continue. In that case, the measure of damages for the nuisance, is the difference in the value of the property for a home with and without such odor....

For the reasons stated above, the several assignments of error mentioned do not invite our attention to the issues sought to be reviewed by them. Having considered those issues that have been sufficiently raised in the appellants' assignments of error and argued by them, and finding no error, we affirm the final decree of the trial court.

Affirmed.

Generally, the remedies available to an individual for either a public or private nuisance are:

- Damages—Monetary damages awarded once a nuisance has been established equal the decrease in the market value of the property as a result of the nuisance, the costs of repairing any damage, and damages for personal harm sustained.

- Injunction—Either standing alone as a remedy or in combination with another, the court may enter an injunction prohibiting the defendant from continuing his or her conduct.
- Abatement—A privilege of self-help available to one harmed by the nuisance, this allows entry upon the defendant's land and the use of all reasonable force in a reasonable manner to remove or terminate the nuisance; most states require a notice before entry.

The remedies in a nuisance action may be available to the plaintiff singly or in combination. As a rule, most courts will not allow an injunction when damages are adequate relief. Paralegal students should review their individual states' statutes regarding damages, injunction, and abatement.

NEGLIGENCE AND STRICT LIABILITY

Historically, the principles of negligence and the concepts surrounding the law of strict liability have not been a part of the law of nuisance. Confusion may exist in the minds of many legal scholars, including those involved in the preparation of the *Restatement*, as to the applicability of the principles of either body of law as a basis for a nuisance recovery. The law of nuisance is based upon an intentional act, and for that reason is not founded in negligence. Chapter 12 discusses the legal principle assigning strict liability to a defendant engaging in an inherently dangerous activity.

The law of nuisance provides recovery for intentional invasions of the property interests of another, and is used as a theory of recovery when the principles of negligence law and strict liability are not applicable. The paralegal student should be alert for the relevant theory of law, be it nuisance, negligence, or strict liability, when preparing a cause of action based upon an unreasonable invasion of another's use and enjoyment of property.

SUMMARY

The law of nuisance is based upon two separate forms of tort liability: private nuisance and public nuisance. They originate in the English common law and are expressed in the statutes of virtually every state. Both involve conduct invading another's use and enjoyment of property.

Public nuisances are redressed by the state through the application of criminal sanctions against the offender. Whether further action is available for public nuisances depends upon the extent of harm to individuals as opposed to the public in general. Private nuisance and public nuisance are remedied by an action in tort for damages, injunctive relief, and abatement.

Review Questions

1. Describe the concept of nuisance.
2. What is the purpose behind the doctrine of nuisance?
3. Describe the nature of the harm that is the subject of an action for nuisance.
4. What are the two principal types of nuisance?
5. Define a private nuisance.
6. Discuss the nature of the use and enjoyment of property.
7. What are the four requirements for a recovery for a private nuisance?
8. What is an absolute nuisance?
9. Define a public nuisance.
10. What are the three remedies available for a nuisance?

Focus Your Skills

Every Saturday morning the peace and tranquility of the Shadow Run Retirement Village were shattered by the cacophonous sounds emanating from 50 Harley-Davidson motorcycles belonging to various members of the Sound Hogs' Motorcycle Club. Led by their intrepid warlord, Moon Dawg Dailey, the Hogs had declared every Saturday as Sound Hog's Day, and proceeded to celebrate the occasion with racing engines, hole shots, and wheelies outside their clubhouse in the streets bordering Shadow Run. To a man, the Sound Hogs were devotees of the roar of the Harley-Davidson motorcycle engine. Joined by similar clubs, the Sound Hogs were actively spearheading a drive to make the growl of a Harley-Davidson the National Sound. The prospect of the National Sound being heard before sporting events all across the country caused a tear to well in the eye of Moon Dawg, whose son was about to play his first T-ball game.

The engine noise and vibrations produced by the Sound Hogs were not without damaging consequences in neighboring Shadow Run. Mrs. Mildred Hearwell had lived without serenity for more than three years before she decided that she had suffered enough. The noise not only loosened the mortar on her home and broke her cherished Waterford crystal, it also loosened her dentures, caused constant gastro-urinary distress, and played a role in the development of gallstones. When the sound interfered with the reception of her favorite television show, *Nature*, Mrs. Hearwell decided to join the battle and confront her enemy.

Nearly crippled from a complex array of symptoms of phonetic etiology, and unable to sell her unmarketable home and relocate, Mrs. Hearwell has come to your law office seeking assistance. Advise her of her rights to maintain an action under the doctrine of nuisance against the Sound Hogs' Motorcycle Club and Moon Dawg Dailey.

10 Vicarious Liability

Men at some time are masters of their fates: The fault, dear Brutus, is not in our stars, but in ourselves, that we are underlings.

William Shakespeare

Tort liability imposes a duty of care to provide protection for others from the harm caused by individuals with whom a person has voluntarily entered into a relationship and for whom he or she is responsible. Just as the common law imposes a duty upon a parent to protect a minor child, it also imposes a duty upon a master to protect others from his or her apprentices. These duties are defined by the law of vicarious liability and are based upon the existence of a particular relationship. This chapter acquaints the paralegal student with the concepts surrounding the law of vicarious liability and illustrates the extent of one's liability to another for the acts of a servant.

Chapter Topics

1. Doctrine of Vicarious Liability
2. Master–Servant Relationship
3. Independent Contractor
4. Joint Enterprise
5. Automobile Ownership
6. Dram Shop Liability

Objectives

After completing this chapter, you will be able to:

1. Understand the doctrine of vicarious liability.
2. Discuss the principle of *respondeat superior*.
3. Analyze the master–servant relationship.
4. Distinguish between a frolic and a detour in determining vicarious liability.
5. Comprehend the distinction between an independent contractor and an employer.
6. Summarize the nature of a joint enterprise.
7. Discuss the principles of liability that attend ownership of an automobile.
8. Analyze the concept of dram shop liability in a contemporary commercial setting.

Doctrine of Vicarious Liability

vicarious liability

The doctrine of **vicarious liability** is a body of tort law based upon the principles of negligence. The relationship between the parties determines the liability of one person for the harmful conduct of another. Vicarious simply means the substitution of one person for another. Applied to the doctrine of vicarious liability, it is the substitution of the liability of one person for the liability of another.

As an example, assume that Bookholder was an Ivory Tower College library employee. In the course of his duties, which included restocking the shelves with returned research materials, he failed to properly place a volume of the *Restatement of Agency* on the top shelf. Because of his negligence, Prudence, while in the midst of her research project, was struck by the falling volume and sustained a serious head injury. In this case, the liability of the college library would be substituted for the negligence of Bookholder.

The doctrine of vicarious liability is referred to in legal literature by the following synonymous terms:

- Imputed negligence—The negligence of one person is imputed (assigned) to another.

- Master–servant—The master is responsible for the conduct of his or her servant.
- Principal–agent—The principal is responsible for the conduct of his or her agent.
- Employer–employee—The employer may be responsible for the conduct of his or her employee.
- *Respondeat superior*—This means, literally, to "look to the man higher up."

The terminology used depends upon the relationship of the parties and the jurisdiction of the action. Some jurisdictions refer to the principle by various terms. The phrases vicarious liability, *respondeat superior*, and imputed negligence interchangeably describe the relationship between the parties seeking to impose liability upon one who is not directly at fault (see Figure 10-1).

Figure 10-1. Vicarious Liability

VICARIOUS LIABILITY—*RESPONDEAT SUPERIOR*—IMPUTED NEGLIGENCE

Relationship	
Master	Servant
Principal	Agent
Employer	Employee
Employer	Independent Contractor
Joint Entrepreneur	Joint Entrepreneur
Owner	Driver

Justification for the application of the doctrine of vicarious liability has been found in several differing theories by individual state appellate courts. The rationale may be based upon a theory of:

- Control—The master has some presumed control over the actions of the servant.
- Origination—The master has initiated the process that led to the harm.
- Entrustment—The master has delegated the responsibility for some task to the servant.
- Privilege—Responsibility for another person accompanies the privilege of hiring.
- Deep pocket—Damages are awarded against the party most likely able to bear the loss.

allocation of risk

Most courts justify the doctrine by merely relying on the phrase, *respondeat superior*. It would appear that the most sound justification for the doctrine in a modern commercial setting is the principle of **allocation of risk**. The principle of allocation of risk is a matter of public policy whereby the risks attendant upon an enterprise are distributed through pricing practice and insurance coverage. Through this method, the enterprise is able to shift the cost of risk to the community at large. In the *Reed* case, the court found that the tortfeasor was not an employee of the business because of the lack of control, but based its justification of the doctrine of vicarious liability on the allocation of risk (see Figure 10-2).

Figure 10-2. Case in Point: *Reed v. House of Decor, Inc.*

REED v. HOUSE OF DECOR, INC.
468 So.2d 1159
Supreme Court of Louisiana
May 14, 1985

LEMON, Justice.

We granted certiorari to determine whether the intermediate court erred in reversing a judgment which held that House of Decor, Inc. was vicariously liable for plaintiff's injuries caused by Chuck Williams, an alleged employee of House of Decor. The critical issue is whether Williams was an employee of the House of Decor in the course and scope of that employment at the time of the accident.

William Cusack and Steven Tomoletz, as individuals, leased certain immovable property in the Vieux Carré section of New Orleans. The lower floor of the main building on the property was used as a gift shop operated by the House of Decor, Inc., a corporation in which Cusack and Tomoletz were the sole shareholders. The two men resided on the upper floor of the main building. The leased property also included slave quarters in the rear. Cusack and Tomoletz sublet the upper apartment in the slave quarters to Williams on a two-year lease for a monthly rental of $125, executing the sublease in their individual capacities and not as officers of the corporation....

The day before the accident, Cusack asked plaintiff, an employee of a hotel across the street from the House of Decor, to help move a refrigerator from Williams' upper apartment to the new residence. The accident occurred on a Sunday, before the hour that the gift shop opened. While Williams and plaintiff were attempting to move the refrigerator down the stairs of the slave quarters to Williams' truck, Williams lost his grip, and the refrigerator fell onto plaintiff's ankle.

Plaintiff filed suit against the House of Decor and Gulf Insurance Company as the corporation's liability carrier, alleging that the House of Decor was vicariously liable for the negligence of its "employee," Chuck Williams. Neither Cusack nor Tomoletz was ever named or served as an individual defendant, nor was any argument made to the jury that they were individually liable. Both sides restricted their opening and closing arguments to the jury (except for the issue of damages) to the issue of the House of Decor's vicarious liability for the negligence of Williams as a corporate employee. After trial on the merits, the jury answered written interrogatories and found that Williams was an employee of House of Decor at the time of the accident and that his negligence caused plaintiff's injuries.... Judgment was rendered in favor of plaintiff and against the House of Decor and Gulf Insurance. Both sides appealed.

We granted certiorari, being primarily concerned about an employer's liability for the off-duty torts of an employee who was performing (perhaps under subtle economic coercion) tasks at the request of and for the personal benefit of a principal officer and shareholder of a corporate employer....

Whether a party is liable for the act of a tortfeasor on the basis that the tortfeasor was the party's employee in the course and scope of employment depends upon the proof and assessment of several factors, including payment of wages by the employer, the employer's power of control, the employee's duty to perform the particular act, the time, place and purpose of the act in relation to service of the employer, the relationship between the employee's act and the employer's business, the benefits received by the employer from the act, the motivation of the employee for performing the act, and the reasonable expectation of the employer that the employee would perform the act....

In summary, Williams did not receive any wages from the House of Decor. The corporation had no power of control or power of discharge over his work activities. The act of moving the refrigerator occurred at a time when the business operated by the corporation was closed and at a place away from the corporation's business premises. The moving of the refrigerator from an apartment occupied by Williams to another residence provided no apparent benefit to the corporation and had no relationship with the corporation's business. Indeed, the corporation was just about to close down the business permanently, and it is difficult to perceive any purpose in moving the refrigerator that was in any way related to the corporation....

Determination of the course and scope of employment is largely based on policy. The risks which are generated by an employee's activities while serving his employer's interests are properly allocated to the employer as a cost of engaging in the enterprise. However, when the party (the alleged employer) upon whom vicarious liability is sought to be imposed had only a marginal relationship with the act which generated the risk and did not benefit by it, the purpose of the policy falls, and the responsibility for preventing the risk is solely upon the tortfeasor who created the risk while performing the act.

In the present case, the jury found that Williams was an employee of the House of Decor. The evidence arguably supports this limited determination that he was an occasional employee.... If Williams were a regular employee of the small corporation, perhaps policy would dictate that he should be viewed as being in the course and scope of his employment when performing a task at the request of and for the personal benefit of the holder of 51% of the corporate shares in the two-shareholder corporation. However, there is no compelling policy reason for a similar conclusion in the case of someone who at best was an occasional employee....

We therefore conclude that Williams' act of moving the refrigerator, during the performance of which plaintiff was injured, was not performed by an employee of House of Decor in the course and scope of employment.

Master–Servant Relationship

servant

The doctrine of *respondeat superior* states that the master is vicariously liable for the torts of the servant once the relationship is established. A **servant** is defined as an individual employed to perform services for another and subject to the other's control. Various individual state courts have established a set of criteria to determine the existence of control in defining the relationship. No single factor predominates in inferring control, and all of the factors must be measured against one another to ultimately decide the relationship. The criteria used by most states include the following:

- the extent to which the employer may determine the details of the work,
- the nature of the occupation,
- custom of the community,
- skill required,
- who supplies the tools or other instrumentalities used in the work,
- period over which the employment is to last, and
- method of payment.

The paralegal student must consult state statutory and case law to ascertain the factors stressed in individual states.

Scope of Employment

scope of employment

Vicarious liability does not extend to any and all torts of the servant. It is limited to those torts occurring within the **scope of employment**, a general term for the acts the servant is employed to perform. The phrase is extremely vague in its meaning and application by the various courts. It includes not only the essential tasks for which the servant was hired, but also acts that are incidental to accomplishing the employer's objectives (see Figure 10-3).

Figure 10-3. Scope of Employment

As in the case of the existence of the relation itself, many factors enter into the question: the time, place and purpose of the act, and its similarity to what is authorized; whether it is one commonly done by such servants; the extent of departure from normal methods; the previous relations between the parties; whether the master had reason to expect that such an act would be done....

W. Page Keeton et. al., *Prosser and Keeton on the Law of Torts* § 70 at 502 (5th ed. 1984)

Generally, the servant remains within the scope of employment if the act serves the employer's purposes. It is not enough that the master forbid the servant to commit a certain act or for the servant to "act carefully." If the servant is furthering the interests of the master, the master will be held responsible regardless of instructions. In the *Baird* case, the court is concerned with the control of the surgeon over the acts of his nurse-anesthetist (see Figure 10-4).

Figure 10-4. Case in Point: *Baird v. Sickler, M.D.*

BAIRD v. SICKLER, M.D.
433 N.E.2d 593
Supreme Court of Ohio
March 9, 1982

On January 26, 1976, appellee Maxine Baird underwent a laminectomy at Good Samaritan Hospital in the city of Dayton, Ohio. The procedure was performed to alleviate blocked vertebrae in her spine resulting from the Klippel-Feil syndrome. Appellees, Maxine and Richard Baird, employed Donald M. Sickler, M.D., to supervise and conduct the operation. J. A. Nichol, a registered nurse and trained nurse-anesthetist licensed under the laws of the state of Ohio to administer anesthesia..., assisted Dr. Sickler as the anesthetist during the laminectomy. At the time of the operation, Nichol was an employee of Anesthesia Associates. Dr. Sickler was aware that, because appellee Maxine Baird suffered from spondylosis as well as Klippel-Feil syndrome, her spinal cord might be compromised if the operation were done with appellee in a sitting position. Cognizant of the difficulties of intubating, i.e., inserting an endotracheal tube in the airway, of an individual so afflicted, Dr. Sickler helped position—prepare the head and torso—and otherwise assist in appellee's intubation. Dr. Sickler did not perform the actual insertion of the tube in appellee's trachea; nurse Nichol performed that task. Dr. Sickler was, however, present at all times during the intubation.

As a result of the operation, appellee was rendered permanently a paraplegic from the C-6 level down. Evidence adduced at trial indicated that the paralysis had two possible geneses: (1) the faulty intubation and positioning of appellee or (2) the aggravation, through fallen blood pressure of a sustained duration during the laminectomy itself, of a minor injury initially precipitated by appellee's intubation and positioning.

At the close of appellees' case, the trial court directed a verdict in favor of appellant. On appeal, the Court of Appeals reversed the lower court's decision, holding the directed verdict to be improper on grounds that reasonable minds could find appellant liable under the doctrine of *respondeat superior* and that appellant, by failing properly to direct the nurse-anesthetist, had breached a statutory duty.... The cause is now before this court pursuant to the allowance of a motion to certify the record.

PER CURIAM.

This cause presents a novel question in Ohio: is a chief surgeon ever legally accountable for the negligence of an assisting nurse-anesthetist, not directly employed by him? If an operating physician may never be held liable in such a factual context, then the trial court in the instant case acted properly in directing a verdict in favor of the appellant, Dr. Sickler. We find, however, that a chief surgeon's immunity for the negligent acts of an assisting nurse-anesthetist is not a matter of law and, thus, that the trial court erred in directing the verdict....

Under the doctrine of *respondeat superior*, the "master" is liable for the negligence of his "servant" when the latter is engaged in performing the work of the former.... A master–servant relationship is extant only when one party exercises the right of control over the actions of another and those actions are directed toward the attainment of an objective which the former seeks.... For the relationship to exist, it is unnecessary that such right of control be exercised; it is sufficient that the right merely exists.

All requisite indices of the master–servant diad were present in the relationship between appellant Dr. Sickler and J. A. Nichol, the nurse-anesthetist who assisted him. That appellant exercised and possessed the right to control Nichol's actions is reflected in appellant's own testimony at trial. Dr. Sickler admitted that, before the intubation, he instructed Nichol as to the procedures he wished to follow because of appellee Baird's special condition. He stated that, during the intubation, he watched to ensure that Nichol did not hyperflex or hyperextend appellee's neck and admitted that had he observed any misfeasance in the conduct of the intubation, he would have possessed the right and duty to halt the procedure. Appellant testified that, following the intubation, he held appellee's head as she was turned and placed on the operating table and monitored her positioning to ensure that neither her airway nor eyes were compromised. Appellant clearly not only controlled but also participated in the administering of the anesthetic. Moreover, even if he had failed to exercise control over the intubation, he clearly, as he himself admitted, had the right to control it. Appellant contends that the doctrine of *respondeat superior* is inapplicable to the present case because Nichol, the nurse-anesthetist, was an employee and servant of Anesthesia Associates, not of Dr. Sickler. The loaned servant rule, however, compels us to reject this argument....

Appellant finally argues that the Court of Appeals' decision in the instant case resurrects the now abjectly discredited "captain of the ship" doctrine which held a chief surgeon responsible for all that transpires in the operating room. Our ruling, which affirms the appellate court's determination, in no way breathes new life into that now prostrate doctrine. We make no attempt to impose upon an operating physician the duty of overseeing all that occurs in the highly technical milieu in which he works. Instead, we seek only to ensure that where, in the operating room, a surgeon does control or realistically possesses the right to control events and procedures, he does so with a high degree of care....

Frolic and Detour

When the servant acts outside the boundaries of the master's service, the master cannot be held responsible. At such times, the servant has no intention of performing any service for the master, and is pursuing only personal interests. In the English case of *Joel v. Morrison*, 172 Eng. Rep. 1338 (1834), Baron Parke stated that the master is not liable when the servant is "going on a frolic of his own." The term **frolic**, meaning any deviation from the scope of employment, has since become a part of American jurisprudence.

frolic

Certain personal activities, such as the use of the rest room, are considered to be so closely tied to the work as not to constitute a deviation from the employment. A question of fact arises as to whether the deviation constitutes such a complete departure from the master's interests as to amount to a frolic, or whether the servant's acts are only a roundabout way of performing the task. In cases wherein the servant deviates from the route on a personal errand, and then returns to the assigned route, he or she is said to have been on a detour from the master's business. Most courts have held the master liable for a servant's slight, reasonably expected departure from that route.

For example, suppose that Arliss was employed by Theodore in a bicycle repair shop as a general helper. Arliss decided to ride a repaired bicycle to the local restaurant to pick up some sandwiches for lunch, and in so doing, struck Mrs. Mantooth, a pedestrian. The question of fact would revolve around what was customarily expected of servants such as Arliss, and whether Theodore permitted the act. A court may hold Arliss to have been on a frolic of her own and not on the master's business, or it may hold her to have been engaged in an act of personal interest that was necessary to the performance of the work. The basic question will generally be resolved based on whether the deviation was major or minor. If the departure was minor, then the employer will be held liable as a necessary risk to his or her business. By way of contrast, consider the New York Supreme Court's decision in the *Cowin* case, where the servant reported for work in an intoxicated condition, and the employer, although aware his means of transportation was an automobile, sent him home in that condition (see Figure 10-5).

Figure 10-5. Case in Point: *Cowin v. Huntington Hospital*

COWIN v. HUNTINGTON HOSPITAL
Supreme Court, Special Term
496 N.Y.S.2d 203
November 1, 1985

MELVYN TANENBAUM, Justice.

Upon a motion to dismiss a complaint for failure to state a cause of action, the Court must accept the facts alleged in the complaint as true and determine whether these facts fit within any cognizable legal theory....

The complaint in the instant action alleges, in effect, that defendant's employee JAMES THOMAS reported for work in an intoxicated condition, and that defendant, although aware his means of transportation was an automobile, sent THOMAS home in that condition. Shortly afterwards, the automobile driven by THOMAS was the cause of a motor vehicle accident causing personal injury to plaintiff. While the Court agrees with the contentions of both parties that under the facts alleged defendant owed no duty to the public to control THOMAS' actions under General Obligations Law a 11-101, commonly known as the Dram Shop Act, it does not agree with plaintiff that a separate common law duty to protect the general public from the actions complained of exists.

In order to establish tort liability, the plaintiff must demonstrate the existence and breach of a duty owed to him by defendant.... While, as a general rule a person is under no duty to control the conduct of another, certain relationships, such as that between master and servant, do create such a duty. This duty, however, is a narrow one and under the doctrine of respondeat superior, an employer will be liable for the negligence of an employee only while the employee is acting within the scope of his employment.... An employee acts within the scope of his employment when he is doing something in furtherance of the duties he owes to his employer and where the employer is, or could be, exercising some control, directly or indirectly, over the employee's activities.... Driving to and from work is not considered to be acting within the scope of one's employment except in those instances where such travel has been found to be within the scope of the employee's duties.... In the instant case, defendant was not, as a matter of law, acting within the scope of his employment since his actions in becoming intoxicated prior to reporting for work can in no way be viewed as having been performed in furtherance of the employer's requirements and the employer did not participate in creating his condition. Nor can this Court find a duty on the part of the defendant, premised independently of an employment relationship, which would require it to take reasonable measures to protect the public at large from the off-duty torts of its employee. Plaintiff cites *Restatement (Second) of Torts* § 319 as a basis for imposing such a duty. That section provides:

> "One who takes charge of a third person whom he knows or should know to be likely to cause bodily harm to others if not controlled is under a duty to exercise reasonable care to control the third person from doing such harm."

This section requires more than mere knowledge of a person's dangerous propensities. "Taking charge" within the meaning of Section 319 requires a custodial relationship, one in which the person charged with controlling the conduct of another voluntarily assumes responsibility for that person. This the defendant specifically and unequivocally declined to do. In the absence of some affirmative action by defendant to intervene or to control its employee, THOMAS' mere reporting for work could not unilaterally transfer to or create on the part of his employer responsibility for a wrongful act done prior to such reporting and there was no duty owed by defendant to this plaintiff to accept such responsibility. The Court notes that while at least one jurisdiction has apparently analogized Section 319 in a fashion as to impose a duty running from an employer to the public at large in circumstances similar to those at bar,... no authority has been cited, nor can any be found by this Court, which would suggest that this jurisdiction has judicially recognized such an expansion of an employer's vicarious liability for the acts of his employee when committed outside the scope of employment.

> The Court therefore finds no basis upon which to predicate a cause of action against defendant for the injuries alleged to have been sustained by plaintiff. Accordingly, the complaint is dismissed.

Intentional Torts

While early United States courts refused to hold the master liable for the willful acts of wrongdoing of the servant, today most jurisdictions adhere to the idea that even an intentional tort may be within the scope of the employment. The general rule is that the master will be held liable for the intentional torts of the servant when the servant is acting wholly or in part to further the master's business (see Figure 10-6).

Figure 10-6. Intentional Torts

> Thus he will be held liable where his bus driver crowds a competitor's bus into a ditch, or assaults a trespasser to eject him from the bus, or a salesman makes fraudulent statements about the products he is selling, or defames a competitor or disparages his product, or where the servant resorts to false imprisonment or malicious prosecution for a like purpose. Thus a railway ticket agent who assaults, arrests or slanders a passenger, in the belief that he has been given a counterfeit bill for a ticket is within the scope of his employment.
>
> W. Page Keeton et. al., *Prosser and Keeton on the Law of Torts* § 70 at 506 (5th ed. 1984)

Yet if the servant acts for entirely personal motives unconnected to the employer's interests, then he or she has deviated from the scope of the employment.

To determine whether an employee has deviated from the scope of employment, the courts will consider such factors as:

- time—whether the servant was within the normal work hours;
- duration—the length of time of the departure, frolic, or detour;
- distance—the remoteness of the deviation;
- motive—interests of the employer measured against the purely personal interests of the servant;
- master's business—whether the acts of the servant had any relationship to furtherance of the master's business.

The court, analyzing the motives of the servant and the interests of the master in the *Webb* case, found that the servant's sexual assault on a customer was not in furtherance of the master's interests (see Figure 10-7).

Figure 10-7. Case in Point: *Webb v. Jewel Companies, Inc.*

WEBB v. JEWEL COMPANIES, INC.
485 N.E.2d 409
Appellate Court of Illinois
October 25, 1985

SULLIVAN, Justice:

This is an appeal from the dismissal, for failure to state a cause of action, of the second amended Count I of a complaint filed on behalf of the minor plaintiff against defendants, Charles Hiley and Jewel Companies, Inc. (Jewel) for damages because of injuries she suffered as a result of a sexual assault allegedly committed by Hiley while he was employed as a security guard for Jewel. The sole issue presented for review is the propriety of the dismissal.

In Count 1, as amended, plaintiff alleged in substance that she was a customer in a Jewel supermarket located in Chicago; that she had just purchased an item when Hiley, acting in his capacity as a security guard, stopped her and then led her to an enclosed office for the purpose of searching her; and that in the course of that search, he sexually molested her. The trial court granted Jewel's motion to dismiss Count I with prejudice, and this appeal followed....

Plaintiff contends that the allegations in Count I are sufficient to state a cause of action against Jewel on the theory of respondeat superior. It is Jewel's position, however, that Count I is both legally and factually deficient and that dismissal was, therefore, proper.

Under the doctrine of *respondeat superior*, an employer may be liable for the negligent, wilful, malicious or even criminal acts of its employees when such acts are committed in the course of employment and in furtherance of the business of the employer; however, the employer is not liable to an injured third party where the acts complained of thereby were committed solely for the benefit of the employee....

In the instant case, plaintiff asserts that the trial court erred in ruling, as a matter of law, that Hiley was not acting within the scope of his employment, but rather acted solely for his own benefit in molesting her.... [S]he argues that this was a question of fact which should have been left to a jury for determination. We disagree....

[T]he fact remains that the sexual molestation of a young girl by a security guard is nonetheless a deviation having no relation to the business of Jewel or the furtherance thereof. Thus, we find that the trial court properly dismissed the second amended Count I of plaintiff's complaint for failing to state a cause of action.

Dangerous Instrumentalities

Some jurisdictions impose liability upon an employer who entrusts an employee with the use of an inherently dangerous instrument or material. For instance, vicarious liability has been imposed in situations involving the use of steam locomotives and poisons. The theory applies only when the servant acts within the scope of his or her employment and has custody of the instrumentality. Most jurisdictions reject the use of a theory of *respondeat superior* in favor of the principles of absolute liability (the subject of Chapter 12). Individual state case law must be reviewed to determine the applicable theory in such cases.

Independent Contractor

independent contractor

The general rule regarding a master's vicarious liability for the acts of his or her servant differs when the servant is an independent contractor. An **independent contractor** is an individual who contracts with another to perform a task according to his or her own methods, and is subject to the employer's control only as to the result of the work. The independent contractor is a person who has entered into an agreement with an employer to accomplish a piece of work. It is the independent contractor who decides how the work is to be performed, the means employed, and the physical conduct of the enterprise.

Originating in the common law, the doctrine of vicarious liability states that the employer has no liability for the torts of an independent contractor (see Figure 10-8).

Figure 10-8. Independent Contractors

[T]he employer of an independent contractor is not liable for physical harm caused to another by an act or omission of the contractor or his servants.

Restatement (Second) of Torts § 409

Most legal scholars reason that since the employer has no control over the performance of the work, and the work is to be regarded as the contractor's own, then the contractor is to be held responsible. If the employer were able to control the performance of the work, then the contractor would not be considered to be independent, and the employer would be held accountable. Whether the work was done for pay or with a contract is immaterial.

For instance, assume that Danforth asked his neighbor, Johnson, to cut his lawn while he was away on vacation. In the course of cutting the lawn the following week, and unaware of Danforth's exact property line, Johnson mowed over Mrs. Goodhart's prize begonias. Johnson would be considered an independent contractor hired only to perform a specific task, and not subject to Danforth's control. Any harm caused by tortious conduct on the part of Johnson would not be the responsibility of Danforth. Mrs. Goodhart's action would be directed at Johnson.

Contrary argument has been made for the liability of the employer in such cases on the theory that he or she is the one responsible for the enterprise and is the one to whom any benefits accrue. Since the employer selected the contractor, may insist upon indemnity, and is best able to spread the risk to his or her customers as a cost of doing business, responsibility should be borne by the employer. The courts in most jurisdictions have rejected this argument, but it is an area that the paralegal student should survey periodically (see Figure 10-9).

Figure 10-9. Case in Point: *Fisherman's Paradise, Inc. v. Greenfield*

FISHERMAN'S PARADISE, INC. v. GREENFIELD
417 So.2d 306
District Court of Appeal of Florida
July 27, 1982

BASKIN, Judge,

Appellee Melvin Greenfield took his ten-year-old boat to Fisherman's Paradise for refurbishing. Fisherman's Paradise subcontracted part of the work, including replacement of the refrigerator, to Endeavor Marine. During a boating trip, the refrigerator broke loose from its mounting and injured Mrs. Greenfield. The Greenfields sued both Fisherman's Paradise and Endeavor Marine. They alleged that Fisherman's Paradise was responsible for the negligent installation and included a claim predicated upon strict liability. They also charged Endeavor Marine with negligently installing the refrigerator. Upon motion, the trial court entered summary judgment against both Fisherman's Paradise and Endeavor Marine, denying the motion for summary judgment filed by Fisherman's Paradise. In this appeal, Fisherman's Paradise contends it should not be held liable for negligent acts of Endeavor Marine, because it operated as an independent contractor. Finding that genuine issues of material fact remain to be decided, we reverse the summary judgment.

According to the general rule, an employer is not liable for the negligent acts of an independent contractor because he lacks control over the manner in which the work is performed.... One of the many exceptions to the general rule, however, occurs when the employer's liability arises from the contractor's negligent performance of inherently dangerous tasks.... Furthermore, an employer may not escape liability for the creation of an inherently dangerous condition (at least on premises where public use is invited) unless it was not discoverable on reasonable inspection....

Whether Fisherman's Paradise may be held liable for Endeavor's negligent conduct under the foregoing principles is subject to a factual determination. We find no merit in the arguments presented in support of liability on other grounds. We therefore reverse the summary judgment and remand for further proceedings.

Negligence of the Employer

Exceptions to the general rule of law for independent contractors have evolved in the courts. The exceptions fall into three categories that impose liability on the employer in an employer–independent contractor relationship. The first category covers cases involving negligence of the employer.

An employer owes a duty of reasonable care when there is a foreseeable risk of harm to another in selecting an independent contractor. When the employer is negligent in failing to exercise reasonable care in the direction of the work, he or she may be found liable (see Figure 10-10).

Figure 10-10. Employer's Negligence

The employer of an independent contractor is subject to the same liability for physical harm caused by an act or omission committed by the contractor pursuant to order or directions negligently given by the employer, as though the act or omission were that of the employer himself.

Restatement (Second) of Torts § 410

This exception is based upon a fundamental principle of negligence law which states that when one negligently directs another, he or she faces liability for the consequences of the act. An employer negligently directs the work when he or she knows, or should know, that the work involves an unreasonable risk of harm to another. This rule is most frequently applied in construction cases wherein the contractor has been supplied with defective plans or specifications by the employer. In such a case, the employer is liable for the acts or omissions of the contractor. An employer's liability for the conduct of an independent contractor may be based upon a failure to exercise reasonable care:

- in giving orders or directions on how the work is to be done,
- to employ a competent independent contractor,
- to take precautions in advance to allow the work to be done safely,
- in performance of his or her own work, or
- in supervising equipment and tools.

If the employer fails in any of the these situations, then he or she will be held liable for any harm caused to another.

Non-Delegable Duty

non-delegable duty

Another exception to the general rule that an employer lacks liability for an an independent contractor is found in cases involving a non-delegable duty. A **non-delegable duty** is an obligation imposed by law or contract that may not be passed to another. Such duties may be created by statute, contract, franchise, or by the common law. For instance, carriers have a duty to transport passengers safely; a railroad must fence its right of way properly; a municipality must maintain its sidewalks in a safe manner; a business owner must maintain the premises in a safe condition for business visitors. In such cases, the employer is not relieved of taking reasonable precautions and will be held liable for the negligence of his or her contractors. The paralegal student should consult state statutes and case law to determine which duties may be considered to be non-delegable.

Inherently Dangerous Activities

The third exception is provided for work that is considered to be inherently dangerous. It remains the responsibility of the employer. An independent contractor will not be held responsible for negligence occurring in the performance of an employer's inherently dangerous work. These activities include the keeping of vicious animals and the handling of electrical wires, dynamite, or fireworks. Any highly risky work may remain the responsibility of the employer.

Collateral Negligence

Collateral negligence refers to any type of negligence that accompanies but is secondary to the risks inherent in the work itself. When an employer may be held liable for a risk that is inherent in the work, he or she will not be held liable if the independent contractor is negligent in easily controlled details of the work. When the negligence of the contractor is significantly removed from the risk for which the employer is responsible, then the contractor remains liable. As an example, consider the *Wilton* case in which dynamite subsequently exploded and caused injury after being left under a sidewalk by an independent contractor (see Figure 10-11).

Figure 10-11. Case in Point: *Wilton v. City of Spokane*

WILTON v. CITY OF SPOKANE
132 P. 404
Supreme Court of Washington
May 26, 1913

FULLERTON, J.

The respondent brought this action against the city of Spokane, Foster & Hindle, a copartnership, and the Washington Water Power Company, a corporation, to recover for personal injuries. Before issue was joined on the complaint, the action was dismissed as to the Washington Water Power Company. Afterwards it was prosecuted to a judgment against the other defendants, both of whom appeal. The facts of the case are not complicated, nor seriously in dispute. The city of Spokane let a contract to Foster & Hindle for the improvement of one of its streets. The work included the grading of a roadway along the center of the street and the construction of a parking strip and a sidewalk on each side thereof. By the terms of the contract Foster & Hindle were made independent contractors, responsible to the city for the result of the work only, not as to the manner in which it was to be performed. In grading the street to its proper level, a ledge of rock was encountered which the contractors removed by blasting; the explosive used being dynamite. In the course of the work a blast put in near the bottom of the required grade failed to explode, and the contractors, instead of removing it, covered it up and constructed the surface of the street over it. Afterwards the city accepted the work as in compliance with the contract without knowledge of the unexploded blast. Some months later the Washington Water Power Company applied for and was granted permission to erect a line of poles along the margin of the improved street on which to string electric wires for lighting purposes. The holes in which to set the poles had to be dug somewhat deeper than the street was cut down in the performance of the improvement work, and where the ledge of rock was encountered the rock necessary to be removed was broken up by blasting. While the employees of the Washington Water Power Company, among whom was the respondent, were drilling for the purpose of putting in a blast in one of such holes, the drill encountered the unexploded blast left in the rock by Foster & Hindle, causing it to explode. The explosion put out one of the respondent's eyes and otherwise seriously injured him, and he brought the present action, with the result before stated.

The record does not make clear the grounds on which the judgment against the city was rested. Several grounds on which it is thought it may rest, however, are suggested in the argument, and these we will notice briefly in their order. It is first said that the work was of such a character that it could not be let to independent contractors, and that the city could not escape liability for the negligent performance by endeavoring to so let it. The particular contention is that the work of blasting rock in an inhabited portion of a city is so inherently dangerous in itself that public policy forbids that the city be permitted to let the work to an independent contractor. But if this be the general rule, we do not think the present case falls within it. The leaving of an unexploded blast of dynamite in the rock below the surface of a street is not an incident to the work of blasting rock to make a grade for a street. Such an action is negligence and nothing else, and the city is liable for the act only in the same way, and to the same extent, that it would have been liable had the contractors left the dynamite on the surface of the street in the traveled part of the roadway on leaving the work; it is liable for injuries resulting therefrom only in the case it knew of its being so left, or by the exercise of reasonable diligence could have known of it. But the employer is not liable where the obstruction or defect in the street causing the injury is wholly collateral to the contract work, and entirely the result of the negligence or wrongful acts of the contractor, subcontractor, or his servants. In such a case the immediate author of the injury is alone liable.... There is no evidence that the city had knowledge of the existence of this unexploded blast, and, of course, there was no sort of diligence that it could have exercised which would have made it acquainted with the fact.

A second reason suggested for sustaining the judgment against the city is that the relation of master and servant existed between the city and the respondent. But it is manifest that the respondent was not in the employ of the city. He was a mere licensee upon the street, and while the city owed him the duty to refrain from doing him willful injury, and from setting snares for him, it owed no duty to provide him with a safe place in which to work.

Again, it is said that the city is responsible for the condition of its streets, and hence liable for any injury arising from defects therein, no matter by whom the defect may have been caused. But the rule is not so broad as this. The city is liable only for those defects in its streets of which it has knowledge, or by the exercise of reasonable diligence could have obtained knowledge. It is not a guarantor of the safe condition of its streets for all purposes and at all times. Its full duty is performed when it exercises reasonable diligence in keeping its streets in repair. We think therefore that the court erred in holding the city liable for the injury.

The appellants Foster & Hindle make the contention that the evidence is insufficient to justify the verdict against them. They argue that when they completed the contract and turned the street over to the city, and the city accepted the work as in compliance with the contract, their liability to third persons for the negligent performance of the work ceased, and from thence-forth the city alone was responsible for any such negligent performance. This argument is perhaps sound in so far as it relates to defects in the street arising from a mere negligent performance of the work, but we think it has no application to an act of the nature here charged against the contractors. The leaving of the unexploded charge of dynamite in the rock beneath the surface of the street was not a matter connected with the contract work. It was a matter wholly collateral thereto, and was, as we have said, of itself a negligent and wrongful act, rendering the persons wrongfully leaving it there liable to any one who in the lawful pursuit of his own business should be injured thereby. The liability of the contractors for the injury arising from the explosion rests on the same principle it would have rested had they knowingly or negligently left the explosive on the surface of the street and a traveler on the street had come into contact therewith and received an injury; it rests on the wrongful and negligent nature of the act itself. There is a distinction between an act of negligence imminently dangerous to the lives of others and one that is not so. In the former case the party guilty of the negligence is liable to the party injured, whether there be a contract between them or not; in the latter, the negligent party is liable only to the party with whom he contracted, and on the ground that negligence is a breach of the contract.... We conclude therefore that the trial judge was right in refusing to sustain the challenge of the appellants Foster & Hindle.

The judgment will be reversed and remanded, with instructions to dismiss as to the appellant city of Spokane, but will stand affirmed as to the other appellants.

As a general rule, the employer is not going to be held liable for the collateral negligence of the independent contractor.

Joint Enterprise

joint enterprise

An understanding of the nature of a joint enterprise is necessary to appreciate its relationship to the law of vicarious liability. A **joint enterprise** is an undertaking to carry out some business purpose by a group of associates with an equal voice in the direction of the venture. Occasionally referred to as a common enterprise, a joint enterprise has four essential elements:

- an agreement among the associates,
- a common purpose to be carried out by the group,
- a community of monetary interest, and
- an equal voice in the control and direction of the enterprise which includes an equal right of control.

Similar to a partnership arrangement, each of the members of the group is considered the servant of the others within the scope of the enterprise. For purposes of the law of vicarious liability, each of the members of the group is vicariously responsible for the conduct of the others within the scope of the enterprise. A joint enterprise differs slightly from the typical joint venture and partnership arrangements that are limited to commercial endeavors. It is broader in scope and includes more informal associations for a limited purpose. Included are undertakings with limited objectives under circumstances in which all have a voice in directing the conduct of the enterprise.

In most cases involving a joint enterprise, the law of vicarious liability has been applied to automobile accidents. In such cases, the negligence of the driver of the vehicle is imputed to the passenger, invoking the principle of contributory negligence. Contributory negligence bars the passenger's claim for damages from the driver by imputing the driver's negligence to the passenger in joint enterprise cases (see Figure 10-12).

Figure 10-12. Joint Enterprise

(1) Any one of several persons engaged in a joint enterprise, such as to make each member of the group responsible for physical harm to other persons caused by the negligence of any member, is barred from recovery against such other persons by the negligence of any member of the group.
(2) Any person engaged in such a joint enterprise is not barred from recovery against the member of the group who is negligent, but is barred from recovery against any other member of the group.

Restatement (Second) of Torts § 491

The use of an automobile by a group of friends out for a pleasure trip is insufficient for the application of the principle of vicarious liability. Something more than a mere agreement to travel together is necessary for its application. Some common monetary interest must be the journey's objective. In those situations in which the doctrine is applied, there is always some mutual right of control of the vehicle used in the financial venture. If the passenger and the driver are traveling as part of the mutual business enterprise, then the two are engaged in a joint enterprise. As an example, assume that Freeley and Fairley decided to shop for a race horse in which to invest. They decided to travel by pickup truck with horse trailer to the Bluegrass region of their state. Rounding a sharp curve on a steep hill, Freeley lost control of the vehicle, struck a tree, and injured Fairley. Fairley's cause of action against Freeley would be barred by the law of vicarious liability as it applies to joint enterprises. In contrast consider the *Galliher* case involving injury to one passenger of a group going to look at used cars (see Figure 10-13).

Figure 10-13. Case in Point: *Galliher v. Holloway*

GALLIHER v. HOLLOWAY
474 N.E.2d 797
Appellate Court of Illinois
January 28, 1985

HARRISON, Justice:

Appeal is taken from a judgment of the circuit court of Madison County, awarding plaintiff $30,000 for personal injuries. On the evening of January 4, 1981, Melissa Galliher (plaintiff) was riding as a passenger in her automobile when it collided with a vehicle owned by James Holloway (defendant). Plaintiff's vehicle was driven by Kevin Hay (third-party defendant). Paul Edmundston and Stephen Jones were also passengers in plaintiff's automobile. Mr. Edmundston was interested in purchasing an automobile, and the four had journeyed to several locations in order to observe used vehicles.

Defendant's vehicle had stalled on Illinois Route 143. Defendant testified that he had his lights on as he attempted to restart the engine. Plaintiff, third-party defendant, and Stephen Jones testified that they did not observe lights on defendant's automobile. Defendant admitted that his emergency flashers were not activated. The front end of plaintiff's vehicle collided with the rear end of defendant's vehicle, and plaintiff, who was seated in the front passenger seat, was jolted forward into the windshield. Plaintiff sustained injuries to her forehead and mouth. Third-party defendant estimated his speed immediately before the collision at 45 miles per hour. Additional testimony established that defendant occasionally had trouble starting his automobile; however, the vehicle had received substantial repairs two days prior to the accident....

Defendant maintains that, as a matter of law, he was not negligent, and that the trial court erred in submitting the issue for resolution by the jury. Defendant contends that he was confronted with a "sudden mechanical failure." This failure, defendant argues, was the result of a defective condition in defendant's automobile of which defendant had no knowledge; moreover, the defect could not have been discovered by defendant's reasonable inspection of the vehicle. Even if this factual assertion were not subject to dispute, the allegations of defendant's negligent conduct extend to defendant's purported behavior after the mechanical failure occurred. Plaintiff alleged that defendant failed to exercise proper care by defendant's failure to keep his lights on as well as defendant's failure to pull his vehicle off the road. Defendant admitted that, even without the use of his vehicle's power steering, it would have been possible for defendant to remove his vehicle from the highway. Defendant further admitted that he failed to turn on his emergency flashers. These facts, together with the conflicting testimony regarding whether defendant even had his lights activated at the time of the accident, provided factual questions bearing directly on the issue of defendant's negligence. The question was properly submitted to the jury for resolution....

Defendant also contends that the trial court erred in denying defendant's motions for a directed verdict and for judgment notwithstanding the verdict. Defendant's allegation of error rests upon the compound premise that (1) the negligence of third-party defendant, the driver of the vehicle in which plaintiff was a passenger, was the proximate cause of plaintiff's injuries, and (2) that third-party defendant's negligence should be imputed to plaintiff because plaintiff and third-party defendant were engaged in a "joint venture." A joint venture, by virtue of which negligence may be imputed from the driver to occupants of an automobile, exists where driver and occupant are engaged in a journey which is part of a business enterprise in which the parties have a mutual interest.... Defendant argues that a common interest of plaintiff and third-party defendant in helping their friend shop for an automobile, together with third-party defendant's act of purchasing gasoline for plaintiff's vehicle, established the requisite business enterprise. The mere sharing of incidental expenses incurred during the journey does not, however, constitute the business purpose essential to a joint venture; neither may the endeavor of aiding a friend in shopping for an automobile reasonably be considered as such.... The negligence of third-party defendant was not, therefore, imputable to plaintiff under this theory....

For the foregoing reasons, the judgment of the circuit court is affirmed.

The idea of imputing the negligence of the driver to the passenger of a vehicle engaged in a joint enterprise, and not in situations involving only social trips, defies rational explanation. The right of control is a fiction imposed by law, and does not in fact exist in most cases when the passenger realistically has little or no control over the vehicle (see Figure 10-14).

Figure 10-14. Critique

One must seriously doubt the logic and fairness of imposing vicarious responsibility, whether as plaintiff or as defendant, upon the passenger who is engaged in a "joint enterprise," for the negligence of his driver. The contractual agreement by which he is said to enter into such an arrangement is all too obviously a fiction in situations where the parties have merely gotten together for the ride; and upon this there is erected a second fiction, that the passenger shares a "right of control" of the operation of the vehicle; and on this is erected in turn a third fiction, that the driver is his agent or servant. This topheavy structure tends to fall of its own weight.

W. Page Keeton et. al., *Prosser and Keeton on the Law of Torts* § 72 at 522 (5th ed. 1984)

The paralegal student should carefully consider the opportunity for change in the application of the principles of vicarious liability in joint enterprise situations.

AUTOMOBILE OWNERSHIP

Automobile ownership has received special attention in the law of vicarious liability by legal scholars, through the decisions of the various state courts, and by the enactment of state statutes regarding the liability of owners of automobiles. The social and financial impact of numerous automobile collisions has spurred judicial concern and legislative attention. The law of vicarious liability presents an ideal theory upon which the courts and the legislatures may base financial responsibility for damages from automobile use on the individual most able to afford insurance coverage. The net effect is to distribute the cost of automobile collision damages over the class of automobile owners in general.

Automobile Consent Statutes

motor vehicle consent statutes

The law in most states is governed by what are termed **motor vehicle consent statutes**. A motor vehicle consent statute is a legislative enactment imposing vicarious liability on the owner of an automobile for the negligence of those driving the vehicle. These statutes hold an owner liable for injuries to third persons caused by the negligence of any person, whether that person was a member of the family of the owner or not. Liability is limited to the scope of the consent to use the vehicle, which means that the owner is not liable if the vehicle is used beyond the scope of permission. The clear purpose of such legislation is to protect injured persons from the financial irresponsibility of drivers.

Family Purpose Doctrine

family purpose doctrine

Some states still adhere to a doctrine of vicarious liability called the **family purpose doctrine**. Under this theory, also called the family car doctrine, the owner of an automobile is liable for the negligence of a family member allowed to drive the vehicle. The owner is said to be the master of the family member servant who is allowed to drive the vehicle. The driver must be a member of the owner's household and the use must be permissive.

As a practical matter, the doctrine has been abandoned by most states in favor of motor vehicle consent statutes. The paralegal student should carefully review individual state legislation to determine the status of the consent statute.

DRAM SHOP LIABILITY

dram shop acts

Closely related in its application to the law of vicarious liability is the body of law surrounding the liquor liability laws of the individual states, called **dram shop acts**. A dram shop act, or civil liability act as it is sometimes called, is a legislative enactment imposing liability on the seller of alcoholic beverages when a third party is injured as a result of the intoxication of the buyer and the sale has led to the intoxication. The individual state statutes vary as to the basis of liability. Depending upon the state, dram shop liability may be based upon:

- a theory of negligence by creating an unreasonable risk of injury,
- sale of liquor to a minor, or
- the intoxication of the buyer.

In many jurisdictions, the liability is not based upon a *sale* of the liquor, but may exist as a result of merely *furnishing* liquor to one who is already intoxicated. For instance, assume that the Wards invited several close friends to their home to see a video of their recent trip to Qingdao. The Wards served a special Chinese punch with an extremely high alcohol content to the guests as they watched the show. Assume further that one of the guests, Sotto, was intoxicated when he arrived. Failing to appreciate what he was viewing, Sotto became even more intoxicated. Upon leaving the party, he negligently backed his automobile into the Ward's neighbor, causing severe injury. Depending upon the jurisdiction, the Wards could face dram shop liability to their neighbor for the injuries caused by Sotto. Consider the Florida Supreme Court's discussion of the history of the development of dram shop liability in the *Ellis* case (see Figure 10-15).

Figure 10-15. Case in Point: *Ellis v. N.G.N. of Tampa, Inc.*

ELLIS v. N.G.N. OF TAMPA, INC.
586 So.2d 1042
Supreme Court of Florida
September 19, 1991

OVERTON, Justice.

...This case concerns the liability of a vendor of alcoholic beverages for sales to a habitual drunkard. It commenced when Mary Evelyn Ellis filed a complaint alleging that her son, Gilbert Ellis, an alleged habitual drunkard, consumed approximately twenty alcoholic drinks served to him at a bar owned by the respondent N.G.N, of Tampa, Inc. (N.G.N.), and operated by the respondent Norbert G. Nissen. The complaint alleged that, after consuming the drinks, an intoxicated Gilbert Ellis drove his car in a manner that caused it to overturn and crash; that he sustained severe injuries, including permanent brain damage; that he has since been declared incompetent, and his mother, the complainant and petitioner, Mary Evelyn Ellis, is his legal guardian. The complaint against N.G.N. and Nissen seeks compensatory and punitive damages on the grounds that N.G.N, and Nissen served Gilbert Ellis "knowing that [he] was a person addicted to the use of any or all alcoholic beverages."

...To resolve this issue, it is first necessary to review the legal history of the duty placed on a vendor of alcoholic beverages. Prior to 1959, the common law established that a commercial vendor of alcoholic beverages could not be liable for the negligent sale of those beverages when either the purchaser or third persons were injured as a result of their consumption. This common law principle was based on the conclusion that the proximate cause of the injury was the consumption of the intoxicating beverage by the person, rather than the sale of intoxicating beverages to the person and, consequently, there could be no valid claim against a vendor for damages.

A change in this common law principle first occurred in 1959 when the Supreme Court of New Jersey, in *Rappaport v. Nichols*, 31 *N.J.* 188, 156 A.2d 1 (1959), modified this consumption—sale distinction in the common law and, in the words of one commentator, "took upon itself to fill a judicially-perceived vacuum of restraint on commercial vendors of alcoholic beverages."... In *Rappaport*, a tavern owner sold alcoholic beverages to a minor under circumstances in which the vendor knew the purchaser to be a minor. After consuming the alcohol, the minor became intoxicated and killed a third party while driving an automobile. In holding the vendor liable to the deceased's estate, the Supreme Court of New Jersey held:

> [W]e are convinced that recognition of the plaintiff's claim will afford a fairer measure of justice to innocent third parties whose injuries are brought about by the unlawful and negligent sale of alcoholic beverages to minors and intoxicated persons, will strengthen and give greater force to the enlightened statutory and regulatory precautions against such sales and their frightening consequences, and will not place any unjustifiable burdens upon defendants who can always discharge their civil responsibilities by the exercise of due care.

...[T]hese cases emphasize, a major change had occurred in the legal principles governing an alcohol vendor's liability. Under the original doctrine, the vendor was absolved of liability because consumption of the alcohol was considered to be the cause of the conduct and the resulting damages, for which the vendor had no control. After *Rappaport,* ... the critical fact was not consumption but whether, under the circumstances, it was foreseeable that injury or damage would occur after a sale, particularly when sales were made to persons who lacked the ability to make a responsible decision in the consumption of alcohol.

As a result of this judicial trend to extend liability towards vendors of alcoholic beverages, the legislature enacted section 562.51, now section 768.125, Florida Statutes (1989).... The statute effectively codified the original common law rule absolving vendors from liability for sales but provided exceptions for sales to those who were not of a lawful drinking age or to a person habitually addicted to alcoholic beverage use....

In summary,... although limited by the provisions of section 768.125, there is a cause of action against a vendor for the negligent sale of alcoholic beverages to a minor that results in the injury to or death of the minor or a third party. While we have not expressly addressed a case involving a habitual drunkard, we find that the same law applies because: (1) it is an express exception to the statute limiting a vendor's liability, and (2) it is also a sale of alcohol to a class of persons who lack the ability to make a responsible decision in the consumption of alcohol.

Summary

The law of vicarious liability is based upon the relationship between the tortfeasor and his or her employer. The doctrine of *respondeat superior* holds the master liable for the torts of the servant when the servant is acting within the scope of the master–servant relationship. The master may also be held accountable under certain circumstances in an employer–independent contractor relationship for non-delegable duties and inherently dangerous activities. The principles of vicarious liability also control the liability of persons engaged in a joint enterprise involving the use of an automobile. Liability for most automobile-related injuries is controlled by the law of negligence and state automobile consent statutes. Similarly, dram shop liability may arise for the torts of another when the owner of an establishment furnishes alcoholic beverages to one already inebriated. The rationale for the law of vicarious liability is the concept of placing the risk of injury on the party best able to afford it, and who in turn passes on the cost to the consumer. The allocation of risk to the consumer is a recurring theme in modern tort law, recognizing the realities of the modern commercial setting.

Review Questions

1. What is the doctrine of vicarious liability?
2. List the synonymous terms used to describe vicarious liability.
3. Discuss the various theories that support the doctrine of *respondeat superior*.
4. What is the principle of the allocation of risk?
5. List the criteria used in most states to determine the existence of a master–servant relationship.
6. Describe the general rule for intentional torts as applied to the doctrine of vicarious liability.
7. Discuss the concept of an independent contractor.
8. What is the employer's liability for non-delegable duties?
9. List the four elements common to a joint enterprise.
10. What is a dram shop act?

Focus Your Skills

Professional rodeo had joined such elite sporting events as jai alai and professional wrestling with the advent of the Roughstock Riders' Association of America, or the RRAA as it was known by its members. The RRAA was the brainchild of Major Dhomoe after his expulsion from the Women's Wrist Wrestling Federation for using male hormone injections to subvert the integrity of the sport. Searching for a sporting venue that would pit man against beast and offer the frequent and violent disasters previously experienced only at NASCAR events, he found the perfect opportunity in professional rodeo. Limiting the circus to just the bull-riding event treated the fans to eight seconds of action, danger, blood, and an occasional good ride.

Resin Dolte had been on the professional rodeo circuit since he was 16, and now, at the age of 32, was an orthopedic disaster. He had no cartilage left in either knee, had survived two laminectomies [twice survived spinal fusion surgery], and had been gored 13 times. Major Dhomoe thought Resin typified the fading American icon of the rodeo cowboy, and that he was ideal for his RRAA extravaganza, Bulls Royale. The Royale, a traveling rodeo, featured only the bull-riding event. Each extravaganza showcased 25 bull riders who competed for a percentage of the gate as their prize money. Resin Dolte was one of ten regular bull riders who toured with the show, but he received only room and board. Any money he made came from his share of the purse. He had to provide his own bull rope, chaps, and flak vest. The Brahma bulls were provided by a livestock contractor under an agreement with Major Dhomoe and varied at each event. Medical insurance was optional.

On the fateful evening of Friday, October 13, Resin drew the dreaded Scrap Heap in the pre-event lottery. In seven years on the pro rodeo circuit, this blue-ribbon Brahma bull had never been successfully ridden, and had sent 23 feckless, would-be heroes to the orthopedic surgeon. Resin stayed on Scrap Heap for the full eight-second ride but became entangled in his rope. He was freed by the rodeo clowns, but not before Scrap Heap's collision with the arena wall rendered both bull and rider unconscious. For the rest of his life, Resin would see the world through the wrong end of a telescope.

Resin Dolte has contacted your office to file a claim against Major Dhomoe for worker's compensation benefits as an employee of Bulls Royale. Major Dhomoe asserts that he faces no liability because Resin was an independent contractor. Provide your analysis of the criteria to be considered in advising Resin of his status.

11 PRODUCT LIABILITY

Of all inventions, the alphabet and the printing press alone excepted, those inventions which abridge distance have done most for the civilization of our species.

Thomas Babington Macaulay

Product liability refers to various causes of action for injury from the use or sale of a manufactured product based upon one or more theories of recovery: negligence, warranty, strict liability, and statutory. While product liability is often considered a separate tort action, multiple combined tort theories apply to the potential for liability created when a product is placed in the stream of commerce. This chapter demonstrates the operation of those areas of tort law previously considered as they relate to unreasonably dangerous products.

CHAPTER TOPICS

1. History
2. Parties
3. Warranty
4. Negligence
5. Strict Liability
6. Unreasonably Dangerous
7. Defenses
8. Consumer Product Safety

OBJECTIVES

After completing this chapter, you will be able to:

1. Provide a history of the development of the law of product liability.
2. Analyze the various theories of recovery in product liability actions.
3. Determine the proper parties for a product liability action.
4. Discuss the concept of warranty.
5. Summarize the role of the law of negligence in product liability actions.
6. Discuss the role of the law of strict product liability.
7. Analyze the liability of a manufacturer for inherently dangerous products.
8. Summarize the defenses available in an action for product liability.
9. Discuss consumer product safety.

HISTORY

caveat emptor

privity of contract

The law of product liability has profoundly changed since the early nineteenth century. At that time, actions against a manufacturer or seller of a product were governed by the doctrine of ***caveat emptor***, which literally means, "let the buyer beware." The doctrine states that the buyer of a product has the obligation of examining and testing the quality and safety of the product, and will find no legal protection for injuries arising from the product. The courts began to undermine the doctrine by allowing recovery for defective products under a theory of breach of contract or breach of warranty. Individuals who stood in a contractual relationship with the seller or manufacturer of a product were said to have **privity of contract**. Privity of contract is the relationship connecting the parties because a contract exists between them. Previously, any action based upon injuries stemming from a defective product must have been based upon the privity between the parties to succeed. For example, assume that Harrington bought a rifle from Millwright, the local gunsmith. The first time he fired the weapon, it exploded and severely burned his face. Harrington would have been able to maintain an action against Millwright based on the privity of contract that exists between manufacturer and buyer. But, assume that Harrington had loaned the rifle to his neighbor, Grover. Upon firing the rifle, Grover sustained the injury. Under early United States case law, Grover would not have privity of contract, and could not maintain an action against Millwright.

The concept of privity of contract came under attack by various state courts throughout the nineteenth century. Courts began to carve out exceptions to the rule for defective products that were found to be "imminently dangerous." Thus, imminent danger became an exception to the rule requiring privity of contract. Finally, in 1916, in the landmark decision authored by Justice Cardozo, *MacPherson v. Buick Motor Co.*, 217 N.Y. 382, 111 N.E. 1050, the privity of contract doctrine was abandoned. *MacPherson* formed the basis for the modern law of product liability, holding that the law of negligence applied to defective products that were unreasonably dangerous (see Figure 11-1).

Figure 11-1. Case in Point: *MacPherson v. Buick Motor Company*

MACPHERSON v. BUICK MOTOR COMPANY
Court of Appeals of New York
111 N.E. 1050
March 14, 1916

Cardozo, J.

The defendant is a manufacturer of automobiles. It sold an automobile to a retail dealer. The retail dealer resold to the plaintiff. While the plaintiff was in the car, it suddenly collapsed. He was thrown out and injured. One of the wheels was made of defective wood, and its spokes crumbled into fragments. The wheel was not made by the defendant; it was bought from another manufacturer. There is evidence, however, that its defects could have been discovered by reasonable inspection, and that inspection was omitted. There is no claim that the defendant knew of the defect and willfully concealed it.... The charge is one, not of fraud, but of negligence. The question to be determined is whether the defendant owed a duty of care and vigilance to any one but the immediate purchaser.

The foundations of this branch of the law, at least in this state, were laid in *Thomas v. Winchester* (6 N.Y. 397). A poison was falsely labeled. The sale was made to a druggist, who in turn sold to a customer. The customer recovered damages from the seller who affixed the label. "The defendant's negligence," it was said, "put human life in imminent danger." A poison falsely labeled is likely to injure any one who gets it. Because the danger is to be foreseen, there is a duty to avoid the injury. Cases were cited by way of illustration in which manufacturers were not subject to any duty irrespective of contract. The distinction was said to be that their conduct, though negligent, was not likely to result in injury to any one except the purchaser. We are not required to say whether the chance of injury was always as remote as the distinction assumes. Some of the illustrations might be rejected to-day. The principle of the distinction is for present purposes the important thing.

Thomas v. Winchester became quickly a landmark of the law. In the application of its principle there may at times have been uncertainty or even error. There has never in this state been doubt or disavowal of the principle itself....

The defendant argues that things imminently dangerous to life are poisons, explosives, deadly weapons—things whose normal function it is to injure or destroy. But whatever the rule in *Thomas v. Winchester* may once have been, it [is] no longer that restricted....

We hold, then, that the principle of *Thomas v. Winchester* is not limited to poisons, explosives, and things of like nature, to things which in their normal operation are implements of destruction. If the nature of a thing is such that it is reasonably certain to place life and limb in peril when negligently made, it is then a thing of danger. Its nature gives warning of the consequences to be expected. If to the element of danger there is added knowledge that the thing will be used by persons other than the purchaser, and used without new tests then, irrespective of contract, the manufacturer of this thing of danger is under a duty to make it carefully. That is as far as we are required to go for the decision of this case. There must be knowledge of a danger, not merely possible, but probable. It is possible to use almost anything in a way that will make it dangerous if defective. That is not enough to charge the manufacturer with a duty independent of his contract. Whether a given thing is dangerous may be sometimes a question for the court and sometimes a question for the jury. There must also be knowledge that in the usual course of events the danger will be shared by others than the buyer. Such knowledge may often be inferred from the nature of the transaction. But it is possible that even knowledge of the danger and of the use will not always be enough. The proximity or remoteness of the relation is a factor to be considered. We are dealing now with the liability of the manufacturer of the finished product, who puts it on the market to be used without inspection by his customers. If he is negligent, where danger is to be foreseen, a liability will follow. We are not required at this time to say that it is legitimate to go back of the manufacturer of the finished product and hold the manufacturers of the component parts. To make their negligence a cause of imminent danger, an independent cause must often intervene; the manufacturer of the finished product must also fail in his duty of inspection. It may be that in those circumstances the negligence of the earlier members of the series was too remote to constitute, as to the ultimate user, an actionable wrong.... We leave that question open to you. We shall have to deal with it when it arises. The difficulty which it suggests is not present in this case. There is here no break in the chain of cause and effect. In such circumstances, the presence of a known danger, attendant upon a known use, makes vigilance a duty. We have put aside the notion that the duty to safeguard life and limb, when the consequences of negligence may be foreseen, grows out of contract and nothing else. We have put the source of the obligation where it ought not be. We have put its source in the law.

From this survey of the decisions, there thus emerges a definition of the duty of a manufacturer which enables us to measure this defendant's liability. Beyond all question, the nature of an automobile gives warning of probable danger if its construction is defective. This automobile was designed to go fifty miles an hour. Unless its wheels were sound and strong, injury was almost certain. It was as much a thing of danger as a defective engine for a railroad. The defendant knew the danger. It knew also that the care would be used by persons other than the buyer. This was apparent from its size; there were seats for three persons. It was apparent also from the fact that the buyer was a dealer in cars, who bought to resell. The maker of this car supplied it for the use of purchasers from the dealer just as plainly as the contractor in *Devlin v. Smith* supplied the scaffold for use by the servants of the owner. The dealer was indeed the one person of whom it might be said with some approach to certainly that by him the car would not be used. Yet the defendant would have us say that he was the one person whom it was under a legal duty to protect. The law does not lead us to so inconsequent a conclusion. Precedents drawn from the days of travel by stage coach do not fit the conditions of travel today. The principle that the danger must be imminent does not change, but the things subject to the principle do change. They are whatever the needs of life in a developing civilization require them to be....

In England the limits of the rule are still unsettled. *Winterbottom v. Wright* (10 M. & W. 109) is often cited. The defendant undertook to provide a mail coach to carry the mail bags. The coach broke down from latent defects in its construction. The defendant, however, was not the manufacturer. The court held that he was not liable for injuries to a passenger. The case was decided on a demurrer to the declaration.... From these cases a consistent principle is with difficulty extracted. The English courts, however, agree with ours in holding that one who invites another to make use of an appliance is bound to the exercise of reasonable care.... That at bottom is the underlying principle of *Devlin v. Smith*. The contractor who builds the scaffold invites the owner's work-men to use it. The manufacturer who sells the automobile to the retail dealer invites the dealer's customers to use it. The invitation is addressed in the one case to determinate persons and in the other to an indeterminate class, but in each case it is equally plain, and in each its consequences must be the same.

There is nothing anomalous in a rule which imposes upon A, who has contracted with B, a duty to C and D and others according as he knows or does not know that the subject matter of the contract is intended for their use. We may find an analogy in the law which measures the liability of landlords. If A leases to B a tumble-down house he is not liable, in the absence of fraud, to B's guests who enter it and are injured. This is because B is then under the duty to repair it, the lessor has the right to suppose that he will fulfill that duty, and if he omits to do so, his guests must look to him.... But if A leases a building to be used by the lessee at once as a place of public entertainment, the rule is different. There injury to persons other than the lessee is to be foreseen, and foresight of the consequences involves the creation of a duty....

In this view of the defendant's liability there is nothing inconsistent with the theory of liability on which the case was tried. It is true that the court told the jury that "an automobile is not an inherently dangerous vehicle." The meaning, however, is made plain by the context. The meaning is that danger is not to be expected when the vehicle is well constructed. The court left it to the jury to say whether the defendant ought to have foreseen that the car, if negligently constructed, would become "imminently dangerous." Subtle distinctions are drawn by the defendant between things inherently dangerous and things imminently dangerous, but the case does not turn upon these verbal niceties. If danger was to be expected as reasonably certain, there was a duty of vigilance, and this whether you call the danger inherent or imminent.... If there was any error, it was none of which the defendant can complain.

We think the defendant was not absolved from a duty of inspection because it bought the wheels from a reputable manufacturer. It was not merely a dealer in automobiles. It was a manufacturer of automobiles. It was responsible for the finished product. It was not at liberty to put the finished product on the market without subjecting the component parts to ordinary and simple tests.... Under the charge of the trial judge nothing more was required of it. The obligation to inspect must vary with the nature of the thing to be inspected. The more probable the danger, the greater the need of caution.

Following the *MacPherson* decision, United States courts began to extend the principles beyond their application to negligence. By 1962, courts had begun to state that negligence was not required in certain circumstances involving inherently dangerous products, and began to apply a theory of strict liability. The seller of a defective product is liable for any harm regardless of the degree of care, and the concept of privity of contract has been abolished.

Over time, the law of product liability has undergone a complete transformation from the early principle of *caveat emptor*, to the application of the rule expressed in the *Restatement*. The paralegal student must consult local state statutory and case law to determine the status of these principles today. This chapter is devoted to a discussion of the issues that may arise under the law of product liability.

Parties

A fundamental issue in any product liability action involves the identification of the parties to an action. The early cases following the court's decision in *MacPherson* limited the liability of the defendant to clearly foreseeable plaintiffs. In the matter of *Elmore v. American Motors Corp.*, 451 P.2d 84 (1969) the court held that the purpose of strict liability in product liability law was to make the industry responsible for all of the foreseeable harm done by its defective products. The rationale was that the costs would be spread to the public through insurance and pricing practices. The case involved an automobile that veered across the center line and struck the plaintiff's automobile head-on. The court held that a bystander was entitled to as much protection as the consumer. Whether strict liability or negligence, the determination of the proper plaintiff in a product liability action is based upon the issue of foreseeability (see Figure 11-2).

Figure 11-2. Case in Point: *Hampshire v. Ford Motor Company*

HAMPSHIRE v. FORD MOTOR COMPANY
Court of Appeals of Michigan
399 N.W.2d 36
June 9, 1986

PER CURIAM.

Plaintiff filed a products liability action against defendant and now appeals as of right from a grant of summary judgment in defendant's favor. The circuit court ruled that, under California law, defendant did not owe a duty to plaintiff under the facts of this case. We affirm the trial court's grant of summary judgment.

The facts, as alleged by plaintiff, which gave rise to this appeal are relatively simple. On December 17, 1976, plaintiff was driving his 1966 Cadillac on Franklin Avenue in the County of Los Angeles, California. Plaintiff sustained serious injuries when his vehicle was struck head-on by a 1973 Lincoln Continental, manufactured by defendant Ford Motor Company, which had crossed over the center line. Plaintiff's allegations of negligence do not relate to any vehicle parts mechanically involved in the operation of the vehicle on the highways. Rather, plaintiff merely alleges that Ford was negligent in the design of the ignition locking system on the 1973 Lincoln such that it failed to operate as an effective anti-theft device which made Ford vehicles more subject to theft than other types of cars. At the time of the accident in this case, the Lincoln was a stolen car. The car had been stolen several hours prior to the accident. However, the person who stole the car was not the driver at the time of the accident. Rather, the thief had given the car to another person shortly before the accident. Both plaintiff and the driver of the vehicle were residents of the state of California when the accident occurred.

Plaintiff asserted that stolen cars are more likely to be involved in injury-causing collisions with other members of the public. Plaintiff alleged that defects in the ignition locking system encourage car thefts that result in injuries to motorists who are struck by stolen cars. The trial court determined that, under California law, the defendant did not owe a duty to the plaintiff under the facts of this case as alleged by plaintiff. For purposes of defendant's motion for summary judgment, the court assumed that the ignition locking mechanism on the Lincoln did not meet with contemporary technical standards. The court also rejected defendant's argument that there was a lack of proximate cause. We find that the trial court correctly granted summary judgment.

As a preliminary question, we must determine whether California or Michigan substantive law controls this action. We find that California law is applicable....

In regard to the substantive issue of this appeal, plaintiff argues that the trial court erred in determining that California law did not impose a duty on defendant under the facts of this case. We disagree.

A manufacturer's duty to use reasonable care to design a product such that it is reasonably safe for its intended and foreseeable use does not extend to the protection of the whole world. The scope of the duty often depends primarily on whether the injuries to a particular plaintiff are foreseeable....

In granting summary judgment to defendant, the trial court relied on California authority which precludes recovery against the owner of a vehicle when he leaves his keys in his car, the car is stolen and an innocent third party is injured when he is involved in an accident with the stolen vehicle....

The trial court reasoned that, since California law did not recognize a duty under those facts, California would not impose a similar duty on an automobile manufacturer. We agree....

Contrary to the assertion made by plaintiff, the trial court in the present case did not equate Ford's duty as a manufacturer with that of the owner of the vehicle and thereby require plaintiff to establish privity with the manufacturer in order to recover. The lower court merely reasoned that, since California did not impose a duty on the owner of a vehicle to prevent theft for the benefit of third parties, it would therefore not impose a similar duty on the automobile manufacturer under similar circumstances. We are persuaded by this reasoning. Defendant owed no duty to plaintiff in this case. We note that no "special circumstances" exist in this case to alter that conclusion.... No special circumstances have been alleged in this case which are sufficient to withstand summary judgment....

The trial court's grant of summary judgment is affirmed.

Determining the proper defendant in a product liability action depends upon the theory of the case (negligence or strict liability) and the role of the defendant in the commercial transaction. For cases based upon a theory of negligence, liability for a lack of reasonable care attaches to any seller (see Figure 11-3).

Figure 11-3. Negligence

So far as liability for negligence is concerned, there is no longer any doubt that it attaches to any seller of a product, including the maker of a component part of the final product, and an assembler of parts supplied by others, or even a mere processor under contract with the maker. It applies to dealers, whether at wholesale or retail, and to a second-hand dealer who reconditions automobiles for sale. It is obvious that less in the way of care may be required of some of these sellers than of others; but if reasonable care has not been exercised, there may be liability.

W. Page Keeton et. al., *Prosser and Keeton on the Law of Torts* § 100 at 704 (5th ed. 1984)

In cases based upon strict liability theory, liability may vary depending upon the role of the defendant. For instance, while a merchant may be strictly liable for supplying particular goods, a neighbor selling a lawn mower to another would not face liability. The respective roles of the individual defendants vary in that the merchant represents the fitness of the product with an implied warranty, and the neighbor makes no such representation.

Therefore, identifying the parties to a product liability action may present difficult questions for the paralegal student. It is not enough that someone was harmed. A determination of the relationship of the parties is essential to the success of any product liability action. Individual state laws must be consulted for specific situations.

WARRANTY

warranty

Because of the obvious hardships created by the doctrine of *caveat emptor*, there was pressure on nineteenth-century courts to protect the interests of the parties in a commercial transaction. As a result, a theory of recovery based upon the concept of **warranty** was developed. A warranty is an assurance by one party in a commercial transaction to another that some fact is true, and upon which the other may rely. It can result from an express statement concerning the goods sold in a commercial transaction, or from the implied warranty inherent in a sale of goods.

The law of warranty today is statutory in nature and is found in the Uniform Commercial Code of every state. The U.C.C. defines several types of warranty, chief among which are:

- express warranty—a promise stated as part of the sales transaction, U.C.C. § 2-313; and
- implied warranty—a promise arising as a matter of law creating a warranty of merchantability or fitness for a particular purpose, U.C.C. § 2-314, 2-315.

While treatises on the U.C.C. fully cover its warranty provisions, the paralegal student should be aware of the basic concepts. An express warranty involves an objective statement, assurance, or promise of some fact that is relied upon by the purchaser of goods. Implied warranties concern statutorily imposed liability for particular goods. A warranty of merchantability refers to the merchantable quality of goods bought from a merchant dealing in those particular goods, while the warranty of fitness for a particular purpose of the buyer exists when that particular purpose is made known to the seller who then furnishes suitable goods. The paralegal student should consult the Uniform Commercial Code of his or her state to determine the application of the principles to specific fact situations.

NEGLIGENCE

The *MacPherson* case forever changed the law of product liability based upon a theory of negligence. Today, in virtually every state, substantial harm is to be anticipated if defective products are placed in the stream of commerce. A seller is liable for negligence in the manufacture or sale of any defective product that may reasonably be anticipated to be capable of inflicting harm. Manufacturers and sellers are required to exercise the level of care expected of a reasonably prudent person under the same circumstances (see Figure 11-4).

Figure 11-4. Failure to Warn

One who supplies directly or through a third person a chattel for another to use is subject to liability to those whom the supplier should expect to use the chattel with the consent of the other or to be endangered by its probable use, for physical harm caused by the use of the chattel in the manner for which and by a person for whose use it is supplied, if the supplier

(a) knows or has reason to know that the chattel is or is likely to be dangerous for the use for which it is supplied, and

(b) has no reason to believe that those for whose use the chattel is supplied will realize its dangerous condition, and

(c) fails to exercise reasonable care to inform them of its dangerous condition or of the facts which make it likely to be dangerous.

Restatement (Second) of Torts § 388

Defendants in product liability cases may be found to be liable for negligence in such situations as:

- creating or failing to discover a flaw in the product,
- failing to adequately warn about a risk or hazard in the way a product is designed, or
- sale of a defectively designed product.

Liability for negligence in the creation or failure to discover a flaw in the product is based upon a lack of reasonable care to avoid unintended dangers. The mere existence of the flaw is not necessarily negligence, unless the defendant has not met the standard of reasonableness. Liability for failure to warn has received treatment in the *Restatement* (see Figure 11-5).

Figure 11-5. Negligent Manufacture

A manufacturer who fails to exercise reasonable care in the manufacture of a chattel which, unless carefully made, he should recognize as involving an unreasonable risk of causing physical harm to those who use it for a purpose for which the manufacturer should expect it to be used and to those whom he should expect to be endangered by its probable use, is subject to liability for physical harm caused to them by its lawful use in a manner and for a purpose for which it is supplied.

Restatement (Second) of Torts § 395

Manufacturers and sellers are liable for a failure to warn of a known hazard or defect in the product design related to its intended use. Defendants can be found negligent if no warning was given, the warning was inadequate, or the means of warning was insufficient. As an example, assume that Quentin Sporting Goods sells a Dragon Slayer Slingshot to Billings, who has stated that he intends to give it to his son for his birthday. The sling, if pulled beyond its designed range, may break. No warning accompanied the sale of the slingshot to Billings, who gave the Dragon Slayer to his son, Little Bill. The first time that Little Bill pulled the sling as far back as his arm would allow, the sling broke and injured Little Bill. Quentin Sporting Goods and the manufacturer of the Dragon Slayer face liability for negligence for a failure to warn of a defect.

There are some circumstances whereby liability for negligence will also attach to sale of a defectively designed product even when a warning has been given. Although a seller may do all that is possible to warn of the defects in a product, the seller may still face liability if a reasonable person could foresee a reasonable risk of harm. In such cases, foreseeability outweighs the utility of the product, and borders upon a theory of strict liability. Consider the Tenth Circuit's application of Kansas law in the case of a defectively designed handgun (see Figure 11-6).

Figure 11-6. Case in Point: *Johnson v. Colt Industries Operating Corporation*

JOHNSON v. COLT INDUSTRIES OPERATING CORPORATION
United States Court of Appeals, Tenth Circuit
797 F.2d 1530
July 28, 1986

TIMBERS, Circuit Judge

Colt Industries Operating Corporation ("appellant") appeals from a judgment entered January 18, 1985 upon a jury verdict in favor of Francis Paul Johnson ("appellee") in the District of Kansas, Dale E. Saffels, District Judge. The jury found appellant liable for the injuries sustained by appellee and his wife when his handgun manufactured by appellant accidently discharged after being dropped. The jury awarded appellee $850,000 in compensatory damages and $1,250,000 in punitive damages.... We summarize only those facts believed necessary to an understanding of the issues raised on appeal.

In May 1974 appellee purchased a .22 caliber Colt single action revolver from a gun store near his home town of Junction City, Kansas. The gun had been manufactured by appellant in 1969 and sold to the gun store in that year. The gun model was the famous Colt "six-shooter," first produced by appellant in 1873. The gun model has achieved a certain notoriety as a result of its association with the Old West and the United States Army. Appellant has not altered the design of the gun model significantly since its inception. The gun has a revolving cylinder with six chambers that accept six bullets. The gun has an exposed hammer that must be cocked manually before each shot is fired. Appellee, an experienced handler of guns, testified that he purchased the gun for personal protection.

On July 31, 1981 appellee took the gun with him on a fishing trip to a nearby creek. While appellee was seated on a rock in the creek the gun fell from its holster and struck the rock. The impact caused the gun to discharge. The bullet entered appellee's right buttock and lodged in his bladder. Although surgery was successful in removing the bullet, appellee's doctor testified that the bullet had traumatized certain nerves and rendered appellee permanently impotent. Appellee and his wife testified to the detrimental effect this injury had on their marriage and appellee's life in general.

Why the gun fired upon impact was not in question. Both parties' expert witnesses testified that exposed hammer single action revolvers expose the user to a hazard known as "drop-fire." Drop-fire occurs when the gun is carried with a bullet in the chamber over which the hammer rests. In this situation, regardless of the cock position of the hammer, a sharp blow to the hammer, such as when the gun is dropped and lands hammer first, will cause the gun to discharge. When appellee's gun discharged, all six chambers were loaded but the hammer was uncocked.

On May 12, 1982 appellee commenced the instant diversity action in the district court. Appellee alleged that appellant was liable for his injuries because of the defective design of the gun. The complaint sounded in negligence, strict products liability and breach of warranty. Appellee's theory of the case was that the gun was unreasonably dangerous when fully loaded because of the drop-fire hazard.

The case was tried before Judge Saffels and a jury from January 7 to January 18, 1985. Viewing the evidence in the light most favorable to appellee, as we must, appellee established through expert testimony that the design of the gun rendered it unsafe in any hammer position if the gun was carried with a bullet in the chamber under the hammer. The evidence showed that, even if the hammer was in the "safety" position when fully loaded, a sharp blow to the hammer would cause the gun to discharge....

Appellant argues that the district court erred in instructing the jury on appellant's duty of care in designing and manufacturing the gun. The court charged the jury in relevant part:

> "A manufacturer of firearms has the duty to exercise the highest degree of care in the design of the product so that it will be reasonably safe for the use for which it was intended or which can reasonably be anticipated. Failure to fulfill this duty constitutes negligence."

Appellant claims that it should have been held only to a duty of reasonable care and not to the "highest degree of care." This claim is without merit. In Kansas, as in most states, one who engages in dangerous activities is held to a higher standard of care to avoid negligence liability.... It requires little imagination to include gun manufacturing in this category of dangerous activities. The court's instruction therefore fairly stated Kansas negligence law. Likewise, in a recent strict products liability case the Kansas Supreme Court stated that "we also think that the duty of the manufacturer must be commensurate with the seriousness of the danger. The greater the danger, the greater the duty."...

It is entirely reasonable to believe that the Kansas courts would hold the manufacturers of deadly hand guns to the most exacting duty of care.

We hold that the court properly instructed the jury on appellant's duty of care....

Kansas tort law provides a remedy and a punishment for unreasonably dangerous defectively designed products that injure consumers while in normal use. Since appellee convinced a properly instructed jury of the gun's defective design and appellant's indifference to the known risk of drop-fire, the judgment must stand.

Strict Liability

The application of the principles of strict liability, discussed in detail in Chapter 12, to the law of product liability originated in the common law. In early decisions, strict liability was applied to those engaged in the business of selling food intended for human consumption. Sellers were held to a higher degree of responsibility for their products, and in fact became the insurers of their product. In the 1913 landmark decision of *Mazetti v. Armour & Co.* (see Figure 11-7), the Supreme Court of Washington departed from the general rule that a supplier of goods was not liable in the absence of negligence.

Figure 11-7. Case in Point: *Mazetti v. Armour & Co.*

MAZETTI v. ARMOUR & CO.
Supreme Court of Washington
135 P. 633
October 8, 1913

CHADWICK, J.

The complaint alleges that the plaintiffs were operating a profitable restaurant in the city of Seattle, and dealing with the general public as their patrons; that defendant Armour & Co. is engaged in the business of manufacturing and selling to the public generally meats and products to be used as food; that it maintains a place of business in Seattle, Wash., from which it sells and distributes its goods, representing and holding out to the general public that its goods are pure, wholesome, and fit food for human beings; that on June 16, 1912, plaintiffs, in the usual course and conduct of their business, purchased from the Seattle Grocery Company a carton of cooked tongue, prepared and ready to be used for food without further cooking or labor; that such package had been manufactured and prepared by defendant Armour & Co.; that the carton or container bore its name, and that it was purchased to be sold to plaintiffs' customers; that in making such purchase plaintiffs relied upon the representations of Armour & Co. that said food was pure and wholesome and fit for food; that Armour & Co. were guilty of negligence in manufacturing and preparing the foods purchased, in that in the center of the carton was a foul, filthy, nauseating, and poisonous substance; that in the due course of trade plaintiffs served to one of their patrons a portion of the tongue; that the patron ate of it; that he then and there became sick and nauseated, and did then and there in the presence of other persons publicly expose and denounce the service to him of such foul and poisonous food; that the incident became known to the public generally; that plaintiffs had no knowledge or means of knowing the character of the food served; that its condition could not be discovered until it was served for use—all to the damage of the plaintiffs, etc., for loss of reputation, business, and lost profits during the life of their lease. Defendants demurred to the complaint. The demurrer of Armour & Co. was sustained, and plaintiffs have appealed.

It has been accepted as a general rule that a manufacturer is not liable to any person other than his immediate vendee; that the action is necessarily one upon an implied or express warranty, and that without privity of contract no suit can be maintained; that each purchaser must resort to his immediate vendor. To this rule certain exceptions have been recognized: (1) Where the thing causing the injury is of a noxious or dangerous kind. (2) Where the defendant has been guilty of fraud or deceit in passing off the article. (3) Where the defendant has been negligent in some respect with reference to the sale or construction of a thing not imminently dangerous.

Within one of these exceptions is to be found the reason for holding the manufacturer of patent or proprietary medicines to answer at the suit of the ultimate consumer. Direct actions are allowed in such cases because the manufacturer of medicines is generally shrouded in mystery, and sometimes, if not generally, they contain poisons which may produce injurious results. They are prepared by the manufacturer for sale and distribution to the general public, and one purchasing them has a right to rely upon the implied obligation of the manufacturer that he will not use ingredients which if taken in prescribed doses will bring harmful results....

Another exception—the doctrine is comparatively recent—is referable to the modern method of preparing food for use by the consumer, and the more general and ever-increasing use of prepared food products.... Although the cases differ in their reasoning, all agree that there is a liability in such cases irrespective of any privity of contract in the sense of immediate contract between the parties.

Indeed, we understand that respondent does not claim that the ultimate consumer, the person who ate the unfit food, would be denied a right of recovery under modern authority; but it is strenuously contended that such actions are sustained because the consumer has been injured in health and comfort, that the exception should not be carried to the extent of allowing a retailer of the goods to sue direct and recover for injury to his business and loss of reputation, that in such cases there must still be privity of contract. It seems that the test should not rest in finding the plaintiff's damage in health or business, but in answering the question whether there has been a damage which may be justly attributed to the negligence or a breach of duty on the part of the one who had power and whose duty it was to prevent the wrong....

The suit was brought by the retailer against his immediate vendor, so that we still have to meet the question of whether the retailer who has lost his trade can sue over the head of his immediate vendor, or join him with the manufacturer as in this case. In the light of modern conditions we see no reason why he should not. He has been damaged. He and all others who in the course of trade handled the unwholesome goods purchased them relying upon the name and reputation of the manufacturer. The goods were designed for ultimate consumption by an individual patron, and packed to facilitate and make convenient such resales as might be made pending ultimate consumption. Every tradesman, whether wholesaler or retailer, is in a sense a consumer, for he buys to resell. In a way he risks his reputation. He stakes it upon either an express warranty, as printed on the package, or an implied warranty that the goods are wholesome and fit for food. He is injured by the fault or a breach of duty of the manufacturer, for his immediate vendor, like himself, has no way to test every sealed package....

Now, under all authority the immediate vendor would be liable upon one theory or another to the consumer. This being so, it should not be held that the vendor could not sue the manufacturer except to recoup against a judgment. He might thus be left without remedy....

To the old rule that a manufacturer is not liable to third persons who have no contractual relations with him for negligence in the manufacture of an article should be added another exception, not one arbitrarily worked by the courts, but arising, as did the three to which we have heretofore alluded, from the changing conditions of society. An exception to a rule will be declared by courts when the case is not an isolated instance, but general in its character, and the existing rule does not square with justice. Under such circumstances a court will, if free from the restraint of some statute, declare a rule that will meet the full intendment of the law. No case has been cited that is squarely in point with the instant case; but there is enough in the adjudged cases to warrant us in our conclusion.

The facts stated in the complaint are admitted by demurrer. Plaintiffs have been injured. No other person or firm had an opportunity to check the offensive package after it was sealed and sent on its way. Right and reason demand that any party injured should have a right of recovery against the first offender without resorting to that circumlocution of action against intervening agents,... which is demanded where the product as well as the market is open, and the rule of caveat emptor should in justice apply.

Plaintiff's argument is also based on the pure food law. It is contended that the negligence of defendant is presumed if a violation of the pure food law be shown. This is admitted as a general proposition by defendant; but it says that the rule applies only where the statute was intended for the benefit of the party who brings the suit; that the pure food laws are intended for the benefit of the consumer alone.

This opinion is already too long drawn out, and we are not disposed to go into this phase of the case, except to say that it seems to us that the plaintiffs would not be barred by the argument made by defendant. The consumer purchases prepared food products to sustain life and health. The retailer purchases the same products, depending upon established brands to sustain his reputation as a dealer in clean and wholesome food. We would be disposed to hold on this question that, where sealed packages are put out, and it is made to appear that the fault, if any, is that of the manufacturer, the product was intended for the use of all those who handle it in trade as well as those who consume it. Our holding is that, in the absence of an express warranty of quality, a manufacturer of food products under modern conditions impliedly warrants his goods when dispensed in original packages, and that such warranty is available to all who may be damaged by reason of their use in the legitimate channels of trade.

We regard this case, in so far as the dealer is permitted to sue the manufacturer, as one of first impression. We think the complaint states a cause of action.

The *Mazetti* case eliminated the requirement of privity of contract between the consumer and the seller, and made the seller strictly liable for the quality of the food products.

Since 1950, decisions have extended liability beyond sellers of food products. In 1958, the Michigan Supreme Court issued its decision in the matter of *Spence v. Three Rivers Builders & Masonry Supply*, 90 N.W.2d 873, extending the rule to apply to a seller of cinder blocks. The court found the seller of the blocks liable for the collapse of the plaintiff's home on a theory of warranty without finding privity of contract or negligence. Recent decisions have extended the principles of strict liability to apply to any defective product causing physical harm. Since the court's decision in *Greenman v. Yuba Power Products, Inc.* in 1963, nearly all courts have adopted the principles of strict liability in tort for product liability (see Figure 11-8).

Figure 11-8. Case in Point: *Greenman v. Yuba Power Products, Inc.*

GREENMAN v. YUBA POWER PRODUCTS, INC.
377 P.2d 897
Supreme Court of California
January 24, 1963

TRAYNOR, Justice.

Plaintiff brought this action for damages against the retailer and the manufacturer of a Shopsmith, a combination power tool that could be used as a saw, drill, and wood lathe. He saw a Shopsmith demonstrated by the retailer and studied a brochure prepared by the manufacturer. He decided he wanted a Shopsmith for his home workshop, and his wife bought and gave him one for Christmas in 1955. In 1957 he bought the necessary attachments to use the Shopsmith as a lathe for turning a large piece of wood he wished to make into a chalice. After he had worked on the piece of wood several times without difficulty, it suddenly flew out of the machine and struck him on the forehead inflicting serious injuries. About ten and a half months later, he gave the retailer and the manufacturer written notice of claimed breaches of warranties and filed a complaint against them alleging such breaches and negligence.

After a trial before a jury, the court ruled that there was no evidence that the retailer was negligent or had breached any express warranty and that the manufacturer was not liable for the breach of any implied warranty. Accordingly, it submitted to the jury only the cause of action alleging breach of implied warranties against the retailer and the causes of action alleging negligence and breach of express warranties against the manufacturer. The jury returned a verdict for the retailer against plaintiff and for plaintiff against the manufacturer in the amount of $65,000. The trial court denied the manufacturer's motion for a new trial and entered judgment on the verdict. The manufacturer and plaintiff appeal. Plaintiff seeks a reversal of the part of the judgment in favor of the retailer, however, only in the event that the part of the judgment against the manufacturer is reversed.

Plaintiff introduced substantial evidence that his injuries were caused by defective design and construction of the Shopsmith. His expert witnesses testified that inadequate set screws were used to hold parts of the machine together so that normal vibration caused the tailstock of the lathe to move away from the piece of wood being turned permitting it to fly out of the lathe. They also testified that there were other more positive ways of fastening the parts of the machine together, the use of which would have prevented the accident. The jury could therefore reasonably have concluded that the manufacturer negligently constructed the Shopsmith. The jury could also reasonably have concluded that statements in the manufacturer's brochure were untrue, that they constituted express warranties, and that plaintiff's injuries were caused by their breach....

Moreover, to impose strict liability on the manufacturer under the circumstances of this case, it was not necessary for plaintiff to establish an express warranty.... A manufacturer is strictly liable in tort when an article he places on the market, knowing that it is to be used without inspection for defects, proves to have a defect that causes injury to a human being. Recognized first in the case of unwholesome food products, such liability has now been extended to a variety of other products that create as great or greater hazards if defective.

Although in these cases strict liability has usually been based on the theory of an express or implied warranty running from the manufacturer to the plaintiff, the abandonment of the requirement of a contract between them, the recognition that the liability is not assumed by agreement but imposed by law,... and the refusal to permit the manufacturer to define the scope of its own responsibility for defective products make clear that the liability is not one governed by the law of contract warranties but by the law of strict liability in tort. Accordingly, rules defining and governing warranties that were developed to meet the needs of commercial transactions cannot properly be invoked to govern the manufacturer's liability to those injured by their defective products unless those rules also serve the purposes for which such liability is imposed.

We need not recanvass the reasons for imposing strict liability on the manufacturer.... The purpose of such liability is to insure that the costs of injuries resulting from defective products are borne by the manufacturers that put such products on the market rather than by the injured persons who are powerless to protect themselves. Sales warranties serve this purpose fitfully at best.... In the present case, for example, plaintiff was able to plead and prove an express warranty only because he read and relied on the representations of the Shopsmith's ruggedness contained in the manufacturer's brochure. Implicit in the machine's presence on the market, however, was a representation that it would safely do the jobs for which it was built. Under these circumstances, it should not be controlling whether plaintiff selected the machine because of the statements in the brochure, or because of the machine's own appearance of excellence that belied the defect lurking beneath the surface, or because he merely assumed that it would safely do the jobs it was built to do. It should not be controlling whether the details of the sales from manufacturer to retailer and from retailer to plaintiff's wife were such that one or more of the implied warranties of the sales act arose.... To establish the manufacturer's liability it was sufficient that plaintiff proved that he was injured while using the Shopsmith in a way it was intended to be used as a result of a defect in design and manufacture of which plaintiff was not aware that made the Shopsmith unsafe for its intended use....

The judgment is affirmed.

The rationale is that when the seller has marketed a product for use and consumption, he or she has undertaken a special responsibility toward the consumer. The consuming public has a right to expect the seller to stand behind the goods, and demands that the cost of any harm be insured by the seller. The *Restatement (Second) of Torts* provides the general rule of liability that is followed in virtually every state today (see Figure 11-9).

Figure 11-9. Strict Liability

(1) One who sells any product in a defective condition unreasonably dangerous to the user or consumer or to his property is subject to liability for physical harm thereby cause to the ultimate user or consumer, or to his property, if

(a) the seller is engaged in the business of selling such a product, and

(b) it is expected to and does reach the user or consumer without substantial change in the condition in which it is sold.

(2) The rule stated in Subsection (1) applies although

(a) the seller has exercised all possible care in the preparation and sale of his product, and

(b) the user or consumer has not bought the product from or entered into any contractual relation with the seller.

Restatement (Second) of Torts § 402 A

Two provisions in the U.C.C. afford sellers some relief by mitigating the principles of strict liability. The first is the requirement that the consumer may not recover on a theory of warranty without first providing the seller with notice within a reasonable period of time after he or she knows or should know of a breach (§ 2-607). This provision protects the seller from delayed claims for damages. The second provision allows disclaimers by the seller that may defeat a warranty (§ 2-316). The seller is free to assert in a contract that he or she does not warrant the product, or limits the warranty in some way. In practice, disclaimers are usually construed to benefit the consumer by courts finding that they were not presented in a clear manner to the plaintiff.

Rule 402A of the *Restatement* applies to products that are unreasonably dangerous to the consumer from the point when these items leave the seller's control. If the seller delivers the product in a safe condition, and it is later somehow modified, then the seller is no longer responsible. For instance, assume that Evergreen Lawn Care offered the brand new model of the Excalibur Reel Mower, complete with safety foot guards to prevent an accidental injury to the operator's foot while mowing. Mr. Handler purchased his new Excalibur from Evergreen, and promptly removed the guards before his wife used the mower. The first time Mrs. Handler operated the mower, now lacking the safety devices, she sustained a serious injury. Evergreen would not be liable to Mrs. Handler in light of the alterations by Mr. Handler. The burden of proof is on the plaintiff to establish the fact that the product was in an unsafe condition at the time it left the seller. The same defense is available to the seller if the property is not used in the manner for which it was designed.

Unreasonably Dangerous

Today, in virtually every jurisdiction, a seller of a defective product that is "in a defective condition unreasonably dangerous to the user or consumer" faces liability for any harm to person or property resulting from that defect whether on a theory of warranty or strict liability in tort. This is the rule set forth in § 402A of the *Restatement*, and is the operative phrase in establishing the seller's liability. Inquiry need not be directed to either the manufacturer or the seller, but is directed toward the defective product itself. A product is defective if it exposes an individual to an unreasonable risk of harm (see Figure 11-10).

Figure 11-10. Unreasonably Dangerous

This simply means that the product must be defective in the kind of way that subjects persons or tangible property to an unreasonable risk of harm.... A product is defective as marketed in the kind of way that makes it unreasonably dangerous for any of the following reasons: (1) a flaw in the product that was present in the product at the time the defendant sold it; (2) a failure by the producer or assembler of a product adequately to warn of a risk or hazard related to the way the product was designed; or (3) a defective design.

W. Page Keeton et. al., *Prosser and Keeton on the Law of Torts* § 99 at 695 (5th ed. 1984)

As Professor Keeton notes, a product may be considered defective in a manner that is unreasonably dangerous in one of three ways:

- a flaw in the product at the time of sale,
- a failure to warn of a risk, or
- a defective design.

The rule contemplates that the product must be dangerous beyond an ordinary consumer's expectations. For instance, a certain brand of alcoholic beverage is not dangerous merely because it can result in drunkenness with overuse, but an alcoholic beverage containing petroleum oil would be dangerous to all consumers. Liability arises when the product is unsafe for its ordinary use.

Flaw in the Product

Any unintentional condition that makes a product more dangerous can be considered a flaw in the product sufficient to create product liability. The product is considered defective as a matter of law because it is manufactured in a manner more dangerous than designed. The manufacturer and seller marketing a product with a design flaw are subject to liability for any harm caused by that flaw. The seller may not have been negligent at all in the process of creating or failing to discover the flaw in the product.

The ability of an injured consumer to pursue an action in product liability without having to prove negligence has made recovery available to victims. The inquiry by a trier of fact need only be directed to a determination that the product was flawed in a manner that made it more dangerous than it otherwise would have been. At that point, the jury may conclude that the product was unreasonably dangerous as a matter of law (see Figure 11-11).

Figure 11-11. Case in Point: *Paducah Coca-Cola Bottling Company v. Harris*

PADUCAH COCA-COLA BOTTLING COMPANY v. HARRIS
Court of Appeals of Kentucky
316 S.W.2d 128
April 25, 1958

CULLEN, Commissioner.

Tony Harris recovered judgment upon a jury verdict for $12,500 against the Paducah Coca-Cola Bottling Company, as damages for loss of the sight of his right eye resulting from the explosion of a bottle of Coca-Cola. The bottling company has appealed, contending that it was entitled to a directed verdict, and that the instructions were erroneous.

Harris purchased a case of mixed soft drinks, including a dozen Coca-Colas, from a country store. He placed the case in the trunk of his automobile and drove to his place of employment. Upon arrival there he opened the trunk and set the case of drinks on the ground. He then went into a nearby shack and brought out a wooden keg, which the workers customarily used as a receptacle for cooling soft drinks. The keg was empty. Harris picked up two Coca-Cola bottles between the fingers of one hand and set them in the keg. He testified that he did not drop or strike the bottles against anything while he was placing them in the keg. As he 'started to raise up,' one of the bottles exploded and particles of glass struck him in the eye. The bottle separated diagonally into two main pieces, one being the top one-third, with the cap still intact, and the other being the bottom two-thirds. The pieces were preserved and were introduced in evidence on the trial.

An expert witness for the plaintiff, having suitable qualifications, testified that in his opinion, based upon an examination of the pieces of the bottle in question and upon experiments he had conducted with other Coca-Cola bottles, the explosion of the bottle in question was due to internal pressure, and not to external impact; that the smooth break lines 'would indicate a default' in the bottle; and that the fault or [defect] could have been discovered by rotating the bottle with a light behind it.

Two expert witnesses for the defendant, also suitably qualified, testified that from their examination of the pieces of the broken bottle it was clear that the explosion was the result of external impact; that when a bottle breaks as the result of impact it breaks immediately upon the impact; that the maximum internal pressure that can be built up in a bottle of Coca-Cola, even at a temperature of 100 degrees and with violent agitation of the bottle, is 85 pounds per square inch, and a normal, sound Coca-Cola bottle will not break from internal pressure unless the pressure exceeds 500 pounds per square inch; that if a bottle was structurally defective or cracked at the time it was passing through the defendant's bottling machinery it would be broken by the capping machine.

Other evidence for the defendant was that the defendant's inspection procedures and devices were such that cracked, chipped or scuffed bottles would be discovered and rejected.

It is the contention of the bottling company that the plaintiff failed to prove that the bottle was in a defective condition when it was in the control of the company, or that the bottling operation was negligently conducted, and that the plaintiff cannot rely upon *res ipsa loquitur* because he failed to establish the 'integrity' of the bottle.... The plaintiff maintains that he is not relying upon *res ipsa loquitur*, and that his proof established actual negligence.

If there had been any evidence introduced to show that a filled bottle of Coca-Cola may as a result of rough handling, or even as a result of deliberate tampering, be cracked or structurally weakened so that at some later time it will explode from only a slight impact or movement, there would be a good basis for the appellant's argument.... The appellant's evidence precludes any possibility of the explosion being the result of tampering or rough handling between the time the bottle left the appellant's plant and the time it was purchased by the appellee.

Since the bottle did break, according to the evidence, without any material external impact at the time, and since the evidence was that a sound bottle could not break from internal pressure even though hot and violently agitated, the conclusion is reasonable that the bottle was defective when it was filled by the appellant bottling company. The question then remains as to whether the bottling company was negligent in not discovering the defect.

The evidence for the bottling company was that its inspection procedures and devices were designed to disclose cracked or chipped bottles, and that a substantial number of such bottles were discovered and rejected each day. The testimony of the plaintiff's expert witness was that a structural flaw in a bottle, such as in his opinion existed in the bottle in question, could have been discovered if the bottles were revolved when passing the inspection point, and particularly if the conveyor belt was operated more slowly. There was no evidence for the company that causing the bottles to revolve or move more slowly on the conveyor belt would be unreasonably burdensome.

...The evidence here would warrant the conclusion that there was a failure of duty on the part of the bottling company, either in the form of an omission of duty by an inspector or in the form of inadequate inspection procedures and devices.

It is our opinion that the defendant was not entitled to a directed verdict. The instructions imposed upon the defendant the duty of exercising the "highest degree of care" in its bottling operations, defined to mean "the highest degree of care usually exercised by ordinarily careful and prudent manufacturers" of such products. The appellant maintains that its duty was only to exercise ordinary care, and that the instruction therefore was erroneous....

Since the normal consumer use of a Coca-Cola bottle involves close contact with hands and face, we think it is obvious that the risk of danger of personal injury from explosion of the bottle is extremely high. The manufacturer's duty of care is commensurate with the risk. Accordingly, the manufacturer of Coca-Cola has the duty to exercise the greatest care to guard against defects that might cause explosion.... The instruction given in the case now before us was not technically correct; however, its error was not in imposing the highest degree of care upon the defendant, but in using the standards of other manufacturers as the measure. This could not have been prejudicial to the defendant.

The judgment is affirmed.

Failure to Warn

A product may be found to be unreasonably dangerous as a matter of law because of a failure to warn of a risk or hazard related to the design of the product. The plaintiff must prove negligence on the part of the manufacturer in the design of the product. He or she must show that the manufacturer knew, or should have known, of the design defect and failed to issue a warning.

Liability for failure to warn departs from pure negligence theory when the target defendant is the seller rather than the manufacturer. If the manufacturer has marketed a defectively designed product without a warning, the seller is also liable to the consumer for a failure to warn of the defect. All persons in the marketing chain are liable on a theory of strict liability without the proof of negligence on their part.

Defective Design

Proof that a product is unreasonably dangerous in product liability cases involves an interpretation of the meaning of the term *defect* as it applies to design hazards. In order for liability to exist for the manufacture or sale of an unreasonably dangerous product, the plaintiff must prove a defect. Two specific tests are utilized by the courts to determine design hazards:

- Consumer contemplation test—A product is defectively dangerous if it is dangerous to an extent beyond that which would be contemplated by the ordinary consumer who purchased it with the ordinary knowledge common to the community.
- Risk-utility test—A product is unreasonably dangerous under this test if the magnitude of the danger outweighs the utility of the product (see Figure 11-12).

Figure 11-12. Consumer Contemplation Test

In an effort to expand the scope of liability and protection to non-purchasers, many courts have substituted "ordinary user" or "foreseeable user" for "ordinary purchaser" thereby making it possible for victims to recover if the hazard was of a kind that would not have been contemplated by reasonably foreseeable users even though it was one that would have been contemplated by the ordinary purchaser-consumer.

W. Page Keeton et. al., *Prosser and Keeton on the Law of Torts*
§ 99 at 698 (5th ed. 1984)

The courts have considered other tests in an attempt to define a defect as it relates to an unreasonably dangerous product. The tests have involved an application of the principles of both negligence theory and strict liability to produce a favorable result for the consumer. The paralegal student must consult individual state laws to ascertain how products are determined to be defective. Any conclusion regarding the unreasonably dangerous nature of a product will turn on a flaw in the product, a failure to warn, or a defective design.

Defenses

The plaintiff's burden of proving all of the elements necessary to sustain a verdict in a product liability action is substantial. He or she must show harm attributable to a defectively dangerous product by proving the following:

- harm from a defective product provided by the target defendant,
- a dangerously defective product,

- a defect in existence at the time the plaintiff took possession of the product,
- a defective condition that was the proximate cause of the harm.

The plaintiff need not prove that the target defendant was negligent in selling a defective product in an unreasonably dangerous condition. It is sufficient that the product was defective enough to cause a breach of warranty or unreasonably dangerous enough to create strict liability in tort.

The defendant is not without a legal argument in product liability cases. Under certain conditions, and depending upon the theory of liability chosen by the plaintiff, the defendant may have one or more defenses available to such actions. The defenses are:

- Contributory negligence—While not a defense in a breach of warranty action, it is available as a defense in cases of extreme misuse of a product; it is not available for a failure to discover a defect.
- Comparative negligence—This is applied in states with comparative negligence statutes in the same manner as a contributory negligence defense.
- Assumption of the risk—When the plaintiff has knowledge of the risk, and voluntarily proceeds to use the product, it is a defense both to a theory of strict liability and in breach of warranty actions.
- Misuse—This is available as a defense only under those circumstances when the misuse was extreme and beyond what should have been contemplated by the defendant.
- Disclaimer of warranty—Disclaimers must be clearly communicated to the purchaser, and are not available as a defense against all ultimate users.
- Notice—This is a valid defense in breach of warranty actions when notice is required within a reasonable time.
- Statutes of limitation—Individual state statutes provide time limitations on maintaining an action for product liability.

Consumer Product Safety

Product liability actions are largely maintained at the state level, which is the case with most tort actions. Each state has developed its own product safety laws to protect its consumers through case law and legislation. The paralegal student should consult individual state statutory and case law for the substantive product liability law of the state.

In an effort to overcome the burdensome system of product liability cases at the state level, and to alleviate the burdens of cost, delay, inequity, and unpredictability, the federal government created the Consumer Product Safety Commission in 1972. The Commission's duty is to protect the public against unreasonable risks of injury occurring from unsafe products. The Commission's goals include:

- developing industry standards,
- issuing and enforcing mandatory standards,
- banning products with substantial or imminent hazards,
- obtaining recall or repair of defective products,
- research on potential hazards, and
- conducting educational programs.

The Consumer Product Safety Act grants the Commission broad authority to enforce product safety standards. The Commission responds to complaints from consumers, investigates unsafe products, and has established the Injury Information Clearinghouse to provide clear and accurate information regarding unsafe products.

SUMMARY

An action for product liability arises out of injuries resulting from using a product that has been placed in the stream of commerce in a defective condition. The action may be based upon a theory of breach of warranty or it may be based upon a theory of strict liability in tort. The law of product liability has advanced substantially since the days of *caveat emptor*, and it now offers the consumer a great deal of protection from products that are unsafe or fail to meet warranted standards. The paralegal student will find this a challenging and constantly evolving area of the law. The future direction of statutory and case law is open to speculation, but laws are clearly moving toward protecting the rights of the ultimate consumers.

REVIEW QUESTIONS

1. What is the meaning of the phrase *caveat emptor*?
2. Discuss the concept of privity of contract.
3. How are the parties to a product liability action determined?
4. Discuss the concept of warranty.
5. In what way is the concept of negligence reflected in the law of product liability?
6. What is the reasoning behind the application of the theory of strict liability in product liability cases?

7. Where can a student locate a general statement as to the state of the law of product liability today?
8. What is meant by the phrase "unreasonably dangerous?"
9. List the traditional defenses to be considered in a product liability action.
10. What was the purpose for establishment of the Consumer Product Safety Commission?

FOCUS YOUR SKILLS

Earnest Birdwell and his wife Emma enjoyed a peaceful existence as caretakers for the estate of J. Ludington Bigelow, one of the founders of the National Manufacturers' Association, a powerful Washington lobby. Perpetuation of the tranquility of the estate ensured sanctuary for many types of wildlife inhabiting the estate's forests and lowlands. While much of the estate was allowed to remain in a natural condition, the neatly manicured perimeter of the property abutted the surrounding woods and wetlands.

Landscape maintenance involved frequent mowing of the extensive lawns, and Earnest felt that the grass should be cut in a manner that was as friendly to the environment as possible. Therefore, on behalf of the estate of Mr. Bigelow, and charged to the account of the estate, Earnest purchased an electric lawn mower, called the Reel Quiet-rider, from Handyman's Hideaway Hardware, owned by Mr. Harley Handy. The Quiet-rider had an owner's manual that was attached to the mower's steering wheel at the time of the purchase. The manual stated in bold print: READ INSTRUCTIONS CAREFULLY BEFORE OPERATING. One of the warnings contained in the manual cautioned against the use of the electric Quiet-rider on extremely wet terrain because of the hazard posed by electric shock.

As a lack of luck would have it, the first time Earnest used the mower on the very wet lawn adjacent to the estate's wetlands area, he received a tremendous electrical shock that almost killed him. He was left confused and perpetually pursuing his own magnetic north.

The Birdwells have contacted your office for advice in maintaining an action for product liability for permanent harm to Earnest. It will be necessary to identify the proper parties to the action, and in turn, identify the theory upon which to base the cause of action. Also, address any defenses the target defendant(s) may have available.

12 STRICT LIABILITY

Man is never watchful enough against the dangers that threaten him every hour.

Horace (B.C. 65–8)

The tort actions considered previously are based upon some negligent or intentional act that interferes with a protected interest of another. The law of strict liability imposes responsibility for harm or damage to an individual or property *without regard* to any intentional or negligent act on the part of the defendant. It is a separate body of tort law serving to protect persons and property from harm from abnormally dangerous things or activities regardless of fault. In order to grasp the concept of strict liability, the paralegal student must first appreciate the theory of fault in both negligence and intentional torts before he or she can recognize the import of liability without fault.

Chapter Topics

1. Liability without Fault
2. Animals
3. Fire
4. Abnormally Dangerous Things
5. Scope of Liability

Objectives

After completing this chapter, you will be able to:

1. Illustrate the development of the law of liability without fault.
2. Discuss the elements of strict liability.
3. Analyze the doctrine of strict liability as applied to animals.
4. Summarize the principles of strict liability as applied to fire.
5. Discuss the nature of abnormally dangerous things.
6. Discuss the scope of strict liability.

Liability without Fault

Early tort law developed through certain writs that were designed to keep the King's peace. Remedies for private recompense restored the injured party to his or her prior status, and in some manner determined standards of conduct. The concept of fault was not an initial element in the law of torts, and only emerged as a condition of moral responsibility in the late nineteenth century. Fault became the basis of liability in tort law with the movement toward identifying standards of conduct expected of responsible members of the community. Thus, tort liability evolved into a fault-based system wherein there was no liability without fault, regardless of whether the conduct of the defendant was either negligent or intentional. Behavior departing from a standard of conduct determined to be reasonable and imposed by law became the basis of liability for individuals causing harm to another's person or property.

A system of liability founded upon the concept of fault is not without inconsistency. As has been seen in a study of the principles of negligence law, fault has not been equated solely with moral responsibility. Morally blameless conduct can form the basis of liability. For instance, if a person trespasses on property mistakenly believing that he or she has permission, even though the error is an honest one, the individual may still be held liable for a trespass. The same may be said of the publisher of a libelous comment who is unaware of the defamatory nature of the statement. Moral blameworthiness is absent, yet the law of tort imposes legal responsibility for the conduct.

In the twentieth century, a doctrine has emerged that holds the defendant liable for conduct involving neither a breach of any moral responsibility on his or her part, nor even a departure from any accepted standard of reasonable conduct. In cases where the defendant's conduct or activity is unusual and the danger to others is abnormally great, he or she will be held responsible for any harm done regardless of the precautions taken. The imposition of tort liability in such situations is based upon a theory of social justice demanding that the cost of an activity must be borne by the person best able to stand the loss. If a defendant chooses to engage in a particular activity, and that intentional behavior exposes those in the vicinity to an unduly great risk, then he or she must bear the cost of any harm caused. The defendant is acting in his or her own enterprise and is in a position to pass along the cost of that enterprise through pricing that spreads the loss among all consumers.

strict liability

Thus emerged the area of tort law termed **strict liability**. Strict liability is merely liability without fault. Also termed absolute liability in reference to the character of the tort as lacking any defense, the term refers to liability without fault or negligence on the part of the defendant. Activities causing an undue risk of harm to the community may result in the imposition of strict tort liability under certain circumstances that do not fall into the category of negligent conduct or intentional torts. The three main categories of activity to which a theory of strict liability is applied are:

- animals,
- fire, and
- abnormally dangerous things.

This chapter explores the concept of strict liability as it relates to the defendant's activities in these areas without fault, negligence, or harmful intent.

ANIMALS

According to the English common law, an owner was strictly liable for any harm his or her animals caused. The rationale was that certain types of animals presented an obvious danger to the community regardless of the care observed by the owner, and the keeper of such animals was required to cover this risk. Today, in most jurisdictions, both statutory enactments and case law have eased this rule. Liability for damage done by animals is based upon the type of animal and the risk represented. Depending upon whether the animal is a domesticated pet, livestock, or a wild animal, the law of a given jurisdiction may vary.

Livestock

Following the common law, most jurisdictions find the owner of livestock liable for the damage done by the animals trespassing on another's property under the rule of strict liability. If an animal is of the type that is likely to roam and do damage, then the keeper of such livestock is strictly liable for the harm caused (see Figure 12-1).

Figure 12-1. Trespassing Livestock

(1) Except as stated in Subsections (3) and (4) a possessor of livestock intruding upon the land of another is subject to liability for the intrusion although he has exercised the utmost care to prevent them from intruding.
(2) The liability stated in Subsection (1) extends to any harm to the land or to its possessor or a member of his household, or their chattels, which might reasonably be expected to result from the intrusion of the livestock.
(3) The liability stated in Subsection (1) does not extend to harm
(a) not reasonably to expected from the intrusion;
(b) done by animals straying onto abutting land while driven on the highway; or
(c) brought about by the unexpectable operation of a force of nature, action or another animal or intentional, reckless or negligent conduct of a third person.
(4) A possessor of land who fails to erect and maintain a fence required by the applicable common law or by statute to prevent the intrusion of livestock, can not recover under the rule stated in Subsection (1).

Restatement (Second) of Torts, § 504

The reasoning behind the application of a theory of strict liability to livestock rests with the ability of the keeper to control the animals. The burden of protecting the community from horses, cattle, pigs, sheep, fowl, and other such livestock should be borne by the owner or keeper, who is in the best position to maintain proper enclosures and insure the risk of loss. It is the owner who is benefitting from the livestock enterprise, and who is thus in a position to pass along the cost of insuring against loss through pricing.

In the western United States, the rule of strict liability for wandering livestock is not applied. Ranchers with grazing cattle on the range have been allowed a great deal of latitude in the eyes of the western courts. With the encroachment of civilization on traditional grazing land, the legislatures of these states have had to address the question statutorily. The statutes of any such jurisdiction must be reviewed to determine the extent, if any, to which the owner of livestock may be liable for the harm done by his or her grazing animals.

Domestic Animals

Most jurisdictions have refused to impose strict liability for domesticated animals such as dogs and cats. The theory is that such animals will do relatively minor harm, and to impose a heavy burden of liability far outweighs the risk represented. Yet the owner of domesticated animals does face liability if the animals have a known propensity for harm. In those situations, liability is based upon a theory of negligence and is imposed for a failure to exercise due care. To be liable, the owner must be aware of a dangerous propensity that is not characteristic of similar animals. For the minor damage occasioned by wandering pets, many jurisdictions have provided a statutory remedy for the resulting property damage.

An animal may be considered domestic in one jurisdiction and wild in another, depending upon the custom of the community. If a particular class of animal has been customarily recognized as a domestic pet, its owner will be afforded greater protection under the law than owners of animals considered non-domestic and inherently dangerous. Domestic animals are those that are customarily devoted to the service of mankind in the jurisdiction where they are maintained.

Wild Animals

Most jurisdictions impose strict liability on the owners of wild animals for any harm caused. Owners of wild animals, regardless of the care exercised, expose the community to an unreasonable risk by maintaining such animals (see Figure 12-2).

Figure 12-2. Wild Animals

(1) A possessor of a wild animal is subject to liability to another for harm done by the animal to the other, his person, land or chattels, although the possessor has exercised the utmost care to confine the animal, or otherwise prevent it from doing harm.
(2) This liability is limited to harm that results from a dangerous propensity that is characteristic of wild animals of the particular class, or of which the possessor knows or has reason to know.

Restatement (Second) of Torts, § 507

Strict liability exists for owners of wild animals based upon the animals' inherently dangerous nature. If the animal presents some form of abnormal risk to the community where it is kept, then the owner has exposed others to that risk and must bear the burden for any harm. Keepers of lions, tigers, bears, wolves, elephants, and other similar animals face strict liability. The law in most jurisdictions has held that such animals can never be domesticated, and therefore strict liability is imposed. In contrast, review the decision of the New Hampshire Supreme Court in the *King v. Blue Mountain Forest Association* case (see Figure 12-3).

Figure 12-3. Case in Point: *King v. Blue Mountain Forest Association*

KING v. BLUE MOUNTAIN FOREST ASSOCIATION
Supreme Court of New Hampshire
123 A.2d 151
May 31, 1956

KENISON, Chief Justice.

This case poses the problem as to what remedies exist in this state by statute or at common law for damage to property allegedly caused by wild animals. The four counts in each declaration present different grounds of liability but certain historical background is common to all counts.

The defendant corporation was organized in 1891 by Austin Corbin, under chapter 152 of the General Laws, for the purpose of enabling him to conveniently manage the park owned by him, consisting of about 25,000 acres of land, including Croydon and Grantham mountains, all fenced and stocked with wild animals, located in the towns of Newport, Cornish, Croydon, and Grantham, in establishing and maintaining which he expended in the vicinity of $500,000.... Included among the animals imported into Corbin park were Prussian wild boar from the Black Forest of Germany.... Generally the boar could survive the climate of this state only if fed in the winter.... By special act of the Legislature the defendant was given special game privileges within the park upon the erection of a fence enclosing the entire area. [T]hat statute provided that "all fish, birds, and game of, in, or upon" the park "shall be the property" of the defendant, its successors or assigns. The Blue Mountain Forest Association is the only one to have imported wild boar into the northeastern part of the United States and they are not indigenous to the North American continent.... Beginning in 1938, and thereafter from time to time, some boar escaped from the park. It is alleged that the escaped boar and their progeny, bred and born during the period of their escape, caused damage to the plaintiffs' lands and crops, which damage was characteristic of wild boar as a class and normally expected of them if at large. It is also alleged that several years prior to the trespasses in September 1954, the boar and their progeny had from time to time passed back and forth from the defendant's park on to land of others, through holes in the fenced enclosure and that the boar habitually returned to defendant's enclosure for the winter or at seasons of food shortage to be fed or cared for by the defendant.

I. The first count in the declaration is in trespass predicated on the common-law liability of an owner or possessor for trespass to real estate by his livestock. *Restatement, Torts*, § 504. At an early date it was firmly established in this state that the owner or possessor of livestock was liable for such trespass irrespective of negligence.... This rule of strict liability for animal trespasses to real estate is still in effect in many of the eastern states today and the tendency has been to restore the common law rule, either by statute or by decision. *Prosser, Torts* (2nd ed, 1955), p. 320. There has been no legislative attempt to modify this doctrine and it is still the law in this state.... As already indicated, strict liability for animal trespasses to real estate was firmly established in the jurisprudence of this state prior to the enactment of this statute.

If a farmer who owns or possesses contented cows is held to strict liability for trespass to real estate it would be a strange doctrine that would not impose at least the same liability upon the owner of battering boar which were imported into the state for the purposes of exclusive and private hunting. Whether the damage to the plaintiffs' real estate was caused by a wild boar that escaped or by its progeny born after its escape, which also belonged to the defendant,... is not determinative of its liability for trespass.... We conclude that the demurrer to the first count in the plaintiffs' declaration should be overruled.

II. The fourth count of the declaration is in case but alleges no negligence. It is predicated on the theory that the possessor of wild animals is held to a standard of strict liability. It is conceded that there is no case in this jurisdiction imposing strict liability for damage to persons or property by escaped wild animals but it is urged that a rule should be adopted in this state following the *Restatement of Torts,* section 507, which reads as follows: "Except as stated in §§ 508, 517, a possessor of a wild animal is subject to liability to others, except trespassers on his land, for such harm done by the animal to their persons, lands or chattels as results from a dangerous propensity which is characteristic of wild animals of its class or of which the possessor has reason to know, although he has exercised the utmost care to confine the animal or otherwise prevent it from doing harm." Section 508 relates to indigenous wild animals after their escape and section 517 relates to wild animals kept in pursuance of a public duty, neither of which sections are applicable to this case.

It is true that strict liability for the keeping of dangerous wild animals is supported by a large number of jurisdictions and that the English courts have regarded this liability as a mere phase and specific application of the rule in *Rylands v. Fletcher,* (1868) LR 3 HL 330.... Inasmuch as we have never adopted *Restatement of Torts,* § 509, which imposes liability for harm done by dangerous domestic animals "although the possessor has exercised the utmost care to prevent it," there is no reason to adopt it in the case of wild animals.... In view of the consistent policy evidenced by an unbroken line of decisions in this state which, with the exception of cases of cattle trespass to real estate, impose liability at common law for negligence only, we do not now adopt a rule of absolute liability for injuries to persons and property caused by wild animals, as a general principle of law. The demurrer to the fourth count of the declaration should be sustained.

Defenses

In the case of wild animals, the owner cannot use the defense that the injured person was at fault or should have known better than to expose himself or herself to such an animal. Contributory negligence is not available as a defense in strict liability situations involving wild animals unless the plaintiff knowingly and unreasonably subjected himself or herself to an abnormally dangerous animal (see Figure 12-4).

Figure 12-4. Plaintiff's Conduct

(1) Except as stated in Subsection (2), the contributory negligence of the plaintiff is not a defense to the strict liability of the possessor of an animal.
(2) The plaintiff's contributory negligence in knowingly and unreasonably subjecting himself to the risk that a wild animal or an abnormally dangerous

domestic animal will do harm to his person, land or chattels, is a defense to strict liability.
(3) The plaintiff's assumption of the risk of harm from the animal is a defense to the strict liability.

Restatement (Second) of Torts, § 515

Assumption of the risk is a defense to a claim by a plaintiff that he or she was injured by a wild or a dangerous domesticated animal. For example, assume that Ms. Honey Potts maintained a dozen active beehives on her property to provide honey for commercial distribution. She had posted signs around her apiary stating, "Beware of Bees: Proceed at Your Own Risk." A visiting neighbor, Ms. Irma Prattle, disregarded the signs and got close enough to a hive to draw the attention of its residents. She required hospitalization for numerous stings and her adverse reaction to the venom. In an action maintained by Ms. Prattle, the defense of assumption of the risk would be available to Ms. Potts.

FIRE

The early common law imposed strict liability upon landholders for their use of fire because of its potential danger. Later statutory changes and court review in many jurisdictions resulted in the removal of strict liability and the imposition of negligence theory for fire damage. Recognizing the inherently dangerous nature of fire, the courts and legislatures have imposed a great level of care upon individuals starting fires or failing to take precautions against their occurrence. An application of the doctrine of strict liability for fire would unnecessarily hamper its utilitarian value in commerce, thus the necessity for the application of negligence theory. The risk of fire and the failure to apply a doctrine of strict liability are fully discussed by the Oregon Supreme Court in the matter of *Koos v. Roth* (see Figure 12-5).

Figure 12-5. Case in Point: *Koos v. Roth*

KOOS v. ROTH
Supreme Court of Oregon
652 P.2d 1255
October 26, 1982

LINDE, Justice.

We are called upon to decide whether a farmer who employs field burning as an agricultural technique is strictly liable to pay damages when the fire enters upon and destroys a neighbor's property, without any need to show that the field burning was conducted negligently.

The course of events is essentially undisputed. Defendant was engaged in the commercial production of grass seed on 55 leased acres in Linn County, near the I-5 interstate highway. After the grass seed was harvested, defendant and a crew of men equipped with mobile water tanks burned the field by setting fire to dry straw, having first plowed a protective strip around the perimeter. While defendant's field was being burned, plaintiffs' adjoining field caught fire, causing damage to real and personal property stipulated at $8,017. Although no one testified to seeing how the fire on plaintiffs' property started, the witnesses, mostly members of defendant's crew, agreed that probably a whirlwind carried burning material from defendant's field. The record shows that the fire also spread to other nearby property of persons not involved in this action....

The modern evolution of this form of strict liability in Oregon can be traced from ... the rule of *Rylands v. Fletcher*, (1868) L.R., 3 H.L. 330, 1 Eng.Rul.Cas. 236, with respect to damage done by the escape of stored water.... Thus, after the acceptance of *Rylands v. Fletcher*, the activities giving rise to strict liability in modern Oregon cases have been the storage or use of explosive material and aerial spraying of destructive chemicals.

In a subsequent case,... the court equated the older terms "extra hazardous" or "ultrahazardous" with the phrase "abnormally dangerous" employed in § 520 of the second *Restatement of Torts*, and it referred to the "factors" there proposed for determining whether an activity is "abnormally dangerous."

The factors are:

(a) Whether the activity involves a high degree of risk of some harm to the person, land or chattels of others;

(b) Whether the gravity of the harm which may result from it is likely to be great;

(c) Whether the risk cannot be eliminated by the exercise of reasonable care;

(d) Whether the activity is not a matter of common usage;

(e) Whether the activity is inappropriate to the place where it is carried on; and

(f) The value of the activity to the community....

The change of phrasing from "extra hazardous" or "ultrahazardous" to "abnormally dangerous," though subtle, created an ambiguity. To what norm does "abnormally" refer? The older phrases kept the focus on the hazardous character of the activity, on its essentially irreducible potential for causing substantial harm. Like them, "abnormally dangerous" literally means extraordinarily dangerous, much more dangerous than other activities. But the newer phrase leads itself to invoking social as well as physical norms, as if it read "abnormal and dangerous activities," thereby mixing questions of cause and effect, or probabilities and magnitudes of harm in the natural world, with what may be called societal considerations, like the "factors" listed....

The probability of the harm is a fact in the natural world. The harm may or may not have an economic measure; the practice of compensating for personal injuries in money does not mean that the law tests the danger of such injury by the estimated compensation. While the physical probabilities may lend themselves to objective or "scientific" assessment, people may deeply disagree how much, if any, "harm" is represented even by a loss measurable in the marketplace, as many contemporary disputes over management of the natural environment show. But the nature of harm is not ordinarily an issue in the kind of injury to person or property for which one party seeks to recover damages from another, and it is not an issue here....

Whether the danger is so great as to give rise to strict liability depends both on the probability and on the magnitude of the threatened harm. If the consequences of a mishap are potentially lethal or highly destructive of health or property a slight likelihood that they will occur suffices....

In sum, the focus in our cases has been on assessing abnormal hazards by their potential for harm of exceptional magnitude or probability despite the utmost care. This potential may, of course, differ with the place where the activity is conducted; but an activity is not otherwise immune from strict liability because it is "appropriate" in its place. If there is an appropriate location for aerial cropdusting, it is over open agricultural fields.... A danger that is only ordinary in an appropriate location may be abnormal where it exposes others to an extraordinary risk or magnitude of harm, but an extraordinary risk does not become ordinary because it occurs in its own appropriate place.

The use of fire, of course, is the aboriginal "dangerous activity." Its relation to the rule of *Rylands v. Fletcher*, however, is more complicated. It is an interesting question what the "common law of England" was in 1843, when this was adopted as the law in Oregon.... It should not be assumed that the common law demanded a showing of negligence to recover for losses from the spread of a fire intentionally set on another's property. The common law decisions were to the contrary, although exactly what rule of liability they established is disputed....

Meanwhile, in the states where strict liability under the *Rylands* doctrine was not adopted or developed, liability for fire damage was litigated under conventional negligence law. Many cases of fires set to clear land or for other agricultural purposes are included in an annotation that asserts "the general rule" that a person who sets a fire for a lawful purpose is not liable for damage on another's property unless he was negligent in starting or in controlling the fire.... The results then hinge on whether the fire was set under unreasonably dangerous conditions or with inadequate precautions against its spread.

These principles do not lead to strict liability for the use of fire as such. The use must be abnormally dangerous, creating an effectively uncontrollable danger of serious harm beyond the ordinary risks associated with common uses of fire that are readily avoided by due care. It appears that field burning fits this description. It differs from other domestic and industrial uses of fire, including the spark-throwing steam locomotives whose incendiary propensities were a classic cost of industrial progress, because it is used specifically for destruction. Any fire means the destruction of raw material by oxidation, with attendant dangers; but in field burning, as in using explosives and herbicides, the same destruction that poses the danger to the user's neighbor is the user's very purpose. That alone does not make every backyard burner an abnormally dangerous activity. It is a matter of scale as well as location. When fire reaches the magnitude of burning essentially the whole surface of a large area open to the winds, the possibility that it will spread beyond its intended bounds cannot be excluded with any practical degree of care.

State statutes have addressed the question of liability for fire, and in some situations have restored strict liability for its use. For instance, railroads are held strictly liable for fires started along their rights of way by their steam engines. Some states prohibit the use of fire in certain dry seasons, or for burning natural land for clearing. The paralegal student must consult local statutes and ordinances relative to the permissible use of fire.

Abnormally Dangerous Things

The rule of strict liability for abnormally dangerous things finds its origin in the English case of *Rylands v. Fletcher*, L.R. 3 H.L. 330 (1868). In *Rylands*, the defendants were mill owners who had constructed a reservoir on their property. The reservoir burst through a shaft of an adjoining mining operation. The mill owners were held strictly liable for their actions based upon the non-natural use of their land. Since the court's decision, the non-natural use of land has been broadened to include things abnormal, requiring some special use that increases the danger to others (see Figure 12-6).

Figure 12-6. Abnormally Dangerous

In short, what emerges from the English decisions as the "rule" of *Rylands v. Fletcher* is that the defendant will be liable when he damages another by a thing or activity unduly dangerous and inappropriate to the place where it is maintained, in the light of the character of that place and its surroundings.

W. Page Keeton et al., *Prosser and Keeton on the Law of Torts*
§ 78 at 547-8 (5th ed. 1984)

In the United States today, most jurisdictions accept the decision in *Rylands v. Fletcher* as applying the law of strict liability to abnormally dangerous things and activities, as summarized by the *Restatement* (see Figure 12-7).

Figure 12-7. Abnormally Dangerous Activities

(1) One who carries on an abnormally dangerous activity is subject to liability for harm to the person, land or chattels of another resulting from the activity, although he has exercised the utmost care to prevent the harm.
(2) This strict liability is limited to the kind of harm, the possibility of which makes the activity abnormally dangerous.

Restatement (Second) of Torts § 519

The defendant's liability is based upon an activity that necessarily involves a risk of serious harm to the person, land, or chattels of another that cannot be eliminated even by the exercise of the utmost care.

The types of activities and things that fall under the strict liability umbrella are gauged by certain factors as enunciated in § 520 of the *Restatement*. Those factors are:

- existence of a high degree of risk of some harm,
- likelihood that the harm will be great,
- inability to eliminate the risk through reasonable care,
- extent to which the activity is not a matter of common usage,
- inappropriateness of the activity to the place where it is being conducted, and
- extent to which its value to the community is outweighed by its dangerous nature.

These factors tend to distinguish strict liability for abnormally dangerous things from pure negligence. Even though the activity may be carried on with all due care, if its risk outweighs its utility, then the defendant will be held strictly accountable for any harm.

Blasting is a frequently cited example of an abnormally dangerous activity that falls within the application of the rule. It may be a proper method for clearing land or mining, yet it poses an abnormal risk of danger to anyone associated with the activity. The risk of serious harm cannot be eliminated by reasonable care, and its usage can only be considered abnormal. In the case of *Young v. Darter*, the Supreme Court of Oklahoma considered the question of strict liability as it applies to the spraying of weed killer (see Figure 12-8).

Figure 12-8. Case in Point: *Young v. Darter*

YOUNG v. DARTER
Supreme Court of Oklahoma
363 P.2d 829
June 6, 1961

WILLIAMS, Chief Justice.

Plaintiff below, defendant in error here, Darter, seeks to recover damages from Young, defendant below, plaintiff in error here. The parties will be referred to herein as they appeared in the trial court.

In 1957, in order to kill weeds growing therein, defendant caused his pasture lying immediately to the south and west of plaintiff's thirty acre field of cotton to be sprayed with 2-4D poison. Such poison allegedly drifted and spread across such cotton, damaging it. Plaintiff alleged defendant was guilty of negligence.

He further alleged diminution of amount of lint produced and decrease in its value as a result of his cotton having been so poisoned.

Judgment was entered on jury verdict against defendant for $1,351.80 and appeal perfected.

Defendant under his 'Proposition One' first argues that plaintiff's evidence wholly failed to prove that defendant caused the spray to drift and blow plaintiff's cotton crop and that there is no proof of lack of ordinary care by the defendant in his spraying operation. We do not agree.

The defendant himself did not actually do the spraying, but testified that it was done with his permission and consent.

Donald Young (defendant's brother) testified that he did the spraying, using a mixture of 2-4D poison and water; that he did not know it would damage cotton or that the spray would drift; that he stopped spraying before he got close to the cotton because he did not know whether it would hurt the cotton or not; that he thought if he sprayed the mixture on the cotton it might kill it; that at the time he did the spraying there was a little breeze out of the south; that there could have been quite a bit out of the southwest.

An inspector in the entomology division of the State Board of Agriculture testified that he had some experience and training with 2-4D; that he was familiar with the reaction of a plant to 2-4D; that the mixture used as a spray would drift and the distance depended upon the wind; that one should know the wind currents when he used it and should not use it when there is any possibility for it to drift and get on any other broad leaf plant; that it has a detrimental effect on cotton; that he examined plaintiff's field of cotton one or two months after the spraying; that, in his opinion, the cotton had been damaged by 2-4D or 2-45T.

We determine the evidence to have been sufficient to warrant the verdict in the light of the following discussion as to our view of applicable principles of law....

Spraying poison on weeds growing upon one's own land is a lawful operation, and, when done in a manner not hazardous to rights of another, is not a nuisance per se. Under proper conditions, the spraying would cause no invasion of the adjacent lands....

When one in an operation lawful and proper in itself, but cognizant of existing conditions and with knowledge that injury may result to another, does an act with the result flowing therefrom that damage is done to the other as the direct and proximate consequence of the act, the one who does the act and causes the injury should be required to compensate the other for the damage done....

[W]e believe ... that the promiscuous spraying of poisonous substances in a manner calculated to endanger the rights of one's neighbors is an activity not commonly regarded as consonant with the principles of natural and common justice.

The facts of the instant case bring it within the rule of *Rylands v. Fletcher* (1868) L.R., 3 H.L. 330:

> ...if a person brings or accumulates on his land anything which, if it should escape, may cause damage to his neighbor, he does so at his peril. If it does escape, and cause damage, he is responsible, however careful he may have been, and whatever precautions he may have taken

to prevent the damages. It may be that the defendant could excuse himself by showing that the escape was owing to the plaintiff's default; or perhaps that the escape was the consequence vis major or the Act of God; but as nothing of this sort was shown here, it is unnecessary to inquire what excuse would be sufficient.

The use, by the defendant, of a poison on his land, which, if it escaped, would cause damage to plaintiff, was done at defendant's peril. He is responsible for its drifting and thereby trespassing on plaintiff's land where it damaged the cotton. Any precautions defendant's agent may have taken to prevent the injuries to plaintiff's cotton, in view of the results, do not serve to extinguish his liability. The question in general is not whether defendant acted with due care and caution, but whether his acts occasioned the damage....

For the reasons that we are holding that the evidence was sufficient to warrant the jury in finding defendant liable under the principles herein enunciated without the requirement that defendant be found guilty of negligence, that the giving of such instruction though it was not perfectly drawn, did not prejudice defendant's rights and that no other instruction in lieu thereof was requested by defendant, we decline to hold that the giving thereof is a sufficient ground of error to warrant reversal of the trial court's judgment based upon the verdict rendered pursuant to the instructions including that one.

In actions for strict liability for abnormally dangerous things, the assumption of the risk by the plaintiff serves as a bar to the action. Yet contributory negligence is not a defense to the action unless the plaintiff knowingly and unreasonably subjects himself or herself to the risk of harm. Since the action is not based upon a theory of negligence, the plaintiff's contributory negligence cannot be a defense. Full responsibility for preventing harm from abnormally dangerous things rests with the defendant as a result of the creation of an abnormal risk. When the plaintiff knowingly and unreasonably exposes himself or herself to the risk, as with an assumption of the risk, then the action is barred.

Scope of Liability

The extent and scope of liability to which the principles of strict liability are applicable can be stated in general terms, yet require some commentary. Generally, strict liability applies to the consequences that are within the risk created. Establishing the scope of liability is similar to determining a proximate cause in a negligence case wherein the defendant is responsible only for clearly foreseeable consequences. Thus, an excavator is held strictly liable for the consequences of blasting activity that were reasonably to be expected from such conduct.

Whether the doctrine of strict liability applies in a given situation may depend upon any one of several relevant inquiries:

- Class of individuals covered—Harm to the person must have been clearly foreseeable.

- Manner of occurrence—Forces of nature and actions of third persons relieve the defendant from strict liability, although the *Restatement* takes a contrary view.
- Plaintiff's conduct—Contributory negligence by knowingly and unreasonably subjecting oneself to a risk of harm will relieve the defendant from responsibility.
- Privilege—When a statute permits a particular activity that is abnormally dangerous, or the activity is in furtherance of some public function, then the principles of strict liability may not apply.

The paralegal student should consult individual state law on these questions. Application to particular circumstances may be the source of some confusion unless the impact of local statutory and case law is considered.

Summary

The doctrine of strict liability imposes responsibility on a defendant for activities that involved no intent to harm nor any breach of a duty of reasonable care. The precepts behind intentional torts and the principles of negligence law do not apply when strict liability is involved. Strict liability arises without any concern for fault on the part of the defendant, and exists to protect the community in situations wherein the risk of harm outweighs the necessity for the activity. The mandates of social policy and the dictates of economic reality allow for the application of the doctrine without any measure of moral wrongdoing on the part of the defendant. The doctrine of strict liability rests squarely on the creation of an undue risk of harm to the community as a result of certain activities by the defendant.

Review Questions

1. Define strict liability.
2. List the three main categories of strict liability.
3. Do the principles of strict liability apply to trespassing animals?
4. How do most jurisdictions treat the liability of an owner of domestic animals?
5. Discuss the rationale behind imposing strict liability on owners of wild animals.
6. Does contributory negligence apply in the case of wild animals?
7. What theory of law applies to fire in most jurisdictions?
8. What is the leading case in the law of strict liability for abnormally dangerous things?

9. What is the reasoning behind imposing strict liability for abnormally dangerous things?
10. Discuss the application of the principle of assumption of the risk in determining strict liability for abnormally dangerous things.

Focus Your Skills

Owen Likely was a firm proponent of the idea that the "morals of the marketplace" dictated proper conduct. As President of SNS Industries, he prided himself as the manufacturer of the nation's most readily available "Saturday Night Special." His handguns came in calibers ranging from .22 to the notorious .44 Magnum. Quality and reliability were sacrificed for affordability and convenience. From the offbeat boutiques of Key West to the Northeast's inner-city pawn shops, SNS pistols could be found at prices that any miscreant could afford.

At midnight on a warm Saturday evening, Milford Pang was suffering from an insatiable desire for a Peanut Plum ice cream cone from his local Nasty-Freeze. Yielding to the craving, he walked the few blocks to the chilled-confection mecca, and stumbled upon a robbery in progress. Jay Bill Poke was in the process of emptying the cash register while holding the clerk at the point of his SNS 9mm. Startled by Pang's entrance, Jay Bill turned and aimed the pistol at the intruder. In a spectacular display of faulty engineering, the pistol fired spontaneously, the bullet wounding Pang in the foot. He has recovered to a significant extent from his injury, and received a lifetime supply of Nasty-Freeze as compensation.

Milford Pang has come to your office to inquire about the viability of an action in strict liability against SNS Industries for the manufacture of an abnormally dangerous thing. Provide your advice.

TABLE OF CASES CITED

FIGURE NUMBER	CASE
4-9	Arbegast v. Board of Education of South New Berlin Central School, 480 N.E.2d 365 (1985)
8-11	Armstrong v. Sundance Entertainment, Inc., 347 S.E.2d 292 (1986)
10-4	Baird v. Sickler, M.D., 433 N.E.2d 593 (1982)
9-10	Baldwin v. McClendon, 288 So.2d 761 (1974)
8-8	Barnhizer v. Paradise Valley Unified School District, 599 P.2d 209 (1979)
8-1	Boudreaux v. Sonic Industries, Inc., 729 P.2d 514 (1986)
5-15	Bradley v. American Smelting and Refining Company, 709 P.2d 782 (1985)
4-2	Brown v. Piggly-Wiggly Stores, 454 So.2d 1370 (1984)
5-6	Burrow v. K-mart Corporation, 304 S.E.2d 460 (1983)
9-1	City of Virginia Beach v. Murphy, 389 S.E.2d 462 (1990)
10-5	Cowin v. Huntington Hospital, 496 N.Y.S.2d 203 (1985)
7-10	Dalehite v. United States, 346 U.S. 15, 73 S.Ct. 956, 97 L.Ed. 1427 (1953)
10-15	Ellis v. N.G.N. of Tampa, Inc., 586 So.2d 1042 (1991)
10-9	Fisherman's Paradise, Inc. v. Greenfield, 417 So.2d 306 (1982)
10-13	Galliher v. Holloway, 474 N.E.2d 797 (1985)
4-4	Garreans v. City of Omaha, 345 N.W.2d 309 (1984)
7-19	Goff v. Taylor, 708 S.W.2d 113 (1986)
11-8	Greenman v. Yuba Power Products, Inc, 377 P.2d 897 (1963)
7-5	Grivas v. Grivas, 496 N.Y.S.2d 757 (1985)
3-8	Hake v. George Wiedemann Brewing Co., 262 N.E.2d 703 (1970)
11-2	Hampshire v. Ford Motor Company, 399 N.W.2d 36 (1986)
6-12	Holbrook v. Commonwealth, 925 S.W.2d 191 (1995)
8-10	Hundt v. Lacrosse Grain Co., Inc., 425 N.E.2d 687 (1981)
4-5	Hundt v. La Crosse Grain Co., Inc., 446 N.E.2d 327 (1983)
2-7	Jakubiec v. Hasty, 59 N.W.2d 385 (1953)

Figure Number	Case
11-6	Johnson v. Colt Industries Operating Corporation, 797 F.2d 1530 (1986)
2-8	Jolley v. Powell, 299 So.2d 647 (1974)
7-7	Kasten v. Y.M.C.A., 412 A.2d 1346 (1980)
5-12	Kimmerle v. New York Evening Journal, 186 N.E. 217 (1933)
12-3	King v. Blue Mountain Forest Association, 123 A.2d 151 (1956)
12-5	Koos v. Roth, 652 P.2d 1255 (1982)
4-13	Larsen v. Vic Tanny International, 474 N.E.2d 729 (1984)
11-1	Macpherson v. Buick Motor Company, 111 N.E. 1050 (1916)
3-2	Massey v. Scripter, 258 N.W.2d 44 (1977)
3-5	Matkovich v. Penn Central Transportation Company, 431 N.E.2d 652 (1982)
11-7	Mazetti v. Armour & Co., 135 P. 633 (1913)
8-3	McGarr v. United States, 736 F.2d 912 (1984)
4-11	Meier v. Ma-Do Bars, Inc., 484 N.Y.S.2d 719 (1985)
8-6	Mendoza v. City of Corpus Christi, 700 S.W.2d 652 (1985)
6-3	Micari, et al. v. Mann, 481 N.Y.S.2d 967 (1984)
1-2	Mueller v. Brunn, 313 N.W.2d 790, 794 (1982)
9-5	Padilla v. Lawrence, 685 P.2d 964 (1984)
11-11	Paducah Coca-Cola Bottling Company v. Harris, 316 S.W.2d 128 (1958)
9-3	Page County Appliance Center, Inc. v. Honeywell, Inc., 347 N.W.2d 171 (1984)
2-19	Palsgraf v. Long Island R. Co., 248 N.Y. 339, 162 N.E. 99 (1928)
2-16	Pitre v. Louisiana Tech University, 655 So.2d 659 (1995)
8-17	Preston v. Goldman, 720 P.2d 416 (1986)
10-2	Reed v. House of Decor, Inc., 468 So.2d 1159 (1985)
9-6	Rodrigue v. Copeland, 475 So.2d 1071 (1985)
7-16	Ross v. Consumers Power Company, 363 N.W.2d 641 (1985)
7-2	S.A.V. v. K.G.V., 708 S.W.2d 651 (1986)
1-1	Stimson v. Michigan Bell Telephone Company, 258 N.W.2d 227, 231 (1977)
8-15	Strunk v. Zoltanski, 479 N.Y.S.2d 175 (1984)
7-9	United States v. Shearer, 473 U.S. 52, 105 S.Ct. 3039, 87 L.Ed.2d 38 (1985)
1-3	Waller v. First Savings & Trust Co., 138 So. 780 (1931)
10-7	Webb v. Jewel Companies, Inc., 485 N.E.2d 409 (1985)
10-11	Wilton v. City of Spokane, 132 P. 404 (1913)
12-8	Young v. Darter, 363 P.2d 829 (1961)

Table of Restatement Citations

Figure Number	Restatement Reference
2-1	282
2-5	283
2-9	283B
2-11	289
2-14	431
2-18	435
3-4	500
3-7	433B
4-1	463
4-6	479
4-7	480
5-1	8A
5-2	21
5-4	35
5-5	36
5-8	46
5-9	652A
5-11	559
5-13	568
5-14	581A
6-2	10A
6-4	63
6-5	65
6-10	147
6-14	119
7-1	895F
7-4	895G

Figure Number	Restatement Reference
7-6	895E
7-8	895A
7-11	895B
7-13	895C
7-15	895D
7-18	895J
8-2	329
8-5	333
8-7	334
8-9	339
8-12	332
8-13	343
8-16	353
9-2	821D
9-4	821F
9-9	821B
10-8	409
10-10	410
10-12	491
11-4	388
11-5	395
11-9	402A
12-1	504
12-2	507
12-4	515
12-7	519

GLOSSARY

abuse of process The improper use of legal proceedings that may have been properly initiated.

act The process of doing something.

act of God A sudden, unexpected, and extraordinary demonstration of the force of nature from which man cannot protect himself.

allocation of risk A matter of public policy whereby the risks attendant an enterprise are distributed through pricing practice and insurance coverage.

appropriation The unauthorized use of the plaintiff's name or likeness for economic gain.

assault A form of mental injury, as opposed to physical, resulting in damages based upon an emotional response rather than actual physical injury.

assumption of risk The plaintiff knowingly exposes himself or herself to danger and assumes responsibility for any harm.

avoidable consequences A doctrine that mandates the plaintiff take reasonable steps to prevent further injury.

bar A prohibition of an action.

bar to action A defense of contributory negligence, it ends the plaintiff's claim.

battery The actual harmful physical contact resulting from an intentional act on the part of another.

breach A violation or failure to perform a legal obligation or duty.

burden of proof The obligation of a party to prove a fact to the satisfaction of the jury.

business visitor One who enters the premises of the business for the purpose for which it is open to the public.

but-for rule If the harm would not have occurred without the conduct of the defendant, then the defendant-tortfeasor is liable.

case law Decisions issued by appellate courts reviewing the decision of lower courts.

cause An act or omission that produces an effect, a result, or a consequence.

cause of action The legal right of the injured party to bring a lawsuit against the wrongdoer.

cause in fact The defendant's conduct was the cause of the plaintiff's injury.

caveat emptor The buyer of a product has the obligation of examining and testing the quality and safety of the product, and will find no protection in the law for injuries arising from the product.

charitable institution An organization that provides charity without profit or gain for itself or its owners.

chattel A term for personal property that is separate and distinct from real property.

collateral source rule The defendant-tortfeasor may not benefit from the fact that the plaintiff may have received compensation for his or her injuries from some other source.

common law Decisions issued by appellate courts reviewing the decisions of lower courts that form the principles and rules of proper behavior relating to the government and its citizens.

comparative contribution A system of apportionment of damages between defendants based upon their respective fault.

comparative negligence A statutory system of apportioning damages between the parties to a negligence action, reducing the recovery by the percentage of negligence attributed to the plaintiff.

compensatory damages The recovery of money to compensate the plaintiff for actual loss or injury as a result of an unlawful act or wrong by another.

consent An act of agreement to accept the intentional acts or omissions of another by a person of sufficient mental capacity to make an intelligent, informed choice.

constitution The highest law of the land.

constitutional tort A right that finds its origin in a constitution and protection in the law of torts.

contribution The ability of one joint tortfeasor to recover a share of the judgment from the remaining joint tortfeasor(s).

contributory negligence Conduct of the part of the plaintiff that falls below the standard to which he or she is required to conform for his or her own protection.

conversion The defendant-tortfeasor deprives the owner of possession, putting the chattel to his or her own use.

court reports Published volumes of case law that can be found in multivolume sets containing the written opinions of the appellate courts within a jurisdiction.

damages The recovery of money to compensate for loss or harm as a result of an unlawful act or wrong by another.

deceit A cause of action for monetary loss from intentionally false statements.

defamation Any false and intentional oral or written communication injurious to another's reputation and good name.

defamation by computer The communication of intentionally false statements affecting the reputation and standing of another in the community via computer.

defamatory statement A statement that harms the plaintiff's reputation and good name in the eyes of another, causes the plaintiff to fall in esteem, or makes others cease associating with him or her.

defendant The party in a lawsuit against whom an action has been brought.

discretionary function Basic policy evaluation, judgment, and expertise by a state.

doctrine of attractive nuisance Landholder is held liable for injuries to children when an artificial condition exists on his or her land that may be expected to be attractive to children.

doctrine of *res ipsa loquitur* The term literally means "the thing speaks for itself" and represents a fusion of the concept of circumstantial evidence, which indirectly proves the existence of a fact.

dram shop act A legislative enactment imposing liability on the seller of alcoholic beverages when a third party is injured as a result of the intoxication of the buyer when the sale led to the intoxication.

duty An obligation requiring an individual to do or refrain from doing something to protect others from harm.

duty of reasonable care A standard of conduct that is owed by the defendant-tortfeasor to the plaintiff in an action for negligence.

emotional distress A state of mind characterized by fear, anxiety, horror, grief, shock, humiliation, or embarrassment.

English common law The ancient unwritten law of England following the Norman Conquest in 1066.

entry Invasion on the land of another without consent that interferes with the plaintiff's exclusive right of use and enjoyment of the property.

equality rule The apportioning of the damages equally among the defendants.

evidence Something that proves or disproves a fact.

exemplary damages A penalty intended to teach the tortfeasor a lesson or to make an example of him or her; also known as punitive damages.

fact The existence of an actual occurrence or event as determined by the evidence presented.

false imprisonment An intentional confinement without consent or legal right.

false light The defendant-tortfeasor publicly and offensively attributes statements, opinions, or a likeness to the plaintiff.

family purpose doctrine The owner of an automobile is liable for the negligence of a family member allowed to drive the vehicle.

finding tools Legal research aids used to locate primary and secondary sources of the law.

foreseeability A reasonable anticipation that harm will occur from an act or omission.

frolic Any deviation from the scope of employment.

government entity Municipal government; traditionally the government of a county, city, town, or village, and its agencies.

governmental function The administration of some phase of government that is essential to its existence in serving the public at large.

guest passenger statute A statute that imposes liability for harm done to a guest in an automobile if the driver's conduct is in reckless disregard of the guest's safety.

hornbook A treatise used by law students to study well-settled principles found in landmark cases.

immunity Freedom from liability or action, providing an absolute defense to an action for negligence or intentional tort.

in loco parentis One who stands in the position of a parent and has the same rights and liabilities as the parent.

indemnification A full reimbursement of the party paying a judgment to the plaintiff.

independent contractor An individual who contracts with another to perform a task according to his or her own methods, and who is subject to the employer's control only as to the result of the work.

injurious falsehood Publication of a false statement regarding the plaintiff's property, title, or affairs; intent on the part of the defendant-tortfeasor to prevent others from dealing with the plaintiff; communication of the falsehood to another; and actual damages.

intent A state of mind at the time one carries out an action to bring about an intended result.

intentional invasion An act intended to cause harm to another's personal or property interest.

intentional tort Injury to the plaintiff's person or property resulting from the defendant intending to violate a duty owed to the plaintiff.

interspousal immunity One spouse is immune from tort liability to the other spouse.

intervening cause The act of a third person or some other force that acts to produce the injury to the plaintiff after the negligent act of the defendant.

invitation Conduct on the part of the landholder or possessor of the premises that justifies the visitor in believing that his or her entry is sought.

invitee A member of the public on public land, or a business visitor.

joint and several liability If the acts or omissions of two or more individuals, acting simultaneously or in sequence, were the proximate cause of the injury to the plaintiff, then they are both liable for the entire result.

joint enterprise An undertaking to carry out some business purpose by a group of associates with an equal voice in the direction of the venture.

joint liability The liability of two or more persons together.

judicial review The power of a court to review legislative enactments to determine their validity.

knowledge An awareness or understanding gained through experience or study.

landholder Any person who has rightful possession of land.

last clear chance A situation in which the defendant had the last opportunity to discover the plaintiff's peril and avoid injury through reasonable care.

legal proof The task of drawing valid inferences from the available facts.

liability Financial responsibility of the tortfeasor for tortious conduct that has resulted in some form of injury to an individual's property or person.

libel A written defamatory statement communicated to a third person.

licensee One who is privileged to enter the land of another by consent.

loss of consortium A damage awarded in some tort cases compensating the spouse of the injured party for loss of love, companionship, services, affection, and sexual relations.

malicious prosecution The unjustified use of the criminal process against another person.

misfeasance An act in the form of misconduct; may form the basis for liability for negligence if the act results in harm to another and fails to meet the standard of a reasonable person.

mistake An act or omission by the defendant based upon a genuine belief that circumstances exist which justify his or her conduct.

motive The mental state of the defendant that compels him or her to act in a certain manner.

motor vehicle consent statute A legislative enactment imposing vicarious liability on the owner of an automobile for the negligence of those driving the vehicle.

natural condition The state of land unaltered by human act.

natural law A fundamental legal principle essential to an ordered social existence.

necessity Defendant-tortfeasor acts to prevent a threatened injury resulting from some force of nature.

negligence The failure to use the care a reasonable person would under the same circumstances.

negligence *per se* A violation of a statutory standard of conduct.

nominal damages Category of damages awarded when the plaintiff has sustained no actual loss or injury.

non-delegable duty An obligation imposed by law or contract that may not be passed to another.

nonfeasance A failure to act and forms the basis for an action for negligence if a reasonable person would not have failed to act under similar circumstances.

nuisance Any activity arising from the use of one's property that produces a substantial and unreasonable interference with another's interests.

omission The failure to act when there exists a legal duty to do so.

opinion What a person thinks or believes as a conclusion drawn from facts.

outrageous conduct That conduct on the part of the defendant-tortfeasor that is beyond decency.

plaintiff The party to a lawsuit that commences the action.

premises liability The liability of a landholder for the use and enjoyment of real property and its attachments.

premises Real property and its attached buildings, grounds, facilities, and structures, and those things attached to the land or growing from it.

preponderance of the evidence A conclusion that a fact is more probable than not, more true than untrue based on the greater probability of something existing.

presumption A rule of law stating that the jury may assume the existence of a fact.

prima facie The plaintiff's proofs are sufficient to establish the claim and shift the burden of proof to the defendant to rebut the plaintiff's case.

primary authority Authorities that are statements *of* the law.

private nuisance An interference with an individual's use and enjoyment of land.

privilege A circumstance that justifies or excuses intentionally tortious conduct, allowing the defendant to commit an act that is contrary to another's interest without facing liability.

privileged communication Statements made by persons within a protected relationship that the law protects from disclosure in court.

privity of contract The relationship between parties that exists because of a contract between them.

proprietary function A service provided by the municipality for the comfort, convenience, and safety of its citizens.

proximate An act or omission that is closely related in space, time, or logical order.

proximate cause The defendant-tortfeasor's conduct causes a foreseeable injury to the plaintiff.

public disclosure An intentional unauthorized and offensive disclosure of purely private information without any legitimate public interest.

public nuisance An intentional act, or failure to perform a legal duty, that harms or endangers the public health, safety, and welfare.

publication The communication of a defamatory statement to a third person.

punitive damages Types of damages occasionally awarded for intentional torts or gross negligence as punishment of the defendant.

question of fact The resolution of an issue concerning the existence of a fact, as opposed to a question of law.

reasonable discipline A privilege to use some degree of force and restraint so long as the individuals act in good faith and in a reasonable manner in the maintenance of order and discipline with children.

reasonable person standard The measure of the conduct of an individual by that of an imaginary person under the same or similar circumstances in avoiding harm to another.

recapture The taking of possession of property in the custody of another.

right of privacy The right of an individual to be free from an unwarranted intrusion into matters with which the public is not necessarily concerned.

rules of evidence Rules of courts that govern the admissibility of evidence in a trial.

scope of employment A general term used to refer to the acts the servant is employed to perform.

secondary authority Authorities that are statements *about* the law.

self-defense Reasonable force used to prevent any threatened bodily harm or damage to property.

servant An individual employed to perform services for another and who is subject to the other's control.

slander An oral defamatory communication to another, requiring proof of actual damages in most situations.

slander *per se* A type of slander in which no proof of actual harm to reputation or good name is required to maintain the action.

sovereign immunity Freedom from liability or action for all levels of government.

statute A formal written act of a legislative body that creates a law.

statute of limitations A legislative enactment establishing maximum time periods during which certain types of actions at law may be brought.

strict liability Liability without fault or negligence on the part of the defendant.

substantial factor rule A rule for the determination of proximate cause stating that if the defendant-tortfeasor's conduct was a substantial factor in bringing about the plaintiff's injury, then proximate cause may be found.

survival The principle terminating the right of recovery with the death of either the plaintiff or the defendant.

survival statute A statute that allows for the survival of a negligence action after the death of either party to the case.

toll The statute of limitations is temporarily suspended until some event occurs.

tort A civil wrong resulting in injury to the person or property of another.

tortfeasor The person whose behavior resulted in injury to another.

tortious conduct The intentional or unintentional behavior that results in harm to another.

toxic torts Toxic interference with one's ownership and enjoyment of property.

treatise An exposition on an area of the law in greater depth than that offered by encyclopedias or periodicals.

trespass A direct and forceful act causing injury to the victim's person or property.

trespass on the case A wrongful act indirectly causing injury to a victim.

trespass to chattels Any intentional interference with another's personal property.

trespasser One who enters upon the land of another without permission, privilege, or consent.

unavoidable accident An accident not proximately caused by the act or omission of the defendant-tortfeasor.

unforeseeability A reasonable person could not conclude that an injury would occur from an act or omission.

unreasonable intrusion An excessive and highly offensive intentional interference with another's interest in solitude or seclusion as to person or private affairs.

warrantless arrest Any detention or taking into custody by a private citizen of a suspect in a felony or breach of the peace.

warranty An assurance by one party to a commercial transaction to another that some fact is true, and upon which the other may rely.

willful, wanton, and reckless conduct Terms used to describe a form of highly unreasonable behavior, departing far beyond ordinary negligence.

writ A petition to the court.

wrongful death action The rule prohibiting family members from pursuing a negligence action against the defendant-tortfeasor responsible for the death.

INDEX

abatement, 209
Abner v. W. T. Grant Co., 98
abrogation of immunity, 151
absolute nuisance, 203-04
abuse of process, 13
  definition of, 108
acceptable conduct, 17
accusations
  crime, 106
  loathsome disease, 106
  unchastity, 106
act, 28
acting in good faith, 154
actionable negligence, 78
activity
  definition of, 191
acts of God, 48, 50-51
administrative claims agency, 151
adolescent immunity, 154-55
age, 26
age of responsibility, 27
aggregation of immunity, 151
Alien Property Act, 154-55
allocation of risk, 213-14
  See also, Reed v. House of Decor, Inc.
American Law Institute (ALI), 18-19
  definition of negligence, 19
ancient tort law, 10, 12
ancient writ of trespass, 10, 12
anesthesiology
  See, Baird v. Sickler, M.D.
animals
  See, Livestock liability.
appropriation
  definition of, 101
Arbegast v. Board of Education of South New Berlin Central School, 81-82, 279
Armstrong v. Sundance Entertainment, Inc., 176-77, 279
ASARCO
  See, Bradley v. American Smelting and Refining Company (ASARCO)
assault
  available defenses, 118
  comparison to battery, 95
  definition of, 94
assault and battery, 13, 93-95
  available defenses, 118
assize of nuisance, 190
assumption of risk, 80, 82-83
  express, 88
  express consent, 83-85
  product liability, 26
  violenti non fit injuria, 119
  voluntary, 80
attorney-client privilege, 158
attractive nuisance doctrine, 171, 173
automobile accidents, 229, 242-43
  vicarious liability, 229-30
automobile consent statutes, 232
automobile industry
  Elmore v. American Motors Corp., 242
  Hampshire v. Ford Motor Co., 243-44, 279
  MacPherson v. Buick Motor Co., 239-42, 245
automobile ownership, 212-13, 232
avoidable consequences, 43, 73-74

Baird v. Sickler, M.D., 217-18, 279
Baldwin v. McClendon, 206-08, 279
Barnhizer v. Paradise Valley Unified School District, 171-72, 279
bar to action, 69-70
  statute of limitations, 133
battery
  available defenses, 118
  definition of, 95
Beecher, Henry Ward, 137
Black's Law Dictionary, 3
  definition of duty, 20
Board of Education of South New Berlin Central School
  See, Arbegast v. Board of Education of South New Berlin Central School.Boudreaux v. Sonic Industries, Inc., 163-65, 279
Bradley v. American Smelting and Refining Company (ASARCO), 110-12, 279
Brandeis, Louis D., 100-01
breach, 20, 29-30, 34
  in Palsgraf case, 39
breach of contract, 238
breach of duty, 36
broadcasting
  form of libel, 103
Brown, Frank C. v. Piggly-Wiggly Stores, 69-70, 279
burden of proof, 58
  product liability action, 259
Burrow v. K-Mart Corporation, 97-99, 279
business reputation, 106
business visitors, 178-79
but-for rule, 30, 36-37
  cause in fact, 36-37
Byrne v. Boadle, 59-60, 62

captain of the ship doctrine, 218
case law, 8, 28
causal culpability, 82
cause, 30
  substantial factor test, 36
cause in fact, 30, 34, 36-37
caveat emptor, 183, 238, 242, 261
  Preston v. Goldman, 184-86
  warranty, 245
charitable immunity, 144-45
  Kasten v. Y.M.C.A., 144-45
charitable institution
  definition of, 144
chattel
  definition of, 112
child abuse, 141-43
  law, 26
  negligence, 26
chronology in nuisance cases, 200
Cincinnati Gas & Electric Company, 61
City of Virginia Beach v. Murphy, 191, 279
civil process
  ulterior purpose, 108
  willful act, 108
civil tort action, 7
civil wrongs, 2
classified waiver of immunity, 151
clergy-penitent privilege, 158
Coca-Cola Cola Bottling Co., 256-58
collateral negligence, 226-28
  Wilton v. City of Spokane, 226-28
collateral source rule, 43

Colt six-shooter, 247
common law, 4-6, 8
common nuisance
  See, Public nuisance.
  comparative causation, 82
  comparative contribution, 80
  comparative negligence, 78
    nature of, 78-79
    in product liability, 260
    statutes of, 78-79,88
    systems of, 79
Comparative Negligence Statute, New York, 88
compensation, 11-12
  See also, Compensatory damages.
compensatory damages, 11-12, 42
computers
  defamation by, 106-07
concept of nuisance, 191-93
concerted action, 62
conditions dangerous to third persons, 180
conduct, 18, 277
  of others, 203
confinement, 96-97
  Burrow v. K-Mart Corporation, 97-99
consortium
  See, Loss of consortium.
constant trespassers, 171
constitution
  definition of, 7
constitutional tort, 7
Consumer Products Safety Commission, 261
consumer safety
  risk-utility test, 259
consumer satisfaction, 259
contribution
  definition of, 63
  indemnity, 63
contributory fault, 71
contributory negligence, 43, 80, 89
  automobile accidents, 229
  definition of, 68-69
  product liability cases, 260
consumer contemplation test, 259
consumer product safety, 269-61
Consumer Product Safety Act, 261
consumer safety
  See also, Product liability.
  defective design, 256, 259
  unreasonably dangerous, 255
control of servant, 213
conversion, 13
  definition of, 112-13
Court of Appeals of Georgia, 176-77
Court of Appeals of Kentucky, 156-57
Court of Appeals of New Mexico, 198-99
Court of Appeals of New York, 81-82
Court of Appeals of Oklahoma, 163-65
court reports, 8
Cowin v. Huntington Hospital, 219-21, 279
culpable conduct, 82
Cybernaut Computer Club, 14

Dalehite v. United States, 148-50, 279
damage to plaintiff, 12
  without regard, 263
damages, 20, 35, 108
  compensatory, 11-12, 42
  exemplary, 10-11
  monetary, 208-09
  negligence, 41-42
  nominal, 42
  nuisance cases, 208-09
    Pitre v. Louisiana Technical University, 33-34, 37
  punitive, 42
dangerous explosives, 226-28
dangerous instrumentalities, 222-23
Davies v. Mann, 76
deceit, 114
  available defenses, 118
deep pocket, 213
defamation, 13
  available defenses, 118
  by computer, 106-07
  definition of,102
  injurious falsehood, 113-14
defamatory statements, 102-03
defective design
  See, Manufacturer's negligence; Product liability.
defendant, 12, 17, 22, 30
  malice, 107
  privilege, 127-28
defendant-tortfeasor
  See, Defendant.
defense of property, 123-24
defenses
  consent, 118, 119-21
  contributory negligence, 68-69
  Holbrook v. Commonwealth, 130-31
  intentional torts, 127-36
  legal process 124-25
  in loco parentis, 129
  mistake, 118, 125
  necessity, 118, 126-27
  negligence, 67-90
  privilege, 127-28
  reasonable discipline, 128-31
  recapture of land and chattels, 132
  self-defense, 118, 121-24
  statute of limitations, 133
  warrantless arrest, 133-34
demands, 132
deprivation of rights, 8
deterrence, 11
Devlin v. Smith, 241
disclaimer of warranty, 260
discretionary-decisional acts, 154
discretionary function, 151
discretionary immunity, 150
disturbing the peace, 192
doctor-client privilege
  See, Physician-patient privilege.
doctrine of attractive nuisance, 171
doctrine of immunity, 137-38
doctrine of nuisance, 189-210
doctrine of *res ipsa loquitur*, 59-62
doctrine of unavoidable accident, 164
doctrine of vicarious liability, 212-14
domestic animals, 266-67
double recovery, in medical cases, 43
Doyle v. Dobson, 24
dram shop acts, 232-33
dram shop liability, 212, 232-35
  Ellis v. N.G.N. of Tampa, Inc., 233-34, 279
drop-fire hazard, 248
drunk driving, 233-35
duty, 20, 34
  Black's Law Dictionary definition of, 20-21
duty of reasonable care, 20, 28, 40
  Boudreaux v. Sonic Industries, Inc., 163-65, 279
  breach of, 29
  Grivas v. Grivas, 142-43, 279
  landholders, 162-65

economic loss
  in nuisance cases, 199
Eleventh Amendment, 150-51
Ellis v. N.G.N. of Tampa, Inc., 233-34, 279
Elmore v. American Motors Corp., 242
eminent domain, 150
eminently dangerous, 242
emotional distress, 99-100
  available defenses, 118
emotional harm
  nuisance actions, 199
employer
  liability, 214-15, 224-25
    Reed v. House of Decor, Inc., 214-15, 279
  negligence, 224-25
  protection against liability, 220-21
employer-employee, 213
  See also, Master-servant relationship.
Endeavor Marine, 224
English common law, 4, 6, 10, 13, 141, 190
  animals, 265
  "the King can do no wrong" concept, 145
  natural law, 6
  public nuisance, 204-05

entrustment, 213
entry upon land, 109,168
equality rule, 80
equal right of control, 229
equation of proximate cause, 37
evidence
  definition of, 48-49
  preponderance, 49-50
evolution of laws, 6-7
exemplary damages, 10-11
existence of risk, recognizing, 27
expert witnesses, 49
express assumption of risk, 88
express consent, 83-85
express warranty, 245
extra hazardous activity, 150

facere
  definition of, 3
fact
  definition of, 49
failure to warn, 246, 258-59
"fair on its face," 124
false arrest, 13
false imprisonment, 13, 96-99, 118
  available defenses, 118
  Burrow v. K-Mart Corporation, 97-99, 279
  definition of, 96
false light
  definition of, 101
family purpose doctrine, 232
federal government, 145-50
  immunity of, 145-60
Federal Reporter (Fed.), 8
Federal Reporter Second Edition (Fed, 2d), 8
Federal Tort Claims Act of 1946, The, 8, 146, 149, 151, 167
Fertilizer Grade Ammonium Nitrate (KGAN), 148-50
Fifth Amendment, 158
finding tools, 8
  examples of, 10
fire
  Koos v. Roth, 270-73
firecrackers
  See, Garreans v. City of Omaha.
firemen's rule, 179
First Amendment, 99, 114
  See also, New York Times v. Sullivan.
Fisherman's Paradise Inc. v. Greenfield, 224, 279
Florida Constitution Declaration of Rights, 6
Florida Supreme Court, 233-34
Florida's wrongful death act, 25
force, threatening and not threatening, 122-23
Ford Motor Company
  See, Hampshire v. Ford Motor Company.
foreseeability, 32-33, 37
  in *Palsgraf v. Long Island Railroad Co.*, 37-41
forgetfulness, as contributory negligence, 74
Foster and Hindle
  See, Wilton v. City of Spokane.
fourth-degree assault, 131
fraud and misrepresentation, 13, 114
Frederick v. City of Detroit, 53
freedom of speech
  See, First Amendment.
frolic and detour, 218-21
function of court injury, 58
furnishing liquor as liability, 233

Galliher v. Holloway, 230-31, 279
Garreans v. City of Omaha, 72-73, 279
General Obligations Law, 85
Goff v. Taylor, 156-57, 279
good faith, 208
governmental functions, 152
governmental immunity, 145-54
  discretionary function, 151
  eminent domain, 150
  municipal, 152
  public officers, 153
  state, 150-51
governmental privileged information, 159
"greater care" duty, 52
Greenman v. Yuba Power Products, Inc., 252-54, 279
Grivas v. Grivas, 142-43, 279
gross negligence, 51
guest passenger statute, 57-58

Hake v. George Wiedemann Brewing Co., 60-62, 279
Hampshire v. Ford Motor Co., 243-44, 279
harm
  definition of, 191
  property, 108-09
  risk of, 274
  substantial and unreasonable, 200-03
Harvard Law Review, 100
Hawkins v. Ivy, 55-56
hazardous material, 222-23
hearsay evidence, 49
helpless plaintiff, 76
herpes praeputialis, 140
Hewellette v. George, 141
Hitaffer v. Argonne Co., 42-43
Hobbes, Thomas, 67
Holbrook v. Commonwealth, 130-31, 279
Holmes, Oliver Wendell, 1
Honeywell, Inc., 194-96
Horace, 263
hornbook, 6
household members as licensees,174
Hundt v. La Crosse Grain Co., Inc., 74-76,174-76, 279

immature recklessness, 172
immediate possession, 132
immunity
  abrogation of, 151
  adolescent, 154-55
  aggregation of , 151
  charitable immunity, 144-45
    Kasten v. Y.M.C.A., 144-45
  classified waiver of, 151
  defense, 118
  definition of, 138
  discretionary, 150
  doctrine of, 137-38
  governmental, 145-60
  infant, 154-55
  interspousal, 139-41
    S.A.V. v. K.G.V., 140-41
  intrafamily, 139-40
  mental incompetence, 155-58
    Goff v. Taylor, 156-57, 279
  parent and child, 141-42
  patient, 158
  public officers, 153-54
  sovereign, 145-50
  state government, 150
  tort liability, 137-60
implied consent, 85
implied warranty, 245
imputed negligence, 212-13
indemnification
  definition of, 63
independent contractor, 212, 223-27
  Fisherman's Paradise Inc. v. Greenfield, 224, 279
Indiana Supreme Court, 74-76
industrial revolution, 5
infant immunity, 154-55
infliction of emotional distress, 13
inherently dangerous activities, 226
inherently dangerous commodity, 150
injunction, 209
injurious falsehood, 113-14
  available defenses, 118
in loco parentis, 121, 129-30, 142
in re Texas City Disaster, 148
insanity defense, 25
intent, 12, 18
  definition of, 92-93
  to cause emotional distress, 99
intentional act, 197
intentional misconduct, 208

intentional torts, 2, 4, 12-13, 221-22
  assault and battery, 94-96
  defamation, 102-104
  definition of, 92
  emotional distress, 99-100
  false imprisonment, 96-99
  harm to person, 93-94
  right of privacy, 100-02
  Webb v. Jewel Companies, Inc., 21-222
interference with enjoyment, 197
interspousal immunity, 139-41
  S.A.V. v. K.G.V., 140-41
intervening cause, 40-41
intrafamily immunity, 139-40
intramarital privilege, 159
invasion
  of interest, 39
  of privacy, 13
invitation
  definition of, 178
invitee
  definition of, 168
  standard of care owed to, 178
ITT Electronic Travel Services, Inc. (ITT), 194-96

Jakubiec v. Hasty, 22, 279
Joel v. Morrison, 219
Johnson v. Colt Industries Operating Corporation, 247-49
joint enterprise, 212-13, 228-32
  definition of, 228
  Galliher v. Holloway, 230-31, 279
joint and several liability, 62-63
joint tortfeasor's liability, 62-63, 79-80
  concerted action, 62
  contribution and indemnity, 63
Jolley v. Powell, 24-26
judicial review, 7

Kansas negligence law, 247, 249
  See also, Johnson v. Colt Industries Operating Corporation.
Kasten v. Y.M.C.A., 144-45
Keeton, W. Page, 19, 21-22, 26, 29-30, 32
  on defective products, 256
  on intervening cause, 41
  parental immunity, 141-42
Kentucky Revised Statutes, 129-30
KGAN
  See, Fertilizer Grade Ammonium Nitrate (KGAN).
Kimmerle v. New York Evening Journal, 103-05
King v. Blue Mountain Forest Association, 267-69
Klippel-Feil syndrome, 217-18
knowledge
  in negligence cases, 27-28
  of peril, 74
  of risk, 85-87
Koos v. Roth, 270-73

La Crosse Grain Co., Inc.
  See, Hundt v. La Crosse Grain Co., Inc.
landholder
  Armstrong v. Sundance Entertainment, Inc., 176-77
  business visitors, 178
  definition of, 162
  general duty of, 162
  Hundt v. La Crosse Grain Co., Inc., 74-76,174-76, 279
  invitation, 178
  liability toward licensee, 174-76
  reasonable care, 162-65
  riparian nuisance, 203-04
  standard of care, 178
  Strunk v. Zoltanski, 180-83
landlords
  agreement to repair, 180
  common areas, 180
  concealed dangerous conditions, 180
  general duty of, 162
  obligations to disclose, 180
Larson v. Vic Tanny International, 86-87
last clear chance
  definition of, 76
law of causation, 40
  See also, Intervening cause.
law of predecessor's ownership, 185
Law of Torts, 4th ed., The, 196
  false imprisonment, 98
legal cause, 31
legal process, as defense, 124-25
legal proof, 48-49
Legislative Reorganization Act, 149
lessor and lessee, 179-83
Leviathan, 67
"let the buyer beware"
  See, Caveat emptor.
liability, 3
  See also, Intentional torts.
  abnormally dangerous things, 273-76
  animals, 265-69
  defenses, 269-70
  definition of, 191
  fire, 270-73
  limitation of, 164
  McGarr v. United States, 166-68
  nature conditions, 165-68
  nuisance concept, 191-93
  Palsgraf v. Long Island Railroad Co., 38-39
  Pitre v. Louisiana Technical University, 37
  scope of, 31-32, 34, 36, 276-77
  trespassers, 169-74
  urban and rural areas, 166
  without fault, 264-65
libel, 103-104
licensee
  definition of, 168
  relationships, 175-77
limitation of liability, 164
  See also, Palsgraf v. Long Island Railroad Co.
Lippman, Walter, 161
livestock liability
  King v. Blue Mountain Forest Association, 267-69
loco parentis *See, In loco parentis.*
Longfellow, Henry Wadsworth, 117
Long Island Railroad Co.
  See, Palsgraf v. Long Island Railroad Co.
"look to the man higher up," 213
  See also, Respondeat superior.
loss
  of consortium, 3, 37, 42-43
  of support and affection, 63
Louisiana Supreme Court
  See, Rodrigue v. Copeland.

Macaulay, Thomas Babington, 237
McGarr v. United States, 166-68
McHugh v. Reading Co., 172
MacPherson v. Buick Motor Co., 239-42, 245
malice, 107
malicious prosecution, 13
  definition of, 107
manufacturer's negligence
  See also, Product liability.
  defective designs, 246
  Greenman v. Yuba Power Products, Inc., 252-54
  Hampshire v. Ford Motor Co., 243-44, 279
  Johnson v. Colt Industries Operating Corporation, 247-49
  MacPherson v. Buick Motor Co., 239-42
  Mazetti v. Armour & Co., 249
  Meier v. Ma-Do Bars, Inc., 84-85
  Paducah Coca-Cola Bottling Co. v. Harris, 256-58
  Spence v. Three Rivers Builders & Masonry Supply, 252
Marbury v. Madison, 7
Massey v. Scripter, 52-53
master liability for servants, 218
master's business, 221
master-servant relationship, 212-13, 216-23
  frolic and detour, 218-19
Matkovich v. Penn Central Transportation Company, 54
Mazetti v. Armour & Co., 249-52
mechanical bulls
  See, Meier v. Ma-Do Bars, Inc.

medical malpractice, 42
Meier v. Ma-Do Bars, Inc., 84-85
Mendoza v. City of Corpus Christi, 169-70
mental condition, 24-27
mental deficiency, 26
mental incompetence
  Goff v. Taylor, 156-57, 279
  immunity of, 155-58
  insanity as a defense, 25, 157
Micari, et al. v. Mann, 120-21
Michigan Fair Employment Practices Act, 3
ministerial-operational acts, 154
minors, immunity of,154-55
misfeasance, 28, 165
  in medical procedure, 218
misrepresentation, 93, 114
mistake, 118
  definition of, 125
mistake defense, 118, 125
  See also, Negligence.
  intentional torts, 125
misuse, 260
  of legal procedure, 107-08
  in product liability, 260
modified comparative negligence, 79
momentary forgetfulness, 74
  Hundt v. La Crosse Grain Co., Inc., 74-76,174-76, 279
monetary awards, 10
  See also, System of monetary compensation.
  in nuisance cases, 208-09
monetary damages
  as deterrence, 11
motive
  definition of, 128
motor vehicle consent statutes, 232
Mueller v. Brunn, 4
municipal government, 152
  proprietary functions, 152

natural conditions, 165-68
  McGarr v. United States, 166-68
natural law, 6
nature of conduct, 120
necessity, 118, 126-27
negligence, 5, 7, 12, 44
  avoidable consequences, 43, 73-74
  bar to action, 69-70
  comparative, 78-80
  comparison to mistake, 125
  contributory, 43, 68-69, 71, 260
  damages for, 41-42
  defenses to, 67-90
  definition of, 18
  degrees of, 51-57
  elements of, 19-21
  employer, 224-25
  intervening cause, 40-41
  knowledge of peril, 74
  last clear chance, 78
  Massey v. Scripter, 52-53
  momentary forgetfulness, 74
  Palsgraf v. Long Island Railroad Co., 38-39
  product liability cases, 244
  proof of, 47-65
  strict liability, 209
  trespassing children, 173
  vel non, 70
  willful, wanton, and reckless conduct, 53-56
negligence *per se*, 56-57
negligent manufacture, 246
  Greenman v. Yuba Power Products, Inc., 252-54
  Mazetti v. Armour & Co., 249-52
  Paducah Coca-Cola Bottling Co. v. Harris, 256-58
  Spence v. Three Rivers Builders & Masonry Supply, 252
New York Civil Practice Law and Rules, 88
New York County Supreme Court, 120-21
New York Court of Appeals, 37-40
New York Times v. Sullivan, 101-02, 114, 116
nominal damages, 42
nondelegable duty, 225-26
nonfeasance, 28
Norman Conquest of 1066, 4, 13-14
notice in breach of warranty actions, 260
nuisance, 13, 191-210
  Baldwin v. McClendon, 206-08, 279
  City of Virginia Beach v. Murphy, 191, 279
  definition of, 191
  degree of intrusion, 201
  private versus public, 190
  recovery, 209
  remedies, 205-09
  Robichaux v. Huppenbauer, 201
  Rodrigue v. Copeland, 200-02
  types of losses occurring, 199-200
nurse-anesthetist liability, 217-18

Ohio, Supreme Court of, 60-62, 217-18
Omaha, Nebraska
  See, Garreans v. City of Omaha.
omission, 12, 28, 125
one standard, 52-53
opinion
  definition of, 49
ordinary negligence, 51, 54
  principles of, 71
origination, 213
outrageous conduct, 99-100

Padilla v. Lawrence, 198-99
Paducah Coca-Cola Bottling Co. v. Harris, 256-58
Page County Appliance Center, Inc. v. Honeywell Inc., 194-96
Palsgraf v. Long Island Railroad Co., 37-41, 164
  intervening cause, 41
  proximate cause, 32, 40
parent and child immunity, 141-42
patient immunity, 158
Penn Central Transportation Company, 54-57
  See also, Matkovich v. Penn Central Transportation Company.
pharmaceutical liability
  See, Thomas v. Winchester.
physical attributes, 22-24
physical harm, 199
  in nuisance cases, 199
physician-patient privilege, 158
Pike, Albert, 47
Pike Circuit Court, 157
Pindilla v. Lawrence, 198-99
Pitre v. Louisiana Technical University, 33-37
  award of damages, 37
plaintiff, 12
  helpless, 76-77
Pollock, Baron, 59-60
possession, trespass to land, 109
predecessor landowners, 185
premises
  definition of, 162
  leased for public benefit, 180
premises liability, 13, 161-87
  definition of, 162
  entry upon land, 168-79
  invitees, 177-79
  landholder duty, 162-68
  lessor and lessee, 179-83
  vendor and vendee, 183-86
preponderance of the evidence, 50
Preston v. Goldman, 184-86
presumptions
  definition of, 59
prima facie, 134
  Byrne v. Boadle, 59-60, 62
  definition of, 59
  libel, 117
primary authority, 7-8
  examples of, 9
principal-agent, in vicarious liability, 213
principles of ordinary negligence, 71
privacy v. defamation, 102
private nuisance, 192-93
  City of Virginia Beach v. Murphy, 191, 279
  definition of, 192
  Padilla v. Lawrence, 198-99

privilege, 127-28
  of hiring, 213
  scope of liability, 276-77
privileged communications, 49,158-59
privity of contract, 238-39
  Mazetti v. Armour & Co., 249
product liability, 13, 237-62
  assumption of the risk, 260
  caveat emptor, 183, 238, 242, 261
  comparative negligence, 260
  consumer contemplation test, 259
  consumer product safety, 269-61
  Consumer Product Safety Act, 261
  contributory negligence, 260
  defective design, 259
  disclaimer of warranty, 260
  defenses, 259-60
  design flaws, 256, 259
  Elmore v. American Motors Corp., 242
  failure to warn, 258
  flaw in the product, 256-58
  Greenman v. Yuba Power Products, Inc., 252-54, 279
  Hampshire v. Ford Motor Co., 243-44, 279
  history of, 238-39
  industry standards, 261
  injury information clearinghouse, 261
  MacPherson v. Buick Motor Co., 239-42, 279
  Mazetti v. Armour & Co., 249-52
  misuse, 260
  negligence, 245-49
  notice, 260
  parties, 242-45
  recall, 261
  res ipsa loquitur, 257
  risk-utility test, 259
  Spence v. Three Rivers Builders & Masonry Supply, 252
  statute of limitations, 260
  strict liability, 249-55
  Thomas v. Winchester, 239
  unreasonably dangerous, 255-56, 262
  warranty, 245
professional malpractice, 28, 42
prompt recapture, 132
property
  defense of, 123
  harm in nuisance cases, 199
  protected interest, 193-94
proprietary functions, 152-53
Prosser and Keaton on the Law of Torts, 6-7, 19, 29-30, 32
  See also, Hornbook.
  abnormally dangerous, 273
  acts of God, 50-51
  battery, 95
  caveat emptor, 185
  child negligence, 26
  conduct of others, 203
  consumer contemplation test, 259
  contributory fault, 71
  criticism, 78
  defense of property, 123-24
  entry upon land, 168
  express consent, 83-85
  knowledge of risk, 85-87
  intentional torts, 221
  last clear chance, 78
  lessor/lessee, 179-81
  mental incompetence, immunity of, 155-58
  minors and infants, 155
  mistake, 125
  outrageous conduct, 100
  necessity, 126-27
  negligence per se, 57
  negligence in product liability cases, 244
  nuisance, 196
  outrageous conduct, 100
  parental immunity, 142
  privacy v. defamation, 102
  privilege, 127-28
  proximate cause, 32, 71
  public nuisance, 204
  reasonable person standard, 21-22
  recapture, 132
  right of control, 231
  scope of employment, 216-17
  social responsibility, 7
  standard of conduct, 19
  unforeseeable causes, 50-51
  unreasonably dangerous, 255
  willful, wanton, and reckless conduct, 54
Prosser on Torts, 4th ed., 208
  nuisance and present harm, 208
Prosser, W. 123, 196
protection, scope of, 34, 36
proximate cause, 20, 29, 32, 37, 40
  definition of, 30
  equation of, 37
public disclosure
  definition of, 101
public nuisance, 189-93, 204-05
  definition of, 192
public officers' immunity, 153-54
public policy, 138
public and private necessity, 126-27
publication, in defamatory statements, 103
punishment, 10-12
punitive damages, 42
pure comparative negligence, 79
question of fact, 49

Rappaport v. Nichols, 234
reasonable assumption of risk, 88
reasonable care
  duty of, 40
  eliminating risk, 274
  landlords, 162-65
reasonable discipline, 128-31
reasonable person standard, 21, 25, 37
  equation of, 37
reasonable risk of harm, 182
recapture of land and chattels, 132
reckless disregard, 54
recognition of risk, 27
recovery
  requirements for, 197
Reed v. House of Decor, Inc., 214-15, 279
remedies, 205-09
requirements for recovery, 197-99
res ipsa loquitur, 59-62, 64-146, 257
respondeat superior, 212-13, 216-18
  Baird v. Sickler, M.D., 217-18, 279
  Webb v. Jewel Companies, Inc., 222
restatement, 182
  as second authority, 9
Restatement (Second) of Torts, 18, 19, 31, 37
  abnormally dangerous activities, 273
  assault, 94
  assumption of risk, 87
  burden of proof, 58
  conduct directed at third person, 100
  confinement, 97
  consent, 119
  constant trespassers, 171
  contributory negligence defined, 68
  defamatory communication, 102
  defamatory statements, 102-03
  deficient mental capacity, 156
  employer negligence, 224-25
  failure to warn, 246
  false imprisonment, 96
  force, threatening and not threatening, 122-23
  foreseeability of harm, 37
  helpless plaintiff, 76-77
  inattentive plaintiff, 77
  independent contractor, 212, 223-27
  intent, 92-93
  intentional torts, 92-93
  interspousal immunity, 139
  invitee, 177
  joint enterprise, 229
  landlord's liability, 184-85
  last clear chance, 76-77
  legal cause, 31
  liability for emotional distress, 100, 199

liability of ownership, 184-85
liability to trespassers, 169-71
libel and slander distinguished, 105
municipal government, 152
natural conditions, 165-68
negligence and strict liability, 19, 209
negligent manufacture, 246
parental immunity, 141-42
plaintiff's conduct, 277
private nuisance, 192-97
public or common nuisance, 192-93, 204-05
public officers' immunity, 153-54
reasonable discipline, 128
reasonable person standard, 21
reckless disregard, 54
right of privacy, 100-02
rules of evidence, 48-49
self-defense, 118, 121-22
significant harm, 196
slander, 105
standard of care owed to invitees, 178
state government immunity, 150
strict liability, 254
superseding cause, 41
termination of liability, 184
trespassing children, 172-74
trespassing livestock, 266
true statements, 106-07
United States government, 146
vicarious liability, 220
vendor liability, 183-84
violenti non fit injuria, 119
warrantless arrest, 134
wild animals, 267, 269-70
right of bodily security, 39
right of control, 231
right of privacy, 100-02
versus defamation, 102-03
Right of Privacy, The, 100-01
riparian nuisance, 203
risk
allocation of, 213-14
See also, *Reed v. House of Decor, Inc.*
assumption of, 80, 82-83
elimination of, 274
express consent, 83-85
of harm, 274
of injury, 233
knowledge of, 85-87
in negligence cases, 27-28
product liability, 260
recognizing existence of, 27
risk-utility test, 259
unreasonable assumption of, 88
violenti non fit injuria, 119
voluntary assumption of, 80

Robichaux v. Huppenbauer, 201
Rodrigue v. Copeland, 200-02
Ross v. Consumers Power Co., 153-54
rules of evidence, 48-49
Rylands v. Fletcher, 269, 271-73, 275

S.A.V. v. K.G.V., 140-41
scope of employment, 216-17
scope of liability, 34, 276-77
manner of occurrence, 277
privilege, 277
scope of protection, 34
secondary authority, 7
examples of, 9
self-defense, 118, 121-22, 127
self-incrimination, 158
servant
frolic and detour, 218-20, 229
definition of, 216
sex abuse, 120-21
sexual assault
See, *Webb v. Jewel Companies, Inc.*
sexual discrimination
See, *Stimson v. Michigan Bell Telephone Company.*
Shakespeare, William, 17, 91, 211
significant harm
definition of, 196
sine qua non rule, 30
Sioux City & Pacific Railroad Co. v. Stout, 171
slander, 103-04
definition of, 105
types of, 106
slander *per se*, 106
slight-gross system, 79
slight negligence, 51
social guests as licensees, 174
socially responsible conduct, 6-7
sovereign immunity, 145-50
Spence v. Three Rivers Builders & Masonry Supply, 252
Spokane, Foster & Hindle, 226-27
standard of care owed to invitees, 178
elimination of traditional distinctions, 179
standard of conduct, 19
state of mind, 18
statute, 8
toll of, 13
statute of limitations, 133
product liability action, 260
statutory law, 29
See also, Statute.
as primary authority, 8-9
Stimson v. Michigan Bell Telephone Company, 3
strict liability, 12, 204, 209

strict liability, 203-04, 209, 249-52, 254
abnormally dangerous things, 274-74
animals, 265-66
defenses, 269-70
definition of, 265
domestic animals, 266-67
fire, 270-73
King v. Blue Mountain Forest Association, 267-69
liability without fault, 264-65
manner of occurrence, 277
Mazetti v. Armour & Co., 249-52
plaintiff's conduct, 277
privilege, 277
Rylands v. Fletcher, 269, 271-73
scope of liability, 276-77
trespassing livestock, 266
wild animals, 267-68
Young v. Darter, 274-76
Strunk v. Zoltanski, 180-83
substantial factor rule, 31, 36-37
substantial harm, 197
substantial and unreasonable interference, 200-02
substantially certain consequences, 93
succession, 39
superseding cause, 41
Supreme Court
Alabama, 206-08
Arizona, 171-73
California, 184-86
Florida, 233-34
Indiana, 74-76
Iowa, 194-96
Kansas, 247
Louisiana, 200-02
Michigan, 8, 52,153-54
Minnesota, 87
Missouri,140
Nebraska, 72-73
New Jersey, 234
Ohio, 60-62, 217-18
Virginia, 191
Washington, 110-12
survival actions, 63-64
survival
rules, 63-64
statutes, 64
system of monetary compensation, 4, 10

team, 15
television
See, Broadcasting.
Thackeray, 189
"thing speaks of itself, the,"
See, *Res ipsa loquitur*.
third-party defendants
See, *Galliher v. Holloway.*

Thomas v. Winchester, 239-40
threatening force, 122-23
toll, 133
torquere
  definition of, 2
tortfeasor, 17
  See also, Defendant.
  compensatory damages, 11-12
  defined, 3
  punishment of, 10, 11
tortious dispossession, 132
tort law
  See also, Intentional torts.
  defined, 1-2
  history of, 4-6
  resources, 7-9
tort liability
  immunity, 137-50
tortious conduct, defined, 2
Torts, 2nd ed., 268
Townsend v. Commonwealth, Kentucky, 130
toxic torts, 110, 119
treatises, 6, 9
trespass
  chattels, 13, 112
  definition of, 4-5
  on the case, 4
  land, 109-12
trespasser
  adults, 170-71
  constant, 171
  definition of, 168
  Mendoza v. City of Corpus Christi, 169-70
true statements, 106-07
two-year statute of limitations, 146

U.C.C., 254
ultra vires, 154
unacceptable conduct, 17
unavoidable accident, 50
unforeseeable causes, 50-51
unforeseeability, 32-33
Uniform Comparative Fault Act, 79
United States Constitution, The, 7-8, 145
  Eleventh Amendment, 150-51
  Fifth Amendment, 158
  First Amendment, 99, 114
    See also, *New York Times v. Sullivan.*
United States government, 145-50
  state government, 150-52
United States v. Shearer, 146-47
unlawful conduct, 203-04
unreasonable assumption of risk, 88
unreasonable interference, 200-02
unreasonable intrusion
  definition of,101
unreasonable risk of injury, 233
unreasonableness of invasion, 197
unreasonably dangerous, product liability, 255

vendor and vendee, 183-86
vendor liability, 183-84
  See also, Product liability.
  Preston v. Goldman, 184-86
vertical possession, 109-10
vicarious liability, 13, 211-36
  See also, *Respondeat superior*.
  automobile ownership, 232
  dangerous instrumentalities, 222-23
  doctrine of, 212-15
  dram shop liability, 232-35
  employer-employee, 213
  imputed negligence, 212
  independent contractor, 223-24
  intentional torts, 221-22
  master-servant relationship, 213, 216-21
  principal-agent, 213
  Reed v. House of Decor, Inc., 214-15, 279
violation of duty, 12
violenti non fit injuria, 80, 119
  See also, Assumption of risk.
voluntary assumption of risk, 80

Waller v. First Savings & Trust Co., 5
warrantless arrest, 133-34
warranty
  breach of, 238
  caveat emptor, 238
  Devlin v. Smith, 241
  Elmore v. American Motors Corp., 242
  eminently dangerous, 242
  MacPherson v. Buick Motor Co., 239-42, 279
  privity of contract, 238-39
  Thomas v. Winchester, 239
  Winterbottom v. Wright, 241
Warren, Samuel D., 100-01
Washington Water Power Co., 226-27
Webb v. Jewel Companies, Inc., 21-222
willful, wanton, and reckless conduct, 53-56
Wilton v. City of Spokane, 226-28
Winterbottom v. Wright, 241
Woolworth, Co., F.W., v. Loggins, 98
Workers Disability Compensation Act, 3
writ, 4
wrongful civil proceedings, 108
wrongful death, 63-64
wrongful death action
  definition of, 64

Young v. Darter, 274-76